11th Edition

Principles of
COST ACCOUNTING

Edward J. VanDerbeck, MS, CPA
PROFESSOR OF ACCOUNTING
XAVIER UNIVERSITY
CINCINNATI, OHIO

Charles F. Nagy, PhD, CPA
EMERITUS ACCOUNTING FACULTY
CLEVELAND STATE UNIVERSITY
CLEVELAND, OHIO

SOUTH-WESTERN College Publishing

An International Thomson Publishing Company

8-18-00

Acquisitions Editor: David L. Shaut
Developmental Editor: Ken Martin
Production Editor: Rebecca Glaab
Production House: Carlisle Communications, Ltd.
Cover Design: Matulionis Photography and Design
Internal Design: Jennifer Martin
Manufacturing Coordinator: Gordon Woodside
Marketing Manager: Matt Filimonov

ISBN: 0-538-87342-6
Copyright © 1999
by South-Western College Publishing
Cincinnati, Ohio

Library of Congress Cataloging-in-Publication Data:

VanDerbeck, Edward J.
      Principles of cost accounting / Edward J. VanDerbeck,
    Charles F. Nagy; — 11th ed.
          p. cm.
        Includes index.
        ISBN 0-538-87342-6
        1. Cost accounting. I. VanDerbeck, Edward J. II. Nagy, Charles F.
    III. Title.
    HF5686.C8S352 1998   98-8478
    657'.42—dc21   CIP

     2 3 4 5 6 7 D1 4 3 2 1 0 9
Printed in the United States of America

ITP
International Thomson Publishing
South-Western College Publishing is an ITP Company. The ITP trademark is used under license.

Preface

WHY STUDY COST ACCOUNTING?

The eleventh edition of *Principles of Cost Accounting* provides a thorough understanding of cost concepts, cost behavior, and cost accounting techniques as applied to manufacturing and service businesses. Students learn how to accurately determine costs of products and services; use the knowledge of product and service costs to set selling prices, to bid on contracts, and to analyze the relative profitability of various products and services; use techniques to measure the performance of managers and subunits within an organization; design an accounting system to fit the production and distribution system of an organization; and use the accounting system as a tool to motivate managers towards the organization's goals.

ELEVENTH EDITION FORMAT

1. Provides coverage for a one-quarter or one-semester cost accounting course.

2. Presents the principles and procedures of job order costing, process costing, and standard costing in a logical and concise manner.

3. Discusses the special purpose reports and analytical techniques of managerial accounting.

4. Retains the ten-chapter format—a distinguishing feature of the text. **A chapter on job order costing for a service business replaces the chapter on the comprehensive application of job order costing.**

5. The main thrust of the revision has been to produce a very readable and relevant text that covers the essentials of cost accounting, introduces real-world examples, reinforces the discussion with demonstration problems, and offers students practice in mastering the

topics with relevant end-of-chapter questions, exercises, and problems. Some problems are adapted to computer solution.

6. Integrates the uses of cost information with a discussion of cost accumulation systems and procedure, while offering practice material that closely resembles the chapter presentation.

ELEVENTH EDITION FEATURES

The eleventh edition includes several features to facilitate the learning process for the student and enhance the teachability of the text for the instructor.

APPENDICES

An appendix at the end of Chapter 2 illustrates just-in-time (JIT) inventory systems. An appendix at the end of Chapter 9 illustrates the four-variance and three-variance methods of analysis.

DEMONSTRATION PROBLEMS

A demonstration problem is included at the end of each chapter, with a step-by-step explanation of how to solve it. The demonstration problem is constructed from a difficult concept(s) in the chapter and reinforces the techniques and procedures discussed in the chapter. In each chapter, a problem very similar to the demonstration problem is identified.

REAL-WORLD EXAMPLES

Real-world examples are predominantly excerpts from articles in journals, explaining the latest in cost accounting techniques used to adapt to the rapid changes in manufacturing technology. Examples of topics include just-in-time inventory systems, world-class manufacturing, highly automated manufacturing systems where direct labor costs are insignificant, and cost allocation methods aimed at determining the "true" cost of a product or service.

INTEGRATED LEARNING OBJECTIVES

Learning objectives begin each chapter. Each learning objective is indicated in the text where first discussed. All end-of-chapter exercises and problems are identified by learning objectives.

KEY TERMS

Key terms are highlighted as they are introduced. They are listed, along with their page reference, at the end of each chapter. A comprehensive glossary is included at the end of the book, providing definitions for all of the key terms.

END-OF-CHAPTER MATERIALS

The end-of-chapter questions, exercises, and problems have been carefully written and revised to reflect the coverage as it appears in the chapters. There has been a concerted effort to provide the instructor with a wide choice of subject matter and degree of difficulty when assigning end-of-chapter materials. Additionally, selected problems may be solved using spreadsheet software.

DIRECTED ASSIGNMENTS

At specific points within each chapter, students are directed to appropriate end-of-chapter assignments. This allows students to work practice items without completing the entire chapter.

SUPPLEMENTARY MATERIALS

A complete package of supplementary materials is available with the eleventh edition of *Principles of Cost Accounting* to assist both instructors and students. The package includes materials that have been carefully prepared and reviewed.

AVAILABLE TO INSTRUCTORS

Solutions Manual. This manual contains the answers to all end-of-chapter questions, exercises, and problems.

Solutions Transparencies. Transparencies of solutions for end-of-chapter exercises and problems are available.

Instructor's Manual. Part I provides summaries and outlines for each chapter to facilitate development of classroom presentations and homework assignments. Part 2 contains a test bank of multiple-choice questions and problems for each chapter, accompanied by solutions. Part 3 contains six Achievement Tests consisting of objective questions and short problems that may be reproduced for classroom use. Each test covers one or two chapters of text material. Part 4 contains end-of-chapter problem check figures that may be reproduced and distributed to students at the discretion of the instructor.

Thomson World Class Testing Tools™. The printed test bank is available in a microcomputer version for Windows. The user may select, mix, edit, and add questions or problems to create the type of test or problem set needed.

Practice Set Key. The solution for the job order costing practice set, Sunblaze Inc., is available to adopters.

Template Diskette. This spreadsheet template disk can be used for solving selected end-of-chapter problems. The diskette, which may be copied, is available upon adoption from South-Western College Publishing. An **SS** icon identifies the spreadsheet exercises and problems.

AVAILABLE TO STUDENTS

Study Guide and Working Papers. A study guide and working papers are bound in a single volume, with perforated pages for easy removal. The study guide provides a review summary for each chapter and questions and problems to test comprehension of chapter material. Solutions for all questions and problems are included in a separate section at the end of the study guide. The working papers include printed forms for use in solving the problems at the end of each chapter of the textbook.

Sunblaze Inc. This job order cost practice set is designed for use with the textbook. The revised practice set has been shortened by minimizing repetitive transactions.

ACKNOWLEDGMENTS

We thank the following faculty who reviewed manuscript for this edition and provided helpful suggestions.

Barry Buchoff
Towson State University

Cynthia Greeson
Ivy Tech State College, Evansville

Margaret Combs
Union College

Leann Johnson
Southeastern Illinois College

Sharon Johnson
Kansas City Kansas
Community College

Judith Kizzie
Clinton Community College

Kenneth Leibham
Columbia Gorge
Community College

Ronald Loesel
Great Lakes Junior College

Josephine Miller
Mercer County Community
College

Joan Ryan
Clackamas Community College

Brief Contents

Contents

1

Introduction to Cost Accounting

LEARNING OBJECTIVES

After studying this chapter, you should be able to:

1. Explain the uses of cost accounting data.
2. Describe the relationship of cost accounting to financial accounting.
3. Identify the three basic elements of manufacturing costs.
4. Illustrate basic cost accounting procedures.
5. Distinguish between the two basic types of cost accounting systems.

The importance of accounting information to the successful operation of a business, including specific cost data, has long been recognized. However, in the current global economic environment, such information is more crucial than ever. Automobiles from Germany, electronic equipment from Japan, shoes from Italy, and clothing from Thailand are just a few examples of foreign-made products that have provided stiff competition to U.S. manufacturers both at home and abroad. As a result of these pressures, companies today are placing more emphasis on controlling costs in an attempt to keep their products competitive. **Cost accounting** provides the detailed cost data that management needs to control current operations and plan for the future. As Figure 1-1 illustrates, cost accounting provides

FIGURE 1-1   Production Process for Goods and Services

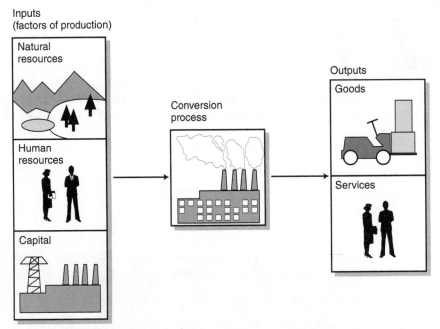

Source: Lawrence J. Gitman and Carl McDaniel, *The World of Business* (Cincinnati, OH: South-Western Publishing Co., 1995).

the information that allows management to allocate resources to the most efficient and profitable areas of operation.

All types of business entities—manufacturing, merchandising, and service businesses—require cost accounting information systems to account for their activities. **Manufacturers** convert purchased raw materials into finished goods by using labor, technology, and facilities. **Merchandisers** purchase finished goods for resale. They may be **retailers**, who sell products to individuals for consumption, or **wholesalers**, who purchase goods from manufacturers and sell to retailers. **For-profit service businesses**, such as airlines, architects, and hair stylists, sell services rather than products. **Not-for-profit service agencies**, such as charities, governmental agencies, and some health care facilities, provide services at little or no cost to the user.

The nature of the manufacturing process requires that the **accounting information systems** of manufacturers be designed to accumulate detailed cost data relating to the production process. Thus, it is common today for manufacturing companies of all sizes to have **cost accounting systems** that show the costs incurred and where and how these expenditures were used. While the cost accounting principles and procedures discussed in the text emphasize manufacturers, many of the same principles apply to merchandising and service businesses. Cost accounting is now recognized as essential to the efficient operation of hospitals, social welfare agencies, and numerous other entities. Chapter 5 illustrates cost accounting procedures for service businesses.

In many ways, the activities of a manufacturing organization are similar to those of a merchandising business. Both purchase, store, and sell goods; both must have efficient management and adequate sources of capital; both may employ hundreds or thousands of workers. The manufacturing process itself highlights the distinction between the two: merchandisers, such as Circuit City, buy electronic equipment in marketable form to resell to their customers; manufacturers, such as Magnavox, must make the goods they sell. Once the merchandising organization has acquired goods, it can perform the marketing function. The purchase of raw materials by a manufacturer, however, is only the beginning of a long and sometimes complex chain of events that results in a finished article for sale.

The **manufacturing process** involves the conversion of raw materials into finished goods through the use of labor and various other factory resources. The manufacturer must make a major investment in physical assets, such as factory buildings and specialized types of machinery and equipment. To carry out the manufacturing process, the manufacturer must purchase appropriate quantities of raw materials, supplies, and parts and build up a work force to convert these resources into finished goods.

In addition to the cost of materials and labor, the manufacturer incurs other expenses in the production process. Many of these costs, such as depreciation, taxes, insurance, and utilities, are similar to those incurred by a merchandising concern. Other costs, such as machine maintenance and repair, materials handling, and production setup, scheduling, and inspection, are unique to manufacturers. Once the goods have been manufactured and are ready for sale, the manufacturer performs basically the same functions as the merchandiser. The methods of accounting for sales, cost of goods sold, and selling and administrative expenses are similar to those of merchandisers. Service businesses, by comparison, have no inventories because the service is consumed at the time it is provided. Service businesses have revenue and operating expenses, but no cost of goods sold.

USES OF COST ACCOUNTING DATA

LEARNING OBJECTIVE 1
Explain the uses of
cost accounting data.
Principles of cost accounting have been developed that enable the manufacturer to process the many different costs associated with manufacturing and to provide built-in control features. The information produced by a cost accounting system provides a basis for determining product costs and selling prices, and it helps management to plan and control operations.

DETERMINING PRODUCT COSTS AND PRICING

Cost accounting procedures provide the means to determine product costs and thus to generate meaningful financial statements and other reports relevant to management. Cost procedures must be designed to permit the determination of **unit costs** as well as total product costs. For example, the fact that a manufacturer spent $10,000 for labor in a certain month is not, in itself, meaningful; but if this labor produced 5,000 finished units, the fact that the cost of labor was $2 per unit is significant. This figure can be compared to the unit labor cost of other periods and, to some extent, of competitors.

Unit cost information is also useful in making a variety of important marketing decisions:

1. **Determining the selling price of a product.** Knowing the cost of manufacturing a unit of product aids in setting the selling price. This price should be high enough to cover the cost of producing the item, including the marketing and administrative expenses attributable to it, and to provide a profit.

2. **Meeting competition.** If a product is being undersold by a competitor, detailed information regarding unit costs can be used to determine whether the problem can be resolved by reducing the selling price, by reducing manufacturing costs, or by eliminating the product.

3. **Bidding on contracts.** Many manufacturers must submit competitive bids in order to be awarded contracts. An analysis of the unit costs relating to the manufacture of a particular product is of great importance in determining the bid price.

4. **Analyzing profitability.** Unit cost information enables management to determine the amount of profit that each product earns and possibly eliminate the least profitable products, thereby concentrating its efforts on those most profitable. It is not uncommon, however, for some companies to retain a certain line of goods yielding a very low profit, or even a loss, in order to maintain the product variety that will attract those customers who also purchase the more profitable items.

PLANNING AND CONTROL

The ultimate value of cost accounting lies in the use of the data accumulated and reported. One of the most important functions of cost accounting is to develop information that management can use to plan and control operations.

Planning is the process of establishing objectives or goals for the firm and determining the means by which the firm will attain them. Effective planning is facilitated by the following:

1. **Clearly defined objectives of the manufacturing operation.** These objectives may be expressed in the number of units to be produced, the quality desired, the estimated cost per unit, or the timing necessary to meet customer demand without carrying excessive inventories.

2. **A production plan that will assist and guide the company in reaching its objectives**. This detailed plan includes a description of the necessary manufacturing operations to be performed, a projection of personnel needs for the period, and the coordination of the timely acquisition of materials and facilities.

Cost accounting enhances the planning process by providing historical costs that serve as a basis for future projections. Management can analyze the data to estimate future costs and operating results and to make decisions regarding the acquisition of additional facilities, changes in marketing strategies, and the availability of capital.

The word "control" is used in many different ways, but from the viewpoint of the manufacturing concern, control is the process of monitoring the company's operations and determining whether the objectives identified in the planning process are being accomplished. Effective control is achieved through the following ways:

1. Assigning responsibility
2. Periodically measuring and comparing results
3. Taking necessary corrective action

Assigning Responsibility. Responsibility should be assigned for each detail of the production plan. All managers and supervisors should know precisely what their responsibilities are in terms of efficiency, operations, production, and costs. The key to proper control involves the use of responsibility accounting and cost centers.

The essence of **responsibility accounting** is the assignment of accountability for costs or production results to those individuals who have the most authority to influence them. It involves an information system that traces the data to the responsible managers.

A **cost center** is a unit of activity within the factory to which costs may be practically and equitably assigned. A cost center may be a department or a group of workers; it could represent one job, one process, or one machine. The criteria for a cost center are (1) a reasonable basis on which manufacturing costs can be allocated and (2) a person who has control over and is accountable for many of the costs charged to that center.

With responsibility accounting, the manager of a cost center is accountable only for those costs that the manager controls. For example, labor and materials costs will be charged to the cost center, but the manager may be responsible only for the quantity of materials used and the number of labor hours worked. This manager would probably not be accountable for the unit cost of raw materials or the hourly rate paid to employees. These expenses are normally beyond the manager's control and are the responsibility of the purchasing and personnel departments. The manager may be responsible for the cost of machinery maintenance and repair due to misuse in the cost center, but he or she would not be responsible for the costs of depreciation, taxes, and insurance on the machinery if the decision to purchase the machinery was made at a higher level in the organization. If production in the cost center for a given period is lower than planned, this could be due to poor supervision, which is the manager's responsibility. However, if less-skilled workers are being hired, this is usually beyond the manager's control.

Cost and production reports for a cost center reflect all cost and production data identified with that center. In a responsibility accounting system, the specific data for which the manager is responsible would be highlighted or segregated to evaluate that manager's performance and initiate action to correct deficiencies. Quite often, however, both a cost and production report and a separate performance report will be prepared for a cost center. The **performance report** will include only those costs and production data that the center's manager can control.

These reports must be furnished at regular intervals (monthly, weekly, or daily) on a timely basis. To provide the maximum benefit, the reports should be available as soon as possible after the end of the period being reported. Reports not produced in a timely fashion are not effective as a control device.

Periodically Measuring and Comparing Results. Actual operating reports should be measured periodically and compared with the objectives established in the planning process. This analysis, which may be made monthly, weekly, daily, or even hourly in the case of production and scrap reports, is a major part of cost control because it compares current performance with the overall plan. The actual dollars, units produced, hours worked, or materials used are compared with the **budget**, which is management's operating plan expressed in quantitative terms (units and dollars). This comparison is a primary feature of cost analysis. The number of dollars expended or the quantity of units produced have little significance until compared with the budgeted amounts. Actual results of prior periods may also be compared to highlight meaningful trends.

Taking Necessary Corrective Action. The reports produced by the measurement and analysis of operating results may identify problem areas and deviations from the plan. Appropriate corrective action should be implemented where necessary. A significant variation from the plan is a signal for attention. An investigation may reveal a weakness to be corrected or a strength to be better utilized.

Management wants to know not only the results of operations, but how the results—whether favorable or unfavorable—compare with the plan, why things happened, and who was responsible. Management must be prepared to improve existing conditions. Otherwise, the periodic measurement of activity has little value. Accountants can be key players in this endeavor, as the real-world example on page 8 illustrates.

RELATIONSHIP OF COST ACCOUNTING TO FINANCIAL ACCOUNTING

LEARNING OBJECTIVE 2
Describe the relationship of cost accounting to financial accounting.

The objective of accounting is to accumulate financial information for use in making economic decisions. **Financial accounting** focuses on gathering information to be used in preparing financial statements that meet the needs of investors, creditors, and other external users of financial information. The statements include a balance sheet, income statement, retained earnings statement, and statement of cash flows. Although these financial statements are useful to management as well as external users, additional reports, schedules, and analyses are required for internal use in planning and control. Management spends most of its time evaluating the problems and opportunities of individual departments and divisions of the company rather than looking at the entire company at once. As a result, the external financial statements for the whole company are of little help to management in making these day-to-day decisions. Cost accounting provides the additional information required for these special reports to management and also provides data necessary to prepare the financial statements. For example, cost accounting procedures are necessary to determine: whether to make or buy a product component;

THE CONTROLLER AS BUSINESS STRATEGIST

"Controllers are breaking out of the traditional accountant mold as the 'numbers cruncher' and are crossing functional lines to reduce cost and improve efficiency, adding value to their organizations. Using technology innovations, they are turning data into knowledge for decision making and their role as business strategist.

The controller's new, expanded role is reflected in the results of the frequent surveys conducted by the Institute of Management Accountants' (IMA) Member Interest Groups (MIGs): Controllers Council (CC) and Cost Management Group (CMG). For example, many controllers and financial managers are involved in cost management innovations exemplified by the major thrust in recent years to reengineer the finance function . . . .

As IMA's continuing surveys indicate, the role of controllers and financial managers is changing as they combine technology tools and creativity to add value to their organizations by reducing costs and by serving as business partners who bring to the team their financial expertise. All indications are that this role will continue and probably expand as their companies compete actively in the world marketplace."

Dan Hrisak, "The Controller As Business Strategist," *Management Accounting*, December 1996, pp. 48-49.

whether to accept a special order at a discounted price; the amount for cost of goods sold on the income statement; and the valuation of inventories on the balance sheet.

COST OF GOODS SOLD

Merchandising concerns compute cost of goods sold as shown below. The amount of purchases represents the cost of goods acquired during the period for resale.

Beginning merchandise inventory
Plus **purchases** (merchandise)
Merchandise available for sale
Less ending merchandise inventory
Cost of goods sold

Because the manufacturing concern makes rather than buys the products it has available for sale, the term "finished goods inventory" replaces "merchandise inventory," and the term "cost of goods manufactured" replaces "purchases" in determining the cost of goods sold, as shown below. The cost of goods manufactured amount is supported by a schedule detailing the costs of materials, labor, and the expenses of maintaining and operating a factory.

Beginning finished goods inventory
Plus **cost of goods manufactured**
Finished goods available for sale
Less ending finished goods inventory
Cost of goods sold

The format of the income statement for a manufacturer is not significantly different from that of a merchandiser. However, the cost accounting procedures involved in gathering the data for determining the cost of goods manufactured are considerably more complex than the recording of merchandise purchased in its finished form. These procedures are introduced in this chapter and discussed in detail in subsequent chapters. The income statements for service businesses do not have a cost of goods sold section, because they provide a service rather than a product.

INVENTORIES

If a merchandiser has unsold items on hand at the end of an accounting period, the cost of the merchandise is reflected in the current assets section of the balance sheet in the following manner:

Current assets:
Cash
Accounts receivable
Merchandise inventory

On the balance sheet of a manufacturing concern, the current assets section is expanded as follows:

Current assets:
Cash
Accounts receivable
Inventories:
Finished goods
Work in process
Materials

The balance of the **finished goods** account represents the total cost incurred in manufacturing goods completed but still on hand at the end of the period. The balance of the **work in process** account includes all manufacturing costs incurred to date for goods in various stages of production but not yet completed. The balance of the **materials** account represents the cost of all materials purchased and on hand to be used in the manufacturing process, including raw materials, prefabricated parts, and other factory materials and supplies. Raw materials for one company are often the finished product of another company. For example, rolled steel to be used in the production of automobiles would be the final product of the steel mill. Prefabricated parts would include units, such as electric motors, assembled by another manufacturer to be used in the manufacture of a product such as office machines. Other materials and supplies might include screws, nails, rivets, lubricants, and solvents.

Service entities do not have inventories on their balance sheets because they provide a service rather than a product. A summary comparison of manufacturing, merchandising, and service businesses appears in Figure 1-2.

Valuation of Inventories. Many procedures used to gather costs are unique to manufacturers. Manufacturers' inventories are valued for external financial reporting purposes by using the inventory costing methods—such as first-in, first-out (FIFO), last-in, first-out (LIFO), and moving average—that are also used by merchandisers. Most manufacturers maintain a **perpetual inventory system** that provides a continuous

FIGURE 1-2   Comparison of Service, Merchandising, and Manufacturing Businesses

Business Sector	Examples	Product or Service	Inventory Account(s)
Service	Airlines, architects, hair stylists, sports franchises	Intangible benefits such as transportation, designs, grooming, entertainment	None
Merchandising	Athletic souvenirs, department stores, poster shops, wholesalers	Tangible products purchased from suppliers in finished form	Merchandise inventory
Manufacturing	Aircraft producers, athletic equipment makers, home builders, pharmaceutical producers	Physical products created by the application of labor and technology to raw materials	Finished goods, work in process, materials

record of purchases, issues, and balances of all goods in stock. Generally these data are verified by periodic counts of selected items throughout the year. Under the perpetual system, inventory valuation data for financial statement purposes are available at any time, as distinguished from a **periodic inventory system** that requires estimating inventory during the year for interim statements and shutting down operations to count all inventory items at the end of the year.

In addition to providing inventory valuation data for the financial statements, the detailed cost data and perpetual inventory records provide the information necessary to control inventory levels, to ensure the timely availability of materials for production, and to detect pilferage, waste, and spoilage. Inventory valuation and control are discussed in detail in Chapter 2.

Inventory Ledgers. Generally both merchandisers and manufacturers maintain various subsidiary ledgers, such as that for accounts receivable. In addition, manufacturers usually maintain subsidiary ledgers for the general ledger inventory control accounts, Finished Goods, Work in Process, and Materials. These subsidiary ledgers are necessary for a perpetual inventory system and provide the detailed balances and information to support the balances in the control accounts.

Some manufacturers use a **factory ledger**, which contains all of the accounts relating to manufacturing, including the inventory accounts. This ledger, which is maintained at the factory, is tied in to the general ledger at the main office through a special account for the factory on the main office books and a special account for the main office on the factory books.

> **You should now be able to work the following: Questions 1–14; Exercises 1-1 and 1-2; Problem 1-1.**

ELEMENTS OF MANUFACTURING COSTS

LEARNING OBJECTIVE 3
Identify the three basic elements of manufacturing costs.

Manufacturing or **production costs** are classified into three basic elements: (1) direct materials, (2) direct labor, and (3) factory overhead.

DIRECT MATERIALS

The costs of materials that become part of and can be readily identified with a certain manufactured product are classified as **direct materials** costs. Examples include lumber used in making furniture, fabric used in the production of clothing, iron ore used in the manufacture of steel products, and rubber used in the production of athletic shoes.

Many types of materials and supplies necessary for the manufacturing process either cannot be readily identified with any particular manufactured item or have a relatively insignificant cost. The costs of items such as sandpaper used in sanding furniture, lubricants used on machinery, and other items for general factory use are classified as **indirect materials** costs. Similarly classified are materials that actually become part of the finished product but whose costs are relatively insignificant, such as thread, screws, rivets, nails, and glue.

DIRECT LABOR

The cost of labor for those employees who work directly on the product manufactured, such as machine operators or assembly line workers, is classified as **direct labor** cost. The wages and salaries of employees who are required for the manufacturing process but who do not work directly on the units being manufactured are considered **indirect labor** costs. This classification includes the wages and salaries of department heads, inspectors, materials handlers, and maintenance personnel. Payroll-related costs, such as payroll taxes, group insurance, sick pay, vacation and holiday pay, retirement program contributions, and other fringe benefits, even for the direct laborers, also are usually treated as indirect costs.

FACTORY OVERHEAD

Factory overhead is known by various names—factory burden, manufacturing expenses, indirect costs, manufacturing overhead, and factory expenses—and includes all costs related to the manufacturing of a product except direct materials and direct labor. Thus, factory overhead includes indirect materials, indirect labor, and other manufacturing expenses, such as depreciation on the factory building and machinery and equipment, supplies, heat, light, power, maintenance, insurance, taxes, and payroll-related costs. As factories have become more automated, factory overhead as a percentage of total manufacturing cost has increased dramatically.

SUMMARY OF MANUFACTURING COSTS

The costs of direct materials and direct labor are sometimes combined and described as the **prime cost** of manufacturing a product. Prime cost plus factory overhead equals the total cost of manufacturing. Direct labor cost and factory overhead, which are necessary to convert the direct materials into finished goods, can be combined and described as **conversion cost**. These manufacturing costs are illustrated in Figure 1-3.

FIGURE 1-3　　　　Prime Cost and Conversion Cost

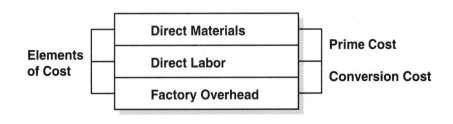

Marketing or selling expenses, general administrative costs, and other nonfactory expenditures are not included in the costs of manufacturing. However, some costs incurred by a manufacturer may benefit both factory and nonfactory operations. Examples include depreciation, insurance, and property taxes on a building that houses both the factory and the administrative offices. In this situation, an allocation of cost must be made to each business function.

FLOW OF COSTS

All three elements of manufacturing cost flow through the work in process inventory account. The costs of direct materials and direct labor used in production are charged (debited) directly to Work in Process. All other factory costs—indirect labor, indirect materials, and other factory expenses—are charged to the factory overhead account and later transferred to Work in Process. When goods are completed, the total costs incurred in producing the goods are transferred from Work in Process to the finished goods inventory account. When goods are sold, the costs incurred to manufacture the goods are transferred from Finished Goods to Cost of Goods Sold. Figure 1-4 illustrates the flow of manufacturing costs.

ILLUSTRATION OF ACCOUNTING FOR MANUFACTURING COSTS

LEARNING OBJECTIVE 4
Illustrate basic cost accounting procedures.

Cost accounting procedures are used to accumulate and allocate all elements of manufacturing cost in a manner that will produce meaningful data for the internal use of management and for the preparation of external financial statements. The following example illustrates basic cost accounting procedures, utilizing the terminology and principles that were discussed previously.

FIGURE 1-4   Flow of Costs

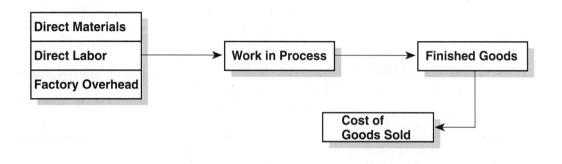

Fahr Furniture Company, a small, newly organized corporation, manufactures wicker furniture—both tables and chairs. The firm sells products directly to retailers. The basic steps in the company's production process are as follows:

1. Pieces of rattan, a natural fiber grown in the Orient, are purchased in precut specifications. The pieces are assembled to form the frame of the table or chair in the Assembly Department.

2. The legs and back uprights of the chair and the legs and outline of the tabletop are then wrapped in binding cane in the Wrapping Department.

3. The seat and back of the chair and the tabletop are now ready to be woven into place in the Weaving Department where the chair or table is finished.

The beginning balance sheet for the company on January 1 of the current year is presented as follows:

Fahr Furniture Company
Balance Sheet
January 1, 20—

Assets		Liabilities and Stockholders' Equity	
Cash	$ 40,000	Liabilities	$ -0-
Building	250,000	Capital stock	365,000
Machinery and equipment	75,000	Total liabilities and	
Total assets	$365,000	stockholders' equity	$365,000

Assume, for the purpose of simplification, that the company makes only one style of table and no chairs. During January the following transactions are completed and recorded, in summary form:

1. Materials (rattan, binding cane, nails, tacks, staples, glue, and solvents) are purchased on account at a cost of $25,000.

Materials	25,000	
Accounts Payable		25,000

The cost of materials purchased is charged to the inventory control account, Materials. This treatment is based on the assumption that the company uses a perpetual inventory system.

2. During the month, direct materials (rattan, binding cane) costing $20,000 and indirect materials (nails, tacks, staples, glue, and solvents for cleaning) costing $995 are issued to the factory.

Work in Process (Direct Materials)	20,000	
Factory Overhead (Indirect Materials)	995	
Materials		20,995

Direct materials issued are charged directly to the work in process control account, but the indirect materials are charged to the factory overhead account. The factory overhead account will be used to accumulate various factory expenses that will later be transferred to Work in Process.

3. Total gross wages and salaries earned for the month were factory employees working on the product, $10,000; factory supervision, maintenance, and custodial employees, $3,500; and sales and administrative employees, $6,500. The entries to record the payroll and the payments to employees (ignoring payroll deductions) would be as follows:

Payroll	20,000	
Wages Payable		20,000
Wages Payable	20,000	
Cash		20,000

4. The entry to distribute the payroll to the appropriate accounts would be as follows:

Work in Process (Direct Labor)	10,000	
Factory Overhead (Indirect Labor)	3,500	
Selling and Administrative Expenses (Salaries)	6,500	
Payroll		20,000

The wages earned by employees working directly on the product are charged to Work in Process, while the salaries and wages of the factory supervisor and the maintenance and custodial personnel, who do not work directly on the product, are charged to Factory Overhead as indirect labor. The salaries of nonfactory employees are debited to a separate expense account.

In order to focus on specific cost accounting procedures as distinguished from general accounting procedures, the general ledger account Selling and Administrative Expenses will be used to accumulate all non-manufacturing expenses. Usually, separate general ledger control accounts would be established for selling expenses and administrative expenses.

5. Depreciation expense for the building is 6% of cost per year. The sales and administrative offices occupy one-tenth of the total building, and the factory operation is contained in the other nine-tenths. The expense for one month is recorded as follows:

Factory Overhead (Depr. of Building)	1,125	
Selling and Administrative Expenses (Depr. of Building)	125	
Accumulated Depr.—Building		1,250

($250,000 × 0.06 × 1/12 = $1,250;
$1,250 × 0.90 = $1,125; $1,250 × 0.10 = $125)

The cost accounting principle illustrated here is that only those costs directly related to production should be charged to Factory Overhead. Depreciation on the portion of the building used as office space is an administrative expense and should not be treated as an element of product cost.

6. Depreciation expense for machinery and equipment is 20% of cost per year.

Factory Overhead (Depr. of Machinery and Equipment)	1,250	
Accumulated Depr.—Machinery and Equipment		1,250

($75,000 × 0.20 × 1/12 = $1,250)

All machinery and equipment is used in the factory for production purposes, so the depreciation expense is properly charged to Factory Overhead.

7. The cost of heat, light, and power for the month was $1,500.

Factory Overhead (Utilities)	1,350	
Selling and Administrative Expenses (Utilities)	150	
Accounts Payable		1,500

Because one-tenth of the building is used for office purposes, 10% of the total utilities cost is allocated to Selling and Administrative Expenses.

8. Miscellaneous selling and administrative expenses for telephone, office supplies, travel, and rental of office furniture and equipment totaled $3,750.

Selling and Administrative Expenses	3,750	
Accounts Payable		3,750

Many other expenses may be incurred by a manufacturing organization, but for simplicity it is assumed that no other expenses were incurred during the month. After posting the journal entries to the appropriate ledger accounts, Factory Overhead will reflect the following debits:

Transaction	Description	Amount
2.	Indirect materials	$ 995
4.	Indirect labor	3,500
5.	Depr. of building	1,125
6.	Depr. of machinery and equipment	1,250
7.	Utilities	1,350
	Total	$8,220

9. The balance in Factory Overhead is transferred to Work in Process by the following entry:

Work in Process	8,220	
Factory Overhead		8,220

The three elements of manufacturing cost—direct materials, direct labor, and factory overhead—are now accumulated in Work in Process. The debits in the account are as follows:

Transaction	Description	Amount
2.	Direct materials	$20,000
4.	Direct labor	10,000
9.	Factory overhead	8,220
	Total	$38,220

10. Assuming that all goods started in process have been finished, the following entry transfers the cost of these goods from Work in Process to Finished Goods:

Finished Goods	38,220	
Work in Process		38,220

Assuming that 1,000 tables were produced during the month, the unit cost is $38.22 ($38,220/1,000). The unit cost for each element of manufacturing cost is calculated as follows:

	Total	Units Produced	Unit Cost
Direct materials	$20,000	1,000	$20.00
Direct labor	10,000	1,000	10.00
Factory overhead	8,220	1,000	8.22
	$38,220		$38.22

If the same type of table is produced in future periods, the unit costs of those periods can be compared with the unit costs determined in the preceding example. Any differences can be analyzed so that management might take appropriate action.

The unit cost also serves as a basis for establishing the selling price of the tables. After considering the anticipated selling and administrative expenses, management establishes a selling price that should provide a reasonable profit. The selling price may be determined by adding a **mark-on percentage**, which is a percentage of the manufacturing cost per unit. For example, if management decides that a 50% mark-on percentage is necessary to cover the product's share of selling and administrative expenses and to earn a satisfactory profit, the selling price per unit, rounded to the nearest cent, would be calculated as follows:

Manufacturing cost	$38.22
Mark-on percentage (50%)	19.11
Selling price	$57.33

In later periods, it might be found that this particular item cannot be sold at a price high enough to provide a reasonable profit. Through analysis of the unit costs, management might effect a cost-cutting measure or perhaps even discontinue production of the item.

From this example, it is apparent that, at any given time, the cost of each item in inventory is available. It should be reemphasized that one function of cost accounting is the accurate determination of the cost of manufacturing a unit of product. This knowledge of unit cost helps management to plan and control operations and to make marketing decisions.

To continue with the example, assume that the following transactions take place in January (in addition to those already recorded):

11. Invoices of $25,000, representing costs of materials, utilities, and selling and administrative expenses, are paid.

Accounts Payable	25,000	
Cash		25,000

12. A total of 800 tables are sold to retailers at a net price of $57.33 each.

Accounts Receivable (800 × $57.33) . . . . : . .	45,864	
Sales		45,864
Cost of Goods Sold (800 × $38.22)	30,576	
Finished Goods		30,576

Because the unit cost of each item is known, the cost of goods sold can be determined without a physical inventory or cost estimate.

13. Cash totaling $33,000 is collected on accounts receivable.

Cash	33,000	
Accounts Receivable		33,000

The accounts in the general ledger will reflect the entries as follows:

Cash				Accounts Receivable			
1/1 Bal.	40,000	3.	20,000	12.	45,864	13.	33,000
13.	33,000	11.	25,000	*12,864*			
	73,000		*45,000*				
28,000							

Finished Goods			
10.	38,220	12.	30,576
7,644			

Work in Process			
2. Direct materials	20,000	10.	38,220
4. Direct labor	10,000		
9. Factory overhead	8,220		
	38,220		

Materials			
1.	25,000	2.	20,995
4,005			

Building			
1/1 Bal.	250,000		

Accumulated Depr.—Building			
		5.	1,250

Machinery and Equipment			
1/1 Bal.	75,000		

Accumulated Depr.—Machinery and Equipment			
		6.	1,250

Accounts Payable			
		1.	25,000
11.	25,000	7.	1,500
		8.	3,750
			30,250
		5,250	

Wages Payable			
3.	20,000	3.	20,000

Capital Stock			
		1/1 Bal.	365,000

Sales			
		12.	45,864

Cost of Goods Sold			
12.	30,576		

Payroll			
3.	20,000	4.	20,000

Factory Overhead			
2. Indirect materials	995	9.	8,220
4. Indirect labor	3,500		
5. Depr. of building	1,125		
6. Depr. of machinery & equip.	1,250		
7. Utilities	1,350		
	8,220		

Selling and Administrative Expenses			
4. Salaries	6,500		
5. Depr. of building	125		
7. Utilities	150		
8. Other	3,750		
	10,525		

After calculating the balance of each general ledger account, the equality of the debits and credits is proven by preparing a trial balance, as follows.

Fahr Furniture Company
Trial Balance
January 31, 20—

Cash	$ 28,000	
Accounts Receivable	12,864	
Finished Goods	7,644	
Work in Process	-0-	
Materials	4,005	
Building	250,000	
Accumulated Depreciation—Building		$ 1,250
Machinery and Equipment	75,000	
Accumulated Depreciation—Machinery and Equipment		1,250
Accounts Payable		5,250
Wages Payable		-0-
Capital Stock		365,000
Sales		45,864
Cost of Goods Sold	30,576	
Payroll	-0-	
Factory Overhead	-0-	
Selling and Administrative Expenses	10,525	
	$418,614	$418,614

Note that the finished goods control account reflects the cost of the 200 units still on hand—200 × $38.22 = $7,644.

From an analysis of the general ledger accounts and the trial balance, financial statements for the period are prepared as follows:

Fahr Furniture Company
Statement of Cost of Goods Manufactured
For the Month Ended January 31, 20—

Direct materials:		
Inventory, January 1	$ -0-	
Purchases	25,000	
Total cost of available materials	$25,000	
Less inventory, January 31	4,005	
Cost of materials used	$20,995	
Less indirect materials used	995	
Cost of direct materials used in production		$20,000
Direct labor		10,000
Factory overhead:		
Indirect materials	$ 995	
Indirect labor	3,500	
Depreciation of building	1,125	
Depreciation of machinery and equipment	1,250	
Utilities	1,350	
Total factory overhead		8,220
Cost of goods manufactured during the month		$38,220

Fahr Furniture Company
Income Statement
For the Month Ended January 31, 20—

Net sales		$45,864
Cost of goods sold:		
Finished goods inventory, January 1	$ -0-	
Add cost of goods manufactured	38,220	
Goods available for sale	$38,220	
Less finished goods inventory, January 31	7,644	30,576
Gross profit on sales		$15,288
Selling and administrative expenses		10,525
Net income		$ 4,763

Fahr Furniture Company
Balance Sheet
January 31, 20—

Assets

Current assets:			
Cash			$ 28,000
Accounts receivable			12,864
Inventories:			
Finished goods	$ 7,644		
Work in process	-0-		
Materials	4,005	11,649	
Total current assets			$ 52,513
Plant and equipment:			
Building	$250,000		
Less accumulated depreciation . .	1,250	$248,750	
Machinery and equipment	$ 75,000		
Less accumulated depreciation . .	1,250	73,750	
Total plant and equipment			322,500
Total assets			$375,013

Liabilities and Stockholders' Equity

Current liabilities:		
Accounts payable		$ 5,250
Stockholders' equity:		
Capital stock	$365,000	
Retained earnings	4,763	
Total stockholders' equity		369,763
Total liabilities and stockholders' equity . .		$375,013

The figures in the cost of goods manufactured statement were obtained by analyzing the appropriate general ledger accounts. The materials inventory account had no beginning balance but has an ending balance of $4,005. The amount of purchases during the period was determined by analyzing the debits to the materials account. The cost of direct materials used of $20,000 and the direct labor cost of $10,000 were obtained from the work in process account. All other items in the statement of cost of goods manufactured represent factory overhead and are determined from the factory overhead account in the general ledger.

This discussion has presented a complete cycle in cost accounting procedures. Before proceeding, carefully review the basic elements of terminology and the flow of costs. A firm grasp of the fundamentals already covered is necessary to comprehend the more complex material in subsequent chapters. Figure 1-5 presents a graphic illustration of the

FIGURE 1-5   Flow of Costs

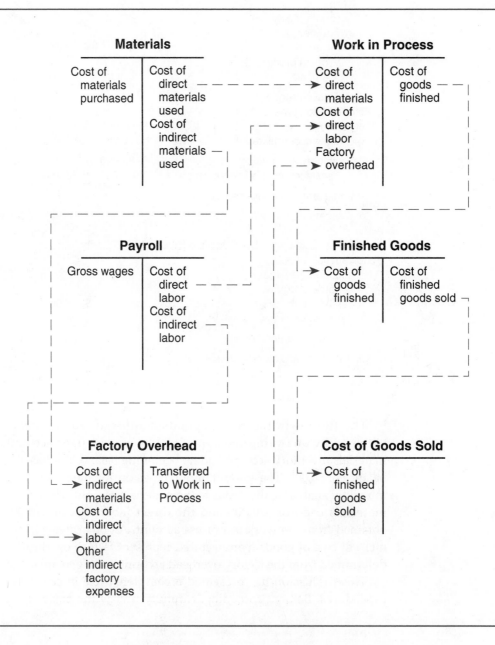

flow of costs. You should study this illustration carefully, following each line to trace the flow of costs.

> **You should now be able to work the following: Questions 15–21; Exercises 1-3 to 1-7; Problems 1-2 to 1-4.**

COST ACCOUNTING SYSTEMS

LEARNING OBJECTIVE 5
Distinguish between the two basic types of cost accounting systems.

The previous example presented the basic foundation of a cost accounting system. In that illustration, costs were accumulated for one month. At the end of the month, the costs were divided by the total units produced to determine the unit cost. This accomplished one function of cost accounting: the determination of product costs—both total costs for the period and cost per unit. However, another important objective of a cost accounting system—cost control—could not be satisfactorily achieved using the described procedure. As was stated, unit costs could be compared with similar costs in future periods to determine if costs were increasing. Assuming that in a subsequent month the cost of direct labor had risen from $10.00 to $11.00 per unit, it is necessary to investigate and determine whether something can be done to correct the situation. The described accounting procedure restricts any investigation, because it is not known exactly where in the factory this increase has occurred. Labor costs went up; but did they go up because of a general rise in wages or because of inefficiency? Did labor costs increase throughout the manufacturing process or for a particular department or job? Answers to such questions are not readily available using the procedures described in the earlier example.

To provide management with the data needed for effective cost control, two basic types of cost accounting systems have been developed: the process cost system and the job order cost system. Both systems are used to gather cost data and to allocate costs to goods manufactured. The selection of one method or the other depends on the type of manufacturing operation used by a given company. To determine the appropriate method, manufacturing operations are classified into two types: special order and continuous or mass production.

SPECIAL ORDER

In this type of operation, the output consists of special or custom-made products; in other words, each product is made to order. An order may be an external or internal order for a predetermined quantity of products. Special-order industries include those manufacturing or producing locomotives, ships, aircraft, machine tools, engines, structural steel, books and magazines, directories and catalogs, and specialty shops producing custom-made products such as clothing, shoes, hats, or custom-built homes. A **job order cost system** is appropriate in these circumstances. Job order cost accounting techniques may be used by service organizations such as accounting, architecture, and law firms to perform functions such as determining the cost to service a client.

CONTINUOUS OR MASS PRODUCTION

This type of operation produces a continuous output of homogeneous products. Such an enterprise may produce a single product, such as an automobile, or many different products, such as soft drinks or pharmaceuticals. The factory generally is departmentally organized. Continuous or mass production industries include those manufacturing automobiles, tires, cement, chemicals, canned goods, lumber, paper, candy, foodstuffs, flour, glass, soap, toothpaste, chewing gum, petroleum products, textiles, plastics, and paints, and firms engaged in such processes as rubber compounding and vulcanizing. This type of manufacturing enterprise normally uses a **process cost system**.

Process cost accounting suits manufacturing situations in which all units of the final product are substantially identical. Fahr Furniture utilized a process cost system in the preceding example to account for its only product. Finished units are placed in stock and removed as needed to fill customer orders. There are no separate jobs presenting substantially different characteristics. Rather, the company (or a department within the company) produces large numbers of virtually identical items that are sold (or transferred to other departments) as orders are received. Process cost accounting techniques may be used by organizations that provide a service such as for determining the cost per X-ray in a hospital's X-ray department or the cost per passenger-mile for an airline. Chapters 6 and 7 cover process cost accounting. Figure 1-6 shows examples of the use of job order cost and process cost systems in service, merchandising, and manufacturing businesses.

COMBINATION OF SYSTEMS

Some companies use both a job order cost and a process cost system. For example, a company that manufactures goods on specific order but also produces, on a continuous basis, a number of small parts to be used in most job orders may benefit from combining the systems. The costs of making these small parts would be accumulated on a process cost basis, while the costs for each job would be gathered on a job cost sheet.

STANDARD COSTING

The job order and process cost accounting systems are the principal systems used by manufacturing organizations. However, as useful as they

FIGURE 1-6   Uses of Cost Systems

Cost System	Service Business	Merchandising Business	Manufacturing Business
Job Order	Architectural firm, executive recruiters	Lumber company, personal computer retailer	Custom home builder, printer
Process	Hospital X-ray department, hotel housekeeping	Newspaper publishing, agricultural wholesaler	Paper producer, brewery

are in providing cost data, these systems are still limited with regard to cost control. Although they make it possible to determine what a product actually costs, they provide no means to determine what the product should have cost. A **standard cost accounting system**, which is not a third system but may be used with either a job order or a process cost system, is designed to furnish a measurement that will help management make decisions regarding the efficiency of operations.

Standard costs would be incurred under efficient operating conditions and are forecast before the manufacturing process begins. During operations, an organization compares the actual costs incurred with these predetermined standard costs. "Variances," or differences, are then calculated. These variances reveal which performances deviate from the standard, and thus they provide a basis on which management can take appropriate action to eliminate inefficient operating conditions. Standard cost accounting will be discussed in depth and illustrated in Chapters 8 and 9.

ILLUSTRATION OF JOB ORDER COST SYSTEM

With a job order cost system, costs are accumulated by job (or lot). One advantage of a job order cost system is that the accumulation of costs for a particular job helps to determine its selling price. Or, if a job is done under contract with a set price, the profit or loss on the job can be readily determined by comparing the cost with the contract price. At the same time, costs that have been accumulated for a certain type of work will assist management in preparing bids for similar jobs in the future.

To illustrate the use of the job order cost accounting system, assume that Fahr Furniture Company accepts two orders to manufacture certain items during the month of February. These special orders are as follows:

1. From Wicker Warehouse: to manufacture 1,000 chairs to Wicker Warehouse's specifications; contract price, $36,000. Job No. 101 is assigned to this order.

2. From The Wicker Shop: to manufacture 500 tables to The Wicker Shop's specifications; contract price, $29,650. Job No. 102 is assigned to this order.

After accepting these orders and planning the manufacturing requirements as to materials, labor, and overhead, the cost accounting department sets up a **job cost sheet** for each job. Figure 1-7 illustrates this form for the Wicker Warehouse order. All costs applicable to each job will be accumulated on these forms. Note that Fahr has changed from process

FIGURE 1-7   Job Cost Sheet

FAHR FURNITURE COMPANY
Job Cost Sheet

Customer Name: Wicker Warehouse   Job No: 101
Address: 5525 Skyway Dr.   Date Started: 2/24
Houston, TX 77057
Quantity: 1,000   Date Completed: 2/28
Product: chairs
Description: 39" wicker

DIRECT MATERIALS			DIRECT LABOR			FACTORY OVERHEAD		
Date	Mat'l Req. No.	Amount	Date	Time Tkt. No.	Amount	Date	Basis Applied	Amount
2/24	5505	8,200	2/25	2101	2,500		60% of	
2/26	6211	4,000	2/27	2826	1,500		total	
			2/28	3902	2,000	2/28	over-head	5,007
Total		12,200			6,000			5,007

SUMMARY
Direct materials ... $12,200   Selling price ...... $36,000   Remarks:
Direct labor 6,000   Mfg. cost 23,207
Factory overhead   5,007   Gross profit $12,793
Total cost $23,207
Unit cost .... $ 23.21

costing to job order costing now that it is making custom products for specific customers.

Transactions and journal entries for the month of February appear as follows. To highlight job order cost accounting procedures, only those entries relating to the manufacture of goods will be illustrated. Routine entries, such as those for recording the purchase of materials, nonmanufacturing expenses, or payments to creditors, will be ignored, as these entries are made in the same way as previously illustrated, regardless of the cost system used.

1. Indirect materials with a cost of $2,620 are issued to the factory, and direct materials are issued as follows:

	Job 101	Job 102
Rattan	$11,000	$8,000
Binding Cane	1,200	1,000
	$12,200	$9,000

The entry at the end of the week to record the issues of materials appears as:

Work in Process—101	12,200	
Work in Process—102	9,000	
Factory Overhead (Indirect Materials)	2,620	
Materials		23,820

If the indirect materials could be directly traced to a specific job, the cost could be charged to that job. However, it is often difficult to determine which job benefited from the use of the various supplies. Thus, indirect materials costs are usually charged to Factory Overhead and later distributed among the various jobs.

2. Indirect labor costs of $2,180 and direct labor costs are incurred as follows:

	Job 101	Job 102
Direct Labor	$6,000	$3,750

The weekly entry to distribute these costs is recorded as follows:

Work in Process—101	6,000	
Work in Process—102	3,750	
Factory Overhead (Indirect Labor)	2,180	
Payroll		11,930

3. Monthly depreciation expense for the building is recorded as follows:

Factory Overhead (Depr. of Building)   1,125

Selling and Administrative Expenses

(Depr. of Building)   125

    Accumulated Depr.—Building   1,250

4. The entry to record monthly depreciation for machinery and equip-ment is recorded as follows:

Factory Overhead (Depr. of Machinery

and Equipment)   1,250

    Accumulated Depr.—Machinery

    and Equipment   1,250

5. The cost of utilities for the month of February is $1,300 and is recorded as follows:

Factory Overhead (Utilities)   1,170

Selling and Administrative Expenses (Utilities)   130

    Accounts Payable   1,300

6. Total charges to Factory Overhead for the month are shown as follows:

Indirect materials	$2,620
Indirect labor	2,180
Depr. of building	1,125
Depr. of machinery and equipment	1,250
Utilities	1,170
Total	$8,345

Assume that factory overhead is allocated as follows: 60% to Job 101, 40% to Job 102.

Total Factory Overhead	60% Job 101	40% Job 102
$8,345	$5,007	$3,338

The distribution of factory overhead would be recorded as follows:

Work in Process—101   5,007

Work in Process—102   3,338

    Factory Overhead   8,345

At the end of the month, the work in process and factory overhead accounts would appear as follows:

Work in Process—101		
1. Direct materials	12,200	
2. Direct labor	6,000	
6. Factory overhead	5,007	
	23,207	

Work in Process—102		
1. Direct materials	9,000	
2. Direct labor	3,750	
6. Factory overhead	3,338	
	16,088	

Factory Overhead		
1. Indirect materials	2,620	6. Transfer to Work in Process 8,345
2. Indirect labor	2,180	
3. Depr. of building	1,125	
4. Depr. of mach. and equip.	1,250	
5. Utilities	1,170	
	8,345	

The costs shown in the work in process accounts represent monthly totals (summary entries) for each element of manufacturing cost. These same costs are shown in more detail on job cost sheets such as the one illustrated previously.

7. Assuming both jobs were completed by the end of the month, the costs of the completed jobs would be transferred to the finished goods inventory control account:

Finished Goods	39,295	
Work in Process—101		23,207
Work in Process—102		16,088

8. When the goods are shipped and billed to the customers, the following entries are made to record the sales and the cost of the jobs:

Accounts Receivable	65,650	
Sales		65,650
Cost of Goods Sold	39,295	
Finished Goods		39,295

The costs of producing the two jobs can be summarized as follows:

	Job 101 (1,000 Units)		Job 102 (500 Units)	
	Total Cost	Unit Cost	Total Cost	Unit Cost
Direct materials	$12,200	$12.20	$ 9,000	$18.00
Direct labor	6,000	6.00	3,750	7.50
Factory overhead	5,007	5.01	3,338	6.68
Total	$23,207	$23.21	$16,088	$32.18

The gross profit realized on each job is determined as follows:

	Job 101 (1,000 Units)		Job 102 (500 Units)	
	Total	Per Unit	Total	Per Unit
Selling price	$36,000	$36.00	$29,650	$59.30
Cost	23,207	23.21	16,088	32.18
Gross profit	$12,793	$12.79	$13,562	$27.12

The job cost sheets would reflect the previous information in more detail so that a short time after each job is completed, the gross profit can be determined. In addition, if management bids on similar jobs in the future, an accurate record of all costs would be available to assist management in determining contract prices.

WORK IN PROCESS CONTROL ACCOUNT

When jobs become too numerous to maintain a separate work in process account for each, a work in process control account in the general ledger will be used. In a job order cost system, the details on the job cost sheets in the subsidiary job cost ledger support the balance in Work in Process in the general ledger.

WORK IN PROCESS IN THE MANUFACTURING STATEMENT

If there is work in process at the beginning and at the end of the month, it will be shown as follows in the statement of cost of goods manufactured for Nehr Manufacturing Company.

The total manufacturing cost of $660,000 represents the cost of direct materials, direct labor, and factory overhead used during the month of June. Nehr Manufacturing incurred costs of $85,000 during the previous month for goods that were not completed at the end of that month. The total of $745,000, therefore, represents manufacturing cost that the company must account for. Work in Process at the end of June is $125,000, which represents the cost incurred to date for items that were not finished at the end of June. Therefore, the cost of goods completed in June, of which some were started in production the previous month, is

Nehr Manufacturing Company
Statement of Cost of Goods Manufactured
For the Month Ended June 30, 20—

Direct materials:		
Inventory, June 1	$ 15,000	
Purchases	310,000	
Total cost of available materials	$325,000	
Less inventory, June 30	25,000	
Cost of materials used	$300,000	
Less indirect materials used	10,000	
Cost of direct materials used in production		$290,000
Direct labor		240,000
Factory overhead:		
Indirect materials	$ 23,000	
Indirect labor	47,000	
Depreciation of building	35,000	
Depreciation of machinery and equipment	15,000	
Utilities	10,000	
Total factory overhead		130,000
Cost of goods manufactured during the month		$660,000
Add work in process inventory, June 1		85,000
		$745,000
Less work in process inventory, June 30		125,000
Cost of goods manufactured during the month		$620,000

$620,000. The work in process ledger account, in T-account form, would appear as follows at the end of the month:

Work in Process			
6/1 Balance	85,000	To Finished Goods	620,000
Direct materials	290,000		
Direct labor	240,000		
Factory overhead	130,000		
	745,000		
125,000			

If a job order cost system is being used, the balance of $125,000 in the account represents the manufacturing cost incurred to date on jobs that have not yet been completed.

You should now be able to work the following: Questions 22–26; Exercises 1-8 and 1-9; Problems 1-5 to 1-9.

KEY TERMS

Accounting information systems, p. 2
Budget, p. 7
Control, p. 5
Conversion cost, p. 12
Cost accounting, p. 1
Cost accounting systems, p. 3
Cost and production report, p. 6
Cost center, p. 6
Cost of goods manufactured, p. 9
Direct labor, p. 12
Direct materials, p. 11
Factory ledger, p. 11
Factory overhead, p. 12
Financial accounting, p. 7
Finished goods, p. 9
For-profit service businesses, p. 2
Indirect labor, p. 12
Indirect materials, p. 12
Job cost ledger, p. 32
Job cost sheet, p. 28
Job order cost system, p. 26

Manufacturers, p. 2
Manufacturing (or production) costs, p. 11
Manufacturing process, p. 3
Mark-on percentage, p. 18
Materials, p. 10
Merchandisers, p. 2
Not-for-profit service agencies, p. 2
Performance report, p. 6
Periodic inventory system, p. 11
Perpetual inventory system, p. 10
Planning, p. 5
Prime cost, p. 12
Process cost system, p. 26
Purchases, p. 8
Responsibility accounting, p. 5
Retailers, p. 2
Standard cost accounting system, p. 27
Standard costs, p. 27
Unit costs, p. 4
Wholesalers, p. 2
Work in process, p. 9

SELF-STUDY PROBLEM

BASIC COST SYSTEM; JOURNAL ENTRIES; FINANCIAL STATEMENTS

MUSKETEER MANUFACTURING CO.

The post-closing trial balance of Musketeer Manufacturing Co. at September 30 is reproduced as follows.

Musketeer Manufacturing Co.
Post-Closing Trial Balance
September 30, 20—

Cash	15,000	
Accounts Receivable	18,000	
Finished Goods	25,000	
Work in Process	4,000	
Materials	8,000	
Building	156,000	
Accumulated Depreciation—Building		23,400
Factory Equipment	108,000	
Accumulated Depreciation—Factory Equipment		54,000
Office Equipment	12,000	
Accumulated Depreciation—Office Equipment		2,000
Accounts Payable		30,000
Capital Stock		175,000
Retained Earnings		61,600
	346,000	346,000

During the month of October, the following transactions took place:

a. Raw materials at a cost of $50,000 and general factory supplies costing $8,000 were purchased on account. (Materials and supplies are recorded in the materials account.)

b. Raw materials to be used in production costing $41,000 and miscellaneous factory supplies costing $5,500 were issued.

c. Wages and salaries incurred and paid for the month were as follows: factory wages (including $2,500 indirect labor), $34,000, and selling and administrative salaries, $5,000. (Ignore payroll withholdings and deductions.)

d. Distributed the payroll in (c).

e. Depreciation was recorded for the month at an annual rate of 5% on the building and 20% on the factory equipment and office equipment. The sales and administrative staff uses approximately one-fifth of the building for its offices.

f. During the month, various other expenses totaling $5,200 were incurred on account. The company has determined that one-fourth of this amount is allocable to the office function.

g. Total factory overhead costs were transferred to Work in Process.

h. During the month, goods with a total cost of $79,000 were completed and transferred to the finished goods storeroom.

i. Sales for the month totaled $128,000 for goods costing $87,000. (Assume that all sales were made on account.)

j. Accounts receivable in the amount of $105,000 were collected.

k. Accounts payable totaling $55,000 and wages payable totaling $39,000 were paid.

Required:

1. Prepare journal entries to record the transactions.

2. Set up T-accounts for all accounts listed in the September 30, 20—, Post-Closing Trial Balance and for Cost of Goods Sold, Factory Overhead, Selling and Administrative Expenses, Sales, and Wages Payable. Post the beginning trial balance and the journal entries prepared in Part 1 to the accounts and calculate the balances in the accounts on October 31.

3. Prepare a statement of cost of goods manufactured, an income statement, and a balance sheet.

SOLUTION TO SELF-STUDY PROBLEM

Suggestions:

Read the entire problem thoroughly, keeping in mind what you are required to do:

1. Journalize the transactions.

2. Post the beginning trial balance and the journal entries to the T-accounts that you set up and calculate the ending balance for each account.

3. Using the ending account balances, prepare a cost of goods manufactured statement, an income statement, and a balance sheet.

The specifics in the problem highlight the following facts:

1. The company is a manufacturer; therefore, three inventory accounts, Materials, Work in Process, and Finished Goods, will be used.

2. A temporary account, Factory Overhead, will be used to record all of the indirect materials, indirect labor, and other manufacturing expenses for the period.

Preparing the journal entries:

a. and b. Note that there is only one inventory account for materials, which includes the cost of both direct and indirect materials. When the materials are issued into production, the direct materials are charged to Work in Process and the indirect materials are charged to Factory Overhead.

a.	Materials	58,000	
	Accounts Payable		58,000

b.	Work in Process	41,000	
	Factory Overhead (Indirect Materials)	5,500	
	Materials		46,500

c. The entries to record the payroll and the payments to employees use the payroll and wages payable accounts.

Payroll	39,000	
Wages Payable		39,000
Wages Payable	39,000	
Cash		39,000

d. The entry to distribute the payroll requires the use of the work in process account for the wages of employees who work directly on the product, the factory overhead account of the wages of employees who work in the factory but not directly on the product, and the selling and administrative expenses account for the wages of salespeople and administrative personnel.

Work in Process	31,500	
Factory Overhead (Indirect Labor)	2,500	
Selling and Administrative Expenses (Salaries) . . .	5,000	
Wages Payable		39,000

e., f., and g. The depreciation on the building and equipment and the other expenses are divided between Factory Overhead and Selling and Administrative Expenses, depending on the portion of the expense that relates to the factory and the portion that relates to the selling and administrative function. The balance in the Factory Overhead account at the end of the month is transferred to Work in Process.

e.	Factory Overhead (Depr. of Building)	520	
	Factory Overhead (Depr. of Factory Equipment) . .	1,800	
	Selling and Administrative Expenses (Depr. of Building)	130	
	Selling and Administrative Expenses (Depr. of Office Equipment)	200	
	Accumulated Depr.—Building		650
	Accumulated Depr.—Factory Equipment		1,800
	Accumulated Depr.—Office Equipment		200
f.	Factory Overhead (Miscellaneous)	3,900	
	Selling and Administrative Expenses (Miscellaneous)	1,300	
	Accounts Payable		5,200

g.   Work in Process   14,220

      Factory Overhead   14,220

h., i., j., and k. When goods are completed, the cost of the goods is taken out of Work in Process and recorded in Finished Goods. When the completed goods are sold, the cost of these goods is removed from the finished goods inventory account and recorded in the cost of goods sold expense account, and the receivable and revenue are recorded for the amount of the sale.

h.   Finished Goods   79,000

      Work in Process   79,000

i.   Accounts Receivable   128,000

      Sales   128,000

      Cost of Goods Sold   87,000

      Finished Goods   87,000

j.   Cash   105,000

      Accounts Receivable   105,000

k.   Accounts Payable   55,000

      Cash   55,000

Posting the beginning trial balance and the journal entries to the T-accounts:

Cash				Accounts Receivable			
9/30	15,000	c.	39,000	9/30	18,000	j.	105,000
j.	105,000	k.	55,000	i.	128,000		
	120,000				146,000		
26,000				41,000			

Finished Goods				Work in Process			
9/30	25,000	i.	87,000	9/30	4,000	h.	79,000
h.	79,000			b.	41,000		
	104,000			d.	31,500		
17,000				g.	14,220		
					90,720		
				11,720			

Materials				Building		
9/30	8,000	b.	46,500	9/30	156,000	
a.	58,000					
	66,000					
19,500						

Accumulated Depr.—Building				Factory Equipment		
		9/30	23,400	9/30	108,000	
		e.	650			
			24,050			

Accumulated Depr.—Factory Equipment				Office Equipment		
		9/30	54,000	9/30	12,000	
		e.	1,800			
			55,800			

Accumulated Depr.—Office Equipment				Accounts Payable		
		9/30	2,000	k.	55,000	9/30	30,000
		e.	200			a.	58,000
			2,200			f.	5,200
							93,200

Wages Payable			
c.	39,000	c.	39,000

(continued — Accounts Payable balance *38,200*)

Capital Stock				Retained Earnings		
		9/30	175,000			9/30	61,600

Sales				Cost of Goods Sold		
		i.	128,000	i.	87,000	

Payroll			
c.	39,000	d.	39,000

Factory Overhead				Selling and Administrative Expenses		
b.	5,500	f.	14,220	d.	5,000	
d.	2,500			e.	130	
e.	520			e.	200	
e.	1,800			f.	1,300	
f.	3,900				*6,630*	
	14,220					

Preparing a statement
of cost of goods
manufactured, an
income statement,
and a balance sheet:

The total manufacturing cost of $86,720 represents the cost of direct materials, direct labor, and factory overhead incurred during the month of October. Note that the cost of the indirect materials is subtracted in calculating the cost of direct materials used in production because it is included as a separate item under factory overhead. To determine the cost of goods manufactured for October, which really means the cost of the goods completed for the month, you have to add the cost of the beginning work in process inventory, $4,000, and subtract the cost of the ending work in process inventory, $11,720, from the total manufacturing cost for October:

Musketeer Manufacturing Co.
Statement of Cost of Goods Manufactured
For the Month Ended October 31, 20—

Direct materials:			
Inventory, October 1		$ 8,000	
Purchases		58,000	
Total cost of available materials		$66,000	
Less inventory, October 31		19,500	
Cost of materials used		$46,500	
Less indirect materials used		5,500	
Cost of direct materials used in production			$41,000
Direct labor			31,500
Factory overhead:			
Indirect materials		$ 5,500	
Indirect labor		2,500	
Depreciation of building		520	
Depreciation of factory equipment		1,800	
Miscellaneous expenses		3,900	
Total factory overhead			14,220
Total manufacturing cost			$86,720
Add work in process inventory, October 1			4,000
			$90,720
Less work in process inventory, October 31			11,720
Cost of goods manufactured			$79,000

In preparing an income statement for a manufacturer, remember that the beginning finished goods inventory for the month must be added to the cost of goods manufactured to obtain the cost of goods available for sale. Then the ending finished goods inventory must be subtracted to obtain the cost of goods sold:

Musketeer Manufacturing Co.
Income Statement
For the Month Ended October 31, 20—

Net sales			$128,000
Cost of goods sold:			
Finished goods inventory, October 1		$ 25,000	
Add cost of goods manufactured		79,000	
Goods available for sale		$104,000	
Less finished goods inventory, October 31		17,000	87,000
Gross profit on sales			$ 41,000

Selling and administrative expenses:

Selling and administrative salaries	$ 5,000	
Depreciation of building	130	
Depreciation of office equipment	200	
Miscellaneous	1,300	6,630
Net income		$34,370

In preparing a balance sheet for a manufacturer, note that there are three separate inventory accounts, rather than the single inventory account as for a merchandiser:

Musketeer Manufacturing Co.
Balance Sheet
October 31, 20—

Assets

Current assets:			
Cash			$ 26,000
Accounts receivable			41,000
Inventories:			
Finished goods		$ 17,000	
Work in process		11,720	
Materials		19,500	48,220
Total current assets			$115,220
Plant and equipment:			
Building	$156,000		
Less accumulated depreciation . .	24,050	$131,950	
Factory equipment	$108,000		
Less accumulated depreciation . .	55,800	52,200	
Office equipment	$ 12,000		
Less accumulated depreciation . .	2,200	9,800	
Total plant and equipment			193,950
Total assets			$309,170

Liabilities and Stockholders' Equity

Current liabilities:			
Accounts payable			$ 38,200
Stockholders' equity:			
Capital stock		$175,000	
Retained earnings*		95,970	
Total stockholders' equity			270,970
Total liabilities and stockholders' equity			$309,170

*$61,600 (bal. on 9/30) + $34,370 (Net income for Oct.) = $95,970

(Note: Problem 1-3 is similar to this problem.)

QUESTIONS

1. How does the cost accounting function assist in the management of a business?

2. How do the activities of manufacturers, merchandisers, and service businesses differ?

3. In what ways does a typical manufacturing business differ from a merchandising concern? In what ways are they similar?

4. How are cost accounting data used by management?

5. Why is unit cost information important to management?

6. For a manufacturer, what does the planning process involve and how are cost accounting data used in planning?

7. How is effective control achieved in a manufacturing concern?

8. Define responsibility accounting.

9. What criteria must be met for a unit of activity within the factory to qualify as a cost center?

10. How is cost accounting related to financial accounting?

11. How does the computation of cost of goods sold for a manufacturer differ from that of a merchandiser?

12. How would you describe the following accounts—Finished Goods, Work in Process, and Materials?

13. Compare the manufacturing, merchandising, and service sectors. How do they differ as to the kinds of businesses in each category, the nature of their output, and type of inventory, if any?

14. What is the difference between a perpetual inventory system and a periodic inventory system?

15. What are the basic elements of production cost?

16. How would you define the following costs: direct materials, indirect materials, direct labor, indirect labor, and factory overhead?

17. How would you define prime cost and conversion cost? Does prime cost plus conversion cost equal the cost of manufacturing?

18. In what way does the accounting treatment of factory overhead differ from that of direct materials and direct labor costs?

19. How do cost of goods sold for a manufacturer and cost of goods manufactured differ?

20. How are nonfactory costs and costs that benefit both factory and nonfactory operations accounted for?

21. What is a mark-on percentage?

22. When is job order costing appropriate and what types of businesses use it?

23. When is process costing appropriate and what types of businesses use it?

24. What are the advantages of accumulating costs by departments or jobs rather than for the factory as a whole?

25. What is a job cost sheet and why is it useful?

26. What are standard costs, and what is the purpose of a standard cost system?

EXERCISES

E1-1
Cost of goods sold—
merchandiser
Objective 2

The following data were taken from the general ledger of Morton Merchandisers on January 31, the end of the first month of operations in the current fiscal year:

Merchandise inventory, January 1	22,000
Purchases	83,000
Merchandise inventory, January 31	17,000

Compute the cost of goods sold for the month of January.

E1-2
Cost of goods sold—
manufacturer
Objective 2

The data below were taken from the general ledger and other data of MillCreek Manufacturing on July 31:

Finished goods, July 1	93,000
Cost of goods manufactured	343,000
Finished goods, July 31	85,000

Compute the cost of goods sold for the month of July.

E1-3
Cost classification
Objective 3

Classify the following as direct materials, direct labor, factory overhead, or selling and administrative expense.
a. Steel used in an automobile plant.
b. Cloth used in a shirt factory.
c. Fiberglass used by a sailboat builder.
d. Lubricating oils used on machines in a tool factory.
e. Wages of a binder employed in a printing plant.
f. Insurance on factory machines.
g. Rent paid for factory buildings.
h. Wages of forklift operators employed in a factory.
i. Leather used in a shoe factory.
j. Wages of a factory janitor.
k. Electric power consumed in operating factory machines.
l. Depreciation on corporate offices.
m. Fuel used in heating a factory.
n. Paint used in the manufacture of automobiles.
o. Wages of an ironworker in the construction business.
p. Electricity used in lighting sales offices.

E1-4
Cost flow
Objective 3

Explain in narrative form the flow of direct materials, direct labor, and factory overhead costs through the accounts.

E1-5
Statement of cost of
goods manufactured;
cost of goods sold
Objective 4

The following data are taken from the general ledger and other records of Mathis Manufacturing Co. on January 31, the end of the first month of operations in the current fiscal year:

a. Prepare a statement of cost of goods manufactured.
b. Prepare the cost of goods sold section of the income statement.

Sales	$75,000
Materials inventory (January 1)	25,000
Work in process inventory (January 1)	24,000
Finished goods inventory (January 1)	32,000
Materials purchased	21,000
Direct labor cost	18,000
Factory overhead (including $1,000 of indirect materials used and $3,000 of indirect labor cost)	12,000
Selling and administrative expense	10,000

Inventories at January 31:

Materials	22,000
Work in process	20,000
Finished goods	30,000

E1-6
Determining
materials, labor, and
cost of goods sold
Objectives 3, 4

The following inventory data relate to Mykanos Corp.:

	Inventories	
	Ending	Beginning
Finished goods	$75,000	$110,000
Work in process	80,000	70,000
Direct materials	95,000	90,000

Revenues and Costs for the Period

Sales	$900,000
Cost of goods available for sale	775,000
Total manufacturing costs	675,000
Factory overhead	175,000
Direct materials used	205,000

Calculate the following for the year:
a. Direct materials purchased.
b. Direct labor costs incurred.
c. Cost of goods sold.
d. Gross profit.

E1-7
Journal entries
Objective 4

The following is a list of manufacturing costs incurred by Printz Products Co. during the month of July:

Direct materials used	$15,000
Indirect materials used	3,000
Direct labor employed	21,000
Indirect labor employed	5,000
Rent expense	4,000
Utilities expense	1,200
Insurance expense	500
Depreciation expense (machinery and equipment)	1,500

Prepare the journal entries to record the preceding information and to transfer Factory Overhead to Work in Process.

E1-8
Journal entries for job
order costing; total
and unit cost
computation
Objectives 4, 5

Mirage Manufacturing, Inc., uses the job order cost system of accounting. The following information was taken from the company's books after all posting had been completed at the end of May:

Jobs Completed	Direct Materials Cost	Direct Labor Cost	Factory Overhead	Units Completed
1984	$3,600	$4,000	$1,600	400
2000	2,380	2,500	1,000	240
2525	1,800	1,700	680	200

a. Prepare the journal entries to charge the costs of materials, labor, and factory overhead to each job.
b. Compute the total production cost of each job.
c. Prepare the journal entry to transfer the cost of jobs completed to Finished Goods.
d. Compute the unit cost of each job.
e. Compute the selling price per unit for each job, assuming a mark-on percentage of 40%.

E1-9
Journal entries for job order costing
Objectives 4, 5

Jet-Products Co. manufactures goods on a job order basis. During the month of April, three jobs were started in process. (There was no work in process at the beginning of the month.) Jobs 707 and 727 were completed and sold during the month (selling prices: Job 707, $22,000; Job 727, $27,000); Job 737 was still in process at the end of April.

The following data came from the job cost sheets for each job. These costs included a total of $1,200 of indirect materials and $900 of indirect labor. One work in process control account is used for all jobs.

	Job 707	Job 727	Job 737
Direct materials	$5,000	$6,000	$3,500
Direct labor	4,000	5,000	2,500
Factory overhead	2,000	2,500	1,250

Prepare journal entries to record the following:
a. Materials used.
b. Factory wages and salaries earned.
c. Factory Overhead transferred to Work in Process.
d. Jobs completed.
e. Jobs sold.

PROBLEMS

P1-1
Cost of goods sold—merchandiser and manufacturer
Objective 2

The following data were taken from the general ledgers and other data of Kingdom Manufacturing and Magic Merchandising on April 30 of the current year:

Merchandise inventory, April 1	$ 38,000
Finished goods, April 1	67,000
Purchases	121,000
Cost of goods manufactured	287,000
Merchandise inventory, April 30	33,000
Finished goods, April 30	61,000

Required:

1. Compute the cost of goods sold for Magic Merchandising, selecting the appropriate items from the above list.
2. Compute the cost of goods sold for Kingdom Manufacturing, selecting the appropriate items from the above list.

P1-2
Statement of cost of goods manufactured; income statement; balance sheet
Objectives 3, 4

The adjusted trial balance for Nehr Furniture Company on September 30, the end of its first month of operation, is recorded as follows:

Nehr Furniture Company
Trial Balance
September 30, 20—

Cash	$ 21,800	
Accounts Receivable	16,200	
Finished Goods	13,900	
Work in Process	—	
Materials	7,400	
Building	300,000	
Accumulated Depr.—Building		$ 3,000
Machinery and Equipment	88,000	
Accumulated Depr.—Mach. and Equip.		2,200
Accounts Payable		7,900
Payroll	—	
Capital Stock		422,550
Sales		68,300
Cost of Goods Sold	41,450	
Factory Overhead	—	
Selling and Administrative Expenses	15,200	
	$503,950	$503,950

The general ledger reveals the following additional data:
a. There were no beginning inventories.
b. Materials purchases during the period were $33,000.
c. Direct labor cost was $18,500.
d. Factory overhead costs were as follows:

Indirect materials	$ 1,400
Indirect labor	4,300
Depr. of Building	3,000
Depr. of Machinery and Equipment	2,200
Utilities	1,750
	$12,650

Required:

1. Prepare a statement of cost of goods manufactured for the month of September.
2. Prepare an income statement for the month of September.
3. Prepare a balance sheet as of September 30.

P1-3
Basic cost system;
journal entries;
financial statements.
Similar to self-study problem.
Objectives 3, 4

The post-closing trial balance of Boulder Manufacturing Co. on April 30 is reproduced as follows:

Boulder Manufacturing Co.
Post-Closing Trial Balance
April 30, 20—

Cash	25,000	
Accounts Receivable	65,000	
Finished Goods	120,000	
Work in Process	35,000	
Materials	18,000	
Building	480,000	
Accumulated Depr.—Building		72,000
Factory Equipment	220,000	
Accumulated Depr.—Factory Equipment		66,000
Office Equipment	60,000	
Accumulated Depr.—Office Equipment		36,000
Accounts Payable		95,000
Capital Stock		250,000
Retained Earnings		504,000
	1,023,000	1,023,000

During the month of May, the following transactions took place:

a. Purchased raw materials at a cost of $45,000 and general factory supplies at a cost of $13,000 on account (recorded materials and supplies in the materials account).
b. Issued raw materials to be used in production, costing $47,000, and miscellaneous factory supplies, costing $15,000.
c. Recorded the payroll, the payments to employees, and the distribution of the wages and salaries earned for the month as follows: factory wages (including $12,000 indirect labor), $41,000, and selling and administrative salaries, $7,000. Additional account titles include Wages Payable and Payroll. (Ignore payroll withholdings and deductions.)
d. Recognized depreciation for the month at an annual rate of 5% on the building, 10% on the factory equipment, and 20% on the office equipment. The sales and administrative staff uses approximately one-fifth of the building for its offices.
e. Incurred various other expenses totaling $11,000. One-fourth of this amount is allocable to the office function.
f. Transferred total factory overhead costs to Work in Process.
g. Completed and transferred goods with a total cost of $91,000 to the finished goods storeroom.

h. Sold goods costing $188,000 for $345,000. (Assume that all sales were made on account.)
i. Collected accounts receivable in the amount of $362,000.
j. Paid accounts payable totaling $158,000.

Required:

1. Prepare journal entries to record the transactions.
2. Set up T-accounts. Post the beginning trial balance and the journal entries prepared in (1) to the accounts and determine the balances in the accounts on May 31.
3. Prepare a statement of cost of goods manufactured, an income statement, and a balance sheet. (Round amounts to the nearest whole dollar.)

P1-4
Journal entries;
account analysis
Objectives 3, 4

Selected account balances and transactions of Hawkins Manufacturing Co. follow:

	Account Balances	
	May 1	May 31
Raw materials	$ 5,000	$ 6,500
Factory supplies	800	900
Work in process	5,300	6,000
Finished goods	13,200	12,000

May Transactions

a. Purchased raw materials and factory supplies on account at costs of $45,000 and $5,000, respectively. (One inventory account is maintained.)
b. Incurred wages during the month of $65,000 ($10,000 was for indirect labor).
c. Incurred factory overhead costs in the amount of $12,000 on account.
d. Made adjusting entries to record $7,000 of factory overhead (credit Various Credits). Factory overhead was closed to Work in Process. Completed jobs were transferred to Finished Goods, and the cost of jobs sold was charged to Cost of Goods Sold.

Required:

Prepare journal entries for the following:
1. The purchase of raw materials and factory supplies.
2. The issuance of raw materials and supplies into production. (Hint: Be certain to consider the beginning and ending balances of raw materials and supplies as well as the amount of the purchases.)
3. The recording of the payroll.
4. The distribution of the payroll.
5. The payment of the payroll.
6. The recording of factory overhead incurred.
7. The adjusting entry for factory overhead.
8. The entry to transfer factory overhead costs to Work in Process.
9. The entry to transfer the cost of completed work to Finished Goods. (Hint: Be sure to consider the beginning and ending balances of Work in Process as well as the costs added to Work in Process this period.)
10. The entry to record the cost of goods sold. (Hint: Be sure to consider the beginning and ending balances of Finished Goods as well as the cost of the goods finished during the month.)

P1-5
Job order cost;
journal entries; ending
work in process;
inventory analysis
Objectives 4, 5

Historic Company manufactures goods to special order and uses a job order cost system. During its first month of operations, the following selected transactions took place:

a. Materials purchased on account $37,000
b. Materials issued to the factory:
    Job 1066 . . . . $ 2,200
    Job 1215   5,700
    Job 1776   7,100
    Job 1865   1,700
    For general use in the factory   1,350
c. Factory wages and salaries earned:
    Job 1066 . . . . $ 2,700
    Job 1215   6,800
    Job 1776   9,200
    Job 1865   2,100
    For general work in the factory   2,250
d. Miscellaneous factory overhead costs on account . . . . $ 2,400
e. Depreciation of $2,000 on the factory machinery recorded.
f. Factory overhead allocated as follows:
    Job 1066 . . . . $ 1,200
    Job 1215   2,000
    Job 1776   3,800
    Job 1865   1,000
g. Jobs 1066, 1215, and 1776 completed.
h. Jobs 1066 and 1215 shipped to the customer and billed at $30,900.

Required:

1. Prepare a schedule reflecting the cost of each of the four jobs.
2. Prepare journal entries to record the transactions. (One control account is used for Work in Process.)
3. Compute the ending balance in Work in Process.
4. Compute the ending balance in Finished Goods.

P1-6
Data analysis,
manufacturing
statement, cost
terminology
Objectives 3, 5

Fielder Company's cost of goods sold for the month ended July 31 was $345,000. The ending work in process inventory was 90% of the beginning work in process inventory. Factory overhead was 50% of the direct labor cost. Other information pertaining to Fielder Company's inventories and production for the month of July is as follows:

Beginning inventories, July 1:
    Direct materials   . . . . $ 20,000
    Work in process   40,000
    Finished goods   102,000
Purchases of direct materials during July   110,000
Ending inventories, July 31:
    Direct materials   26,000
    Work in process . . . .   ?
    Finished goods   105,000

Required:

1. Prepare a statement of cost of goods manufactured for the month of July. (Hint: Set up a statement of cost of goods manufactured, putting the given information in the appropriate spaces and solving for the unknown information.)
2. Prepare a schedule to compute the prime cost incurred during July.
3. Prepare a schedule to compute the conversion cost charged to Work in Process during July.

P1-7
Job order cost;
journal entries; profit
analysis
Objectives 4, 5

Dice Manufacturing Co. obtained the following information from its records for the month of July:

| | Jobs Completed and Sold | | |
	Job 7	Job 11	Job 12
Direct materials cost	$ 15,000	$10,000	$ 25,000
Direct labor cost	50,000	50,000	50,000
Factory overhead	30,000	30,000	30,000
Units manufactured	10,000	5,000	4,000
Selling price	126,667	80,000	131,250

Required:

1. Prepare, in summary form, the journal entries that would have been made during the month to record the distribution of materials, labor, and overhead costs; the completion of the jobs; and the sale of the jobs. (Assume separate work in process accounts for each job.)
2. Prepare schedules showing the gross profit or loss for July for the following:
   a. The business as a whole.
   b. Each job completed and sold.
   c. For each unit manufactured and sold. (Round to the nearest cent.)

P1-8
Job cost; journal
entries; inventory
analysis;
manufacturing
statement
Objectives 4, 5

Power-D Manufacturing Co. manufactures engines that are made only on customers' orders and to their specifications. During January, the company worked on Jobs 90AX, 90BZ, 90CK, and 90DQ. The following figures summarize the cost records for the month:

	Job 90AX (100 units)	Job 90BZ (60 units)	Job 90CK (25 units)	Job 90DQ (100 units)
Direct materials put into process:				
Jan. 2	$15,000	$ 5,000	—	—
18	20,000	16,000	$ 5,000	—
22	15,000	1,000	10,000	$ 6,000
28	—	—	3,500	2,000
Direct labor cost:				
Week ending				
Jan. 2	$ 1,000	$ 1,000	—	—
9	27,000	9,000	—	—
16	32,000	27,000	—	—
23	20,000	3,000	$ 5,000	$ 500
30	—	—	18,000	11,500
Factory overhead	$60,000	$32,000	$17,500	$10,500
Engines completed	100	60	25	—

Jobs 90AX and 90BZ have been completed and delivered to the customer at a total selling price of $426,000, on account. Job 90CK is finished but has not yet been delivered. Job 90DQ is still in process. There was no work in process at the beginning of the month.

Required:

1. Prepare the summary journal entries for the month to record the distribution of materials, labor, and overhead costs. (Assume that a work in process account is kept for each job.)
2. Prepare a summary showing the total cost of each job completed during the month or in process at the end of the month. Also determine the cost of the inventories of completed engines and engines in process at the end of the month.
3. Prepare the journal entries to record the completion of the jobs and the sale of the jobs.
4. Prepare a statement of cost of goods manufactured.

P1-9
Data analysis;
manufacturing
statement
Objective 5

Pincus Corporation manufactures one product and accounts for costs by a job order cost system. You have obtained the following information from the corporation's books and records for the year ended December 31:

a. Total manufacturing cost during the year was $1,000,000, including direct materials, direct labor, and factory overhead.
b. Cost of goods manufactured during the year was $970,000.
c. Factory overhead charged to work in process was 75% of direct labor cost and 27% of the total manufacturing cost.
d. The beginning work in process inventory, January 1, was 60% of the ending work in process inventory, December 31.

Required:

Prepare a statement of cost of goods manufactured for the year ended December 31 for Pincus Corporation. (Hint: Set up a statement of cost of goods manufactured, putting the given information in the appropriate spaces and solving for the unknown information.)

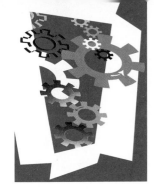

2

Accounting for Materials

LEARNING OBJECTIVES

After studying this chapter, you should be able to:

1. Recognize the two basic aspects of materials control.
2. Specify internal control procedures for materials.
3. Account for materials and relate materials accounting to the general ledger.
4. Account for scrap materials, spoiled goods, and defective work.
5. Account for inventories in a just-in-time system.

The total cost of a finished product consists of the expenditures made for raw materials, direct labor, and the factory overhead generated by the manufacturing activities. The principles and procedures for controlling and accounting for these cost elements are the major subjects of Chapters 2, 3, and 4. Each chapter will examine the controls and accounting procedures that apply to each element. However, common controls and practices pertain to all cost control systems. The major function, in general, of any cost control system is to keep expenditures within the limits of a preconceived plan. The control system should also encourage cost reductions by eliminating waste and operational inefficiencies. An effective system of cost control is designed to control the people responsible for the expenditures because people control costs. Costs do not control themselves.

An effective cost control system should include the following:

1. A specific assignment of duties and responsibilities.
2. A list of individuals who are authorized to approve expenditures.
3. An established plan of objectives and goals.
4. Regular reports showing the differences between goals and actual performance.
5. A plan of corrective action designed to prevent unfavorable differences from recurring.
6. Follow-up procedures for corrective measures.

Responsibility accounting is an integral part of a cost control system because it focuses attention on specific individuals who have been designated to achieve the established goals. Of the three major objectives of cost accounting—cost control, product costing, and inventory pricing—cost control is often the most difficult to achieve. A weakness in cost control can often be overcome by placing more emphasis on responsibility accounting. This makes the people who incur costs accountable for those costs.

MATERIALS CONTROL

LEARNING OBJECTIVE 1
Recognize the two basic aspects of materials control.

The two basic aspects of **materials control** are (1) the physical control or safeguarding of materials and (2) control of the investment in materials. Physical control protects materials from misuse or misappropriation. Controlling the investment in materials maintains appropriate quantities of materials in inventory.

PHYSICAL CONTROL OF MATERIALS

Every business requires a system of internal control that includes procedures for the safeguarding of assets. Because highly liquid assets, such as cash and marketable securities, are particularly susceptible to misappropriation, the protection provided for such assets is usually more than adequate. However, other assets, including inventories, must also be protected from unauthorized use or theft.

Because inventories usually represent a significant portion of a manufacturer's current assets, a business must control its materials from the time they are ordered until the time they are shipped to customers in the form of finished goods. In general, to effectively control materials, a business must maintain: (1) limited access, (2) segregation of duties, and (3) accuracy in recording.

Limited Access. Only authorized personnel should have access to materials storage areas. Materials should be issued for use in production only if requisitions for materials are properly documented and approved. Finished goods should also be safeguarded in limited access storage areas and not released for shipment in the absence of appropriate documentation and authorization. Procedures should be established within each production area or department for safeguarding work in process.

Segregation of Duties. A basic principle of internal control is the segregation of duties to minimize opportunities for misappropriation of assets. With respect to materials control, the following functions should be segregated: purchasing, receiving, storage, use, and recording. The independence of personnel assigned to these functions does not eliminate the danger of misappropriation or misuse because the possibility of collusion still exists. However, the appropriate segregation of duties limits an individual employee's opportunities for misappropriation and concealment. In smaller organizations, it is frequently not possible to achieve optimum segregation due to limited resources and personnel. Small businesses must therefore rely on specially designed control procedures to compensate for the lack of independence of assigned functions.

Accuracy in Recording. An effective materials control system requires accurate recording of purchases and issuances of materials. Inventory records should document the inventory quantities on hand, and cost records should provide the data needed to assign a value to inventories for the preparation of financial statements. Periodically, recorded inventories should be compared with a physical inventory count, and any significant discrepancies should be investigated. Differences may be due to recording errors or may result from inventory losses through theft or spoilage. Once the cause has been determined, appropriate corrective action should be taken.

CONTROLLING THE INVESTMENT IN MATERIALS

Maintaining the proper balance of materials on hand is one of the most important objectives of materials control. An inventory of sufficient size and diversity for efficient operations must be maintained, but the size should not be excessive in relation to scheduled production needs.

Because funds invested in inventories are unavailable for other uses, management must consider other working capital needs in determining the amount of funds to be invested in inventories and whether alternative uses of these funds might yield a greater return. In addition to the usage of funds, management should consider the costs of materials handling, storage, and insurance against fire, theft, or other casualty. Also, higher than needed inventory levels could increase the possibility of loss from damage, deterioration, and obsolescence. The planning and control of the materials inventory investment requires that all of these factors be carefully studied to determine (1) when orders should be placed and (2) how many units should be ordered.

Order Point. A minimum level of inventory should be determined for each article of raw material, and inventory records should indicate how much of each article is on hand. This requires the establishment of a subsidiary ledger in which a separate account is maintained for each individual item of raw material used in the manufacturing process.

The point at which an item should be ordered, called the **order point**, occurs when the predetermined minimum level of inventory on hand is reached. Calculating the order point is based on the following data:

1. **Usage**—the anticipated rate at which the material will be used.

2. **Lead time**—the estimated time interval between the placement of an order and the receipt of the material.

3. **Safety stock**—the estimated minimum level of inventory needed to protect against **stockouts** (running out of stock). Stockouts may occur due to inaccurate estimates of usage or lead time or various other unforeseen events, such as the receipt of damaged or inferior materials from the supplier.

Assume that a company's expected daily usage of an item of material is 100 units, the anticipated lead time is 5 days, and the estimated safety stock is 1,000 units. The following calculation shows that the order point is reached when the inventory on hand reaches 1,500 units:

100 units (daily usage) × 5 days (lead time)	500 units
Safety stock required	1,000 units
Order point	1,500 units

If estimates of usage and lead time are accurate, the level of inventory when the new order is received would be equal to the safety stock of 1,000 units. If, however, the new order is delivered three days late, the company would need to issue 300 units of material from its safety stock to maintain the production level during the temporary delay.

Economic Order Quantity (EOQ). The order point establishes the time when an order should be placed, but it does not indicate the most economical number of units to be ordered. To determine the quantity to be ordered, the cost of placing an order and the cost of carrying inventory must be considered. **Order costs** generally include several factors:

1. Salaries and wages of employees engaged in purchasing, receiving, and inspecting materials.

2. Communications costs associated with ordering, such as telephone (including fax) charges, postage, and forms or stationery.

3. Materials accounting and record keeping.

A variety of factors must be considered in determining **carrying costs**:

1. Materials storage and handling costs.

2. Interest, insurance, and property taxes.

3. Loss due to theft, deterioration, or obsolescence.

4. Records and supplies associated with carrying inventories.

Order costs and carrying costs move in opposite directions—annual order costs decrease when the order size increases, while annual carrying costs increase when the order size increases. The optimal quantity to order at one time, called the **economic order quantity,** is the order size that minimizes the total order and carrying costs over a period of time, such as one year.

The factors to be considered in determining order and carrying costs for a particular company vary with the nature of operations and the organizational structure. Special analyses are usually required to identify relevant costs, because these data are not normally accumulated in an accounting system. Care must be exercised in determining which costs are relevant. For example, a company may have adequate warehouse space to carry a large additional quantity of inventory. If the space cannot be used for some other profitable purpose, the cost of the space is not a relevant factor in determining carrying costs. If, however, the space in the company warehouse could be used for a more profitable purpose or if additional warehouse space must be leased or rented to accommodate increased inventories, the costs associated with the additional space are relevant in determining carrying costs.

The interest cost associated with carrying an inventory in stock should be considered whether or not funds are borrowed to purchase the inventory. If these funds were not used for inventory, they could have been profitably applied to some alternate use. The rate of interest to be used in the calculations will vary depending on the cost of borrowing or the rate that could be earned by the funds if they were used for some other purpose.

Quantitative models or formulas have been developed for calculating the economic order quantity. One formula that can be used is the following:

$$EOQ = \sqrt{\frac{2CN}{K}}$$

where
EOQ = economic order quantity
C = cost of placing an order
N = number of units required annually
K = carrying cost per unit of inventory

Principles of Cost Accounting

To illustrate this formula, assume that the following data have been determined by analyzing the factors relevant to materials inventory:

Number of units of material required annually 10,000
Cost of placing an order $10.00
Annual carrying cost per unit of inventory . . . . $.80

Using the EOQ formula:

$$EOQ = \sqrt{\frac{2(\text{cost of order}) (\text{number of units required annually})}{(\text{carrying cost per unit})}}$$

$$= \sqrt{\frac{2(\$10)(10,000)}{\$.80}}$$

$$= \sqrt{\frac{\$200,000}{\$.80}}$$

$$= \sqrt{250,000}$$

$$= 500 \text{ units}$$

The EOQ can also be determined by constructing a table using a range of order sizes. A tabular presentation of the data from the previous example, assuming no safety stock, follows:

1 Order Size	2 Number of Orders	3 Total Order Cost	4 Average Inventory	5 Total Carrying Cost	6 Total Order & Carrying Cost
100	100	$1,000	50	$ 40	$1,040
200	50	500	100	80	580
300	33	330	150	120	450
400	25	250	200	160	410
500	**20**	**200**	**250**	**200**	**400**
600	17	170	300	240	410
700	14	140	350	280	420
800	13	130	400	320	450
900	11	110	450	360	470
1,000	10	100	500	400	500

1. Number of units per order
2. 10,000 annual units ÷ order size
3. Number of orders × $10 per order
4. Order size ÷ 2 = average inventory on hand during the year
5. Average inventory × $0.80 per unit carrying cost for one year
6. Total order cost + total carrying cost

The data presented in Figure 2-1 show the total annual order cost decreasing as the order size increases. Meanwhile, the total annual carrying cost increases as the order size increases because of the necessity to

FIGURE 2-1   Costs of Ordering and Carrying Inventory

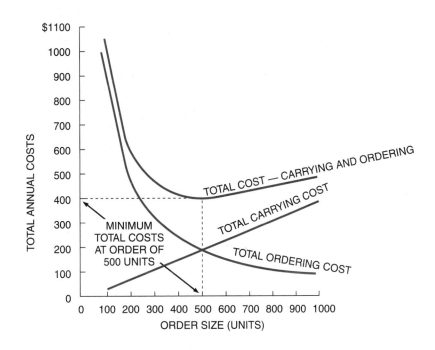

maintain a large quantity of inventory in stock. At the 500-unit level, the combined carrying and order costs are at their minimum point. This is the point at which the total carrying charges equal the total order costs, as demonstrated in the figure, when no safety stock is provided for. Assume in the preceding example that the company desires a safety stock of 400 units. The average number of units in inventory would be calculated as follows:

Average number of
units in inventory   = (1/2 × EOQ) + Safety stock
                       = (1/2 × 500) + 400
                       = 650 units

The total carrying cost then would be

Carrying cost   = Average inventory × Carrying cost per unit
                       = 650 × $0.80
                       = $520

Note that the order cost of $200, which doesn't change in this example, is significantly less than the carrying cost of $520 when safety stock is present.

Limitations of Order Point and EOQ Calculations. The techniques illustrated for determining when to order (order point) and how much to order (EOQ) may give a false impression of exactness. However, because these calculations are based on estimates of factors such as production volume, lead time, and order and carrying costs, they are really approximations that serve as a guide to planning and controlling the investment in materials.

In addition, other factors may influence the time for ordering or the quantity ordered. Such factors include the availability of materials from suppliers, the proximity of suppliers, fluctuations in the purchase price of materials, and trade (volume) discounts offered by suppliers.

MATERIALS CONTROL PROCEDURES

LEARNING OBJECTIVE 2
Specify internal control procedures for materials.

Specific internal control procedures should be tailored to a company's needs. However, materials control generally involves the following functions: (1) purchase and receipt of materials, (2) storage of materials, and (3) requisition and consumption of materials.

MATERIALS CONTROL PERSONNEL

Although actual job titles and duties may vary from one company to another, the personnel involved in materials control usually include (1) purchasing agent, (2) receiving clerk, (3) storeroom keeper, and (4) production department supervisor.

Purchasing Agent. The responsibility for buying the materials needed for the manufacturing enterprise should rest on the shoulders of one person. In a small plant the employee who does the buying may also perform other duties, while in a large plant the **purchasing agent** may head a department established to perform buying activities. Regardless of the size of an organization, it is important that ultimately one individual be responsible for the purchasing function. The duties of a purchasing agent may include the following:

1. Working with the production manager to prevent delays caused by the lack of materials.

2. Compiling and maintaining information that identifies where the desired materials can be obtained at the most economical price.

3. Placing purchase orders.
4. Supervising the order process until the materials are received.
5. Verifying purchase invoices and approving them for payments.

Receiving Clerk. The **receiving clerk** is responsible for supervising the receipt of incoming shipments. All incoming materials must be checked as to quantity and quality and sometimes as to price.

Storeroom Keeper. The **storeroom keeper**, who has charge of the materials after they have been received, must see that the materials are properly stored and maintained. The materials must be placed in stock and issued only on properly authorized requisitions. The purchasing agent should be informed of the quantities on hand as a guide to the purchasing of additional materials.

Production Department Supervisor. Each production department has a person who is responsible for supervising the operational functions within the department. This individual may be given the title of **production department supervisor** or another similar designation. One of the assigned duties of a department supervisor is to prepare or approve the requisitions designating the quantities and kinds of material needed for the work to be done in the department.

CONTROL DURING PROCUREMENT

Materials are ordered to maintain the adequate levels of inventory necessary to meet scheduled production needs. The storeroom keeper is responsible for monitoring quantities of materials on hand. When the order point is reached for a particular item of raw material, the procurement process is initiated. In many companies, computers store data pertaining to inventories on hand, predetermined order points, and economic order quantities. When properly programmed, computers can simplify the task of maintaining appropriate inventory levels.

Supporting documents are essential to maintaining control during the procurement process. In general, the documents should be prenumbered and protected from unauthorized use. The documents commonly used in procuring materials include (1) purchase requisitions, (2) purchase orders, (3) vendor's invoices, (4) receiving reports, and (5) debit-credit memoranda. Increasingly the supporting documents are in the form of computer records.

Purchase Requisitions. The form used to notify the purchasing agent that additional materials are needed is known as a **purchase requisition**. This requisition is an important part of the materials control process because it authorizes the agent to buy. Purchase requisitions should originate with the storeroom keeper or some other individual with similar authority and responsibility.

Purchase requisitions should be prenumbered serially to help detect the loss or misuse of any of these forms. They are generally prepared in duplicate. The first copy goes to the purchasing agent, and the storeroom keeper retains the second copy. Figure 2-2 shows a purchase requisition.

Purchase Order. The purchase requisition gives the purchasing agent authority to order the materials described in the requisition. The purchasing agent should maintain or have access to an up-to-date list of vendors, which includes prices, available discounts, estimated delivery time, and any other relevant information. From this list, the purchasing agent selects a vendor from whom high-quality materials can be obtained when needed at a competitive cost. If this information is not available from the list for a particular item of material, the purchasing agent may communicate with several prospective vendors and request quotations on the materials needed.

The purchasing agent then completes a **purchase order**, as shown in Figure 2-3, and addresses it to the chosen vendor, describing the materials wanted, stating price and terms, and fixing the date and method of delivery. This purchase order should be prenumbered serially and prepared in quadruplicate. The first copy goes to the vendor, one copy goes to the accounting department, one copy goes to the receiving clerk, and the purchasing agent retains a copy.

The purchasing agent's copy of the order should be placed in an unfilled orders file. Before the order is filed, the purchase requisition on which it is based should be attached to it. This last important step begins the assembly of a complete set of all the forms pertaining to the purchase transaction. To identify each document relating to a transaction with all others of the same set, the purchase order number should be shown on each of the documents. The sets can then be compiled according to the respective purchase order numbers.

Vendor's Invoice. The company should receive a **vendor's invoice** before the materials arrive at the factory. As soon as it's received, the vendor's invoice goes to the purchasing agent, who compares it with the purchase order, noting particularly that the description of the materials is the same, that the price and the terms agree, and that the method of ship-

FIGURE 2-2   Purchase Requisition. (Notifies purchasing agent that additional materials should be ordered.)

LONGHORN MFG	PURCHASE REQUISITION	No. **3246**

Date _January 3, 20--_

Date wanted _February 1, 20--_

For { Job No.   300
      Account No.   1482

Authorization No.   3313

QUANTITY	DESCRIPTION
20,000 Gal.	Adhesive Compound -- Grade A102

Approved by _L. Merz_   Signed by _G. Thomas_

Purchase order No. _1982_   Date ordered _January 6, 20--_
Ordered from _Sooner Corporation_

ment and the date of delivery conform to the instructions on the purchase order. When satisfied that the invoice is correct, the purchasing agent initials or stamps the invoice indicating that it has been reviewed and agrees with the purchase order. The invoice is then filed together with the purchase order and the purchase requisition in the unfilled orders file until the materials arrive.

FIGURE 2-3   Purchase Order. (Prepared by purchasing agent and sent to vendor to order materials.)

LONGHORN MFG	PURCHASE ORDER	Order No. **1982**

Mark Order No. on invoice
and on all packages

To: Sooner Corporation
Batesville, Indiana 47006

Date ___January 6, 20--___

Terms ___3/10 eom n/60___

Ship Via ___Truck (to arrive January 25, 20--)___

QUANTITY	DESCRIPTION	PRICE	
20,000 Gal.	Adhesive Compound -- Grade A102	$31,300	00

By ___A. Lauren___

Purchasing Agent

Receiving Report. As noted previously, a copy of the purchase order goes to the receiving clerk to give advance notice of the arrival of the materials ordered. This is done to facilitate planning and to provide space for the incoming materials. The receiving clerk is in charge of the receiving department where all incoming materials are received, opened, counted or weighed, and tested for conformity with the order. If the materials received are of too technical a nature to be tested by the receiving clerk, an engineer from the production manager's office may perform the inspection, or the materials may be sent to the plant laboratory for testing.

The receiving clerk counts and identifies the materials received and prepares a **receiving report** similar to the one reproduced in Figure 2-4. Each report is numbered serially and shows the vendor, when the materials were received, what the shipment contained, and the number of the purchase order that identifies the shipment. The report should be prepared in quadruplicate. Two copies go to the purchasing agent, one copy goes with the materials or supplies to the storeroom keeper to ensure that all of the materials that come to the receiving department are put

FIGURE 2-4   Receiving Report. (Incoming materials opened, counted, weighed, or tested for conformity with purchase order.)

LONGHORN MFG   RECEIVING REPORT   No. **496**

Date January 21, 20--

To the purchasing agent:

RECEIVED FROM Sooner Corporation

Via Ace Trucking   Transportation Charges $210.85

QUANTITY	DESCRIPTION
20,000 Gal.	Adhesive Compound -- Grade A102

Counted by R. S.   Inspected by D. P.

Purchase order No. 1982

into the storeroom, and the receiving clerk retains one copy. In some plants, the receiving clerk is given a copy of the purchase order with the quantity ordered omitted, thus ensuring that the items received will be counted.

The purchasing agent compares the receiving report with the vendor's invoice and the purchase order to determine that the materials received are those ordered and billed. If the documents agree, the purchasing agent initials or stamps the two copies of the receiving report. One copy is then attached to the other forms already in the file, and the entire set of forms is sent to the accounting department where the purchase of merchandise on account is recorded. The other copy of the receiving report is sent to the person in the accounting department who maintains inventory records. The procedures for recording materials purchases are discussed later in this chapter.

Debit-Credit Memorandum. Occasionally, a shipment of materials does not match the order and the invoice. The purchasing agent will discover this discrepancy when comparing the receiving report with the purchase order and the invoice. Whatever the cause, the difference will lead to correspondence with the vendor, and copies of the letters should be added to the file of forms relating to the transaction. If a larger quantity has been received than has been ordered and the excess is to be kept for future use, a **credit memorandum** is prepared notifying the vendor of the amount of the increase in the invoice.

If, on the other hand, the shipment is short, one of two courses of action may be taken. If the materials received can be used, they may be retained and a **debit memorandum** prepared notifying the vendor of the amount of the shortage. If the materials received cannot be used, a **return shipping order** is prepared and the materials are returned.

Figure 2-5 shows one form of the debit-credit memorandum. This memo shows that the vendor has delivered materials that do not meet the buyer's specifications. The purchasing agent will prepare a return shipping order and return the materials to the vendor.

CONTROL DURING STORAGE AND ISSUANCE

The preceding discussion outlined ways to maintain the control of materials during the procurement process. The procedures and forms described are necessary for control of the ordering and receiving functions and the transfer of incoming materials to the storeroom. The next problem to be considered is the storage and issuance of materials and supplies.

Materials Requisition. As discussed earlier, materials should be protected from unauthorized use. No materials should be issued from the store-

FIGURE 2-5   Debit-Credit Memorandum. (Discrepancy between order, shipment, and vendor invoice. Price adjustment request shown on debit-credit memo.)

LONGHORN MFG

(DEBIT) MEMORANDUM
CREDIT

Date _January 3, 20--_

To: Jayhawk Machine Company
    Lawrence, Kansas 66044

We have today (Debited) your account for the following:
           Credited

Explanation _wrong size_

QUANTITY	DESCRIPTION	UNIT PRICE	AMOUNT
5 boxes	Brass machine screws, 8/32" x 1" flat head	$27.50	$137	50

Purchase order No. _1029_
Your invoice date _December 27, 20--_

By _A. Lauren_
                    Purchasing Agent

---

room except on written authorization to lessen the chance of theft, carelessness, or misuse. The form used to provide this control is known as the **materials requisition** or **stores requisition** (see Figure 2-6) and is prepared by factory personnel authorized to withdraw materials from the storeroom. The personnel authorized to perform this function may differ from company to company, but such authority must be given to someone of responsibility. The most satisfactory arrangement would be to have the production manager prepare all materials requisitions, but this is usually not feasible. Another arrangement requires that the

FIGURE 2-6   Materials Requisition. (Authorization to withdraw materials from storeroom.)

LONGHORN MFG
MATERIALS REQUISITION

Date January 19, 20--   No. **632**

To: D. Graham

QUANTITY	DESCRIPTION	UNIT PRICE	AMOUNT	
100 Gal.	Adhesive Compound-- Grade A102	$1.565	$156	50

Approved by *E. B.*   Issued by *B. W.*

Received by *L. M.*

Charged to Job/Dept. *300*   Factory Overhead Expense Account _____

department supervisors approve (sign) all materials requisitions for their respective departments. When the storeroom keeper receives a properly signed requisition, the requisitioned materials are released. Both the storeroom keeper and the employee to whom materials are issued should be required to sign the requisition.

The materials requisition is usually prepared in quadruplicate. Two copies go to the accounting department for recording; one copy goes to the storeroom keeper and serves as authorization for issuing the materials; and the production manager or department supervisor who prepared it retains one copy.

Identification is an important factor in the control of materials. For this reason, the materials requisition should indicate the job number (job order costing) or department (process costing) for which the materials are issued. When indirect materials are issued, such as cleaning materials, lubricants, and paint, the requisition will indicate the name or number of the factory overhead account to be charged.

Returned Materials Report. After materials are requisitioned, occasionally some or all of the materials must be returned to the storeroom. Perhaps more materials were requested than were needed or the wrong type of materials were issued. Whatever the reason, a written report, called a **returned materials report**, describing the materials and the reason for the return, must accompany the materials to the storeroom.

You should now be able to work the following: Questions 1–15; Exercise 2-1; Problem 2-1.

ACCOUNTING FOR MATERIALS

LEARNING OBJECTIVE 3
Account for materials and relate materials accounting to the general ledger.

A company's inventory records should show (1) the number of units of each kind of materials on hand and (2) their cost. The most desirable method of achieving this result is to integrate the materials accounting system with the general ledger accounts. All purchases of materials are recorded as a debit to Materials in the general ledger (the corresponding credit is to Accounts Payable). Materials is a control account supported by a subsidiary **stores** or **materials ledger** that contains an individual account for each item of material carried in stock. Periodically, the balance of the control account and the total of the individual accounts are compared, and any significant variation between the two is investigated.

Each of the individual materials accounts in the subsidiary stores ledger shows (1) the quantity on hand and (2) the cost of the materials. To keep this information current, it is necessary to record in each individual account the quantity and the cost of materials received, issued, and on hand. The stores ledger accounts are usually maintained on cards similar in design to the one shown in Figure 2-7.

Copies of the purchase order and receiving report are approved by the purchasing agent and sent to the accounting department. Upon receiving the purchase order, the stores ledger accountant enters the date, purchase order number, and quantity in the "On Order" columns of the appropriate stores ledger card. When materials arrive, the accounting department's copy of the receiving report serves as the basis for posting

FIGURE 2-7   Stores Ledger Card

	ON ORDER		RECEIVED				ISSUED				BALANCE		
Date	Purchase Order No.	Quantity	Receiving Report No. (Returned Shipping Order No.)	Quantity	Unit Price	Amount	Materials Requisition (Returned Materials Report No.)	Quantity	Unit Price	Amount	Quantity	Unit Price	Amount

Description White Lead   **Location in Storeroom** Bin 8

Maximum 15,000 lbs.   **Minimum** 1,000 lbs.   **Stores Ledger Acct. No.** 1411

the receipt of the materials to the stores ledger card. The posting shows the date of receipt, the number of the receiving report, and the number of units received and their cost. The cost may be expressed in both unit cost and total cost or in total only.

When materials are issued, two copies of the materials requisition go to the accounting department. One copy is used in posting the cost of requisitioned materials to the appropriate accounts in the job cost and factory overhead ledgers. Direct materials are charged to the job (or department), and indirect materials are charged to the appropriate factory overhead accounts. The other copy of the requisition goes to the stores ledger accountant and becomes the basis for posting to the ledger cards. The posting shows the date of issue, the number of the requisition, and the number of units issued and their cost.

When materials are returned to the storeroom, a copy of the returned materials report goes to the accounting department. The cost of the returned materials is entered on the report and posted to the appropriate stores ledger card. The cost assigned to the returned materials should be the same as that recorded when the materials were issued to the factory.

The copy of the returned materials report is then routed to the cost accountant in charge of the job cost and factory overhead ledgers. Direct materials returned are credited to the job or department, and indirect materials returned are credited to the appropriate factory overhead account.

After each receipt and issue of materials is posted to the stores ledger cards, the balance is extended. These extensions could be made at the end of the accounting period, when ending inventories are to be determined for financial reporting purposes. However, to wait until that time would defeat one of the advantages of this method of materials control because it would not be possible to determine from the stores ledger when stock is falling below the minimum requirements. Also, most companies have automated inventory systems that utilize online information processing, such as bar coding and optical scanning, allowing current balances to be available in a timely and cost-efficient manner.

DETERMINING THE COST OF MATERIALS ISSUED

An important area of materials accounting is the cost of materials requisitioned from the storeroom for factory use. The unit cost of incoming materials is known at the time of purchase. The date of each purchase is also known, but the materials on hand typically include items purchased on different dates and at different prices. Items that look alike usually are commingled in the storeroom. As a result, it may be difficult or impossible to identify an issue of materials with a specific purchase when determining what unit cost should be assigned to the materials being issued.

Several practical methods of solving this problem are available. In selecting the method to be employed, the accounting policies of the firm and the federal and state income tax regulations must be considered. As the methods are discussed, it is important to remember that the flow of materials does not dictate the flow of costs. The **flow of materials** is the order in which materials are actually issued for use in the factory. The **flow of costs** is the order in which unit costs are assigned to materials issued. The following examples assume the use of a perpetual inventory system where the materials ledger card is updated each time materials are received or issued. FIFO and LIFO may also be used with a periodic inventory system where the inventory is counted and costed at the end of the period. In a periodic inventory system, the moving average method is replaced by the weighted or month-end average method.

First-In, First-Out Method. The **first-in, first-out (FIFO)** method of costing has the advantage of simplicity. The FIFO method assumes that materials issued are taken from the oldest materials in stock. Therefore, the materials are costed at the prices paid for the oldest materials. In many companies, the flow of costs using FIFO closely parallels the physical flow of materials. For example, if materials have a tendency to deteriorate in storage, the oldest materials would be issued first. However, as noted previously, the flow of costs does not have to be determined on the basis of the flow of materials. As a result, any organization may use FIFO.

The FIFO method can be illustrated using the following data:

Dec. 1 Balance, 1,000 units @ $20.
10 Issued 500 units.
15 Purchased 1,000 units @ $24.
20 Issued 250 units.
26 Issued 500 units.
28 Purchased 500 units @ $26.
30 Issued 500 units.
31 Balance, 750 units.

Using FIFO, costs would be assigned to materials issued during the month and to materials on hand at the end of the month as follows (see Figure 2-8):

Dec. 10 Issued from the December 1 balance: 500 units @ $20 total cost, $10,000.
20 Issued from the December 1 balance: 250 units @ $20, total cost, $5,000.
26 Issued from the December 1 balance: 250 units @ $20, total cost, $5,000.

Dec. 26   Issued from the December 15 purchase: 250 units @ $24, total
      cost, $6,000.
    26   Total cost of materials issued: $5,000 + $6,000 = $11,000.
    30   Issued from the December 15 purchase: 500 units @ $24, total
      cost, $12,000.
    31   The ending inventory of materials, 750 units, consists of the fol-
      lowing:

Date of Purchase	Units	Unit Cost	Total Cost
December 15	250	$24	$ 6,000
December 28	500	26	13,000
	750		$19,000

As illustrated in the example, ending inventories using FIFO are costed at the prices paid for the most recent purchases. Thus, 500 of the units on hand are assigned a unit cost of $26, the unit cost of the December 28 purchase. The remaining 250 units on hand are costed at $24 per unit, reflecting the unit cost of the next most recent purchase on December 15.

Last-In, First-Out Method. The **last-in, first-out (LIFO)** method of costing materials, as the name implies, assumes that materials issued for manufacturing are the most recently purchased materials. Thus, materials issued are costed at the most recent purchase prices, and inventories on hand at the end of the period are costed at prices paid for the earliest purchases. The LIFO method of costing closely approximates the physical flow of materials in some industries. For example, in the smelting of iron ore, the raw material is stored in mountainous piles. As ore is needed for production, it is drawn from the pile in such a way that the material being used is the last ore to have been received. As emphasized previously, however, physical flow does not determine the costing method used.

Using the same data given to illustrate the FIFO method, costs under the LIFO method would be determined as follows (see Figure 2-8):

Dec. 10   Issued from the December 1 balance: 500 units @ $20, total cost,
      $10,000.
    20   Issued from the December 15 purchase: 250 units @ $24, total
      cost, $6,000.
    26   Issued from the December 15 purchase: 500 units @ $24, total
      cost, $12,000.
    30   Issued from the December 28 purchase: 500 units @ $26, total
      cost, $13,000.
    31   The ending inventory of materials, 750 units, consists of the fol-
      lowing:

Principles of Cost Accounting

Date of Purchase	Unit	Unit Cost	Total Cost
Balance, December 1	500	$20	$10,000
December 15	250	24	6,000
	750		$16,000

FIGURE 2-8   Comparison of Inventory Valuation Methods

First-In, First-Out Method

	Received			Issued			Balance		
Date	Quantity	Unit Price	Amount	Quantity	Unit Price	Amount	Quantity	Unit Price	Amount
Dec. 1							1,000	20 00	20,000 00
10				500	20 00	10,000 00	500	20 00	10,000 00
15	1,000	24 00	24,000 00				500	20 00 ⎱	
							1,000	24 00 ⎰	34,000 00
20				250	20 00	5,000 00	250	20 00 ⎱	
							1,000	24 00 ⎰	29,000 00
26				250	20 00 ⎱				
				250	24 00 ⎰	11,000 00	750	24 00	18,000 00
28	500	26 00	13,000 00				750	24 00 ⎱	
							500	26 00 ⎰	31,000 00
30				500	24 00	12,000 00	250	24 00 ⎱	
							500	26 00 ⎰	19,000 00

Last-In, First-Out Method

	Received			Issued			Balance		
Date	Quantity	Unit Price	Amount	Quantity	Unit Price	Amount	Quantity	Unit Price	Amount
Dec. 1							1,000	20 00	20,000 00
10				500	20 00	10,000 00	500	20 00	10,000 00
15	1,000	24 00	24,000 00				500	20 00 ⎱	
							1,000	24 00 ⎰	34,000 00
20				250	24 00	6,000 00	500	20 00 ⎱	
							750	24 00 ⎰	28,000 00
26				500	24 00	12,000 00	500	20 00 ⎱	
							250	24 00 ⎰	16,000 00
28	500	26 00	13,000 00				500	20 00 ⎱	
							250	24 00 ⎰	
							500	26 00 ⎰	29,000 00
30				500	26 00	13,000 00	500	20 00 ⎱	
							250	24 00 ⎰	16,000 00

FIGURE 2-8   Continued

Moving Average Method

Date	Received			Issued			Balance		
	Quantity	Unit Price	Amount	Quantity	Unit Price	Amount	Quantity	Unit Price	Amount
Dec. 1							1,000	20 00	20,000 00
10				500	20 00	10,000 00	500	20 00	10,000 00
15	1,000	24 00	24,000 00				1,500	22 66⅔	34,000 00
20				250	22 66⅔	5,666 67	1,250	22 66⅔	28,333 33
26				500	22 66⅔	11,333 33	750	22 66⅔	17,000 00
28	500	26 00	13,000 00				1,250	24 00	30,000 00
30				500	24 00	12,000 00	750	24 00	18,000 00

Moving Average Method. The **moving average** method assumes that the materials issued at any time are simply withdrawn from a mixed group of like materials in the storeroom and that no attempt is made to identify the materials as being from the earliest or the latest purchases. This method has the disadvantage of requiring more frequent computations than the other methods. However, the use of computers has overcome this disadvantage, and many firms are adopting this method. A basic requirement of the moving average method is that an average unit price must be computed every time a new lot of materials is received, and this average unit price must be used to cost all issues of materials until another lot is purchased. Thus, the issues in the illustration would be computed as follows (see Figure 2-8):

Dec. 10   Issued from the December 1 balance: 500 units @ $20, total cost, $10,000.

15   The balance of materials on hand on December 15 consists of 500 units from December 1 and 1,000 units acquired on December 15, for a total of 1,500 units that cost $34,000. The average cost is $22.66 2/3 per unit ($34,000 ÷ 1,500).

20   Issued 250 units @ $22.66 2/3, total cost, $5,666.67.

26   Issued 500 units @ $22.66 2/3, total cost, $11,333.33.
28   The balance of materials on hand on December 28 consists of 750 units costing $17,000 (purchased prior to December 28) and 500 units @ $26 (purchased on December 28) costing $13,000. The total cost is $30,000 for 1,250 units, representing an average cost of $24 per unit ($30,000/1,250).
30   Issued 500 units @ $24, total cost, $12,000.
31   The ending inventory of materials is $18,000, consisting of 750 units at $24 per unit.

Analysis of FIFO, LIFO, and Moving Average. FIFO, LIFO, and moving average are the most commonly used methods of inventory costing. Any of these methods may be adopted to maintain the stores ledger.

Because no one method best suits all manufacturing situations, the method chosen should be the one that most accurately reflects the income for the period in terms of the current economic conditions. One factor to consider is the effect the costing method has on reported net income. Overstating net income will subject a firm to higher taxes than those of a competitor who is using a different costing method.

In an inflationary environment, LIFO is sometimes adopted so that the higher prices of the most recently purchased materials may be charged against the increasingly higher sales revenue. The resulting lower gross margin is assumed to reflect a more accurate picture of earnings because the firm will have to replace its inventory at the new higher costs. Also, the lower gross margin, brought about by the use of the LIFO method, results in a smaller tax liability for the firm. This LIFO benefit, however, does not mean that all companies should adopt LIFO.

To illustrate the effects that the different costing methods have on profit determination, assume that A, B, and C are competing companies that use FIFO, moving average, and LIFO, respectively. The companies have no beginning inventories, and they purchase identical materials at the same time, as follows (assume also that each purchase is for one unit):

Purchase No. 1 @ $0.10
Purchase No. 2 @ $0.50
Purchase No. 3 @ $0.90

Assume that one unit of materials is used and sold at a price of $1.00 after the last purchase has been made. The net income is calculated as follows:

	Co. A FIFO (Per Unit)	Co. B Moving Avg. (Per Unit)	Co. C LIFO (Per Unit)
Net sales	$1.00	$1.00	$1.00
Less cost of goods sold	0.10	0.50*	0.90
Gross margin on sales	$0.90	$0.50	$0.10
Operating expenses	0.08	0.08	0.08
Income before income taxes . . .	$0.82	$0.42	$0.02
Less income taxes (50%)	0.41	0.21	0.01
Net income	$0.41	$0.21	$0.01

*$0.10 + $0.50 + $0.90 = $1.50/3 units = $0.50 per unit.

As shown in the example, LIFO costing has a definite tax advantage when prices are rapidly rising. Notice that Company C pays $0.01 per unit for taxes, while Companies A and B pay taxes per unit of $0.41 and $0.21, respectively. Thus, Company C has $0.99 of each sales dollar to pay for merchandise, operating expenses, and dividends, while Company A has only $0.59 and Company B has only $0.79 available.

As previously mentioned, each unit of material currently costs $0.90 (Purchase No. 3). Therefore, Company A requires additional funding of $0.31 ($0.90 – $0.59) and Company B requires additional funding of $0.11 ($0.90 – $0.79) to replace a unit of material. Only Company C can replace materials, pay operating expenses and taxes, and retain its profit per unit.

The companies, using their respective costing methods, have the following ending materials inventory balances:

Company A (FIFO) . . . . $1.40 ($0.50 + $0.90)
Company B (moving average) . . . . $1.00 ($0.50 + $0.50)
Company C (LIFO) . . . . $0.60 ($0.10 + $0.50)

Company C has the most conservatively valued inventory at $0.60, and Company A shows the highest inventory value at $1.40. The Company A inventory value also may be detrimental because inventory often is subject to state and local property taxes that are based on the inventory valuation chosen by the company. It is important to realize that differences between the three methods usually will not be as extreme as they were in this example. Companies that turn their inventory over very rapidly will not be as concerned with the choice of methods as will companies who hold their inventory for a longer time.

Many companies have adopted the LIFO method to match current materials costs with current revenue as well as to minimize the effect of income taxes in periods of rising prices. Companies considering the adoption of the LIFO method, however, should carefully analyze economic conditions and examine the tax regulations that pertain to LIFO. If there should be a downward trend of prices, these companies would probably desire to change to the FIFO method to have the same competitive advantages that were gained by using LIFO when prices were rising. However, the LIFO election cannot be rescinded unless authorized or required by the Internal Revenue Service.

ACCOUNTING PROCEDURES

The purpose of materials accounting is to provide a summary from the general ledger of the total cost of materials purchased and used in manufacturing. The forms commonly used in assembling the required data have already been discussed. The purchase invoices provide the information needed to prepare the entry in the purchases journal or to prepare the vouchers, which are then recorded in a voucher register, if a voucher system is in use. Note that for illustrative purposes in this text all entries are recorded in general journal format. At the end of the month, the total materials purchased during the month is posted by debiting Materials and crediting Accounts Payable. The materials account in the general ledger serves as a control account for the stores ledger.

All materials issued during the month and materials returned to stock are recorded on a **summary of materials issued and returned** form (see Figure 2-9). When the summary is completed at the end of the month, the total cost of direct materials requisitioned is recorded by debiting Work in Process and crediting Materials. The total of indirect materials requisitioned is recorded by debiting the appropriate factory overhead account and crediting Materials. The work in process account in the general ledger serves as a control account for the job cost ledger.

Any undamaged materials returned to the storeroom should also be recorded on the summary of materials issued and returned so that the totals may be recorded at the end of the month. The entries required to record undamaged materials returned are the reverse of the entries required to record materials requisitioned. Thus, the total cost of direct materials returned to the storeroom should be debited to Materials and credited to Work in Process, while the total cost of indirect materials returned should be debited to Materials and credited to the proper factory overhead account.

Any materials returned to the original vendors should be debited to Accounts Payable and credited to Materials. Unless a special journal is provided for recording such returns, the entries may be made in the general journal. All transactions relating to materials should be recorded so that the balance of the materials account in the general ledger will represent the cost of materials on hand at the end of a period. The balance of the materials account in the general ledger may be proved by listing the stores ledger account balances.

FIGURE 2-9   Summary of Materials Issued and Returned

SUMMARY OF MATERIALS ISSUED AND RETURNED

Month Ending _____ 20 ____

Date	Req. No.	Materials Issued — Direct Materials — Job	Amount	Indirect Materials — Overhead Acct. No.	Amount	Report No.	Materials Returned to Storeroom — Direct Materials — Job	Amount	Indirect Materials — Overhead Acct. No.	Amount
Mar. 5	825	315	$2,150 00							
8	826	316	3,210 00	3121	$ 440 00				3121	$ 12 50
11	827	317	280 00	3121	132 50					
14	828	317	415 00							
17	829	316	340 00							
17	830	317	820 00	3121	135 00				3121	15 00
18	831	318	290 00							
19	832	319	224 20			232	319	$ 12 10		
20	833	319	975 90							
24	834	320	4,350 00	3121	432 00	233	320	448 90		
27	835	321	6,500 00			234	321	318 20		
29	836	322	550 00							
30	837	321	785 40							
31	838	320	870 00							
			$21,760 50		$1,139 50			$ 779 20		$ 27 50

A summary of the procedures involved in accounting for materials is shown in Figure 2-10, which presents the recordings required for the more typical materials transactions, both at the time of the transaction and at the end of the period. At the time of the transaction, the recordings to be made affect the subsidiary ledgers, such as the stores ledger and the job cost ledger. At the end of the period, the recordings to be made affect the control accounts for materials, work in process, and factory overhead in the general ledger.

Inventory Verification. The stores ledger contains an account for each material used in the manufacturing process. Each account shows the number of units on hand and their cost. In other words, the stores ledger provides a perpetual inventory of the individual items of material in the storeroom. From the information in the stores ledger, the necessary materials inventory data can be obtained for preparing a balance sheet, an income statement, and a manufacturing statement.

Errors in recording receipts or issues of materials in the stores ledger may affect the reliability of the inventory totals. To guard against error, the materials on hand should be checked periodically against the individual stores ledger accounts. The usual practice is to count one lot of materials at a time, spacing the time of the counts so that a complete check of all inventories in the storeroom can be made within a fixed period of time, such as three months. These periodic checks have the advantage of eliminating the costly and time-consuming task of counting all the materials at one time. To guard against carelessness or dishonesty, the count should be made by someone other than the storeroom keeper or the stores ledger clerk.

The person making the count should prepare an **inventory report** similar to the one shown in Figure 2-11. If the total indicated in the report differs from the balance in the stores ledger account, an immediate correcting entry should be made in the proper stores ledger account. The entries in the general ledger accounts may be made in total at the end of the month. If the materials on hand exceed the balance in the control account, the control account balance should be increased by the following entry:

Materials	xxx	
Factory Overhead (Inventory Short and Over)		xxx

If the amount of materials on hand is less than the control account balance, as was the case in Figure 2-11, the balance should be decreased by the following entry:

Factory Overhead (Inventory Short and Over)	xxx	
Materials		xxx

FIGURE 2-10   Summary of Materials Transactions

Transaction	Entry at Time of Transaction			Entry at End of Accounting Period		
	Source of Data	Book of Original Entry	Subsidiary Ledger Posting	Source of Data	Book of Original Entry	General Ledger Posting
Purchase of materials	Vendor's Invoice Receiving Report	Voucher Register	Stores Ledger	Voucher Register	None	Materials Accounts Payable
Materials returned to vendor	Return Shipping Order	General Journal	Stores Ledger	General Journal	None	Accounts Payable Materials
Payment of invoices	Approved Voucher	Check Register	None	Check Register	None	Accounts Payable Cash
Direct materials issued	Materials Requisitions	None	Stores Ledger Job Cost Ledger	Materials Summary	General Journal	Work in Process Materials
Indirect materials issued	Materials Requisitions	None	Stores Ledger Factory Overhead Ledger	Materials Summary	General Journal	Factory Overhead Materials
Direct materials returned from factory to storeroom	Returned Materials Report	None	Stores Ledger Job Cost Ledger	Materials Summary	General Journal	Materials Work in Process
Indirect materials returned from factory to storeroom	Returned Materials Report	None	Stores Ledger Factory Overhead Ledger	Materials Summary	General Journal	Materials Factory Overhead
Inventory adjustment: (a) Materials on hand less than stores ledger balance	Inventory Report	General Journal	Factory Overhead Ledger Stores Ledger	General Journal	None	Factory Overhead Materials
(b) Materials on hand more than stores ledger balance	Inventory Report	General Journal	Factory Overhead Ledger Stores Ledger	General Journal	None	Materials Factory Overhead

FIGURE 2-11   Inventory Report. (Compares book inventory and physical inventory quantities.)

LONGHORN MFG

INVENTORY REPORT

Material _____ 3/4" valves _____
Location in storeroom _____ Bin L123 _____
Stores ledger acct. No. _____ 12345 _____
Date of Verification _____ January 27, 20-- _____

Units in storeroom	590
Units in receiving department	300
Total number units on hand	890
Balance per stores ledger	910
Difference	20

Counted by _____ P. Valence _____
Supervised by _____ W. Cox _____

Such inventory differences are almost always a shortage and may arise from carelessness in handling materials, shrinkage in goods as a result of handling, or issuing excess quantities of materials to production. Such shortages are considered unavoidable and are part of the cost of operating a manufacturing plant. Shortages (or overages) are recorded in a factory overhead account, usually entitled Inventory Short and Over, as indicated in the preceding entries.

Visual Aid. For a cost accounting system to function properly, each employee must understand the assigned duties and the purpose of the various forms and records. Figure 2-12 shows the interrelationship of the accounts and how internal control procedures can be established.

FIGURE 2-12 Interrelationship of Materials Documents and Accounts

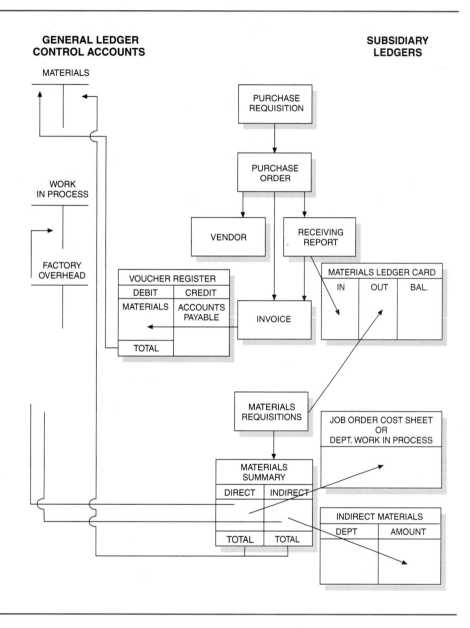

> **You should now be able to work the following: Questions 16–20; Exercises 2-2 to 2-9; Problems 2-2 to 2-7.**

SCRAP, SPOILED GOODS, AND DEFECTIVE WORK

LEARNING OBJECTIVE 4
Account for scrap materials, spoiled goods, and defective work.

Manufacturing operations usually produce some imperfect units that cannot be sold as regular items. The controls over imperfect items and operations that waste materials are important elements of inventory control. **Scrap** or **waste materials** may result naturally from the production process, or they may be spoiled or defective units that result from avoidable or unavoidable mistakes during production. Because the sale of imperfect items tends to damage a company's reputation, most companies introduce quality control techniques that prevent imperfect items from being sold. Since scrap, spoiled goods, and defective work usually have some value, each of their costs is accounted for separately.

SCRAP MATERIALS

The expected sales value of the scrap produced by the manufacturing process determines which accounting procedures are used. When the scrap value is small, no entry is made for it until the scrap is sold. Then Cash (or Accounts Receivable) is debited, and an account such as Scrap Revenue is credited. The income from scrap sales is usually reported as "Other income" in the income statement.

If income from scrap is to be treated as a reduction in manufacturing costs rather than as other income, Work in Process may be credited if the scrap can be readily identified with a specific job. If the scrap cannot be identified with a specific job, Factory Overhead may be credited.

When the value of the scrap is relatively high, an inventory card should be prepared and the scrap transferred to a controlled materials storage area. If both the quantity and the market value of the scrap are known, the following journal entries are recorded:

Scrap Materials	xxx	
Scrap Revenue (or Work in Process or Factory Overhead)		xxx
Transferred scrap to inventory.		
Cash (or Accounts Receivable)	xxx	
Scrap Materials		xxx
Sold scrap.		

If the market value of the scrap is not known, no journal entry is made until the scrap is sold. At the time of sale, the following entry is then recorded:

Cash (or Accounts Receivable)	xxx	
Scrap Revenue (or Work in Process or Factory		
Overhead)		xxx
Sold scrap.		

SPOILED AND DEFECTIVE WORK

Scrap is an unexpected by-product of the production of the primary product. Spoiled or defective goods are not by-products but imperfect units of the primary product. **Spoiled units** have imperfections that cannot be economically corrected. They are sold as items of inferior quality or "seconds." **Defective units** have imperfections considered correctable because the market value of the corrected unit will be greater than the total cost incurred for the unit.

Spoiled Work. The loss associated with spoiled goods may be treated as part of the cost of the job or department that produced the spoiled units, or the loss may be charged to Factory Overhead and allocated among all jobs or departments. Generally, Factory Overhead is charged unless the loss results from a special order and the spoilage is due to the type of work required on that particular order. In both cases, the spoiled goods are recorded in Spoiled Goods Inventory at the expected sales price.

To illustrate, assume a garment manufacturer using job order costing completes an order for 1,000 denim jackets (Job 350) at the following unit costs:

Materials	$20
Labor	20
Factory overhead	10
Total cost per unit	$50

The journal entry to record the costs of production is as follows:

Work in Process—Job 350	50,000	
Materials		20,000
Payroll		20,000
Factory Overhead		10,000
Recognized production costs for Job 350.		

During the final inspection, 50 jackets are found to be inferior and are classified as irregulars or seconds. They are expected to sell for $10 each. If the unrecovered costs of spoilage are to be charged to Factory Overhead, the following entry is recorded:

Spoiled Goods Inventory	500	
Factory Overhead	2,000	
Work in Process—Job 350		2,500

     Recognized spoiled goods at market value (50 jackets @ $10), charged Factory Overhead for loss of $40 per unit, and reduced cost of Job 350 (50 jackets @ $50).

If the loss from spoilage is considered a cost of the specific job, the entry to record the market value is as follows:

Spoiled Goods Inventory	500	
Work in Process—Job 350		500

     Recognized spoiled goods at market value and reduced the cost of Job 350 by $500 sales price of spoiled goods.

Spoilage costs charged to Factory Overhead are allocated among all jobs in production. When spoilage is attributed to a specific job, however, the entire cost of spoilage is reflected in the cost of that job. In the example, Job 350 will be charged with only a portion of the $2,000 loss from spoilage when Factory Overhead is allocated to the various jobs. When Factory Overhead is not charged for the spoilage costs, however, the entire $2,000 loss is included in the total cost of Job 350.

Defective Work. The procedures for recording the cost associated with defective work are similar to those employed in accounting for spoiled work. There are, however, additional costs for correcting the imperfections on defective units. If these costs are incurred on orders that the company regularly produces, they are charged to Factory Overhead. For special orders, the additional costs are charged to the specific job on which the defective work occurs. An inventory account is not established for goods classified as defective because the defects are corrected and the units become first-quality merchandise.

As in the previous illustration, assume that it costs $50 to manufacture each jacket. Upon final inspection of the 1,000 jackets completed, 50 jackets are defective because one sleeve on each jacket is a slightly different shade of blue than the other parts of the jacket. Management decides to recut the sleeves from a bolt of material identical in color to the rest of the jacket. The costs of correcting the defects are $500 for materials, $400 for labor, and $300 for factory overhead, representing a total cost of $1,200.

If the additional costs are charged to Factory Overhead, the cost of correcting defective work is spread over all jobs that go through the production cycle. The journal entry is as follows:

Factory Overhead (Costs to Correct Defective Work) .	1,200	
Materials		500
Payroll		400
Factory Overhead		300
Recognized costs of correcting defective units.		

If the order for 1,000 jackets was a special order and the defects resulted from the exacting specifications of the order, the additional costs would be charged to the job as follows:

Work in Process—Job 350	1,200	
Materials		500
Payroll		400
Factory Overhead		300
Charged Job 350 with cost of correcting defective work.		

The total cost of Job 350 will be higher because the additional costs to correct the defects were charged to the order rather than to the factory overhead account. The unit cost of each completed jacket is increased from $50 ($50,000/1,000) to $51.20 ($51,200/1,000) because of the additional costs charged to the work in process account.

> **You should now be able to work the following: Questions 21–22; Exercises 2-10 to 2-12; Problems 2-8 to 2-10.**

APPENDIX: JUST-IN-TIME MATERIALS CONTROL

LEARNING OBJECTIVE 5
Account for inventories in a just-in-time system.

In a **just-in-time (JIT) inventory system**, materials are delivered to the factory immediately prior to their use in production. A JIT system significantly reduces inventory carrying costs by requiring that the raw materials be delivered just in time to be placed into production. Additionally, work in process inventory is minimized by eliminating inventory buffers between work centers. For example, the work is performed on a unit in Department A only after the department receives the request from Department B for a certain number of the units. This contrasts with traditional manufacturing systems that produce goods for inventory with the hope that the demand for these goods then will be created. For JIT to work successfully, a high degree of coordination and cooperation must exist between the supplier and the manufacturer and among manufacturing work centers.

Just-in-time production techniques first were utilized by Japanese industry, and they have become popular with U.S. manufacturers in recent years. U.S. companies that have adopted the principles of JIT include Harley-Davidson, Hewlett-Packard, IBM, and Motorola. It is not unusual in JIT manufacturing for a finished product to be shipped to the customer during the same eight-hour shift that the raw materials used in the product were received from the supplier. The following Real-World Example makes numerous references to JIT and inventories.

REAL-WORLD EXAMPLE

JIT AND THE BALANCED SCORECARD

JIT can be described as a set of manufacturing techniques and concepts or a philosophy of doing business that minimizes inventory levels and enjoys the commensurate effects of doing so. Generally, JIT manufacturing is more oriented to broad-based effectiveness, while traditional manufacturing systems tend to emphasize efficiency. JIT exposes production problems because there is no buffer stock of inventory. If a part on the line is discovered to be defective, and therefore unusable, then the production line must be stopped because there is no additional excess inventory to replace it. JIT would require that the problem be addressed immediately so that production could resume and similar problems could be avoided in the future. Accordingly, JIT is quality oriented and emphasizes simplifying the process and preventing problems.

. . . The supplier base used with JIT is much smaller than with traditional systems and often consists of certified vendors. These suppliers are certified (i.e., contractually required) to provide timely deliveries of goods at a high-quality level. A partnership relationship with suppliers is encouraged, and suppliers often are invited to the plant to help them understand the needs of the manufacturer. Long-term contracts involving a minimum amount of paperwork are pursued.

. . . With a JIT system, defect prevention becomes more important than appraisal, and workers are rewarded for pointing out and solving problems rather that hiding them. Managers are rewarded for minimizing investment by explicitly imputing inventory investment into the performance evaluation scorecard.

. . . Using certified supplier relationships simplifies supplier relations, ensures that quality and delivery levels are attained, and minimizes transaction cost and paperwork. Activity analysis is appropriate with JIT to determine effectiveness. Activity analysis also is helpful in developing relevant management control metrics.

B. Douglas Clinton and Ko-Cheng Hsu, "JIT and the Balanced Scorecard," *Management Accounting*, September 1997, pp. 18-24.

JIT and Cost Control. Reducing inventory levels may increase processing speed, thereby reducing the time it takes for a unit to make it through production. For example, if 10,000 units are produced each day and the average number of units in work in process is 40,000, then the **throughput time,** or time that it takes a unit to make it through the system, is 40,000/10,000, or four days. If the same daily output can be achieved while reducing the work in process by 50%, the throughput time will be reduced to two days, 20,000/10,000, and the **velocity** or speed with which units are produced in the system will have doubled. If production speed can be increased dramatically, all products may be made to order, thus eliminating the need for finished goods inventory. Also, reducing throughput time can lower costs because there will be fewer **nonvalue-added activities**—operations that include costs but do not add value to the product, such as moving, storing, and inspecting.

If the velocity of production is doubled as in the preceding example, the inventory carrying costs can be reduced. For example, assume an annual inventory carrying cost percentage of 20% and an average work in process of $400,000, resulting in annual carrying costs of $80,000 (20% × $400,000). Further assume that through the use of JIT production techniques, the velocity of production is doubled without changing the total annual output, thus necessitating only half as much work in process (WIP). The new annual carrying costs would be calculated as follows:

$$\text{Carrying cost percentage} \times \text{Average WIP}$$
$$20\% \times (1/2 \times \$400,000) = \$40,000$$

or a $40,000 reduction from the previous level of $80,000.

Another advantage of reduced throughput time is increased customer satisfaction due to quicker delivery. Also, production losses are reduced due to not having great quantities of partially completed units piling up at the next work station before an error in their production is detected.

JIT AND COST FLOWS

Figure 2-13 contrasts the journal entries made in a traditional manufacturing cost accounting system with the entries made in a JIT system. **Backflush costing** is the name for the accounting system used with JIT manufacturing. It derives its name from the fact that costs are not "flushed out" of the accounting system and charged to the products until the goods are completed and sold.

Entries A and B in Figure 2-13 indicate that a single account, Raw and In-Process, is used in backflush costing for both raw materials and work in process inventories. This is done because raw materials are issued to production as soon as they are received in a JIT system, thus negating the

FIGURE 2-13   Journal Entries for Traditional and Backflush Accounting Systems

Transaction	Journal Entries: Traditional System	Journal Entries: Backflush System

A Purchase of raw materials	Materials 50,000
	    Accounts Payable 50,000
		Raw and In-Process . 50,000
		    Accounts Payable 50,000

B Raw materials requisitioned to production	Work in Process . . . . 50,000 Materials 50,000	No Entry

C Direct labor cost distributed	Work in Process 25,000
	    Payroll 25,000
		Conversion Costs . . 25,000
		    Payroll 25,000

D Manufacturing overhead costs incurred	Factory Overhead . . . 75,000
	    Various Credits 75,000
		Conversion Costs . . 75,000
		    Various Credits 75,000

E Transfer of factory overhead costs to work in process	Work in Process . . . . 75,000 Factory Overhead 75,000	No Entry
F Completion of products	Finished Goods . . . . . 150,000 Work in Process 150,000	No Entry

G Sale of products	Cost of Goods Sold . . . 150,000
	    Finished Goods 150,000
		Cost of Goods Sold . 150,000
		    Raw and In-Process . . . 50,000
		    Conversion Costs 100,000

need for a separate raw materials inventory account. Entries C, D, and E illustrate that a single account, Conversion Costs, contains both direct labor and factory overhead costs in a backflush system. Direct labor usually is so insignificant in a highly automated JIT setting that it is not cost effective to account for it separately.

Entries F and G illustrate that in a true JIT setting, there is no need for a finished goods account because goods are shipped to customers immediately upon completion. Entry G also illustrates that materials, labor, and overhead costs are not attached to products in a backflush system until they are completed and sold. The rationale for this approach is that products move through the system so rapidly in a JIT environment that it would not be cost effective to track production costs to them while in process.

Note that different companies choose different points in the production process, called **trigger points**, at which to record journal entries in a backflush system. The points chosen in this example are typical.

You should now be able to work the following: Questions 23–24; Exercises 2-13 and 2-14; Problems 2-11 and 2-12.

K E Y   T E R M S

Backflush costing, p. 87
Carrying costs, p. 55
Credit memorandum, p. 64
Debit memorandum, p. 64
Defective units, p. 83
Economic order quantity, p. 55
First-in, first-out (FIFO), p. 70
Flow of costs, p. 70
Flow of materials, p. 70
Inventory report, p. 78
Just-in-time (JIT) inventory system, p. 85
Last-in, first-out (LIFO), p. 71
Lead time, p. 54
Materials control, p. 52
Materials ledger, p. 67
Materials requisition, p. 65
Moving average, p. 74
Nonvalue-added activities, p. 87
Order costs, p. 54
Order point, p. 54
Production department supervisor, p. 59

Purchase order, p. 60
Purchase requisition, p. 60
Purchasing agent, p. 58
Receiving clerk, p. 59
Receiving report, p. 63
Returned materials report, p. 67
Return shipping order, p. 64
Safety stock, p. 54
Scrap materials, p. 82
Spoiled units, p. 83
Stockout, p. 54
Storeroom keeper, p. 59
Stores ledger, p. 67
Stores requisition, p. 65
Summary of materials issued and returned, p. 76
Throughput time, p. 87
Trigger points, p. 88
Usage, p. 54
Velocity, p. 87
Vendor's invoice, p. 60
Waste materials, p. 82

S E L F - S T U D Y   P R O B L E M

ORDER POINT; ECONOMIC ORDER QUANTITY; ORDERING AND CARRYING COSTS

**LEXINGTON
SLUGGER
COMPANY**

The Lexington Slugger Company, manufacturer of top-of-the-line baseball bats from Northern white ash, predicts that 8,000 billets of lumber will be used during the year. (A billet is the quantity of rough lumber needed to make one bat.) The expected daily usage is 32 billets. There is an expected lead time of 10 days and a safety stock of 500 billets. The company expects the lumber to cost $4 per billet. It anticipates that it will cost $40 to place each order. The annual carrying cost is $0.25 per billet.

Required:

1. Calculate the order point.
2. Calculate the most economical order quantity (EOQ).
3. Calculate the total cost of ordering and carrying at the EOQ point.

SOLUTION TO SELF-STUDY PROBLEM

Suggestions:

Read the entire problem thoroughly, keeping in mind that you are required to calculate (1) order point, (2) EOQ, and (3) total ordering and carrying costs.

The specifics in the problem highlight the following facts relevant to computing the order point:

> Expected daily usage is 32 billets.
> Expected lead time is 10 days.
> Required safety stock is 500 billets.

The order point is the inventory level at which an order should be placed. It is determined by adding the estimated number of billets to be used between placement and receipt of the order:

> Estimated usage during lead time = 32 units (daily usage) × 10 days (lead time) = 320

Add the number of units of safety stock (500 in this problem) needed to protect against abnormally high usage and unforeseen delays in receiving good materials from the supplier:

Order Point = Expected usage during lead time + safety stock
    = 320   + 500
    = 820 units

The specifics in the problem highlight the following facts relevant to computing the EOQ:

Estimated annual usage of materials	8,000 billets
Cost of placing an order	$40
Annual carrying cost per billet	$0.25

The EOQ is the order size that minimizes total order and carrying costs. It can be calculated by using the EOQ formula:

$$\text{EOQ} = \sqrt{\frac{2 \times \text{order cost} \times \text{annual demand}}{\text{annual carrying cost per unit}}}$$

$$= \sqrt{\frac{2 \times \$40 \times 8{,}000}{\$0.25}}$$

$$= \sqrt{\frac{\$640{,}000}{\$0.25}}$$

$$= \sqrt{2{,}560{,}000}$$

$$= 1{,}600 \text{ billets}$$

The specifics in the problem highlight the following facts that are relevant to computing the total ordering and carrying costs at the EOQ point:

Annual usage	8,000 billets
EOQ	1,600 billets
Ordering costs	$40 per order
Carrying cost	$0.25 per billet
Safety stock	500 billets

To determine the annual ordering cost, you must first determine the number of orders by dividing the annual usage by the EOQ:

$$\text{Number of orders} = \text{annual usage} / \text{EOQ}$$
$$= 8,000 \text{ billets} / 1,600 \text{ units}$$
$$= 5$$

The annual order cost is determined by multiplying the number of orders by the cost per order:

$$5 \text{ orders} \times \$40 \text{ per order} = \$200$$

To determine the annual carrying cost, you must first determine the average number of units in inventory:

$$(1/2 \times \text{EOQ}) + \text{safety stock}$$
$$(1/2 \times 1,600) + 500 \qquad = 1,300 \text{ units}$$

The average number of billets in inventory would consist of one-half of the amount ordered plus the 500 billets that are kept as a cushion against unforeseen events. The total carrying cost would then be as follows:

$$\text{Average inventory} \times \text{carrying cost per billet}$$
$$1,300 \qquad \times \$0.25 \qquad = \$325$$

Total cost of ordering and carrying:

$$\text{Order costs} + \text{carrying costs}$$
$$\$200 + \$325 \qquad = \$525$$

(Note: Problem 2-1 is similar to this problem.)

QUESTIONS

1. What are the two major objectives of materials control?

2. Materials often represent a substantial portion of a company's assets; therefore, they should be controlled from the time orders are placed to the time finished goods are shipped to the customer. What are the control procedures used for safeguarding materials?

3. What factors should management consider when determining the amount of investment in materials?

4. Maintaining and replenishing the stock of materials used in manufacturing operations is an important aspect of the procurement process. What is the meaning of the term "order point"?

5. What kind of information and data are needed to calculate an order point?

6. How would you define the term "economic order quantity"?

7. What factors should be considered when determining the cost of an order?

8. What are the costs of carrying materials in stock?

9. Briefly, what are the duties of the following employees?
   a. Purchasing agent
   b. Receiving clerk
   c. Storeroom keeper
   d. Production supervisor

10. Proper authorization is required before orders for new materials can be placed. What is the difference between a purchase requisition and a purchase order?

11. Purchasing agents are responsible for contacting vendors from which to purchase materials required by production. Why is the purchasing agent also responsible for reviewing and approving incoming vendors' invoices?

12. Illustrations of forms for requisitioning, ordering, and accounting for materials are presented in the chapter. Would you expect these forms, as shown, to be used by all manufacturers? Discuss.

13. What internal control procedures should be established for incoming shipments of materials purchased?

14. What is the purpose of a debit-credit memorandum?

15. Who originates each of the following forms?
   a. Purchase requisition
   b. Purchase order
   c. Receiving report
   d. Materials requisition
   e. Debit-credit memorandum

16. Normally a manufacturer maintains an accounting system that includes a stores ledger and a general ledger account for Materials. What is the relationship between the stores ledger and the materials account?

17. A company may select an inventory costing method from a number of commonly used procedures. Briefly, how would you describe each of the following methods?
   a. First-in, first-out
   b. Last-in, first-out
   c. Moving average

18. Why do companies adopt the LIFO method of inventory costing? Your discussion should include the effects on both the income statement and balance sheet.

19. Which of the forms shown in the chapter is the source for the following entries to subsidiary ledger accounts?
   a. Debits to record materials purchased in stores ledger.
   b. Credits to record materials requisitioned in stores ledger.
   c. Debits to record materials placed in process in job cost ledger.

20. What are some of the steps manufacturers can take to control inventory costs?

21. A manufacturing process may produce a considerable quantity of scrap material because of the nature of the product. What methods can be used to account for the sales value of scrap material?

22. After a product is inspected, some units are classified as spoiled and others as defective. What distinguishes a product as being spoiled or defective?

23. How does the just-in-time approach to production differ from the traditional approach? (Appendix)

24. What is the difference between throughput time and velocity? (Appendix)

EXERCISES

E2-1
Economic order
quantity; order cost;
carrying cost
Objective 1

Hornik Company predicts that it will use 90,000 units of material during the year. The material is expected to cost $5 per unit. Gordon anticipates that it will cost $18 to place each order. The annual carrying cost is $1 per unit.

a. Determine the most economical order quantity by using the EOQ formula.
b. Determine the total cost of ordering and carrying at the EOQ point.

E2-2
Journalizing materials
requisitions
Objective 3

Hood Corporation records the following use of materials during the month of June:

Date	Req. No.	Use	Materials Requisitions Direct Materials	Indirect Materials
1	110	Material A, Job 10	$20,000	
5	111	Material B, Job 11	18,000	
9	112	Material B, Job 12	16,000	
12	113	Factory supplies		$ 800
18	114	Material C, Job 10	3,000	
21	115	Material D, Job 10	9,000	
23	116	Material E, Job 13	2,000	
28	117	Factory supplies		1,300
30	118	Factory supplies		1,700

Prepare a summary journal entry for the materials requisitions.

E2-3
Recording materials
transactions
Objective 3

Prepare a journal entry to record each of the following materials transactions:

a. Total materials purchased during the month amounted to $200,000.
b. Direct materials requisitioned for the month totaled $175,000.
c. Indirect materials requisitioned during the month totaled $12,000.
d. Direct materials returned to the storeroom from the factory amounted to $2,500.
e. Total materials returned to vendor during the month amounted to $800.
f. Payment during the month for materials purchases totaled $160,000 less 2% discount. (Use Purchases Discounts.)

E2-4
FIFO costing
Objective 3

Using first-in, first-out, perpetual inventory costing, and the following information, determine the cost of materials used and the cost of the May 31 inventory:

May 1 Balance on hand, 1,000 units (bearings, $4 each).
     3 Issued 250 units.
     5 Received 500 units at $4.50 each.
     6 Issued 150 units.
    10 Issued 110 units.
    11 Factory returned 10 units to the storeroom that were issued on the 10th.

	15	Received 500 units at $5.00 each.
	20	Returned 300 units to vendor from May 15 purchase.
	26	Issued 600 units.

E2-5
LIFO costing
Objective 3

Using last-in, first-out, perpetual inventory costing, and the information presented in E2-4, compute the cost of materials used and the cost of the May 31 inventory.

E2-6
Moving average costing
Objective 3

Using the moving average method, perpetual inventory costing, and the information presented in E2-4, compute the cost of materials used and the cost of the May 31 inventory. (Round unit prices to five decimal places and amounts to the nearest whole dollar.)

E2-7
Comparison of FIFO, LIFO, and moving average methods
Objective 3

In tabular form, compare the total cost transferred to Work in Process and the cost of the ending inventory for each method used in E2-4, E2-5, and E2-6. Discuss the effect that each method will have on profits, depending on whether it is a period of rising prices or a period of falling prices.

E2-8
Impact of costing methods on net income
Objective 3

Scripps Company was franchised on January 1, 1999. At the end of its third year of operations, December 31, 2001, management requested a study to determine what effect different materials inventory costing methods would have had on its reported net income over the three-year period.

The materials inventory account, using LIFO, FIFO, and moving average, would have had the following ending balances:

	Materials Inventory Balances		
December 31	LIFO	FIFO	Average
1999	$20,000	$22,000	$21,000
2000	22,000	24,000	23,000
2001	26,000	30,000	28,000

a. Assuming the same number of units in ending inventory at the end of each year, were material costs rising or falling from 1999 to 2001?
b. Which costing method would show the highest net income for 1999?
c. Which method would show the highest net income for 2001?
d. Which method would show the lowest net income for the three years combined?
e. For the year 2000, how would the profit using LIFO compare to the profit if FIFO was used?

E2-9
Recording materials transactions
Objective 3

Nashville Manufacturing Company maintains the following accounts in the general ledger: Materials, Work in Process, Factory Overhead, and Accounts Payable. On June 1, the materials account had a debit balance of $8,000. Following is a summary of material transactions for the month of June:

1. Materials purchased, $18,750.
2. Direct materials requisitioned, $21,250.
3. Direct materials returned to storeroom, $1,400.

4. Indirect materials requisitioned, $1,975.
5. Indirect materials returned to storeroom, $185.

a. Prepare journal entries to record the materials transactions.
b. Post the journal entries to ledger accounts (in T-account form).
c. What is the balance of the materials inventory account at the end of the month?

E2-10
Scrap materials
Objective 4

A machine shop manufactures a stainless steel part that is used in an assembled product. Materials charged to a particular job amounted to $600. At the point of final inspection, it was discovered that the material used was inferior to the specifications required by the engineering department; therefore, all units had to be scrapped.

Record the entries required for scrap under each of the following conditions:

a. The revenue received for scrap is to be treated as a reduction in manufacturing cost but cannot be identified with a specific job. The value of stainless steel scrap is stable. The scrap is sold two months later for $125.
b. Revenue received for scrap is to be treated as a reduction in manufacturing cost but cannot be identified with a specific job. A firm price is not determinable for the scrap until it is sold. It is sold eventually for $75.
c. The production job is a special job and the $85 received for the scrap is to be treated as a reduction in manufacturing cost. (A firm price is not determinable for the scrap until it is sold.)
d. Only $40 was received for the scrap when it was sold in the following fiscal period. (A firm price is not determinable for the scrap until it is sold and the amount to be received for the scrap is to be treated as other income.)

E2-11
Spoiled work
Objective 4

Parr Company manufactures golf clothing. During the month, the company cut and assembled 8,000 sweaters. One hundred of the sweaters did not meet specifications and were considered "seconds." Seconds are sold for $9.95 per sweater, whereas first-quality sweaters sell for $39.95. During the month, Work in Process was charged $108,000: $36,000 for materials, $48,000 for labor, and $24,000 for factory overhead.

Record the entries to charge production costs for the period and the loss due to spoiled work, under each of the following conditions:

a. The loss due to spoiled work is spread over all jobs in the department.
b. The loss due to spoiled work is charged to this job because it is a special order.

E2-12
Defective work
Objective 4

Techno Mfg. Company manufactures an integrated transistor circuit board for repeat customers but also accepts special orders for the same product. Job No. 1OA1 incurred the following unit costs for 1,000 circuit boards manufactured:

Materials	$5.00
Labor	2.00
Factory overhead	2.00
Total cost per unit	$9.00

When the completed products were tested, 50 circuit boards were found to be defective. The costs per unit of correcting the defects follow:

Materials	$3.00
Labor	1.00
Factory overhead	1.00

Record the journal entry for the costs to correct the defective work:

a. If the cost of the defective work is charged to factory overhead.
b. If the cost of the defective work is charged to the job.

E2-13
JIT and Cost Control
Appendix
Objective 5

Nomar Industries produces 5,000 units each day and the average number of units in work in process is 25,000.

1. Determine the throughput time.
2. If the same daily output can be achieved while reducing the work in process by 40%, determine the new throughput time.

E2-14
Backflush costing
Appendix
Objective 5

Roman Company uses backflush costing to account for its manufacturing costs. Prepare journal entries to account for the following:

a. Purchased raw materials, on account, $80,000.
b. Requisitioned raw materials to production, $40,000.
c. Distributed direct labor costs, $10,000.
d. Manufacturing overhead costs incurred, $60,000. (Use Various Credits for the account in the credit part of the entry.)

P R O B L E M S

P2-1
Economic order quantity; ordering and carrying costs. Similar to self-study problem.
Objective 1

Normandy Company predicts that it will use 25,000 units of material during the year. The expected daily usage is 200 units, and there is an expected lead time of five days and a safety stock of 500 units. The material is expected to cost $5 per unit. Normandy anticipates that it will cost $50 to place each order. The annual carrying cost is $0.10 per unit.

Required:

1. Compute the order point.
2. Determine the most economical order quantity by use of the formula.
3. Calculate the total cost of ordering and carrying at the EOQ point.

P2-2
Inventory costing methods
Objective 3

The purchases and issues of rubber gaskets (Stores Ledger #11216) as shown in the records of Begker Corporation for the month of November follow:

		Units	Unit Price
Nov. 1	Beginning balance	30,000	$3.00
4	Received, Rec. Report No. 112	10,000	3.10
5	Issued, Mat. Req. No. 49	30,000	
8	Received, Rec. Report No. 113	50,000	3.30
15	Issued, Mat. Req. No. 50	20,000	
22	Received, Rec. Report No. 114	25,000	3.50
28	Issued, Mat. Req. No. 51	30,000	

Required:

1. Complete a stores ledger card similar to Figure 2-7 (the "on order" columns may be omitted) for each of the following inventory costing methods, using a perpetual inventory system:
   a. FIFO
   b. LIFO
   c. Moving average (carrying unit prices to five decimal places)
2. For each method, prepare a schedule that shows the total cost of materials transferred to Work in Process and cost of the ending inventory.
3. If prices continue to increase, would you favor adopting the FIFO or LIFO method? Explain.
4. When prices continue to rise, what is the effect of FIFO versus LIFO on the inventory balance reported in the balance sheet? Discuss.

P2-3
Inventory costing methods
Objective 3

The following transactions affecting materials occurred in February:

Feb. 1	Balance on hand, 1,200 units @ $2.76, $3,312.00 (plastic tubing, 100 feet per unit; stores ledger account # 906).
5	Issued 60 units on Materials Requisition No. 108.
11	Issued 200 units on Materials Requisition No. 210.
14	Received 800 units, Receiving Report No. 634, price $2.8035 per unit.
15	Issued 400 units, Materials Requisition No. 274.
16	Returned for credit 90 units purchased on February 14, which were found to be defective.
18	Received 1,000 units, Receiving Report No. 712, price $2.82712 per unit.
21	Issued 640 units, Materials Requisition No. 318.

Required:

Record the transactions on stores ledger cards similar to Figure 2-7. (The "on order" columns may be omitted.) Use the following inventory methods, assuming the use of a perpetual inventory system. Carry units prices to five decimal places.

1. FIFO
2. LIFO
3. Moving average

P2-4
Journalizing materials transactions
Objective 3

Newark Knitting Company uses a job order cost system. A partial list of the accounts being maintained by the company, with their balances as of November 1, is shown below:

Cash	$32,250
Materials	29,500
Work in process	27,000
Accounts payable (credit)	21,000
Factory overhead	none

The following transactions were completed during the month of November:

a. Materials purchases during the month, $24,000
b. Materials requisitioned during the month:

1. Direct materials, $31,000.
2. Indirect materials, $6,000.

c. Direct materials returned by factory to storeroom during the month, $1,100.
d. Materials returned to vendors during the month prior to payment,$1,000.
e. Payments to vendors during the month, $23,000.

Required:

1. Prepare general journal entries for each of the transactions.
2. Post the general journal entries to T-accounts.
3. Balance the accounts and report the balances of November 30 for the following:
   a. Cash
   b. Materials
   c. Accounts Payable

P2-5
Analyzing materials and other transactions
Objective 3

Liza Manufacturing Company uses a job order cost system. The following accounts have been taken from the books of the company:

Materials			
Bal. Inventory	7,000	b. Requisitions for month	23,000
a. Purchases for month	20,000		

Work in Process			
Bal. Inventory	3,600	e. To finished goods	50,000
b. Material Requisitions	23,000		
c. Direct Labor	17,000		
d. Factory Overhead	12,000		

Finished Goods			
Bal. Inventory	11,650	f. Cost of Goods Sold	55,000
e. Goods Finished	50,000		

Required:

1. Analyze the accounts and describe in narrative form what transactions took place. (Use the reference letters a through f in your explanations.)
2. List the supporting documents or forms required to record each transaction involving the receipt or issuance of materials.
3. Determine the ending balances for Materials, Work in Process, and Finished Goods.

P2-6
Comprehensive analysis of materials accounting procedures
Objectives 2, 3

The following decisions and transactions were made by Manatee Sheet Metal Company in accounting for materials costs for April.

Mar. 31 The factory manager informs the storeroom keeper that for the month of April, 2,000 sheets of aluminum are the forecasted usage. A check of the stock shows 500 aluminum sheets, costing $23 each, on hand. A minimum stock of 300 sheets must be maintained, and the purchasing agent is notified of the need for 1,800 sheets. This quantity will cover the April production requirements and, at the same time, maintain the minimum inventory level.

Apr.	1	After checking with a number of different vendors, the purchasing agent orders the requested number of sheets at $25 each.
	6	The shipment of aluminum sheets is received, inspected, and found to be in good condition. However, the order is short 100 sheets, which are backordered and expected to be shipped in five days.
	6	The invoice from the vendor covering the aluminum sheets is received and is approved for payment.
	11	The aluminum sheets that were backordered are received and approved.
	11	The vendor's invoice for the backordered shipment is received and approved for payment.
	16	The April 6 invoice is paid, less a cash discount of 2%.
	30	During the month, 1,900 sheets are issued to the factory. The company uses FIFO costing and a job order cost system.
	30	The factory returns 20 unused sheets to stores. The returned sheets have a cost of $25 each.
	30	At the end of the day, 398 sheets are on hand.

Required:

1. In tabular form, answer the following questions pertaining to each of the preceding decisions and transactions:
   a. What forms, if any, were used?
   b. What journal entries, if any, were made?
   c. What books of original entry, if any, were used to record the data?
   d. What subsidiary records were affected?
2. Calculate and show your computations for the following:
   a. The materials inventory balance as of April 30.
   b. The cost of materials used in production during April.

P2-7
Review problem;
transactions and
statements
Objective 3

Stewart Company manufactures chain hoists. The raw materials inventories on hand October 1 were as follows:

Chain	12,000 pounds, $24,000
Pulleys	4,000 sets, $20,000
Bolts and taps	10,000 sets, $5,000
Steel plates	4,000 units, $2,000

The balances in the ledger accounts on October 1 were as follows:

Cash	$ 12,000	
Work in process	35,000	
Materials	51,000	
Prepaid insurance	3,000	
Machinery	125,000	
Office equipment	30,000	
Office furniture	20,000	
Accounts payable		$ 30,000
Capital stock		200,000
Retained earnings		46,000
	$276,000	$276,000

Transactions during October were as follows:

a. Payroll recorded during the month: direct labor, $28,000; indirect labor, $3,000.
b. Factory supplies purchased for cash, $1,000. (Use a separate inventory account, Factory Supplies.)
c. Materials purchased on account: chain—4,000 pounds, $8,800; pulleys—2,000 units, $10,200; steel plates—5,000 units, $3,000.
d. Sales on account for the month, $126,375.
e. Accounts receivable collected, $72,500.
f. Materials used during October (FIFO costing): chain, 14,000 pounds; pulleys, 4,400 units; bolts and taps, 4,000 sets; steel plates, 3,800 units.
g. Payroll paid, $31,000.
h. Factory supplies on hand, October 31, $350.
i. Factory heat, light, and power costs for October, $3,000 (not yet paid).
j. Office salaries paid, $6,000.
k. Advertising paid, $2,000.
l. Factory superintendence paid, $1,800.
m. Expired insurance—on office equipment, $100; on factory machinery, $300.
n. Factory rent paid, $2,000.
o. Depreciation on office equipment, $400; on office furniture, $180; on machinery, $1,200.
p. Factory overhead charged to jobs, $11,950.
q. Work in Process, October 31, $31,000. (Hint: The difference between the total charges to Work in Process during the period and the ending balance in Work in Process represents the cost of the goods completed.)
r. Cost of goods sold during the month, $84,250.
s. Accounts payable paid, $33,750.

Required:

1. Set up T-accounts and enter the balances as of October 1.
2. Prepare journal entries to record each of the above transactions.
3. Post the journal entries to the accounts, setting up any new ledger accounts necessary. Only controlling accounts are to be maintained; however, show the calculation for the cost of materials used.
4. Prepare a statement of cost of goods manufactured for October.
5. Prepare an income statement.
6. Prepare a balance sheet showing the classifications of current assets, plant and equipment, current liabilities, and stockholders' equity.

P2-8
Materials inventory shortage; returns; scrap; spoiled goods
Objectives 3, 4

An examination of Hood-Robbins Corporation's records reveals the following transactions:

a. On December 31, the physical inventory of raw material was 9,950 units. The book quantity, using the moving average method, was 11,000 units @ $0.52 per unit.
b. Production returned to stores materials costing $775.
c. Materials valued at $770 were charged to Factory Overhead (Repairs and Maintenance), but should have been charged to Work in Process.
d. Defective material, purchased on account, was returned to the vendor. The material returned cost $234, and the return shipping charges (our cost) of $35 were paid in cash.

e. Goods sold to a customer, on account, for $5,000 (cost $2,500) were returned because of a misunderstanding of the quantity ordered. The customer stated that the goods returned were in excess of the quantity needed.

f. Materials requisitioned totaled $22,300, of which $2,100 represented supplies used.

g. Materials purchased on account totaled $25,500. Freight on the materials purchased was $185.

h. Direct materials returned to stores amounted to $950.

i. Scrap materials sent to the storeroom were valued at an estimated selling price of $685 and treated as a reduction in the cost of all jobs worked on during the period.

j. Spoiled work sent to the storeroom valued at a sales price of $60 had production costs of $200 already charged to it. The cost of the spoilage is to be charged to the specific job worked on during the period.

k. The scrap materials in (i) were sold for $685 cash.

Required:

Record the entries for each transaction. (Round amounts to the nearest whole dollar.)

P2-9
Spoiled goods; loss charged to factory overhead; loss charged to job
Objective 4

Humungo Company manufactures Giants, which sell for $0.99 each. The cost of each Giant consists of:

Materials	$0.35
Labor	0.15
Factory overhead	0.20
Total	$0.70

Job 100 produced 10,000 Giants, of which 600 units were spoiled and classified as seconds. Seconds are sold to department stores for $0.50 each.

Required:

1. Under the assumption that the loss from spoilage will be distributed to all jobs produced during the current period, use general journal entries to (a) record the costs of production, (b) put spoiled goods into inventory, and (c) record the cash sale of spoiled units.

2. Under the assumption that the loss due to spoilage will be charged to Job 100, use general journal entries to (a) record the costs of production, (b) put spoiled goods into inventory, and (c) record the cash sale of spoiled units.

P2-10
Spoiled goods and defective work
Objective 4

Reinsdorf Company manufactures electrical equipment from specifications received from customers. Job X10 was for 1,000 motors to be used in a specially designed electrical complex. The following costs were determined for each motor:

Materials	$117
Labor	100
Factory overhead	83
Total	$300

At final inspection, Reinsdorf discovered that 33 motors did not meet the exacting specifications established by the customer. An examination indicated that 15 motors were beyond repair and should be sold as spoiled goods for $75 each. The remaining 18 motors, although defective, could be reconditioned as first-quality units by the addition of $1,650 for materials, $1,500 for labor, and $1,200 for factory overhead.

Required:

Prepare the journal entries to record the following:
1. The scrapping of the 15 units, with the income from spoiled goods treated as a reduction in the manufacturing cost of the specific job.
2. The correction of the 18 defective units, with the additional cost charged to the specific job.
3. The additional cost of replacing the 15 spoiled motors with new motors.
4. The sale of the spoiled motors for $75 each.

P2-11
JIT and Cost Control
Appendix
Objective 5

Spencer Fixtures produces 50,000 units each day and the average number of units in work in process is 200,000. The average annual inventory carrying cost percentage is 20% and the average work in process is $1,000,000.

Required:

1. Determine the throughput time.
2. Compute the annual carrying costs.
3. If the same daily output can be achieved while reducing the work in process by 50%, determine the new throughput time.
4. What has happened to the velocity of production in part 3?
5. Compute the annual carrying costs for part 3.

P2-12
Backflush Costing
Appendix
Objective 5

Crumm Company uses backflush costing to account for its manufacturing costs. The trigger point for recording inventory transactions are the purchase of materials and the sale of completed products.

Required:

Prepare journal entries, if needed, to account for the following transactions.
a. Purchased raw materials on account, $150,000.
b. Requisitioned raw materials to production, $150,000.
c. Distributed direct labor costs, $25,000.
d. Manufacturing overhead costs incurred, $100,000. (Use Various Credits for the credit part of the entry.)
e. Cost of products completed, $275,000.
f. Completed products sold for $400,000, on account.

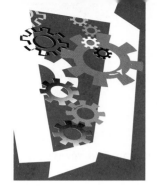

3

Accounting for Labor

LEARNING OBJECTIVES

After studying this chapter, you should be able to:

1. Distinguish between features of hourly rate and piece-rate plans.
2. Specify procedures for controlling labor costs.
3. Account for labor costs and payroll taxes.
4. Prepare accruals for payroll earnings and taxes.
5. Account for special problems in labor costing.

Factory payroll costs are divided into two categories: direct labor and indirect labor. **Direct labor** represents payroll costs traced directly to the product. The cost of direct labor is debited to Work in Process. **Indirect labor** consists of labor costs incurred for a variety of jobs related to the production process but not readily identifiable with the individual jobs worked on during the period. Indirect labor costs include the salaries and wages of the factory superintendent, supervisors, janitors, clerks, factory accountants, and timekeepers. Indirect labor costs are charged to Factory Overhead.

The accounting system of a manufacturer must include the following procedures for recording payroll costs:

1. Recording the hours worked or quantity of output by employees in total and by job, process, or department.

2. Analyzing the hours worked by employees to determine how time is to be charged.

3. Charging payroll costs to jobs, processes, departments, and factory overhead accounts.

4. Preparing the payroll, which involves computing and recording employee gross earnings, withholdings and deductions, and net earnings.

WAGE PLANS

LEARNING OBJECTIVE 1
Distinguish between features of hourly rate and piece-rate plans.

Employees' wages are based on plans that have been established by management, approved by the unions, if present, and that comply with the regulations of governmental agencies. A manufacturer may use many variations of wage plans. This chapter covers the wage plans most frequently encountered, including hourly rate, piece-rate, and modified wage plans.

HOURLY RATE PLAN

An **hourly rate plan** establishes a definite rate per hour for each employee. An employee's wages are computed by multiplying the number of hours worked in the payroll period by the established rate per hour. The hourly rate plan is widely used and is simple to apply. Critics argue that it provides no incentive for the employee to maintain or achieve a high level of productivity. An employee is paid for merely "being on the job" for an established period of time. The plan gives no extra recognition or reward for doing more than the minimum required of the position. Proponents of the plan argue that because productivity is not an important factor of such a plan, employees will not be tempted to sacrifice the quality of the product by speeding up production to earn a higher wage.

To illustrate the hourly rate plan, assume that an employee earns $10 per hour and works 40 hours per week. The employee's gross earnings would be $400 (40 × $10 per hour).

PIECE-RATE PLAN

A company that gives a high priority to the quantity produced by each worker should consider using an **incentive wage plan**, such as a **piece-rate plan**, which bases earnings on the employee's quantity of production. To illustrate, assume that a machine operator will earn $0.20 for each part (or "piece") finished. If the operator finishes 2,200 parts in a week, he or she will earn $440 ($0.20 × 2,200 parts). The plan provides an incentive for employees to produce a high level of output, thereby maximizing their earnings and also increasing the company's revenue. However, a serious shortcoming of such plans is that they may encourage employees to sacrifice quality in order to maximize their earnings, unless the plan is based on good units only. Also, piece rates are not appropriate if machines control production speed.

MODIFIED WAGE PLANS

Modified wage plans combine some features of the hourly rate and piece-rate plans. An example of a modified wage plan would be to set a minimum hourly wage that will be paid by the company even if an employee does not attain an established quota of production. If the established quota is exceeded, an additional payment per piece would be added to the minimum wage level. This type of plan directs management's attention to the employee unable to meet the established quotas.

Labor-management negotiations create many variations of the hourly rate and piece-rate plans. These variations occur because management wishes to minimize costs and maximize profits, while labor attempts to maximize employee earnings.

To illustrate a modified wage plan, assume that an employee earns $10 per hour for up to 100 units of production per day. The employee who produces more than 100 units per day will receive an additional piece rate of $0.80 per unit [($10 × 8 hours) / 100 units]. When the employee produces fewer than 100 units, the difference, often referred to as a make-up guarantee, will be charged to Factory Overhead rather than to Work in Process because it represents the cost of inefficient production, rather than a necessary cost of the jobs worked on.

Assume that an employee's production and earnings for one week are as follows:

	Hours Worked	Pieces Finished (Quota 100)	Earnings @ $10 per Hour	Earnings @ $0.80 per Unit	Make-Up Guarantee	Payroll Earnings
Mon.	8	120	$ 80	$ 96		$ 96
Tues.	8	90	80	72	$ 8	80
Wed.	8	80	80	64	16	80
Thurs.	8	110	80	88		88
Fri.	8	80	80	64	16	80
	40		$400	$384	$40	$424

The employee earned $384 on the piece-rate basis, but the daily guarantee of $80 per day compensated for the days when the employee did not reach the quota. A make-up guarantee of $40 is charged to Factory Overhead because the employee did not meet the quota on Tuesday ($8), Wednesday ($16), and Friday ($16). The payroll distribution for the week would be as follows:

Work in Process	384	
Factory Overhead	40	
Payroll		424

Distributed payroll.

If the number of pieces finished depends on a group effort, then a single incentive plan for the group would be appropriate. In recent years, U.S. manufacturers have adopted the concept of **production work teams**, where output is dependent upon contributions made by all members of the work crew or department. The wages may be computed in a manner similar to the previous illustration, except that the piece-rate bonus would be shared by all members of the group. The Real-World Example on page 107 illustrates a group bonus or **gainsharing plan** at a box company.

CONTROLLING LABOR COST

LEARNING OBJECTIVE 2
Specify procedures for controlling labor costs.

The timekeeping and payroll departments have the responsibility of maintaining labor records. The timekeeping and payroll functions may be established as separate departments or organized as subdivisions of a single department. In either case, they should function as independent units to provide an internal check on the accuracy of computing and recording labor costs.

The **timekeeping department** accounts for the time spent by the hourly employees in the factory. The overall objective of the department is to determine the number of hours that should be paid for and the type of work performed by the employees during the working day.

The **payroll department** computes each employee's gross earnings, the amount of withholdings and deductions, and the net earnings to be paid to the employee.

The departmental responsibilities of timekeeping and payroll include completing and maintaining the following forms and records:

Timekeeping	**Payroll**
Clock cards	Payroll records
Time tickets	Employees earnings records
Production reports	Payroll summaries

CLOCK CARDS AND TIME TICKETS

A **clock card** is provided for each company employee required to use a time clock (time recorder). The card provides a record of the total amount of time the employee spends in the plant. The preprinted card contains such information as the employee's name, social security number,

GAINSHARING AT A BOX COMPANY

A Missouri company employing about 180 factory workers and manufacturing corrugated boxes, shipping containers, inner packing, and displays illustrates how gainsharing works in practice. Under pressure from an original equipment manufacturer (OEM) customer for lower prices, the box producer was forced to boost its workforce to higher productivity in order to slice unit costs, thereby permitting lower prices.

The gainsharing project began with an examination of the company's production records for the past two years. Such digging found that labor costs (including supervision, plant engineering, scheduling, and all indirect labor) hovered around 37% of total cost. That is, for every $1 million of corrugated products, $370,000 went to related labor expenses. The objective was to trim those costs.

With some expert guidance, the company proceeded to design a formula for rewarding the workforce for achieving lower labor costs. The formula involved convincing the workers that if they performed *harder, smarter, neater, and more carefully*, reducing labor costs to (say) $300,000, savings would be $70,000 on the next $1 million production run. The savings (gain) in that period would be shared equally: $35,000 for the workers, as a bonus of $194.44 for each employee, and a $35,000 saving for the company. The employee bonuses were over and above the normal wage rate.

The standard of productivity was set by careful investigation of past experience, showing how many hours were required for the average production mix with volume of (good) output. A typical base period was selected to serve as a standard. The fact that past experience involved a mix of corrugated products, containers, and displays that did not duplicate the current run of corrugated products exactly presented no problem. The records showed that the mix held fairly constant. The common elements—staff-hours worked or dollars spent on labor—could be distilled out and serve as a standard.

Woodruff Imberman, "Is Gainsharing the Wave of the Future?" *Management Accounting* (November 1995), pp. 35–39.

department number, clock number, and the week or pay period. The completed card shows the time a worker started and stopped work each day and the total regular and overtime hours and wages for the period. The clock number also identifies the employee in the payroll records. Figure 3-1 shows an example of a clock card.

Each entrance to the factory may be a clock card station with time clocks and a rack of clock cards for the employees assigned to that

FIGURE 3-1   Employee Clock Card

NAME	Todd R. Moser
SOCIAL SEC. NO.	410-80-7865

DEPT. NO.	CLOCK NO.
04	2316

WEEK ENDING   2/16

AUTHORIZED   _Henry Johnson_

DAY	IN	OUT	IN	OUT	TOTAL	FOR PAYROLL USE ONLY
M	7:56	12:01	12:59	5:03	8	120.00
T	8:28	12:03	12:58	5:07	7 1/2	112.50
W	7:54	12:01	12:57	5:00	8	120.00
TH	7:58	12:05	1:00	5:05	8	120.00
F	7:55	12:00	12:55	5:02	8	120.00
S						
S						

	RATE		HOURS	AMOUNT
REGULAR	15.00/hr.	REGULAR	39 1/2	592.50
OVERTIME		OVERTIME		

entrance. The clock card should show the time of each employee's entrance and exit. Currently, mechanical time recorders and clock cards are being replaced by bar-coding technology. **Bar codes** are symbols that can be processed electronically to identify numbers, letters, or special characters. Each employee receives a bar-coded identification card that is read by **optical scanners** positioned at the factory entrances, thus recording arrival and departure times in the computer database.

Upon reporting to a work station, the employee receives a **time ticket** (Figure 3-2) for recording the hours worked on specific assignments. The time spent on each assignment may be entered by the employee manually on the time ticket, a production supervisor, or by an individual from the timekeeping department. Many companies have computer terminals located throughout the factory that, when used in conjunction with bar

FIGURE 3-2   Time Ticket (Daily)

Name Todd R. Moser					Clock No. 2316		
Dept. Grinding (04)							

Job or Type of Work	Time Started	Time Stopped	Hours Worked		Payroll Use Only		Amount Earned
			Reg.	O.T.	Rate Reg.	O.T.	
402	8:00	12:00	4		15.00		60 00
437	1:00	4:00	3		15.00		45 00
Machine repair	4:00	5:00	1		15.00		15 00

Date 2/14   Signed Todd R. Moser
Employee

Approved Shawna Campo
Supervisor

coding technology, can enter employee time distributions directly into the computer without the need for the hard copy.

The time ticket shows the employee's starting and stopping time on each job, the rate of pay, and the amount of earnings. When job transfers occur during a working day, the times of the transfers to and from different jobs are recorded on the ticket. The labor hours recorded on the time ticket should be approved by a supervisor because the ticket is the source document for allocating the cost of labor to jobs or departments in the cost ledger and factory overhead ledger. The preparation of separate or unit time tickets for each job or operation on which an employee works may be a requirement of the accounting system (Figure 3-3). Different colors may be selected for these time tickets to facilitate the sorting of the tickets into direct labor and indirect labor categories.

After employees clock in, the timekeeper collects the preceding day's time tickets from supervisors and compares the time tickets and clock cards. The purpose of the comparison is to determine that all time spent by the employee in the factory is accounted for. Total time worked, as shown on the employee's clock card, should correspond to the time

FIGURE 3-3   Time Ticket (Unit)

DEPT.	CLOCK NO.	NAME
04	2316	Todd R. Moser

JOB	DESCRIPTION OF WORK 3 HP gear
402	Semi-finishing housings

			HOURS	AMOUNT	PAYROLL USE ONLY TOTAL
STOP	12:00	OVERTIME			
START	8:00	REGULAR	4	15.00	60.00

Date 2/14

Signed _Todd R. Moser_
                                    Employee

Approved _Shawna Campo_
                                    Supervisor

reported on the time ticket. Discrepancies should be investigated immediately. If the clock card shows more hours than the time ticket, the difference is reported as idle time. Some companies compare time tickets with clock cards at the end of each shift rather than waiting until the next day. That way, accurate efficiency reports can be prepared overnight and made available to the supervisor at the beginning of the next day.

The employer must compensate the employee for the time spent on assigned jobs. When time is not fully utilized, the employer suffers a loss just as if a theft of some tangible good had occurred. Therefore, if time spent in the factory has been unproductive, the idle time, along with the reason for it, should be recorded.

After the clock cards and time tickets have been compared, the cards are returned to the racks and the time tickets are forwarded to payroll. The pay rates are entered, and the employee's gross earnings are computed and recorded on the time tickets. At the end of the week, the clock cards are removed from the rack, and the total hours worked by the employee are computed and recorded. The cards are then forwarded to payroll where the pay rate and gross earnings are entered on the clock cards and recorded in the payroll records. The cards are then filed by employee name or number.

Individual production reports are used instead of time tickets when labor costs are computed using piece rates. A daily report is prepared for each employee that shows work assignments by job number or type of work performed and the total number of units completed. After approval by the supervisor, the report is forwarded to payroll for computing earnings.

PAYROLL DEPARTMENT

The payroll department's primary responsibility is to compute the employees' wages and salaries. It involves combining the daily wages, determining the total earnings, and computing deductions and withholdings for each employee.

The department must maintain current information concerning regulatory requirements regarding wages and salaries because a specified amount of the employee's wages are subject to social security (FICA) and income tax deductions. Additional deductions, approved by the employee, can be taken for group insurance premiums, union dues, contributions to a tax-sheltered annuity, and so on.

Payroll Records. Forms used to record earnings information may vary considerably from company to company; however, all forms possess some common characteristics. The **payroll record** shown in Figure 3-4 is for the period ending February 16 and provides typical information. It assembles and summarizes each period's payroll data and serves as a subsidiary record for the preparation of a general journal entry. For example, the entry to record the payroll data in Figure 3-4 would be as follows:

Payroll	1840.50	
FICA Tax Payable		147.24
Employees Income Tax Payable		386.11
Health Insurance Payable		120.00
Employee Receivable		50.00
Wages Payable		1,137.15
Recognized incurred payroll.		

Employees Earnings Records. In addition to the payroll record, the payroll department keeps a record of the earnings for each employee. Figure 3-5 shows an **employee earnings record**. This cumulative record of employee earnings is needed to compute the amount of employee earnings subject to FICA and other payroll taxes.

FIGURE 3-4   Payroll Record

FOR PERIOD ENDING 2/16/20—

EARNINGS

NAME	CLOCK NO.	M/S	NO. OF ALLOW.	RATE	REGULAR HOURS	REGULAR AMOUNT	OVERTIME HOURS	OVERTIME AMOUNT	TOTAL EARNINGS
DONOVAN, P.	1987	M	0	14.00	40.0	560.00	0	00.00	560.00
FRY, R.	2403	M	2	16.00	40.0	640.00	2	48.00	688.00
MOSER, T.	2316	S	1	15.00	39.5	592.50	0	00.00	592.50

WITHHOLDINGS

DEDUCTIONS

NET PAY

FICA TAXABLE EARNINGS	FICA TAX	INCOME TAXES FEDERAL	INCOME TAXES STATE	INCOME TAXES LOCAL	HEALTH INSURANCE	OTHER	CHECK NO.	CHECK AMOUNT
560.00	44.80	84.00	28.00	5.60	40.00		8441	357.60
688.00	55.04	103.20	34.00	6.88	40.00	50.00 ADVANCE	8442	398.88
592.50	47.40	88.88	29.62	5.93	40.00		8443	380.67

FIGURE 3-5   Employee Earnings Record

02/16/19—

CLOCK NUMBER: 2316   EMPLOYEE NAME: TODD R. MOSER   SOCIAL SECURITY NO.: 410-80-7865

MAR. ST.: S   NO. ALLOW.: 1   SEX: M   DEPARTMENT: GRINDING   OCCUPATION: MACHINIST   DATE OF BIRTH: 4/4/47

PERIOD NO.	DATE 19—	REGULAR RATE	REGULAR HOURS	REGULAR AMOUNT	OVERTIME HOURS	OVERTIME AMOUNT	TOTAL EARNINGS	FICA TAX	FEDERAL	STATE	LOCAL	HEALTH INS.	OTHER	CHECK NO.	AMOUNT
1	1/05	14.40	40	576.00			576.00	43.20	86.40	28.80	5.76	40.00		7971	371.84
7	2/16	15.00	39.5	592.50			592.50	47.40	88.88	29.62	5.93	40.00		8443	380.67
QTR TTL				4096.00		306.00	4402.00	330.15	660.30	220.10	44.02	280.00	50.00		2817.43
YRL TTL				4096.00		306.00	4402.00	330.15	660.30	220.10	44.02	280.00	50.00		2817.43

Payment of Net Earnings. The payroll department sends the payroll record (Figure 3-4) to the treasurer's office, which is responsible for making the payments to the employees. The earnings usually are paid by check. A check for the total amount to be paid is drawn to create a special payroll fund from which the employees will be paid. The special account is used only for payroll, and the individual payroll checks, when cashed, are charged to the special account. A new payroll account may be established for each payroll period, numbering the accounts sequentially. The checks drawn for each payroll period can then be identified as belonging to a special payroll period. This system facilitates the reconciliation of bank statements. The entry to record the payment of net pay to employees would be as follows:

```
Wages Payable . . . . . . . . . . . . . . . . . .1137.15
    Cash  . . . . . . . . . . . . . . . . . . . . . . . .    1137.15
        Paid employees.
```

In the rare instance where employees are paid cash, a check is cashed for the total amount of net earnings. The cash is then divided into amounts earned by individual employees. These cash amounts are placed in envelopes and distributed to the employees. The employee's receipt or signature acknowledges the payment. Many employers now allow employees to authorize the direct electronic deposit of their net pay to their checking accounts.

> **You should now be able to work the following: Questions 1–10, Exercises 3-1 to 3-3, and Problem 3-1.**

ACCOUNTING FOR LABOR COSTS AND EMPLOYERS' PAYROLL TAXES

LEARNING OBJECTIVE 3
Account for labor costs and payroll taxes.

For all regular hourly employees, the hours worked should be recorded on a time ticket or individual production report. The time tickets and production reports are sent to payroll on a daily basis. The payroll department enters pay rates and gross earnings and forwards the reports to accounting. Cost accountants sort the time tickets and production reports and charge the labor costs to the appropriate jobs or department and to factory overhead. This analysis of labor costs is recorded on a **labor cost summary** (Figure 3-6) in the job cost ledger and in the factory overhead ledger.

Salaried employees, such as department supervisors, are not required to punch time clocks or prepare daily time tickets. Payroll sends a list of salaried employees to accounting showing the names of employees, the nature of work performed, and the salaries. The accounting department

FIGURE 3-6   Labor Cost Summary

LABOR COST SUMMARY					
Dept. Grinding			Month Ending May 31, 20--		
Date	Dr. Work in Progress (Direct labor-regular time)		Dr. Factory Overhead (Indirect labor and overtime premium)		Cr. Payroll (Total)
5/14	11,050	00	1,950	00	13,000	00
5/28	13,000	00	2,600	00	15,600	00
5/31	3,900	00	780	00	4,680	00

records the earnings on the labor cost summary and in factory overhead ledger accounts, because the salaried factory employees are indirect labor.

The labor cost summary becomes the source for making a general journal entry to distribute payroll to the appropriate accounts:

Work in Process	27,950	
Factory Overhead	5,330	
Payroll		33,280

Distributed payroll.

The entry is then posted to the control accounts, Work in Process and Factory Overhead, in the general ledger. The time tickets and individual production reports have been used to record the labor costs in the subsidiary job cost and factory overhead ledgers and in the labor cost summary. Therefore, the debit to the work in process control account must equal the direct labor cost charged to the jobs, and the charge to the factory overhead control account must equal the labor costs recorded in the factory overhead ledger.

In preparing the labor cost summary from the time tickets, any overtime must be separated from an employee's regular time because the accounting treatment may be different for each type of pay. Regular time worked by direct laborers is charged to Work in Process. Overtime pay may be charged to Work in Process, to Factory Overhead, or allocated partly to Work in Process and partly to Factory Overhead. Overtime distribution depends upon the conditions creating the need for overtime hours.

If an employee works beyond the regularly scheduled time but is paid at the regular hourly rate, the extra pay is called **overtime pay**. If an additional rate is allowed for the extra hours worked, the additional rate earned is referred to as an **overtime premium**. The premium pay rate is added to the employee's regular rate for the additional hours worked. The premium rate is frequently one-half the regular rate, resulting in a total hourly rate for overtime that is 150% of the regular rate. Under these circumstances, overtime pay is often referred to as "time-and-a-half" pay. In some cases, the overtime premium may be equal to the regular rate, resulting in "double-time" pay.

To illustrate how a payroll is computed where overtime premium is a factor, assume that an employee regularly earns $10 per hour for an 8-hour day. If called upon to work more than 8 hours in a working day, the company pays time-and-a-half for overtime hours. Assuming that the employee works 12 hours on Monday, the earnings would be computed as follows:

Direct labor—8 hours @ $10		$ 80
Direct labor—4 hours @ $10	$40	
Factory overhead (overtime premium)—4 hours @ $5	20	60
Total earnings		$140

The preceding analysis shows that the regular rate of pay was used to charge Work in Process for the direct labor cost of $120. The additional rate was used to compute the $20 cost of the overtime hours, which was charged to Factory Overhead. By charging the overtime premium to the factory overhead account, all jobs worked on during the period share the cost of overtime premiums paid. If the job contract stipulated that it was a rush order and the overtime premium resulted from the time limitation in the contract, it would be appropriate to charge the premium pay to the specific job worked on during the overtime period instead of to a factory overhead account.

EMPLOYERS' PAYROLL TAXES

Payroll taxes imposed on employers include social security tax and federal and state unemployment taxes. Employers must periodically report and pay the taxes to the appropriate government agencies. Employers who fail to file required reports or pay taxes due are subject to civil and, in some cases, criminal penalties.

The **Federal Insurance Contributions Act (FICA)** requires employers to pay social security taxes on wages and salaries equal to the amount withheld from employees' earnings. The employers and employees, therefore, share equally in the cost of the social security program. FICA includes a tax to finance the federal old age, survivors, and disability insurance program (OASDI) and the Medicare program. The legislation that governs FICA is frequently amended. These amendments change the wage base subject to FICA and the percentage rate of tax to be charged. For example, in 1980 the tax rate for the employer was 6.13% and the wage base was $25,900. For 1997, the FICA tax rate was 7.65% on the first $65,400 in annual earnings; earnings beyond $65,400 were taxed 1.45% for Medicare. (Due to the uncertainty that surrounds both the rate and the base wage, an arbitrary FICA tax rate of 8% will be applied to the first $70,000 of earnings in all discussions, examples, and problems in this text. Earnings beyond $70,000 will not be taxed. The selected arbitrary rate and wage base will simplify the tax calculations related to FICA, but they are not predictive of future legislation that may alter the social security system.)

The **Federal Unemployment Tax Act (FUTA)** requires employers to pay an established rate of tax on wages and salaries to provide for compensation to employees if they are laid off from their regular employment. For 1998, employers were subject to a tax of 6.2%, which may be reduced to 0.8% for credits for state unemployment compensation tax, on the first $7,000 of wages or salaries paid to each employee during the calendar year.

Unemployment benefits, however, are actually paid by individual states and not the federal government. As of 1998, the maximum state rate recognized by the federal unemployment system was 5.4% of the first $7,000 of each employee's annual earnings, which goes to the state government to accumulate funds for paying unemployment compensation. Each state has its own unemployment tax laws, although such laws must conform to certain requirements established under FUTA. Both tax rates and wage bases vary among states, and the actual amount of combined federal and state unemployment taxes paid depends on a number of factors, including an experience rating for an employer who provides steady employment that may result in a state rate substantially below the 5.4% maximum. (Because of the variation among states and because FUTA taxes are subject to amendments, the examples, exercises, and problems in the text will assume a 4% rate for state taxes and a 1% rate for federal taxes. These tax rates will be applied to the first $8,000 of an employee's annual earnings.)

The employer's payroll taxes are directly related to the costs of direct labor and indirect labor, and theoretically should be charged to these categories of labor cost. However, due to the additional expense and time such allocations would require, it is usually more practical to record all factory-related payroll taxes as factory overhead. The entry to record the payroll taxes for the payroll in Figure 3-4, assuming that no employee had exceeded the maximum for unemployment taxes, would be as follows:

Factory Overhead	239.27	
FICA Tax Payable		147.24
Federal Unemployment Tax Payable		18.41
State Unemployment Tax Payable		73.62
Recognized payroll taxes.		

ILLUSTRATION OF ACCOUNTING FOR LABOR COSTS

Morton Manufacturing Company pays employees every two weeks. Monday, May 1, is the beginning of a new payroll period. The company maintains the following records:

Payroll record

Employee earnings records

General journal

General ledger

Job cost ledger

Factory overhead ledger

Morton uses the following general ledger accounts in accounting for labor costs:

Cash

Work in Process

Wages Payable

FICA Tax Payable

Employees Income Tax Payable

Federal Unemployment Tax Payable

State Unemployment Tax Payable

Health Insurance Premiums Payable

Payroll

Factory Overhead

Sales Salaries

Administrative Salaries

Payroll Tax Expense—Sales Salaries

Payroll Tax Expense—Administrative Salaries

Applicable withholding and payroll tax rates and wage bases follow:

	Rates		Annual
	Employee Withholdings	Employer Payroll Taxes	Wages/Salaries Subject to Tax
Federal income tax	Graduated*		100%
FICA	8%	8%	$70,000
Federal unemployment . .		1%	$ 8,000
State unemployment . . .		4%	$ 8,000

*Federal income tax withholdings are determined from tables. State and local income taxes are not shown in this example.

The following payroll summary is prepared by the payroll department and forwarded to accounting for recording:

Payroll Summary
For the Period May 1–14

	Factory Employees	Sales and Administrative Employees	Total
Gross earnings	$100,000	$30,000	$130,000
Withholdings and deductions:			
FICA tax	$ 8,000	$ 2,400	$ 10,400
Income tax	11,250	3,500	14,750
Health insurance premiums .	2,100	700	2,800
Total	$ 21,350	$ 6,600	$ 27,950
Net earnings	$ 78,650	$23,400	$102,050

After the data are verified, a general journal entry records the payroll:

(A)	Payroll	130,000	
	FICA Tax Payable		10,400
	Employees Income Tax Payable		14,750
	Health Insurance Premiums Payable		2,800
	Wages Payable		102,050

Incurred payroll for period ended May 14.

To record the payment of the net earnings to employees, the following entry must be made:

(B)	Wages Payable	102,050	
	Cash		102,050

Paid payroll for period ended May 14.

The following labor cost summary and summary of payroll taxes provides the information necessary to distribute the total payroll of $130,000
to the appropriate accounts and to record the employer's payroll taxes
for the period.

Schedule of Earnings and Payroll Taxes
For Payroll Period, May 1–14

| | | | Unemployment Taxes | | |
Nonfactory Employees	Gross Earnings	FICA 8%	Federal 1%	State 4%	Total Payroll Taxes
Sales	$ 20,000	$ 1,600	$ 200	$ 800	$ 2,600
Administrative	10,000	800	100	400	1,300
	$ 30,000	$ 2,400	$ 300	$1,200	$ 3,900
Factory Employees					
Direct labor:					
Regular	$ 85,000	$ 6,800	$ 850	$3,400	$11,050
Overtime premium	10,000	800	100	400	1,300
Indirect labor	5,000	400	50	200	650
	$100,000	$ 8,000	$1,000	$4,000	$13,000
Total	$130,000	$10,400	$1,300	$5,200	$16,900

The distribution of the payroll and the employer's payroll taxes are
recorded as follows:

```
(C)   Work in Process                           85,000
      Factory Overhead                          15,000*
      Sales Salaries                            20,000
      Administrative Salaries                   10,000
          Payroll                                        130,000
          Distributed payroll for period ended May 14.
      *Overtime premium ($10,000) + indirect factory labor ($5,000)

(D)   Factory Overhead                          13,000**
      Payroll Tax Expense—Sales Salaries         2,600***
      Payroll Tax Expense—Administrative Salaries 1,300****
          FICA Tax Payable                               10,400
          Federal Unemployment Tax Payable              1,300
          State Unemployment Tax Payable               5,200
          Recognized employer's payroll taxes for period ended May 14.

  **FICA ($8,000) + FUTA ($1,000) + SUTA ($4,000)
 ***FICA ($1,600) + FUTA ($200) + SUTA ($800)
****FICA ($800) + FUTA ($100) + SUTA ($400)
```

The general ledger accounts that reflect the entries related to the May 1–14 payroll period follow:

Cash				Work in Process		
	(B)	102,050		(C)	85,000	

Wages Payable				FICA Tax Payable		
(B)	102,050	(A)	102,050		(A)	10,400
					(D)	10,400

Employees Income Tax Payable			Federal Unemployment Tax Payable		
	(A)	14,750		(D)	1,300

State Unemployment Tax Payable			Health Insurance Premiums Payable		
	(D)	5,200		(A)	2,800

Payroll				Factory Overhead		
(A)	130,000	(C)	130,000	(C)	15,000	
				(D)	13,000	

Sales Salaries			Administrative Salaries		
(C)	20,000		(C)	10,000	

Payroll Tax Expense—Sales Salaries			Payroll Tax Expense—Admin. Salaries		
(D)	2,600		(D)	1,300	

The next payroll period is May 15 to May 28. At the end of the two-week period, the following schedule for payroll is prepared:

Payroll Summary
For the Period May 15–28

	Factory Employees	Sales and Administrative Employees	Total
Gross earnings	$120,000	$30,000	$150,000
Withholdings and deductions:			
FICA tax	$ 9,600	$ 2,400	$ 12,000
Income tax	13,000	3,500	16,500
Health insurance premiums . .	2,300	700	3,000
Total	$ 24,900	$ 6,600	$ 31,500
Net earnings	$ 95,100	$23,400	$118,500

The payroll data are verified, and a general journal entry is prepared as follows:

(E) Payroll   150,000
       FICA Tax Payable   12,000
       Employees Income Tax Payable   16,500
       Health Insurance Premiums Payable   3,000
       Wages Payable   118,500
       Incurred payroll for period ending May 28.

The payment of the net earnings to employees requires the following entry:

(F) Wages Payable   118,500
       Cash   118,500
       Paid payroll for period ended May 28.

The following labor cost summary and summary of payroll taxes provides the information necessary to distribute the total payroll of $150,000 to the appropriate accounts and to record the employer's payroll taxes for the period.

Schedule of Earnings and Payroll Taxes
For Payroll Period May 15–28

Nonfactory Employees	Gross Earnings	FICA 8%	Unemployment Taxes Federal 1%	State 4%	Total Payroll Taxes
Sales	$ 20,000	$ 1,600	$ 200	$ 800	$ 2,600
Administrative	10,000	800	100	400	1,300
	$ 30,000	$ 2,400	$ 300	$1,200	$ 3,900
Factory Employees					
Direct labor:					
Regular	$100,000	$ 8,000	$1,000	$4,000	$13,000
Overtime premium .	12,000	960	120	480	1,560
Indirect labor	8,000	640	80	320	1,040
	$120,000	$ 9,600	$1,200	$4,800	$15,600
Total	$150,000	$12,000	$1,500	$6,000	$19,500

The distribution of the payroll and the employer's payroll taxes are recorded as follows:

(G)	Work in Process	100,000
	Factory Overhead	20,000*
	Sales Salaries	20,000
	Administrative Salaries	10,000
	Payroll	150,000

Distributed payroll for period ended May 28.

*Overtime premium ($12,000) + indirect factory labor ($8,000)

(H)	Factory Overhead	15,600	
	Payroll Tax Expense—Sales Salaries	2,600	
	Payroll Tax Expense—Administrative Salaries . .	1,300	
	FICA Tax Payable		12,000
	Federal Unemployment Tax Payable		1,500
	State Unemployment Tax Payable		6,000

Recognized employer's payroll taxes for period ended May 28.

PAYROLL ACCRUAL

LEARNING OBJECTIVE 4
Prepare accruals for payroll earnings and taxes.

When the financial statement date does not coincide with the ending date for a payroll period, an accrual for payroll earnings and payroll tax expense should be made. The accrual computations will not include the employees' withholdings because they do not affect the employer's income or total liabilities to be reported. However, the employer's payroll taxes are accrued to avoid understating the expenses and liabilities for the period.

The next payroll period for Morton Manufacturing Company begins on May 29 and ends June 11. However, the financial statements to be prepared for May will require an accrual of payroll earnings and taxes for the period May 29–31. The employee earnings and the payroll taxes for the accrual period are shown here, followed by the journal entries to record and distribute the accrued payroll and to record the employer's payroll taxes.

Schedule of Earnings and Payroll Taxes
For Payroll Period May 29–31

	Gross Earnings	FICA 8%	Unemployment Taxes Federal 1%	Unemployment Taxes State 4%	Total Payroll Taxes
Nonfactory Employees					
Sales	$ 6,000	$ 480	$ 60	$ 240	$ 780
Administrative	3,000	240	30	120	390
	$ 9,000	$ 720	$ 90	$ 360	$1,170
Factory Employees					
Direct labor:					
Regular	$30,000	$2,400	$300	$1,200	$3,900
Overtime premium .	4,000	320	40	160	520
Indirect labor	2,000	160	20	80	260
	$36,000	$2,880	$360	$1,440	$4,680
Total	$45,000	$3,600	$450	$1,800	$5,850

(I)	Payroll	45,000	
	Wages Payable		45,000

Incurred payroll for May 29–31.

(J)	Work in Process	30,000	
	Factory Overhead	6,000*	
	Sales Salaries	6,000	
	Administrative Salaries	3,000	
	Payroll		45,000

Distributed payroll for period May 29–31.

*Overtime premium ($4,000) + indirect labor ($2,000)

(K)	Factory Overhead	4,680	
	Payroll Tax Expense—Sales Salaries	780	
	Payroll Tax Expense—Administrative Salaries . .	390	
	FICA Tax Payable		3,600
	Federal Unemployment Tax Payable		450
	State Unemployment Tax Payable		1,800

Recognized employer's payroll taxes for period May 29–31.

Before June transactions are recorded, the entry for accruing payroll should be reversed:

| (L) | Wages Payable | . . . . | 45,000 | |
| | Payroll | . . . . | | 45,000 |

Reversed May 31 adjusting entry for accrued payroll.

The amount earned by the employees during the May 29–31 period is a portion of the total costs and expenses for production, sales, and administration for the month of May. However, the employees will not be paid until June 11 for the payroll period from May 29 to June 11. The credit balance in the payroll account, created by the reversing entry, will assure that only the payroll costs accumulated during the June 1 to June 11 period will be included in the June production, sales, and administrative costs. The ledger accounts would appear as follows after posting all of the preceding entries:

	Cash				Work in Process	
	(B)	102,050		(C)	85,000	
	(F)	118,500		(G)	100,000	
				(J)	30,000	
					215,000	

	Wages Payable				FICA Tax Payable	
(B)	102,050	(A)	102,050		(A)	10,400
(F)	118,500	(E)	118,500		(D)	10,400
(L)	45,000	(I)	45,000		(E)	12,000
					(H)	12,000
					(K)	3,600
						48,400

	Employees Income Tax Payable				Federal Unemployment Tax Payable	
		(A)	14,750		(D)	1,300
		(E)	16,500		(H)	1,500
			31,250		(K)	450
						3,250

	State Unemployment Tax Payable				Health Insurance Premiums Payable	
		(D)	5,200		(A)	2,800
		(H)	6,000		(E)	3,000
		(K)	1,800			5,800
			13,000			

	Payroll				Factory Overhead
(A)	130,000	(C)	130,000	(C)	15,000
(E)	150,000	(G)	150,000	(D)	13,000
(I)	45,000	(J)	45,000	(G)	20,000
	325,000	(L)	45,000	(H)	15,600
			370,000	(J)	6,000
			45,000	(K)	4,680
					74,280

	Sales Salaries		Administrative Salaries
(C)	20,000	(C)	10,000
(G)	20,000	(G)	10,000
(J)	6,000	(J)	3,000
	46,000		23,000

	Payroll Tax Expense—Sales Salaries		Payroll Tax Expense— Administrative Salaries
(D)	2,600	(D)	1,300
(H)	2,600	(H)	1,300
(K)	780	(K)	390
	5,980		2,990

You should now be able to work the following: Questions 11–17, Exercises 3-4 to 3-11, and Problems 3-2 to 3-9.

SPECIAL LABOR COST PROBLEMS

LEARNING OBJECTIVE 5
Account for special problems in labor costing.

An employer may be required to account for a variety of labor-related costs that do not fall into the normal routine of accounting for payroll costs. These special costs may include shift premiums, pensions, bonuses, and vacation and holiday pay. If encountered, the employer should systematically record and recognize each of these costs as a cost of the production process. Some companies identify the fringe benefits of direct laborers with the specific job being worked on (Work in Process), while others allocate the fringe benefits to all jobs worked on during the period (Factory Overhead). It is theoretically more correct to trace the fringe benefit costs to the specific jobs because if highly paid workers with their higher fringe benefits are required for a certain job, that job should also bear a greater amount of fringe benefit costs.

SHIFT PREMIUM

A **work shift** is defined as a regularly scheduled work period for a designated number of hours. If a company divides each work day into two or three 8-hour shifts, the employees working on shifts other than the regular daytime shift may receive additional pay, called a **shift premium**. For example, assume that a company operates three shifts: day shift, 8 a.m. to 4 p.m.; evening or "swing" shift, 4 p.m. to midnight; night or "graveyard" shift, midnight to 8 a.m. The company pays an additional $1.00 per hour to employees who work the evening shift and an additional $1.50 per hour to workers on the night shift. The additional payroll costs for the shift premiums do not increase the productivity of the shifts but are paid because of the social and other life-style adjustments required of the late-shift workers. The "other-than-normal" sleep and work schedules deprive the workers from participating in many normal, established social activities and routines. The shift premiums are designed to attract workers to the later shifts scheduled by a company. In reality, even though later shift workers are paid at higher rates, the productivity level of the day workers usually exceeds the productivity of the higher paid, late-shift employees. To avoid a distortion in costing products depending upon the time of day that they are worked on, shift premiums are usually charged to Factory Overhead and allocated to all jobs worked on during the period, regardless of shift.

EMPLOYEE PENSION COSTS

Pension costs originate from an agreement between a company and its employee group, by which the company promises to provide income to employees after they retire. The amount of pension benefits paid to a retired employee is commonly based on the employee's past level of earnings and length of service with the company. **Non-contributory plans** are completely funded (paid for) by the company. **Contributory plans** require a partial contribution from the employee. When a pension plan is initiated, it is usually retroactive and recognizes the previous years of each employee's service with the company.

A basic provision of all plans is to systematically accrue, over the period of active service, the total estimated pension cost from the beginning date of the pension plan to the employee's retirement date. If, for example, an employee works a 40-hour week and the company incurs a pension cost of $2 per hour, the amount of pension cost chargeable to the payroll period for this employee is $80. The pension costs related to the factory employees could be charged to general or administrative expenses under the premise that the costs of pensions is beneficial to the company as a whole. However, it is also considered appropriate to charge pension costs directly to the individual employee's department or to apportion the cost of pensions, using a percentage of the total payroll, to all departments within the company.

BONUSES

Employees may receive **bonus pay** for a variety of reasons, such as higher-than-usual company profits, exceeding departmental quotas for selling or production, or for any other achievement that the company feels merits additional pay. Bonus plans may include some or all employees. The cost of bonuses is generally charged to the department in which the employee works. Therefore, factory workers' bonuses are charged to Factory Overhead, sales employees' bonuses are charged to Selling Expense, etc.

VACATION AND HOLIDAY PAY

All permanent employees of a company expect a vacation period each year that will be paid by their employer. Usually the **vacation pay** is earned gradually by the employee for daily service on the job.

Vacation plans generally stipulate that an employee will be granted a specified period of paid vacation time each year for services rendered during the year. The vacation cost is accrued throughout the year and assigned to the employee's department. For example, assume that an employee earns $600 per week and is entitled to a four-week vacation. The total cost of the vacation to the company would be $2,400. Each week that the employee works, the employee's department would be charged $50 ($2,400/48 weeks) for vacation pay expense.

Holiday pay is based on an agreement between management and company employees. The argument stipulates that certain holidays during the year will be paid for by the company but are nonworking days for the employees.

ACCOUNTING FOR BONUSES, VACATIONS, AND HOLIDAY PAY

To illustrate accounting for bonuses, vacations, and holiday pay, assume that a factory worker, who is classified as direct labor, earns $700 each week. In addition, the worker will receive a $1,000 bonus at year-end, a two-week paid vacation, and five paid holidays. The following entry records the weekly payroll and the costs and liabilities related to the bonus, vacation, and holiday pay as an expense of the 50 weeks that the employee actually worked:

Work in Process	700	
Factory Overhead (Bonus)*	20	
Factory Overhead (Vacation)**	28	
Factory Overhead (Holiday)***	14	
Payroll		700
Bonus Liability		20
Vacation Pay Liability		28
Holiday Pay Liability		14

Incurred payroll and bonus, vacation, and holiday pay.

*Bonus: $1,000 / 50 weeks = $20 per week.
**Vacation Pay: ($700 per week × 2 weeks) / 50 weeks = $28 per week.
***Holiday Pay: $140 per day × 5 paid holidays = $700
$700 / 50 weeks = $14 per week.

Note in the previous example that Factory Overhead was debited for the cost of the bonus, vacation, and holiday pay. If the workers' fringe benefits had been traced to the individual jobs, work in process would have been debited. If these fringe benefits had related to sales workers or general office workers, Sales Salaries and Administrative Salaries would have been debited respectively.

You should now be able to work the following: Questions 18–22, Exercise 3-12, and Problems 3-10 and 3-11.

K E Y   T E R M S

SELF-STUDY PROBLEM

PAYMENT AND DISTRIBUTION OF PAYROLL

NAUTICAL COMPANY

The general ledger of the Nautical Company showed the following credit balances on March 15:

FICA Tax Payable	$1,550
Employees Income Tax Payable	975
FUTA Tax Payable	95
State Unemployment Tax Payable	380

Direct labor earnings amounted to $5,100, and indirect labor was $3,400 for the period from March 16 to March 31. The sales and administrative salaries for the same period amounted to $1,500.

Use the following tax rates and bases for this problem:

FICA: 8% on the first $70,000.
State unemployment: 4% on the first $8,000.
FUTA: 1% on the first $8,000.
Federal income tax: 10% of each employee's gross earnings

Required:

1. Prepare the journal entries for the following:
   a. Recording the payroll.
   b. Paying the payroll.
   c. Recording the employer's payroll tax liability.
   d. Distributing the payroll for March 16 to 31.
2. Prepare the journal entries to record the payment of the amounts due for the month for FICA and income tax withholdings.

Suggestions:

Read the entire problem thoroughly, keeping in mind what you are required to do:

1. Journal entries to record the payroll, pay the payroll, record the employer's payroll taxes, and distribute the payroll.
2. Journal entries for the payment of FICA taxes and federal income tax withholdings.

The specifics of the problem highlight the fact that there are three separate categories of labor: direct labor, indirect factory labor, and salespersons and administrators.

SOLUTION TO SELF-STUDY PROBLEM

1. a. Journal entry to record the payroll for the period March 16–31: To determine the amount of the debit to Payroll, the earnings of direct labor, indirect labor, and sales and administrative must be added together to obtain $10,000. The $800 of FICA to be withheld can be obtained by multiplying

the $10,000 payroll (assuming that no employee's salary has already exceeded the $70,000 base for the year by the 8% rate). The $1,000 withholding for income taxes is determined by multiplying the $10,000 payroll by the assumed withholding percentage of 10%. Lastly, the credit to Wages Payable for $8,200 represents the amount of net pay that is to appear on employees' paychecks.

Payroll	10,000	
FICA Tax Payable		800
Employees Income Tax Payable		1,000
Wages Payable		8,200

b. Journal entry to pay the payroll: A check drawn by the company for the total payroll net earnings is deposited in a separate payroll account at the bank, and individual checks are issued to the employees.

Wages Payable	8,200	
Cash		8,200

c. Journal entry to record the payroll tax liability: Payroll taxes consist of the employer's share of the FICA taxes and the federal and state unemployment insurance premiums. The employer pays an amount of FICA taxes that matches the employees' contributions and unemployment insurance premiums that are based on an experience rating related to the business' employment history. (In this example, $800 represents the employer's FICA contributions, $400 is the state unemployment insurance premium, and $100 is the federal unemployment insurance premium.) An important fact to note in the following journal entry is that the payroll taxes on factory labor, whether direct or indirect, are all charged to Factory Overhead, whereas the payroll taxes on the sales and administrative salaries are charged to Payroll Tax Expense (Sales and Administrative Salaries).

Factory Overhead	1,105*	
Payroll Tax Expense (Sales and Administrative Salaries)	195**	
FICA Tax Payable		800
Federal Unemployment Tax Payable		100
State Unemployment Tax Payable		400

*[.08 ($5,100 + $3,400) + .01 ($8,500) + .04 ($8,500)]
**[.08 ($1,500) + .01 ($1,500) + .04 ($1,500)]

d. Journal entry to distribute the payroll: In distributing the payroll to the appropriate accounts, it is important to distinguish direct labor, which is charged to Work in Process, from indirect labor, which is debited to Factory Overhead.

Work in Process	5,100	
Factory Overhead	3,400	
Sales and Administrative Salaries	1,500	
Payroll		10,000

2. At appropriate times as designated by law, the employer payroll taxes and employee withholdings must be remitted to the proper authorities. In this example, FICA taxes and employee income taxes are remitted monthly. The entry would be as follows:

FICA Tax Payable	3,150	
Employees Income Tax Payable	1,975	
Cash		5,125

(Note: Problem 3-5 is similar to this problem.)

QUESTIONS

1. What is the difference between direct and indirect labor?

2. Briefly stated, what are the advantages and disadvantages of (a) the hourly rate wage plan and (b) the piece-rate wage plan?

3. What is a modified wage plan?

4. What is the concept of production work teams as it relates to incentive wage plans?

5. What are the functions of the timekeeping and payroll departments?

6. The timekeeping and payroll departments are expected to operate, to a degree, independently of each other. Why is this independence important?

7. a. In a payroll system, what purpose is served by the clock card and time ticket? b. How is the information recorded on clock cards and time tickets used?

8. What technology is replacing mechanical time recorders and clock cards in the modern factory? Explain.

9. How do the clock cards and time tickets complement each other?

10. Although payroll records may vary in design, what types of employee data would be found in the payroll records of most manufacturing companies?

11. What are the sources for posting direct labor cost to (a) individual jobs in the job cost ledger and (b) the work in process account in the general ledger?

12. What are the sources for posting indirect labor cost to the indirect labor account in the factory overhead ledger?

13. In accounting for labor costs, what is the distinction between regular pay and overtime premium pay?

14. Maintaining internal control over labor cost is necessary for a cost accounting system to function effectively. What are the internal control procedures regarding the charge to the work in process account and the credit to the payroll account in the general ledger?

15. What accounts are used to record employees' withholding taxes and the employer's payroll taxes?

16. What are the procedures involved in accounting for labor cost, and what supporting forms are used for each procedure?

17. What are the sources of data and the books of original entry for each of the following?

   a. Recording the wages and salaries earned during the payroll period.

   b. Recording the payroll taxes imposed on the employer.

18. What is a shift premium?

19. What is a basic requirement in all pension plans?

20. What accounting treatments do factory bonuses, vacation pay, and holiday pay for factory employees have in common?

21. Under what set of circumstances might direct labor be an insignificant amount that would not be accounted for as a separate cost category?

22. What are the two alternatives for accounting for the fringe benefits of direct laborers?

E X E R C I S E S

NOTE: For the exercises and problems in this chapter, use the following tax rates:

FICA—Employer and employee, 8% of the first $70,000 of earnings per employee per calendar year.

State unemployment—4% of the first $8,000 of earnings per employee per calendar year.

FUTA—1% of the first $8,000 of earnings per employee per calendar year.

Federal income tax withholding—10% of each employee's gross earnings, unless otherwise stated.

E3-1
Computing payroll earnings and taxes
Objectives 1, 2

R. King of Royalty Manufacturing Company is paid at the rate of $12 an hour for an 8-hour day, with time-and-a-half for overtime and double-time for Sundays and holidays. Regular employment is on the basis of 40 hours a week, five days a week. The regular workday is from 7:00 a.m. to 12:00 noon and from 12:30 p.m. to 3:30 p.m. At the end of a week, the clock card shows the following:

	A.M. In	A.M. Out	P.M. In	P.M. Out	Overtime In	Overtime Out
Sunday	8:00	12:00				
Monday	6:58	12:01	12:25	3:35		
Tuesday	7:00	12:03	12:28	3:32		
Wednesday	6:56	12:02	12:30	3:33		
Thursday	6:55	12:05	12:28	3:35	6:00	9:30
Friday	6:55	12:01	12:29			6:32
Saturday	6:55			1:30		

On Monday through Friday night, King worked on the production line. The hours worked on Saturday and Sunday were used to repair machinery.

a. Compute King's total earnings for the week. (Ignore odd minutes.)
b. Present the journal entry to distribute King's total earnings.

E3-2
Recording payroll
Objectives 1, 2

Using the earnings data developed in E3-1, and assuming that this was the first week of employment for R. King with Royalty Manufacturing Company, prepare the journal entries for the following:

a. The week's payroll.
b. Payment of the payroll.

Note: *These single journal entries here and in E3-7 and E3-8 are for the purpose of illustrating the principle involved. Normally the entries would be made for the total factory payroll plus the administrative and sales payroll.*

E3-3
Determining payroll earnings
Objective 2

David Company requires all factory workers to record the time of arrival and departure by means of a time clock. The company operates on a 40-hour basis, with time-and-a-half allowed for overtime. The regular workday is from 8:30 a.m. to 12:00 noon and from 1:00 p.m. to 5:00 p.m., Monday through Friday, and from 8:30 a.m. to 11:00 a.m. on Saturday.

The clock card record of a group of employees for Monday is as follows:

Employee No.	Morning In	Noon Out	Noon In	Night Out	Extra In	Extra Out
51	8:29	12:00	12:51	4:57		
52	8:30	12:01	12:56	4:58		
53	8:21	12:05				
54	8:20	12:02	12:57	4:53		
55	8:24	12:04	12:57	4:50		
56	8:29	12:04	12:53	4:57		
57	8:25	12:04				
58	8:27	12:00	12:48	4:56		
59	8:28	12:01	12:57			6:50
60	8:26	12:03	12:56			5:20
61	8:26	12:05	12:59	4:58		
62	8:23	12:00	12:52	4:59	5:30	9:30

a. Compute the regular and overtime hours for each employee for the day. (Round to nearest half hour.)
b. Assuming that all of the employees are paid at the rate of $9.20 an hour, compute the amount of each employee's earnings for the day.

E3-4
Overtime allocation
Objective 3

Igar Machine Tool Company produces tools on a job order basis. During May, two jobs were completed, and the following costs were incurred:

	Job 401	Job 402
Direct materials	$28,000	$37,000
Direct labor: regular	18,000	23,000
overtime premium	—	6,000

Other factory costs for the month totaled $16,800. Factory overhead costs are allocated one-third to Job 401 and two-thirds to Job 402.

a. Describe two alternative methods for assigning the overtime premium cost to Jobs 401 and 402 and explain how the appropriate method would be determined.
b. Compute the cost of Job 401 and Job 402 under each of the two methods described in part a.

E3-5
Journal entries for payroll
Objectives 2, 3

A partial summary of the payroll data for The Monte Carlo Manufacturing Company for each week of June is as follows:

	June 7	June 14	June 21	June 28
Total earnings	$36,500	$34,200	$37,300	$38,400
Deductions:				
FICA tax, 8%	$?	$?	$?	$?
Tax-sheltered annuity . . .	1,825	1,780	1,855	1,870
Income tax	4,215	4,120	4,320	4,410
Health insurance	600	600	600	600
Total deductions	$?	$?	$?	$?
Net earnings	$?	$?	$?	$?

a. Compute the missing amounts in the summary, assuming that no employees have reached the $70,000 FICA maximum.

b. For each payroll period, prepare journal entries to (1) record the payroll and (2) record the payments to employees.

E3-6
Payroll taxes
Objective 3

Fucia Company paid wages to its employees during the year as follows:

Brooks	$11,400
Coombs	12,700
Durkins	9,000
Evans	19,300
Hull	29,200
Massey	32,100
Oliver	62,700
Sanders	75,000

a. How much of the total payroll is exempt from the FICA rate of 8%?

b. How much of the total payroll is exempt from federal and state unemployment taxes?

c. How much of the total payroll is exempt from federal income tax withholding?

E3-7
Recording the payroll and payroll taxes
Objectives 2,3

Using the earnings data developed in E3-1, and assuming that this was the tenth week of employment for King and the previous earnings to date were $7,900, prepare the journal entries for the following:

a. The week's payroll.

b. Payment of the payroll.

c. The employer's payroll taxes.

E3-8
Recording the payroll and payroll taxes
Objectives 2,3

Using the earnings data developed in E3-1, and assuming that this was the fiftieth week of employment for King and the previous earnings to date were $69,800, prepare the journal entries for the following:

a. The week's payroll.

b. Payment of the payroll.

c. The employer's payroll taxes.

E3-9
Payroll distribution
Objective 3

The total wages and salaries earned by all employees of The Fang Manufacturing Company during the month of March as shown in the labor cost summary and the schedule of fixed administrative and sales salaries are classified as follows:

Direct labor	$ 625,125
Indirect labor	162,120
Administrative salaries	140,200
Sales salaries	172,500
Total wages earned	$1,099,945

a. Prepare a journal entry to distribute the wages earned during March.

b. What is the total amount of payroll taxes that will be imposed on the employer for the payroll, assuming that two administrative employees with combined earnings this period of $1,500 have exceeded $8,000 in earnings prior to the period?

E3-10
Employees' earnings and taxes
Objectives 2, 3

A weekly payroll summary made from time tickets shows the following data:

Employee	Classification	Hourly Rate	Hours Regular	Overtime
Longley, P.	Direct	$12	40	2
Rodman, A.	Direct	12	40	3
Potter, D.	Direct	15	40	4
Harpen, D.	Indirect	9	40	
Jordan, C.	Indirect	18	40	

Overtime is payable at one-and-a-half times the regular rate of pay for an employee and is distributed to all jobs worked on during the period.

a. Determine the net pay of each employee. The income taxes withheld for each employee amount to 15% of the gross wages.
b. Prepare journal entries for the following:
   1. Recording the payroll.
   2. Paying the payroll.
   3. Distributing the payroll. (Assume that overtime premium will be charged to all jobs worked on during the period.)
   4. The employer's payroll taxes. (Assume that none of the employees has achieved the maximum wage bases for FICA and unemployment taxes.)

E3-11
Employees' earnings using hourly and piece-rate methods
Objectives 1, 3

The payroll records of Western-Southern Manufacturing Company show the following information for the week ended April 17:

Employee	Classification	Hours Worked	Production (Units)	Rate	Income Tax W/held
Charles, A.	Direct	42		$9.00/hr.	$40
Donn, B.	Direct	48		8.80/hr.	42
Johns, C.	Direct	39	2,000	$.22/piece	55
Peter, D.	Direct	40	1,800	.22/piece	50
Raymond, E.	Indirect	40		$200/wk.	25
Stephens, F.	Indirect	40		400/wk.	60
Williams, G.	Indirect	40		350/wk.	30

Hourly workers are paid time-and-a-half for overtime.

a. Determine the net earnings of each employee.
b. Prepare the journal entries for the following:
   1. Recording the payroll.
   2. Paying the payroll.
   3. Distributing the payroll.

4. Recording the employer's payroll taxes. Assume that none of the employees has achieved the maximum wage bases for FICA and unemployment taxes.

E3-12
Accounting for bonus
and vacation pay
Objective 5

Mary Watson, a factory worker, earns $1,000 each week. In addition, she will receive a $4,000 bonus at year-end and a four-week paid vacation.

Prepare the entry to record the weekly payroll and the costs and liabilities related to the bonus and the vacation pay, assuming that Watson is the only employee.

P R O B L E M S

P3-1
Payroll computation
with incentive bonus
Objective 1

Fifteen workers are assigned to a group project. The production standard calls for 500 units to be completed each hour to meet a customer's set deadline for the products. If the required units can be delivered before the target date on the order, a substantial premium for early delivery will be paid by the customer. The company, wishing to encourage the workers to produce beyond the established standard, has offered an excess production bonus that will be added to each project employee's pay. The bonus is to be computed as follows:

a. $\dfrac{\text{Group's excess production over standard} \times 50\%}{\text{Standard units for week}}$ = bonus percentage

b. Individual's hourly wage rate × bonus percentage = hourly bonus rate
c. Hourly wage rate + hourly bonus rate = new hourly rate for week
d. Total hours worked × new hourly rate = earnings for week

The average wage rate for the project workers is $12 per hour. The production record for the week shows the following:

	Hours Worked	Production (Units)
Monday	112	61,040
Tuesday	112	60,032
Wednesday	112	60,480
Thursday	112	65,632
Friday	108	57,344
Saturday	60	26,000
	616	330,528

Required:

1. Determine the hourly bonus rate and the total amount of the bonus for the week.
2. What are the total wages of L. Bachman, who worked 40 hours at a base rate of $10 per hour?
3. What are the total wages of C. Scripps, who worked 35 hours at a base rate of $14 per hour?

P3-2
Payroll calculation
and distribution;
overtime and idle time
Objectives 2, 3

A rush order was accepted by Coleman's Conversions for five van conversions. The time tickets and clock cards for the week ended March 27 show the following:

		Time Tickets—Hour Distribution				
Employees	Clock Hours	Van #1	Van #2	Van #3	Van #4	Van #5
Bagwell (Supervisor)	42					
Belle	45	10	10	10	10	5
Griffey	48	24	24			
Martinez	48			24	24	
McGuire	45	15	15	15		
Sanders	42	24	8			
Thomas	40	20	10			

All employees are paid $10.00 per hour, except Bagwell, who receives $15 per hour. All overtime premium pay except Bagwell's is chargeable to the job, and all employees, including Bagwell, receive time-and-a-half for overtime hours.

Required:

1. Calculate the total payroll and total net earnings for the week. Assume that an 18% deduction for federal income tax is required in addition to FICA deductions. Assume that none of the employees has achieved the maximums for FICA and unemployment taxes. Hours not worked on vans are idle time and are not charged to the job.
2. Prepare the journal entries to record and pay the payroll.
3. Prepare the journal entry to distribute the payroll to the appropriate accounts.
4. Determine the dollar amount of labor that is chargeable to each van, assuming that the overtime costs are proportionate to the regular hours used on the vans. (First compute an average labor rate for each worker, including overtime premium, and then use that rate to charge all workers hours to vans.)

P3-3
Computing and
journalizing
employer's payroll
taxes
Objective 3

The following form is used by The Munich Manufacturing Company to compute payroll taxes incurred during the month of April:

Classification of Wages and Salaries	Earnings for Month	FICA Tax 8%	Unemployment Taxes Federal Tax 1%	State Tax 4%	Total Payroll Taxes Imposed on Employer
Direct labor	88,180				
Indirect labor	16,220				
Payroll taxes on factory wages					
Administrative salaries	12,000				
Sales salaries	11,500				
Total payroll taxes . .					

Required:

1. Using the above form, calculate the employer's payroll taxes for April. Assume that none of the employees has achieved the maximums for FICA and unemployment taxes.
2. Assuming that the employer payroll taxes on factory wages are treated as factory overhead, the taxes covering administrative salaries are an administrative expense, and the taxes covering sales salaries are a selling expense, prepare a general journal entry to record the employer's liability for the April payroll taxes.

P3-4
Payroll for piece-rate wage system
Objectives 1, 3

Green Manufacturing Company operates on a modified wage plan. During one week's operation, the following direct labor costs were incurred:

Employee	Piece Rate per 100 Units	M	T	W	T	F
				Units Completed		
J. Nicklaus	$0.90	6,800	7,100	6,500	8,000	4,800
A. Palmer	1.10	6,300	6,400	2,900	2,800	7,000
T. Woods	1.30	6,200	6,100	7,100	6,000	2,800

The employees are machine operators. Piece rates vary with the kind of product being produced. A minimum of $45 per day is guaranteed each employee by union contract.

Required:

1. Compute Nicklaus', Palmer's, and Woods' earnings for the week.
2. Prepare journal entries to:
   a. Record the week's payroll, assuming that none of the employees has achieved the maximum base wage for FICA taxes.
   b. Record payment of the payroll.
   c. Record the employer's share of payroll taxes, assuming that none of the employees has achieved the maximum base wage for FICA or unemployment taxes.

P3-5
Payment and distribution of payroll.
Similar to self-study problem.
Objective 3

The general ledger of Franklin Company showed the following credit balances on May 15:

FICA Tax Payable	3,100.00
Employees Income Tax Payable	1,937.50
FUTA Tax Payable	193.75
State Unemployment Tax Payable	775.00

Direct labor earnings amounted to $10,500 from May 16 to May 31. Indirect labor was $5,700 and sales and administrative salaries for the same period amounted to $3,800. All wages are subject to FICA, FUTA, state unemployment taxes, and 10% income tax withholding.

Required:

1. Prepare the journal entries for the following:
   a. Recording the payroll.
   b. Paying the payroll.
   c. Recording the employer's payroll tax liability.
   d. Distributing the payroll costs for May 16 to 31.

2. Prepare the journal entry to record the payment of the amounts due for the month for FICA and income tax withholdings.
3. Calculate the amount of total earnings for the period from May 1 to May 15.

P3-6
Payroll work sheet and journal entries
Objectives 2, 3

The payroll records of Stricker Corporation for the week ending October 7, the fortieth week in the year, show the following:

Employee	Classification	Salary or wage per 40-Hour Week	Hours Worked	Income Tax Withheld	Gross Earnings through Thirty-Ninth week
Coster	President	$2,040	40	$400	$79,560
Davis	Vice-President—Administration	1,782	40	320	69,500
Evans	Supervisor—Production	700	40	180	27,300
Frank	Factory—Direct	500	48	150	19,820
Gregg	Factory—Direct	400	46	160	17,200
Haynes	Factory—Direct	400	44	110	16,600
Porter	Factory—Direct	380	42	120	15,200
Revoz	Factory—Indirect	300	42	80	7,800
Stover	Factory—Indirect	300	42	60	6,600

Required:

1. Complete a work sheet with the following column headings:
   Employee
   3 columns for Earnings for Week:
      Use one for Regular Pay
      Use one for Overtime Premium Pay (The company pays time-and-a-half for overtime for all employees below the supervisory level.)
      Use one for Total for Week
   Total Earnings through Fortieth Week
   FICA Taxable Earnings
   FICA
   Income Tax Withheld
   Net Earnings
2. Prepare journal entries for the following:
   a. Payroll for fortieth week.
   b. Payment of payroll for week.
   c. Distribution of the payroll costs, assuming that overtime premium is charged to all jobs worked on during the period.
   d. Employer's payroll tax liability.
3. The company carries a disability insurance policy for the employees at a cost of $7.80 per week for each employee. Journalize the employer's cost of insurance premiums for the week.

P3-7
Estimating labor costs for bids
Objectives 1, 3

Mutombo Manufacturing Company prepares cost estimates for projects on which it will bid. In order to anticipate the labor cost to be included in a request to bid on a contract for 1,200,000 units that will be delivered to the customer at the rate of 100,000 units per month, the company has compiled the following data related to labor:

a. The first 100,000 units will require 5 hours per unit.

b. The second 100,000 units will require less labor due to the skills learned on the first 100,000 units finished. It is expected that labor time will be reduced by 15% if an incentive bonus of one-half of the labor savings is paid to the employees.

c. For the remaining 1,000,000, it is expected that the labor time will be reduced 25% from the original estimate (the first 100,000 units) if the same incentive bonus (1/2 of the savings) is paid to the employees.

d. Overtime premiums are to be excluded when savings are computed.

The contract will require 2,250 employees at a base rate of $10.00 per hour, with time-and-a-half for overtime. The plant operates on a 5-day, 40-hour-per-week basis. Employees are paid for a two-week vacation in August and for eight holidays.

The scheduled production for the 50-week work-year shows:

January—June: 26 weeks with 4 holidays
July—December: 24 weeks with 4 holidays

Required:

Prepare cost estimates for direct labor and labor-related costs for the contract, showing the following:

1. Wages paid at the regular rate.
2. Overtime premium payments. (Don't forget holidays in computing regular hours available.)
3. Incentive bonus payments.
4. Vacation and holiday pay.
5. Employer's payroll taxes (13% of total wages, assuming that no employee has exceeded the wage bases for FICA and the unemployment insurance taxes).

P3-8
Summary of payroll procedures
Objectives 2, 3

An analysis of the payroll for the month of November of Stern Manufacturing Company reveals the information shown:

Employee Name	11/8	11/15	11/22	11/29
	Gross Earnings*—Week Ending			
A. Arthur	$ 300	$ 280	$ 290	$ 320
B. Bennett	280	270	260	280
C. Carletto	320	300	340	280
D. Davenport	1,577	1,577	1,577	1,577
E. Evans	800	760	850	870

*All regular time

Arthur, Bennett, and Carletto are production workers, and Davenport is the plant manager. Evans is in charge of the office.

Cumulative earnings paid (before deductions) in this calendar year prior to the payroll period ending November 8 were as follows: Arthur, $12,000; Bennett, $7,800; Carletto, $11,500; Davenport, $69,400; and Evans, $32,800.

Required:

The solution to this problem requires the following forms, using the indicated column headings:

Employee Earnings Record	Payroll Record	Labor Cost Summary
Week Ending	Employee's Name	Week Ending
Weekly Gross Earnings	Gross Earnings	Dr. Work in Process
Accumulated Gross	Withholdings	(Direct Labor)
Earnings	(2 columns):	Dr. Factory Overhead
Weekly Earnings Subject	FICA Tax	(Indirect Labor)
to FICA	Income Tax (10%)	Dr. Administrative
Withholdings	Net Amount Paid	Salaries (Office)
(2 columns):		Cr. Payroll (Total)
FICA Tax		
Income Tax (10%)		
Net Amount Paid		

1. Prepare an employee earnings record for each of the five employees.
2. Prepare a payroll record for each of the four weeks.
3. Prepare a labor cost summary for the month.
4. Prepare journal entries to record the following:
   a. The payroll for each of the four weeks.
   b. The payment of wages for each of the four payrolls.
   c. The distribution of the monthly labor costs per the labor cost summary.
   d. The company's payroll taxes covering the four payroll periods.

P3-9
Summary of payroll
procedures
Objectives 2, 3

Costanza Construction Company uses the job order cost system. In recording payroll transactions, the following accounts are used:

Cash	Administrative Salaries
Wages Payable	Miscellaneous Administrative Expense
FICA Tax Payable	Sales Salaries
Federal Unemployment Tax Payable	Miscellaneous Selling Expense
State Unemployment Tax Payable	Factory Overhead
Employees Income Tax Payable	Work in Process
Payroll	

Factory employees are paid weekly, while all other employees are paid semi-monthly on the fifteenth and the last day of each month. All salaries and wages are subject to all taxes.

Following is a narrative of transactions completed during the month of March:

Mar. 7   Recorded total earnings of factory employees amounting to $68,200, less deductions for employees income taxes and FICA taxes.

7   Issued check for payment of the payroll.

14   Recorded total earnings of factory employees amounting to $66,300, less deductions for employees income taxes and FICA taxes.

14   Issued check for payment of the payroll.

15   Recorded administrative salaries, $9,000, and sales salaries,
      $17,000, less deductions for employees income taxes and FICA
      taxes.
15   Issued check for payment of the salaries.
21   Recorded total earnings of factory employees amounting to
      $72,500, less deductions for employees income taxes and FICA
      taxes.
21   Issued check for payment of the payroll.
28   Recorded total earnings of factory employees amounting to
      $74,200, less deductions for employees income taxes and FICA
      taxes.
28   Issued check for payment of the payroll.
31   Recorded administrative salaries, $9,000, and sales salaries,
      $17,000, less deductions for employees income taxes and FICA
      taxes.
31   Issued check for payment of the salaries.
31   The following wages and salaries were earned or accrued during
      March:

Direct labor	$302,500
Indirect labor	22,500
Administrative salaries	18,000
Sales salaries	34,000
Total	$377,000

Costanza Construction Company used the following form to compute the
amount of payroll taxes incurred:

Items	Taxable Earnings FICA tax	Federal Unemployment Taxes Payroll	State Unemployment Tax	Total Payroll Taxes
Factory wages	325,000			
Administrative salaries				
Sales salaries	———			
Total	377,000			

Required:

1. Complete the above form to show the payroll taxes imposed on the
   employer for the month of March.
2. Prepare the journal entries to record the foregoing transactions, including the
   distribution of payroll costs and payroll taxes, assuming that the payroll taxes
   imposed on the employer for factory wages are to be charged to Factory
   Overhead, the taxes for administrative salaries are to be charged to Miscellaneous Administrative Expense, and the taxes for sales salaries are to be
   charged to Miscellaneous Selling Expense.
3. Assume that the factory employees worked on March 29, 30, and 31. What
   was the amount of accrued wages on March 31?

P3-10
Accounting for bonus,
vacation pay, and
holiday pay
Objective 5

The factory payroll for the week is $100,000, consisting of $70,000 earned by 100 direct laborers and $30,000 earned by 30 indirect laborers. The total of factory bonuses to be received at year-end is estimated at $200,000. All factory workers receive a two-week paid vacation and five paid holidays.

Prepare the entry to record the weekly payroll and the costs and liabilities related to the bonus, vacation, and holiday pay, assuming that the fringe benefits of the direct laborers are charged to Factory Overhead.

P3-11
Allocating overtime
premium and bonus
costs
Objectives 3, 5

Cyclops Manufacturing Company uses a job order cost system to cost its products. It recently signed a new contract with the union that calls for time-and-a-half for all work over 40 hours a week and double-time for Saturday and Sunday. Also, a bonus of 1% of the employees' earnings for the year is to be paid to the employees at the end of the fiscal year. The controller, the plant manager, and the sales manager disagree as to how the overtime pay and the bonus should be allocated.

An examination of the first month's payroll under the new union contract provisions shows the following:

Direct labor:		
Regular—40,200 hours @ $10		$402,000
Overtime:		
Weekdays—1,700 hours @ $15	$25,500	
Saturdays—400 hours @ $20	8,000	
Sundays—300 hours @ $20	6,000	39,500
Indirect labor		14,800
		$456,300

Analysis of the payroll supporting documents revealed the following:

a. More production was scheduled each day than could be handled in a regular workday, resulting in the need for overtime.
b. The Saturday and Sunday hours resulted from rush orders with special contract arrangements with the customers.

The controller believes that the overtime premiums and the bonus should be charged to factory overhead and spread over all production of the accounting period, regardless of when the jobs were completed.

The plant manager favors charging the overtime premiums directly to the jobs worked on during overtime hours and the bonus to administrative expense.

The sales manager states that the overtime premiums and bonus are not factory costs chargeable to regular production but are costs created from administrative policies and, therefore, should be charged only to administrative expense.

Required:

1. Evaluate each position—the controller's, the plant manager's, and the sales manager's. If you disagree with all of the positions taken, present your view of the appropriate allocation.
2. Prepare the journal entries to illustrate the position you support, including the accrual for the bonus.

4

Accounting for Factory Overhead

LEARNING OBJECTIVES

After studying this chapter, you should be able to:

1. Identify cost behavior patterns.
2. Separate semivariable costs into variable and fixed components.
3. Prepare a budget for factory overhead costs.
4. Account for actual factory overhead costs.
5. Distribute service department factory overhead costs to production departments.
6. Apply factory overhead using predetermined rates.
7. Account for actual and applied factory overhead.

All costs incurred in the factory not chargeable directly to the finished product are called **factory overhead**. These operating costs of the factory cannot be traced specifically to a unit of production. A variety of other terms have been used to describe this type of cost, such as indirect expenses, indirect manufacturing costs, or factory burden. These costs are also referred to simply as "overhead" or "burden."

One method to determine whether a factory expenditure is a factory overhead item is to compare it to the classification standards established for direct materials and direct labor costs. If the expenditure cannot be charged to either of these two "direct" factory accounts, it is classified as factory overhead. Thus, all indirect factory expenditures are factory overhead items. Generally, factory overhead accounts include (1) indirect materials consumed in the factory, such as cleaning materials and lubricants required for production; (2) indirect factory labor, such as wages of janitors, forklift operators, and supervisors; and overtime premiums paid to all factory workers; and (3) other indirect manufacturing expenses, such as rent, insurance, property taxes, depreciation, heat, light, and power.

Accounting for factory overhead involves the following procedures:

1. Identifying cost behavior patterns.
2. Budgeting factory overhead costs.
3. Accumulating actual overhead costs.
4. Applying factory overhead estimates to production.
5. Calculating and analyzing differences between actual and applied factory overhead.

IDENTIFYING COST BEHAVIOR PATTERNS

LEARNING OBJECTIVE 1
Identify cost behavior patterns.

Direct materials and direct labor are classified as variable costs. **Variable costs** are costs that vary in direct proportion to volume changes. In contrast are those costs that remain the same, in total, when production levels increase or decrease. These unchanging costs are referred to as **fixed costs**. **Semivariable costs** have characteristics of both variable and fixed costs. They are sometimes called **semifixed** or **mixed costs**.

Factory overhead expenses include costs that may be classified as variable, fixed, or semivariable. Therefore, factory overhead creates a difficult problem for most companies because they must predict costs that will be incurred at various levels of production. The factory overhead costs that behave in the same pattern as direct materials cost and direct labor costs are considered variable costs and are readily forecasted because they move up or down proportionately with production volume changes. The factory overhead charges deemed to be fixed costs remain unchanged when production varies; therefore, they are also considered predictable. The factory overhead costs that are semivariable require additional analysis and attention because they are not as readily predictable. In many companies, semivariable costs constitute a substantial portion of the factory overhead charges, and the method used to forecast these costs must be carefully selected.

Figure 4-1 shows the basic patterns of factory overhead costs as volume changes are encountered. Examples of variable, fixed, and semivariable factory overhead costs include the following:

Variable: Power costs directly associated with production, depreciation expense computed on the basis of hours equipment is used, supplies, spoilage, small tools expense.

FIGURE 4-1   Cost Behavior Patterns

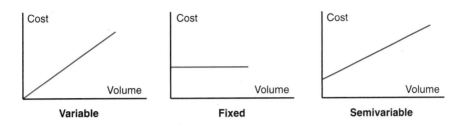

Fixed: Factory property taxes, depreciation of equipment computed on a straight-line basis, periodic rent payments,
production executives' salaries, insurance on factory
building and equipment.

Semivariable:

Type A: Changes as various levels of production are reached. This
type of cost, also known as a **step variable cost,** will
remain constant over a range of production, then abruptly
change. The increases are not continuous, and costs will
plateau before another cost change occurs. Examples are
inspection and handling costs, factory supervision and
other indirect labor costs, and some indirect materials.

Type B: Varies continuously, but not in direct proportion (ratio)
to volume changes. Examples include utilities costs and
maintenance of factory equipment. For example, the
electricity used to power the machines would vary in
direct proportion to the level of production, whereas
electricity used to light and heat the factory would not
vary with the number of units produced. A Type B semivariable cost is illustrated in Figure 4-1.

The composition of the different semivariable factory overhead costs
make the prediction of a specific amount of overhead cost for a given
level of production very challenging. Mathematical techniques can be
used to establish fixed and variable components that comprise semivariable costs and, to a degree, remove some of the uncertainty.

ANALYZING SEMIVARIABLE FACTORY OVERHEAD COSTS

LEARNING OBJECTIVE 2
Separate semivariable
costs into variable and
fixed components.

Many different techniques and theories exist regarding the prediction of
future events. Most mathematical techniques attempt to establish a pattern
from the historic evidence available, then use the pattern as a model for

predicting future outcomes. If history repeats itself, the model will satisfactorily simulate the future events, and the predictions will be beneficial to
the decision-making process.

The mathematical (statistical) techniques to be discussed use the relationships of historical costs to isolate variable and fixed elements that can
be used to determine future costs. The nonmathematical (observation)
method relies on personal experience and managerial judgment.

OBSERVATION METHOD

The **observation method** relies heavily on the ability of an observer to
detect a pattern of cost behavior by reviewing past cost and volume data.
The reaction of an expense to past changes in production is observed,
and a decision is made to treat the expense as either a variable item or a
fixed item, depending on which type of cost behavior it more closely
resembles. The analyzed overhead item will thereafter be treated as
either a variable or fixed cost, ignoring the fact that many costs are semivariable. Companies that use this method believe that the discrepancy
between the actual costs and the forecast costs will be insignificant and
will not affect management strategies or operations.

The observation method still is used by some companies. However,
due to an increasing emphasis on quantifying business data and the need
to separate semivariable costs into their fixed and variable components,
mathematical methods have increased in popularity. Two of these methods are discussed in the following sections: (1) the high-low method and
(2) the statistical scattergraph method. Both of these methods isolate an
element of a semivariable cost, then suggest that the remainder of the
cost is the other element.

HIGH-LOW METHOD

The **high-low method** compares a high production volume and its
related cost to a low production volume with its related cost. The difference in volume between the two points being compared is linear and will
fall along a straight line.

To illustrate, assume that the following overhead costs were incurred
at two different levels of production:

	1,000 Units	2,000 Units
Depreciation (fixed)	$2,000	$2,000
Inspection costs (semivariable)	3,000	5,000
Factory supplies (variable)	1,000	2,000

Depreciation is a fixed cost and remained unchanged in total as production doubled. Factory supplies is a variable cost and it doubled in
total when production volume doubled. Inspection costs, however, were

neither fixed nor did they change proportionately with volume. By using the high-low technique, part of the inspection cost will be determined to be variable and the remaining part fixed:

Variable cost:

	Units	Costs
High volume	2,000	$5,000
Low volume	1,000	3,000
Difference	1,000	$2,000

Variable cost per unit ($2,000 / 1,000 units) = $2

Fixed cost:

	1,000 Units	2,000 Units
Cost	$3,000	$5,000
Variable @ $2 per unit	2,000	4,000
Fixed cost (remainder)	$1,000	$1,000

Inspection costs at various levels of production can be estimated using the following formula:

Inspection costs = $1,000 + ($2 × number of units produced)

Assume that management wishes to estimate total factory overhead costs for one month at a production level of 4,000 units. Using the above data and the formula for the semivariable cost, projected factory overhead costs for the month would be $15,000, computed as follows:

Depreciation (fixed)	$ 2,000
Inspection costs [semivariable, $1,000 + $2 (4,000)]	9,000
Factory supplies (variable, $1 × 4,000)	4,000
Total estimated factory overhead at 4,000 units	$15,000

SCATTERGRAPH METHOD

The **scattergraph method** estimates a straight line along which the semivariable costs will fall. The cost being analyzed is plotted on the y-axis of the graph, and the activity level, such as direct labor hours or machine hours, is plotted on the x-axis. After the observations of cost and production data are plotted on graph paper, a line is drawn by visual inspection representing the trend shown by most of the data points. Usually an equal number of data points fall above and below the line. The point where the straight line intersects the y-axis represents the total fixed costs. The variable cost per unit is computed by subtracting fixed costs from total costs at any point on the graph and then dividing by the volume level for that point read from the x-axis.

The following data will be used to illustrate the determination of the fixed and variable components of inspection cost, using cost and production data for the past six months:

Month	Inspection Cost for Month	Units Produced
July	$4,500	1,600
August	3,000	1,000
September	4,600	1,800
October	5,000	2,000
November	4,050	1,500
December	3,350	1,200

Figure 4-2 shows the scattergraph of these data. A line is visually fit to these data by positioning a ruler so that it is on or near all the data

FIGURE 4-2   Scattergraph Method

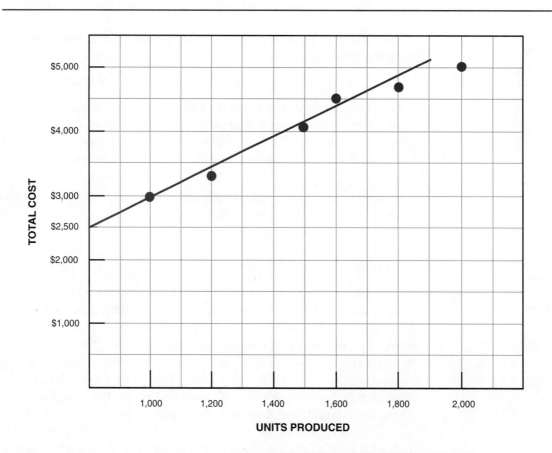

points, with an equal number of data points above and below the line. (The fact that more than one such line might be drawn is among the limitations explained below.) The cost line in Figure 4-2 intersects the y-axis at $2,500. This is the estimate of the fixed cost portion of the semivariable cost. Subtract the fixed cost from the total cost at any volume level to determine the total variable cost at that level. For example, the total variable cost at a volume level of 1,500 units is $4,050 – $2,500 = $1,550. The variable cost per unit would then be $1.03 ($1,550 / 1,500 units).

LIMITATIONS OF HIGH-LOW AND STATISTICAL SCATTERGRAPH METHODS

The high-low and statistical scattergraph methods both use historical cost patterns to predict future costs and are, therefore, subject to the limitations that apply to all forecasting techniques. The use of mathematical techniques does not ensure accurate forecasts. To a great extent, the accuracy of a forecast depends on the validity of the data used with the chosen method.

Cost analysis is more useful for decision making when all costs are segregated into two categories: variable and fixed. Therefore, the semivariable costs should be analyzed and subdivided into the two categories. The high-low method bases its solution on two observations and assumes that all other unanalyzed relationships will fall along a straight line between these selected observations. Such an assumption may prove to be highly unrealistic because the two observations used may not be representative of the group from which the data were selected. The method may be considered reliable, however, if additional pairs of data are analyzed and the results approximate those obtained from the first observations.

The scattergraph method is an improvement over the high-low method because it uses all of the available data. Also, visual inspection of the graph enables nonrepresentative data points, called outliers, to be identified. The major disadvantage of the scattergraph method is that the cost line is drawn through the data points based on visual inspection rather than mathematical techniques. More sophisticated techniques of determining mathematically a line of best fit through a set of plotted points are beyond the scope of this text.

Both methods stress the importance of the relationship of cost factors to volume; however, many other factors may affect cost behavior and should not be ignored. For example, consideration should also be given to price changes and changes in technology. Generalizations about cost patterns should be avoided because only a few costs have inherent characteristics. Management policies directly influence most costs.

> **You should now be able to work the following: Questions 1–7, Exercises 4-1 to 4-3, and Problems 4-1 to 4-3.**

BUDGETING FACTORY OVERHEAD COSTS

LEARNING OBJECTIVE 3
Prepare a budget for factory overhead costs.

Budgets are management's operating plans expressed in quantitative terms, such as units of production and related costs. After factory overhead costs have been classified as either fixed or variable, budgets can be prepared for expected levels of production. The segregation of fixed and variable cost components permits the company to prepare a **flexible budget**. A flexible budget is a budget that shows estimated costs at different production volumes.

Assume that management desires to budget factory overhead costs at three levels of production—10,000, 20,000, and 40,000 units. The variable factory overhead cost is $5 per unit, and fixed overhead costs total $50,000. The budgeted costs at these volumes are as follows:

	10,000 units	20,000 units	40,000 units
Variable cost @ $5 per unit	$ 50,000	$100,000	$200,000
Fixed cost	50,000	50,000	50,000
Total factory overhead	$100,000	$150,000	$250,000
Factory overhead per unit	$10.00	$7.50	$6.25

As the volume increases, the factory overhead cost per unit decreases because the total fixed cost, $50,000, is spread over a larger number of units. For example, the fixed cost per unit will add $5 to the per-unit cost ($50,000 / 10,000 units) at the 10,000-unit level but only $1.25 ($50,000 / 40,000 units) when 40,000 units are produced. The variable cost remains constant at $5 per unit for the entire range of production.

Budgeting is a valuable management tool for planning and controlling costs. A flexible budget aids management in establishing realistic production goals and in comparing actual costs with budgeted costs.

ACCOUNTING FOR ACTUAL FACTORY OVERHEAD

LEARNING OBJECTIVE 4
Account for actual factory overhead costs.

Cost accounting systems are designed to accumulate, classify, and summarize the factory overhead costs actually incurred. The specific procedures used to account for actual factory overhead costs depend on the nature and organization of the manufacturing firm.

In a small manufacturing company having only one production department, factory overhead may be accounted for in much the same manner as selling and administrative expenses. All the factory overhead accounts may be kept in the general ledger. However, separate accounts should be kept for indirect materials, indirect labor, and for each of the other indirect manufacturing expenses.

Indirect materials and indirect labor costs are recorded first in the general journal. These entries are made from the summary of materials issued and returned and from the labor cost summary. Other factory overhead expenses also are recorded in the general journal, from which they are posted to the appropriate accounts in the general ledger. The invoices that have been received are the sources for these entries. Schedules of fixed costs should be prepared and used as the source for general journal adjusting entries to record the amount of taxes, depreciation, insurance, and other similar expenses for the period.

A substantial modification must be made in the accounting system when the number of factory overhead accounts becomes sizeable. A factory overhead subsidiary ledger should be created and maintained, along with a control account in the general ledger. The subsidiary ledger is known as the **factory overhead ledger**, and the control account is entitled "Factory Overhead" or "Manufacturing Overhead." At the end of each accounting period, the balance of the factory overhead control account is proved by comparing its balance to the total of the account balances in the subsidiary factory overhead ledger.

Accounts in the factory overhead ledger should have titles clearly descriptive of the nature of the expenditure. Examples of typical factory overhead accounts include the following:

Defective Work	Overtime Premium
Depreciation	Plant Security
Employee Fringe Benefits	Power
Fuel	Property Tax
Heat and Light	Rent
Indirect Labor	Repairs
Indirect Materials	Small Tools
Insurance	Spoilage
Janitorial Service	Supplies
Lubricants	Telephone/Fax
Maintenance	Water
Materials Handling	Workers' Compensation Insurance

In manufacturing companies with several departments, the accounting system is designed to accumulate costs by department. Separate budgets are generally prepared for each department and then combined into a master budget for the company. The actual costs incurred can thus be readily compared with budgeted costs for each department.

Factory overhead expenses must be carefully analyzed before the expenses are assigned to departments. For example, total factory depreciation is analyzed to determine the distribution of depreciation charges among the departments. The accounting system should be designed to provide the necessary data promptly and accurately.

FACTORY OVERHEAD ANALYSIS SHEETS

Instead of expanding the factory overhead ledger to include a separate account for each department's share of different expenses, **factory overhead analysis sheets** may be used to keep a subsidiary record of factory overhead expenses. A separate analysis sheet may be used to record each type of expense, with individual columns for the departmental classification of the expense. Alternatively, a separate analysis sheet can be used for each department, with individual columns for the expense classification.

Figure 4-3 shows an example of an analysis sheet used to keep individual records for each kind of factory overhead expense. The **expense-type analysis sheet** provides a separate amount column for each department, making it possible to distribute charges among departments as expenses are recorded. Each column represents a department; therefore, each analysis sheet replaces as many separate accounts as there are departments in the factory. In Figure 4-3, which illustrates the distribution of one month's depreciation to departments, the depreciation cost assignable to the various departments was determined by multiplying the plant and equipment valuation in each department (A: $36,000; B: $24,000; C: $18,000; D: $60,000) by the annual rate of depreciation (10%) applicable to the property. The estimated monthly depreciation

FIGURE 4-3   Factory Overhead Analysis Sheet—Expense Type

Account No. 3111				Distribution Base: *Valuation of Plant and Equipment*					
Account *Depreciation*									
DEPARTMENTAL ANALYSIS				Date	Description	Post. Ref.	Debit	Credit	Balance
Dept. A	Dept. B	Dept. C	Dept. D						
3 0 0 00	2 0 0 00	1 5 0 00	5 0 0 00	Jan. 31	Depreciation for January	GJ	1 1 5 0 00		1 1 5 0 00

(1/12 of the annual depreciation) was recorded in the general journal and became the source of posting to the analysis sheet.

The **department-type analysis sheet** in Figure 4-4 provides a separate amount column for each kind of expense. This makes it possible to distribute expenses on a departmental basis as they are recorded. Each column represents a different expense. Therefore, each analysis sheet replaces as many separate accounts as there are types of expenses in the factory. Figure 4-4 shows all expenses incurred for Department A during January. Only the totals are entered. Expenses are posted from the books of original entry either in total or as of the date incurred. The fixed expenses are posted from the general journal at the end of the month.

Factory overhead analysis sheets, both expense and department types, serve as subsidiary ledgers and are controlled by the factory overhead account in the general ledger. The advantage of using an analysis sheet for each expense, classified by departments, is that it provides only as many amount columns as there are departments within the factory (see Figure 4-3). However, a summary should be prepared at the end of an accounting period to determine the total expenses incurred for each department.

FIGURE 4-4   Factory Overhead Analysis Sheet—Department Type

FACTORY OVERHEAD—DEPARTMENT A

Indirect Materials No. 311.1	Indirect Labor No. 311.12	Power No. 311.13	Depreciation No. 311.18	Factory Property Tax No. 311.20	Insurance No. 311.30	General Factory Expenses No. 311.50
3 0 0 00	2 0 0 00	1 5 0 00	3 0 0 00	2 8 0 00	3 5 0 00	1 5 0 00

FACTORY OVERHEAD—DEPARTMENT A

Misc. Factory Expenses Account No.	Amount	Date	Description	Post. Ref.	Debit	Credit	Balance
		Jan. 31	Total expenses-January		1 7 3 0 00		1 7 3 0 00

The advantage of using an analysis sheet for each department, classified by expense, is that fewer sheets are required and the preparation of a summary is not required at the end of an accounting period (see Figure 4-4). When a factory is departmentalized, the factory overhead must be recorded departmentally to determine the total cost of operating each department. Spreadsheet software facilitates the distribution of departmental factory overhead.

SCHEDULE OF FIXED COSTS

Fixed costs are assumed not to vary in amount from month to month. Some fixed costs, such as insurance and property taxes, are either prepaid or accrued expenses. Because these costs are considered very predictable, schedules for the periodic amount of fixed costs to be allocated to the various departments can be prepared in advance. A **schedule of fixed costs** similar to Figure 4-5 can be prepared for several periods. By referring to the schedule at the end of the period, a journal entry can be prepared to record the total fixed costs. The schedule can also be used as the source from which fixed costs can be posted to the departmental factory overhead analysis sheets.

In Figure 4-5, the schedule of fixed costs shows that for the month of January, the total depreciation expense for machinery, $1,150, is allocated to the departments as follows: A, $300; B, $200; C, $150; D, $500. Figure 4-5 also shows the monthly departmental fixed costs for property tax and insurance, which were distributed on the basis of the square footage of space occupied by each department. At the end of the month, the accountant would post the amounts from the schedule of fixed costs to each department's analysis sheet.

GENERAL FACTORY OVERHEAD EXPENSES

All factory overhead expenses are recorded in a regular, systematic manner so that at the end of an accounting period, all expenses chargeable to the period have already been distributed to the factory departments. The allocation of overhead to departments would have been made in proportion to the measurable benefits received from such expenses. However, for some items of factory overhead, it is difficult to measure the benefits departmentally. Instead, the factory as a whole is the beneficiary. An example is the salary of the plant manager, who has the responsibility to oversee all factory operations. Another example would be the wages of the company security guards.

General factory overhead expenses not identified with a specific department are charged to departments by a process of allocation. This

FIGURE 4-5   Schedule of Fixed Costs

Schedule of Fixed Costs

Item of Cost	January	February	March	April	May	June
Depreciation:						
Dept. A	$ 300.00	$ 300.00	$ 300.00	$ 300.00	$ 300.00	$ 300.00
Dept. B	200.00	200.00	200.00	200.00	200.00	200.00
Dept. C	150.00	150.00	150.00	150.00	150.00	150.00
Dept. D	500.00	500.00	500.00	500.00	500.00	500.00
Total	$1,150.00	$1,150.00	$1,150.00	$1,150.00	$1,150.00	$1,150.00
Property tax:						
Dept. A	$ 280.00	$ 280.00	$ 280.00	$ 280.00	$ 280.00	$ 280.00
Dept. B	270.00	270.00	270.00	270.00	270.00	270.00
Dept. C	250.00	250.00	250.00	250.00	250.00	250.00
Dept. D	200.00	200.00	200.00	200.00	200.00	200.00
Total	$1,000.00	$1,000.00	$1,000.00	$1,000.00	$1,000.00	$1,000.00
Insurance:						
Dept. A	$ 350.00	$ 350.00	$ 350.00	$ 350.00	$ 350.00	$ 350.00
Dept. B	325.00	325.00	325.00	325.00	325.00	325.00
Dept. C	300.00	300.00	300.00	300.00	300.00	300.00
Dept. D	425.00	425.00	425.00	425.00	425.00	425.00
Total	$1,400.00	$1,400.00	$1,400.00	$1,400.00	$1,400.00	$1,400.00
Grand Total	$3,550.00	$3,550.00	$3,550.00	$3,550.00	$3,550.00	$3,550.00

allocation is usually made on a logical basis, such as allocating heating costs to departments based on the factory space devoted to each department or the plant manager's salary based on the estimated amount of time devoted to each department. The allocation may be made for each item of expense as incurred and recorded, or expenses may be accumulated as incurred and the allocation of the total expenses made at the end of the accounting period. If the allocation is made at the end of the period, each kind of general factory overhead expense incurred during the period is recorded on a separate analysis sheet. At the end of the period, the total is allocated and recorded on the departmental analysis sheets. The desirability of recording the overhead on a separate sheet depends on the frequency with which such expenses are incurred during the period.

SUMMARY OF FACTORY OVERHEAD

All factory overhead expenses incurred during the accounting period, both variable and fixed, are recorded on factory overhead analysis sheets and in the factory overhead control account in the general ledger. After the posting is completed at the end of an accounting period, the balance of the control account is proved by preparing a **summary of factory overhead** (Figure 4-6) from the analysis sheets. This summary shows the items of expense by department and in total.

DISTRIBUTING SERVICE DEPARTMENT EXPENSES

LEARNING OBJECTIVE 5
Distribute service department factory overhead costs to production departments.

All job order and process cost systems are designed to accumulate the total cost of each job or unit of product. To include factory overhead as part of the total cost, the amount of factory overhead incurred by each production department must be determined.

In a factory, the manufacturing process consists of a series of operations performed in departments or cost centers. Departments are divided into two classes: service departments and production departments. A **service department** is an essential part of the organization, but it does not work directly on the product. The function of a service department is to serve the needs of the production departments and other service

FIGURE 4-6   Summary of Factory Overhead

Summary of Factory Overhead
For the Month Ended January 31, 20—

Expenses	Dept. A	Dept. B	Dept. C	Dept. D	Total
Indirect materials	$ 100	$ 50	$ 40	$ 30	$ 220
Indirect labor	200	150	140	160	650
Power	150	140	120	100	510
Depreciation	300	200	150	500	1,150
Factory property tax	280	270	250	200	1,000
Insurance	350	325	300	425	1,400
General factory expenses	150	350	200	300	1,000
Total	$1,530	$1,485	$1,200	$1,715	$5,930

departments. The product indirectly receives the benefit of the work performed by the service department. Examples of service departments include a department that generates power for the factory, a building maintenance department that is responsible for maintaining the buildings, or the cost accounting department that maintains the factory accounting records.

A **production department** performs the actual manufacturing operations that physically change the units being processed. Because the production departments receive the benefit of the work performed by the service departments, the total cost of production must include not only the costs charged directly to the production departments but also a portion of the costs of operating the service departments. Therefore, the total product costs should include a share of service department costs.

The distribution of the service department costs to production departments involves an analysis of the service department's relationship to the other departments before an apportionment process can be developed. The cost of operating each service department should be distributed in proportion to the benefits received by the various departments. The apportionment of service department costs is complicated because some service departments render service to other service departments as well as to the production departments. For a distribution to be equitable, the cost of operating a service department should be divided among all departments that it serves, service and production alike.

The first requirement of the distribution process is to determine how a particular service department divides its services among the other departments. In some cases, the services performed for another department may be determined precisely. More often, however, the distribution must be based on approximations. For example, the power department may be furnishing power for the operation of the machines and for lighting the building and the surrounding grounds of the plant. If the power used in each department is metered, the meters can be read at the end of the period and the departments charged for the exact amount of power used. This type of charge to a department would be termed a **direct charge**.

On the other hand, a department such as building maintenance, which keeps the building clean and in repair, cannot measure exactly the benefits it provides to the other departments that it serves. The cost of operating the building maintenance department is therefore distributed to the other departments on some equitable basis, such as square footage of floor space occupied.

Common bases for distributing service department costs include the following:

Service Departments	Basis for Distribution
Building Maintenance	Floor space occupied by other departments
Inspection and Packing	Production volume
Machine Shop	Value of machinery and equipment
Personnel	Number of workers in departments served
Purchasing	Number of purchase orders
Shipping	Quantity and weight of items shipped
Stores	Units of materials requisitioned
Tool Room	Total direct labor hours in departments served

After the bases for distribution have been selected for the service departments, the next step is to distribute the total cost of each service department to the other departments. To illustrate the distribution process, assume the following conditions:

1. The maintenance department services the power plant building.

2. The power department furnishes power to the maintenance department for maintenance equipment.

3. The power department and the maintenance department service the personnel department facilities.

4. The personnel department services the power and maintenance departments through their functions of hiring personnel and maintaining the departments' personnel records.

The first step is to compute the total cost of any one of these overlapping departments. Three different methods are available for use:

1. The **direct distribution method**, which distributes service department costs directly to production departments.

2. The **sequential distribution** or **step-down method**, which distributes service department costs regressively to other service departments and then to production departments. The sequence of allocating service department costs usually is established on one of two bases:

    a. The number of other departments served.

    b. The magnitude of total costs in each service department.

3. The **algebraic distribution method** takes into consideration that some service departments not only may provide service to, but may also receive service from, other service departments. A further explanation of this method is beyond the scope of this text.

The **direct distribution method** makes no attempt to determine the extent to which one service department renders its services to another service department. Instead, the service department's costs are allocated directly and only to the production departments. This method has the advantage of simplicity, but it may produce less accurate results than the other methods. Use of the direct method is justified if the costs allocated to the production departments do not differ materially from the costs that would be allocated using another, more precise method.

The **sequential distribution method** recognizes the interrelationship of the service departments. The power department costs are divided among the personnel, maintenance, and production departments. After the power department cost distribution, the personnel department's total costs—which now include a portion of the power department costs—will be allocated to the maintenance and the production departments. Finally, the maintenance department's costs will be distributed to the production departments.

The distribution sequence for allocating service department costs is a high priority decision when the sequential distribution method is used. The sequential procedure should first distribute the costs of the service department that services the greatest number of other departments. It should continue until all service department costs have been distributed to the production departments. The sequential distribution method can be long and laborious, but it has the advantage of being more accurate if the sequence established is based on a sound analysis of services rendered to the various departments. If a substantial degree of uncertainty exists as to which department's cost should be distributed first to other departments, and the uncertainty cannot be resolved, the department with the largest total overhead should be distributed first. This order of distribution is based on the assumption that the departments render services in direct proportion to the amount of expense they incur.

Figure 4-7 (direct distribution to production departments only) and Figure 4-8 (sequential distribution to service departments and production departments based on magnitude of total costs in service departments) show the direct and sequential methods of distributing service department costs to production departments. Note that the amount of costs in each service department is used as the criterion for determining the order of distribution because each service department services the same number of other departments. The organization and operational structure of a company is the determinant of which distribution method should be selected and used. If the variation from one method to another is insignificant, the direct distribution method would be suitable because it saves time and effort.

The completed distribution work sheets are the basis for a series of general journal entries. The entries on page 164 are based on the data shown in Figure 4-8.

FIGURE 4-7   Method 1—Direct Distribution of Service Department Costs to Production Departments

	Power	Personnel	Main-tenance	Dept. A	Dept. B	Dept. C	Dept. D	Total
Total from factory overhead analysis sheets	30,000 00	10,000 00	20,000 00	50,000 00	40,000 00	60,000 00	90,000 00	300,000 00
Power distribution— (kw. hours)				3,600 00	5,400 00	6,000 00	15,000 00	
A— 12,000 @ $0.30*								
B— 18,000 @ 0.30								
C— 20,000 @ 0.30								
D— 50,000 @ 0.30								
100,000								
Personnel distribution (number of employees served)				3,000 00	1,000 00	2,000 00	4,000 00	
A— 30 @ $100**								
B— 10 @ $100								
C— 20 @ $100								
D— 40 @ $100								
100								
Maintenance distribution— (square feet)				5,000 00	6,000 00	4,000 00	5,000 00	
A— 5,000 @ $1.00**								
B— 6,000 @ 1.00								
C— 4,000 @ 1.00								
D— 5,000 @ 1.00								
20,000				61,600 00	52,400 00	72,000 00	114,000 00	300,000 00

*$30,000 ÷ 100,000 (kilowatt hours) = $0.30 per kilowatt hour
**$10,000 ÷ 100 (number of employees served) = $100 per employee
***$20,000 ÷ 20,000 (square feet) = $1.00 per square foot

FIGURE 4-8   Method 2—Sequential Distribution of Service Department Costs Based on Magnitude of Total Costs in Service Departments

	Power	Maintenance	Personnel	Dept. A	Dept. B	Dept. C	Dept. D	Total
Total from factory overhead analysis sheets	30,000 00	20,000 00	10,000 00	50,000 00	40,000 00	60,000 00	90,000 00	300,000 00
Power distribution—(kw. hours)								
Maintenance—10,000 @ $0.25*		2,500 00						
Personnel— 10,000 @ 0.25*			2,500 00					
A— 12,000 @ 0.25				3,000 00				
B— 18,000 @ 0.25					4,500 00			
C— 20,000 @ 0.25						5,000 00		
D— 50,000 @ 0.25							12,500 00	
120,000								
		22,500 00						
Maintenance distribution—(square feet)								
Personnel— 5,000 @ $0.90**			4,500 00					
A— 5,000 @ 0.90**				4,500 00				
B— 6,000 @ 0.90					5,400 00			
C— 4,000 @ 0.90						3,600 00		
D— 5,000 @ 0.90							4,500 00	
25,000								
			17,000 00					
Personnel distribution (number of employees served)								
A— 30 @ $170**				5,100 00				
B— 10 @ $170					1,700 00			
C— 20 @ $170						3,400 00		
D— 40 @ $170							6,800 00	
100								
				62,600 00	51,600 00	72,000 00	113,800 00	300,000 00

*$30,000 ÷ 120,000 (kilowatt hours) = $.025 per kilowatt hour
**$22,500 ÷ 25,000 (square feet) = $0.90 per square foot
***$17,000 ÷ 100 (number of employees served) = $170 per employee

Factory Overhead—Power Department   30,000
Factory Overhead—Maintenance Department   20,000
Factory Overhead—Personnel Department   10,000
Factory Overhead—Department A   50,000
Factory Overhead—Department B   40,000
Factory Overhead—Department C   60,000
Factory Overhead—Department D   90,000
  Factory Overhead   300,000
      Closed factory overhead expenses to service and production departments.

The allocation of service department costs would be journalized as follows:

Factory Overhead—Maintenance Department   2,500
Factory Overhead—Personnel Department   2,500
Factory Overhead—Department A   3,000
Factory Overhead—Department B   4,500
Factory Overhead—Department C   5,000
Factory Overhead—Department D   12,500
  Factory Overhead—Power Department   30,000
      Closed factory overhead expenses of power department to service and
      production departments.

Factory Overhead—Personnel Department   4,500
Factory Overhead—Department A   4,500
Factory Overhead—Department B   5,400
Factory Overhead—Department C   3,600
Factory Overhead—Department D   4,500
  Factory Overhead—Maintenance Department . . .   22,500
      Closed factory overhead expenses of maintenance department to ser-
      vice and production departments.

Factory Overhead—Department A   5,100
Factory Overhead—Department B   1,700
Factory Overhead—Department C   3,400
Factory Overhead—Department D   6,800
  Factory Overhead—Personnel Department   17,000
      Closed factory overhead expenses of personnel department to produc-
      tion departments.

An accounting system can be designed to reduce the number of factory overhead accounts to be maintained for the service departments. In such a system, after the distribution work sheet in Figure 4-8 has been completed, a journal entry can be made to close the factory overhead control account. The charges are made directly to the production departments as follows:

Factory Overhead—Department A	. . . .	62,600
Factory Overhead—Department B	. . . .	51,600
Factory Overhead—Department C	. . . .	72,000
Factory Overhead—Department D	. . . .	113,800
Factory Overhead	. . . .	300,000

> Closed factory overhead to production departments. (The departmental totals include the apportioned costs of the service departments.)

After posting the journal entries to the general ledger, the total balances of the departmental factory overhead accounts will equal the balance of the factory overhead control account before it was closed. The journal entries have not affected the total of the factory overhead expenses. However, the general ledger now shows the amount of factory overhead expense being allocated to each of the production departments.

You should now be able to work the following: Questions 8-11, Exercises 4-4 to 4-6, and Problem 4-4.

APPLYING FACTORY OVERHEAD TO PRODUCTION

LEARNING OBJECTIVE 6
Apply factory overhead using predetermined rates.

In previous discussions, companies avoided estimating and applying factory overhead to production by charging the actual or incurred factory overhead costs to the work in process account. Companies used these procedures to emphasize the flow of costs and the basic techniques used in cost accounting without unduly complicating the fundamentals. However, factory overhead includes many different costs, some of which will not be known until the end of the accounting period. Because it is desirable to know the total cost of a job or process soon after completion, some method must be established for estimating the amount of factory overhead that should be applied to the finished product. Through the estimating procedure, a job or process will be charged an estimated amount of factory overhead expense. At the end of a period, the actual or incurred factory overhead costs can be compared to the estimated factory overhead applied. If the company encounters a difference, it can make an analysis and subsequent distribution to the appropriate accounts.

The advantages of estimating and charging factory overhead include billing customers on a more timely basis and preparing bids for new contracts more accurately. If it were not possible to bill a customer for a completed job until a month or more later because all factory overhead costs were not known, the extension of time in collecting such accounts would prove very costly to the company. Many companies rely heavily on a bidding process to obtain new jobs. If a company cannot include a fairly accurate factory overhead charge in the cost of a bid, the financial health of the enterprise can be detrimentally affected. If a company has underbid an awarded contract because of understating the actual factory overhead expenses, it could lose income as a result. On the other hand, overstating factory overhead on bids may lead to a lack of new work. Therefore, approximating the overhead charges assigned to bids and to completed jobs is important to a company's financial well-being and continued growth.

The flexible budget, which includes the expected departmental factory overhead costs at given levels of production, is used to establish **predetermined factory overhead rates**. The rates are computed by dividing the budgeted factory overhead cost by the budgeted production. The budgeted production may be expressed in terms of machine hours, direct labor hours, direct labor cost, units, and so on. The accuracy of the rate depends on the cost projections and production estimates forecast in the flexible budget. In budget projections, the fixed and variable cost components, historical cost behavior patterns, and possible future economic and operational differences must be considered carefully. Specifically, these factors include the anticipated volume of production, the variability of expenses, the fixed costs relevant to the production levels, the activity of the industry as forecast, and the possible price changes that may occur. Because of the many unknowns, absolute accuracy cannot be expected. Nevertheless, management should give a high priority to attaining the most accurate rate possible.

In a departmentalized company, factory overhead should be budgeted for each department. The procedures for distributing the budgeted departmental expenses are identical to those used to allocate the actual factory overhead expenses. The departmental overhead budgets should also include an allotment of budgeted fixed expenses, such as depreciation and a portion of the budgeted service department expenses.

Upon completing the factory overhead expense budget, the company must choose a method to use when applying the estimated expenses to the departments. The usual application methods require that data from the period's production budgets be obtained. The production budgets will provide information as to the estimated quantity of product, direct labor cost, direct labor hours, and machine hours.

From the production estimates for the plant or for each department, the company can select a method that will charge the product with a fair share of the factory overhead that is expected to be incurred. The departmental composition of human labor versus machines will influence the method of applying factory overhead to the product. A department with little automation will usually apply overhead using either the direct labor cost or direct labor hour method, whereas a highly automated production department will normally use the machine hour method.

DIRECT LABOR COST METHOD

The **direct labor cost method** uses the amount of direct labor cost that has been charged to the product as the basis for applying factory overhead. The overhead rate to be used is predetermined by dividing the estimated (budgeted) factory overhead cost by the estimated (budgeted) direct labor cost. The relationship of the overhead to the direct labor cost is expressed as a percentage of direct labor cost (the base).

For example, assume that the budgeted factory overhead cost for Department A amounts to $100,000, and the estimated direct labor cost is expected to be $200,000. The predetermined rate would be 50% of direct labor dollars ($100,000 / $200,000). Also, assume that during the first month of operations, Job 100 incurred $1,000 for direct materials and $3,000 for direct labor. The job is completed. Using the predetermined rate to estimate factory overhead, the total cost is computed as follows:

Job 100

Direct materials	$1,000
Direct labor	3,000
Factory overhead (50% of direct labor $)	1,500
Total cost of completed job	$5,500

The direct labor cost method is appropriate in departments that require mostly human labor and in which the direct labor cost charges are relatively stable from one product to another. If a labor force generates direct labor cost that varies widely due to the hourly rate range of the employees or absenteeism, another method should be used. For example, a low-paid hourly employee could be replaced, due to absenteeism, with a higher-paid hourly employee. The higher-paid employee would increase the direct labor cost and thereby increase the amount of factory overhead charged to the department. Such increases in factory overhead charges to a department are usually unwarranted because the higher-paid employee does not normally increase the actual factory overhead expense incurred by the department. Any fluctuation in the departmental direct labor cost not accompanied by a proportional increase in actual factory overhead expenses will cause a distortion in the product's total cost. This can be detrimental to the company's ability to control costs and to make good production and marketing decisions.

DIRECT LABOR HOUR METHOD

The **direct labor hour method** overcomes the problem of varying wage rates by applying factory overhead using the number of direct labor hours worked on a job or process. The predetermined rate is computed by dividing the budgeted factory overhead cost by the estimated direct labor hours to be worked. For example, assume that the budgeted factory overhead cost was $100,000, and it is expected that production will require 25,000 direct labor hours. The predetermined rate would be $4 per direct labor hour ($100,000 / 25,000 hours).

If factory overhead is applied to Job 100 using the direct labor hour method, the records must include the number of direct labor hours worked on each job. Assuming that it took 500 direct labor hours to complete Job 100, and the direct materials and direct labor costs were $1,000 and $3,000, respectively, the cost of Job 100 is as follows:

Job 100

Direct materials	$1,000
Direct labor (500 hours)	3,000
Factory overhead (500 hours @ $4)	2,000
Total cost of completed job	$6,000

An advantage of the direct labor hour method is that the amount of factory overhead applied is not affected by the mix of labor rates in the total direct labor cost. A disadvantage in using this method could be that the application base (the number of direct labor hours) could be substantially smaller than when direct labor cost is used. This application base would thereby be more affected by slight deviations in direct labor hours. Also, if factory overhead primarily consists of items that are more closely tied to labor dollars, such as employee fringe benefits, then the direct labor hour method may not be as accurate.

MACHINE HOUR METHOD

A highly automated department is normally best served by the **machine hour method**. In such a department, the factory overhead cost should be more proportionate to the machine hours generated by the equipment than the direct labor hours or costs incurred by the employees operating the machinery. It is common in automated departments for one employee to operate more than one piece of equipment. Therefore, one direct labor hour may generate, possibly, five machine hours.

The machine hour method requires substantial preliminary study before installation and an additional quantity of records to be maintained. However, the advantages to be gained by a more dependable factory overhead application rate may more than outweigh the additional effort and costs involved. The machine hour rate is determined by dividing the budgeted factory overhead cost by the estimated machine hours to be used by production.

For example, assume that the factory overhead budget is $100,000, and it is expected that 10,000 machine hours will be required. The predetermined rate would be $10 per machine hour ($100,000 / 10,000 hours). Assuming that Job 100, now completed, used $1,000 for direct materials, $3,000 for direct labor, and required 300 machine hours, its cost is as follows:

Job 100

Direct materials	$1,000
Direct labor	3,000
Factory overhead (300 machine hours @ $10)	3,000
Total cost of completed job	$7,000

ACTIVITY-BASED COSTING METHOD

The preceding methods of applying overhead to products assumed that all overhead costs incurred were related to volume. For example, the amount of overhead costs incurred were solely a function of how many direct labor hours or machine hours were worked. In a modern factory that produces many products, a substantial portion of the overhead may be more a function of the complexity of the product being made rather than the number of units produced. **Activity-based costing (ABC)** considers non-volume-related activities that create overhead costs, such as the number of machine setups or product design changes required of a particular product line.

A product that is difficult to make may also be produced in small numbers, perhaps due to its unusual nature and the resulting lack of demand. If overhead were applied to products strictly on the basis of direct labor hours or machine hours, very little overhead would be charged to such a product due to its low production volume. Its complexity to produce, however, may have created a lot of additional overhead costs in the form of machine setups and design changes, even though the number of units in the production run was small.

To successfully employ an ABC system, a company must first identify activities in the factory that create costs. Examples of those would include design changes, inspections, materials movements, material requisitions, and machine setups. The cost of performing each of these activities in the coming period then must be determined. The next step is to decide upon the **cost driver**, or basis used to allocate each of the activity cost pools. For example, for machine setup costs the cost driver may be total estimated setup time for the coming period or the estimated number of setups to be performed. Lastly, the estimated cost of each activity pool is divided by the estimated number of cost driver units related to that pool to compute an overhead or activity rate that is used to charge each product or job based on its consumption of the resources required to sustain each activity.

For example, assume that the factory overhead budget is $100,000. The allocation bases, expected levels of activity for each cost pool, and overhead rates follow:

Cost Pool	Expected Amount	Expected Level of Allocation Base	Overhead Rate
Direct labor usage	$ 30,000	10,000 labor hours	$3/direct labor hour
Machine usage	40,000	5,000 machine hours	$8/machine hour
Machine setups	20,000	100 setups	$200/setup
Design changes	10,000	25 design changes	$400/design change
	$100,000		

Assume that Job 100, now completed, required $1,000 for direct materials, $3,000 for direct labor, 500 direct labor hours, 75 machine hours, two setups, and one design change. The cost of the job would be computed as follows:

Job 100

Direct materials	$ 1,000
Direct labor (500 hours)	3,000
Factory overhead related to:	
Direct labor usage (500 hours × $3/direct labor hour)	1,500
Machine usage (75 hours × $8/machine hour)	600
Machine setups (2 setups × $200/setup)	400
Design changes (1 change × $800/design change)	800
Total cost of complete job	$ 7,300

Note that the overhead charged to this job using activity-based costing and, thus, the total cost of the job are greater than they were under any of the other methods of charging overhead. Activity-based costing better reflects the additional costs of producing a job that requires a design change and more than one setup.

You should now be able to work the following: Questions 12–18, Exercises 4–7 and 4-8, and Problems 4–5 to 4-7.

REAL-WORLD EXAMPLE

ABC: A PILOT APPROACH

Included below are excerpts from an article in *Management Accounting*, in which the author explains the implementation of ABC at Lord Corporation, a worldwide diversified, technology-based company.

"First we had to learn our ABC's, so our team split up and attended ABC seminars held across the country. Here's what we brought back: It is vital to learn the good, the bad, and the ugly of what others have done before you attempt your own implementation . . . For example, you must get senior management support. Also, start small—choose an area that will be easy to study. Decide up front your purpose for using ABC—it's impossible to assign the best cost drivers without knowing your goals. And, this is worth repeating: You must have cross-functional involvement to make the project work. If the effort comes only from accounting, implementation will be seen as an accounting project. . . .

"The employee interviews were preceded by a group meeting in which members of the ABC team explained to employees the basics of activity-based costing. We also helped employees think about their primary activities and how much time they spent performing each one, and we asked them to fill out a form with this information prior to their interviews. We wanted no more than four main activities for each person and a brief(!) description for each activity. We stressed we did not want a five-page summary of every job a person had ever performed. We also emphasized and reemphasized that people need not be fearful for or protective of their jobs. On the form we also asked employees to describe the causes for each of their job activities. . . .

"The pilot study showed us that part cost was a poor driver of material overhead. It also revealed the single largest driver of material overhead cost was inspection. (We found, for example, that simply moving materials from inspection to stock represented a significant portion of a component's overhead cost.) That's where we drove home the need for ABC. Vital to the pilot's success was the implementation, so in frequent presentations to senior management and the corporation's officers we stressed the need to beef up our certified supplier program to reduce inspection activities. With a certified supplier, incoming parts bypass inspection and go straight to production. We also rely heavily on a 'skip-lot' program. A computer model determines whether a part should be inspected or not, based on a vendor's history of shipping quality parts. . . .

"The ABC approach to costing sent shock waves through the marketing group. It couldn't understand why low-volume, low-cost parts that once took a flat percentage of their cost as material overhead suddenly jumped 500% to 700%. It only made sense that a $0.10 part should take a penny's worth of overhead, as our standard cost system used to show. What ABC revealed was that even those inexpensive parts were being purchased, received, inspected, and stocked in a manner that created significant costs. Particularly hard hit were low-cost and low-volume parts. . . .

"Savings that we can attribute directly to ABC are more noticeable in the form of better-priced products than in reductions in manufacturing cost. That was due to our goals for the pilot and our choices for cost drivers. We use the results to justify pricing and to discuss with customers our focus on identifying and eliminating costs. Consequently, we have been able to improve the bottom line by improving the match between selling price and cost. . . ."

Alan W. Rupp, "ABC: A Pilot Project," *Management Accounting,* January 1995, pp. 50–55.

ACCOUNTING FOR ACTUAL AND APPLIED FACTORY OVERHEAD

LEARNING OBJECTIVE 7
Account for actual
and applied factory
overhead.

After selecting the application method and computing the predetermined rate to be used, all jobs or processes should be charged with the estimated overhead cost rather than the actual factory overhead costs being incurred. The estimated factory overhead is applied to production by a debit to Work in Process and a credit to an account entitled **Applied Factory Overhead**. Use of the separate applied factory overhead account rather than the credit side of the factory overhead control account avoids confusing the actual factory overhead charges, which are debited to the factory overhead control account, with the estimated charges that are debited to production. At the end of a period, the debit balance in Factory Overhead is compared to the credit balance in Applied Factory Overhead to determine the accuracy of the predetermined rates.

Factory Overhead		Applied Factory Overhead	
Debited for actual overhead incurred		Debited when closed to factory overhead	Credited for overhead applied to jobs

To illustrate the use of a predetermined rate, assume that a company has estimated a rate of $5 per direct labor hour, and a production job required 1,000 direct labor hours to complete. Using the direct labor hour method, $5,000 of estimated factory overhead cost would be applied to the job as follows:

Work in Process	5,000	
Applied Factory Overhead		5,000
Applied factory overhead to job (1,000 hours @ $5).		

At the end of the period, the applied factory overhead account is closed to the factory overhead control account:

Applied Factory Overhead	5,000	
Factory Overhead		5,000

Closed applied factory overhead account to control account.

After the above entries are posted, if a balance (debit or credit) remains in the factory overhead control account, it indicates that the actual factory overhead incurred did not equal the estimated factory overhead applied. A remaining debit balance in Factory Overhead indicates that a smaller amount of overhead was applied to production than was actually incurred during the period. The debit balance indicates that the factory overhead costs were **underapplied** or **underabsorbed**. In other words, the work in process account was undercharged for the costs of factory overhead incurred in the accounting period. Probable causes for the underapplication could include: (1) a lower level of operating capacity was achieved than was forecast when the predetermined rate was established or (2) the actual factory overhead expenses were more than budgeted for the operating level achieved. If, on the other hand, a credit balance remains after the applied factory overhead account is closed to the control account, the credit balance would represent **overapplied** or **overabsorbed factory overhead**. This means that more overhead was applied to production than was actually incurred in the period. To begin each new month with a zero balance in Factory Overhead, the debit or credit balance in the account is usually transferred to an account entitled **Under- and Overapplied Factory Overhead**, as follows:

Under- and Overapplied Factory Overhead	xx	
Factory Overhead		xx

Closed debit balance (underapplied) in factory overhead control account.

Factory Overhead	xx	
Under- and Overapplied Factory Overhead		xx

Closed credit balance (overapplied) in factory overhead control account.

The special account, Under- and Overapplied Factory Overhead, will accumulate the month-to-month differences. At the end of the year, the balance of the under- and overapplied account will be closed to Cost of Goods Sold or allocated on a pro rata basis to Work in Process, Finished Goods, and Cost of Goods Sold. The balance should be prorated if it would materially distort net income to charge the entire amount to Cost of Goods Sold.

The following table illustrates how under- and overapplied factory overhead costs typically offset each other over a given period of time as seasonal demands and production levels change:

Under- and Overapplied Factory Overhead

Month	Underapplied	Overapplied	Dr(Cr) Balance
January	$1,200		$1,200
February	800		2,000
March		$3,500	(1,500)
April		2,000	(3,500)
May		1,000	(4,500)
June		500	(5,000)
July	700		(4,300)
August	1,100		(3,200)
September	2,500		(700)
October	1,000		300
November	500		800
December		1,000	(200)
	$7,800	$8,000	

If a small balance, such as the $200 in the preceding example, remains in Under- and Overapplied Factory Overhead at year-end, it may be closed directly to Cost of Goods Sold because it will not materially affect net income. A large remaining balance, however, could distort the year's net income if it were closed entirely to Cost of Goods Sold when the company had material amounts of ending work in process and finished goods inventories which also would contain applied factory overhead. Therefore, an adjustment is required to restate the balances of the Work in Process, Finished Goods, and Cost of Goods Sold accounts.

To illustrate the proration (adjusting) procedure, assume that a debit balance of $10,000 (underapplied factory overhead) remained in the under- and overapplied factory overhead account. The year-end balances, before adjustment, of the following accounts were as follows:

		Percent of Total
Work in Process	$ 10,000	10%
Finished Goods	30,000	30
Cost of Goods Sold	60,000	60
Total	$100,000	100%

The pro rata amount of underapplied factory overhead chargeable to each account would be computed as follows:

Work in Process ($10,000 × 10%)	$ 1,000
Finished Goods ($10,000 × 30%)	3,000
Cost of Goods Sold ($10,000 × 60%)	6,000
	$10,000

The journal entry to close the debit balance in Under- and Overapplied Factory Overhead would be as follows:

Work in Process	1,000	
Finished Goods	3,000	
Cost of Goods Sold	6,000	
Under- and Overapplied Factory Overhead		10,000

Closed debit balance in Under- and Overapplied Factory Overhead.

The amount allocated to Cost of Goods Sold becomes a **period cost** that directly reduces the amount of net income for the current period. The amounts allocated to Work in Process and Finished Goods become part of the **product cost** of the inventories and will be deferred, along with the other inventory costs, to the next period when the inventory is sold.

The preceding sections of this chapter have presented and illustrated the various aspects of accounting for factory overhead, including departmentalizing factory overhead costs, distributing service department costs, applying factory overhead to production using predetermined rates, and accounting for differences between actual and applied factory overhead. Figures 4-9 through 4-15 tie together these various aspects and show the flow of factory overhead costs through the accounting system.

Figure 4-9 shows actual factory overhead costs accumulated during the month and distributed at the end of the month, using the same data and service department cost distribution method presented in Figure 4-8. Factory overhead was applied to the production departments as jobs were worked on throughout the month, as follows:

Department A	$ 66,000
Department B	56,000
Department C	70,000
Department D	110,000

Figure 4-9 also shows the under- or overapplied factory overhead by department and in total as follows:

	Actual Costs	Applied	Under/(Over)
Department A	$ 62,600	$ 66,000	$(3,400)
Department B	51,600	56,000	(4,400)
Department C	72,000	70,000	2,000
Department D	113,800	110,000	3,800
Total	$300,000	$302,000	$(2,000)

Figure 4-10 shows the flow of actual factory overhead expenses through the accounting records. The example assumes that the amounts posted to the factory overhead control account were originally recorded in the general journal. The total charge to the control account of $300,000 equals the

FIGURE 4-9   Summary of Actual and Applied Factory Overhead

	Power	Maintenance	Personnel	Dept. A	Dept. B	Dept. C	Dept. D	Total
Total actual expenses from factory overhead analysis sheets	30,000 00	20,000 00	10,000 00	50,000 00	40,000 00	60,000 00	90,000 00	300,000 00
Power distribution— (kw. hours) Maintenance— 10,000 @ $0.25 . . .		2,500 00	2,500 00	3,000 00	4,500 00	5,000 00	12,500 00	
Personnel—								
A— 10,000 @ 0.25								
B— 12,000 @ 0.25								
C— 18,000 @ 0.25								
D— 20,000 @ 0.25								
50,000 @ 0.25								
120,000		22,500 00						
Maintenance distribution— (square feet) Personnel—			4,500 00	4,500 00	5,400 00	3,600 00	4,500 00	
A— 5,000 @ $0.90								
B— 5,000 @ 0.90								
C— 6,000 @ 0.90								
D— 4,000 @ 0.90								
5,000 @ 0.90								
25,000			17,000 00					
Personnel distribution (number of employees served)				5,100 00	1,700 00	3,400 00	6,800 00	
A— 30 @ $170								
B— 10 @ $170								
C— 20 @ $170								
D— 40 @ $170								
100				62,600 00	51,600 00	72,000 00	113,800 00	300,000 00
Applied factory overhead				66,000 00	56,000 00	70,000 00	110,000 00	302,000 00
(Over-) or underapplied factory overhead				(3,400 00)	(4,400 00)	2,000 00	3,800 00	(2,000 00)

FIGURE 4-10   Actual Factory Overhead Expenses

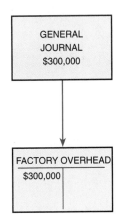

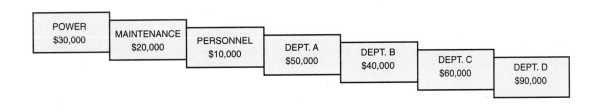

FIGURE 4-11   Distribution of Actual Factory Overhead to Service and Production Departments

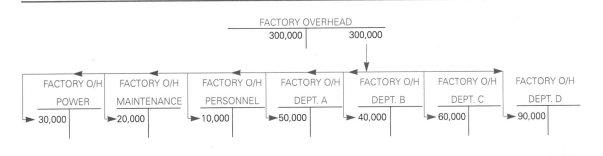

sum of the actual factory overhead expenses incurred by the individual departments and recorded on the factory overhead analysis sheets.

In Figure 4-11, the $300,000 balance in the factory overhead control account is transferred to the factory overhead accounts for both the service and production departments. The factory overhead analysis sheets provide the data necessary for the distribution.

FIGURE 4-12   Distribution of Service Department Costs

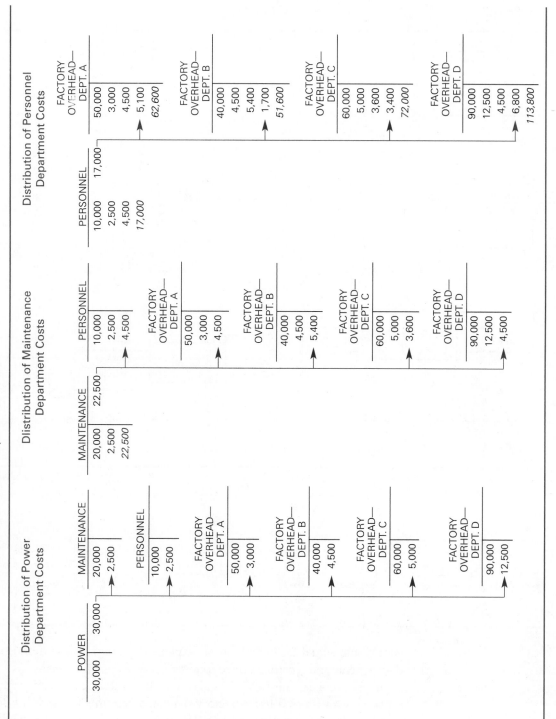

Figure 4-12 shows the distribution of the service department's costs to the production department's factory overhead accounts, using the sequential distribution method of service department costs with the service department, with the greatest total cost being distributed first. Figure 4-13 shows the application of factory overhead, based on predetermined rates, to the individual production departments. In Figure 4-14, the applied factory overhead accounts are closed to the departmental factory overhead accounts. Finally, as shown in Figure 4-15, the balances in the departmental factory overhead accounts are closed to Under- and Overapplied Factory Overhead. The net amount of overapplied factory overhead, $2,000, is relatively small and would be closed entirely to Cost of Goods Sold rather than allocated (prorated) among Cost of Goods Sold and the inventory accounts. Figure 4-16 shows in summary form the transactions involved in accounting for factory overhead.

You should now be able to work the following: Questions 19–20, Exercises 4-9 to 4-12, Problems 4-8 to 4-13, and Problem 4-14, which is a comprehensive review of Chapters 1–4.

FIGURE 4-13   Departmental Applied Factory Overhead

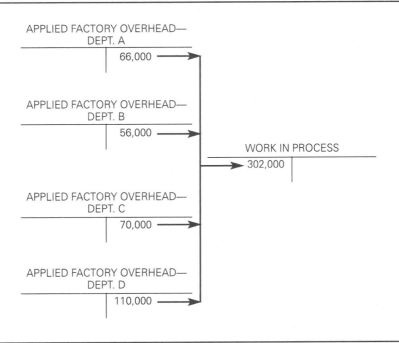

FIGURE 4-14

Closing Applied Factory Overhead Accounts to Departmental Factory Overhead Accounts

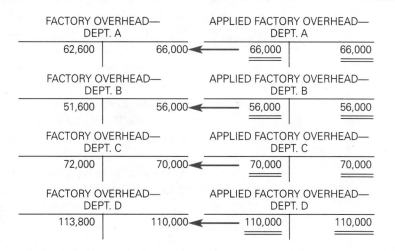

FIGURE 4-15

Closing Balances in Departmental Factory Overhead Accounts

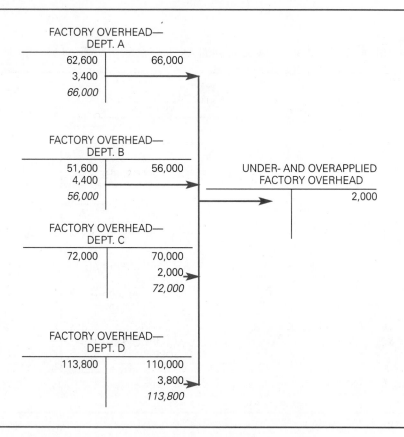

FIGURE 4-16   Summary of Factory Overhead Transactions

ACCOUNTING FOR FACTORY OVERHEAD

Transaction	Source of Data	Book of Original Entry	General Ledger Entry	Subsidiary Cost Records
Indirect materials requisitioned from storeroom for factory use	Materials issued summary	General Journal or Requisition Journal	Factory Overhead Materials	Factory overhead analysis ledger sheets Stores ledger cards
Indirect labor employed in factory	Labor cost summary	General Journal	Factory Overhead Payroll	Factory overhead analysis ledger sheets
Payroll taxes imposed on the analysis ledger employer	Payroll record	General Journal	Factory Overhead FICA Tax Payable FUTA Tax Payable State Unemployment Tax Payable	Factory overhead sheets
Incurred factory overhead such as rent, power, and repairs	Invoices	General Journal	Factory Overhead Accounts Payable	Factory overhead analysis ledger sheets
Adjustments for factory overhead such as expired insurance, accrued property tax, and depreciation	Schedules	General Journal	Factory Overhead Prepaid Insurance Accrued Property Tax Payable Accumulated Depreciation	Factory overhead analysis ledger sheets
Distribution of factory overhead to service and production departments	Schedules	General Journal	Departmental Factory Overhead Accounts Factory Overhead	None
Distribution of service department expenses to production department expense accounts	Schedules	General Journal	Production Department Factory Overhead Accounts Service Department Expense Accounts	Factory overhead analysis ledger sheets
Application of factory overhead to jobs	Schedule of predetermined departmental application rates	General Journal	Work in Process Production Department Applied Factory Overhead Accounts	Job cost sheets
Close applied factory overhead accounts to factory overhead control	Applied factory overhead accounts	General Journal	Applied Factory Overhead Accounts Factory Overhead	None
Close factory overhead control balances to under- and over-applied factory overhead account	Factory overhead control accounts	General Journal	Under- and Overapplied Factory Overhead Factory Overhead (if underapplied) Factory Overhead Under- and Overapplied Factory Overhead (if overapplied)	None

KEY TERMS

Activity-based costing, p. 169
Algebraic distribution method, p. 160
Applied Factory Overhead, p. 172
Budget, p. 152
Cost driver, p. 170
Department-type analysis sheet, p. 155
Direct charge, p. 159
Direct distribution method, p. 160
Direct labor cost method, p. 167
Direct labor hour method, p. 168
Expense-type analysis sheet, p. 154
Factory overhead, p. 145
Factory overhead analysis sheets, p. 154
Factory overhead ledger, p. 153
Fixed costs, p. 146
Flexible budget, p. 152
General factory overhead expense, p. 156
High-low method, p. 148
Machine hour method, p. 168
Mixed costs, p. 146

Observation method, p. 148
Outliers, p. 151
Overapplied or overabsorbed factory overhead, p. 173
Period cost, p. 175
Predetermined factory overhead rate, p. 166
Product cost, p. 175
Production department, p. 159
Scattergraph method, p. 149
Schedule of fixed costs, p. 156
Semifixed costs, p. 146
Semivariable costs, p. 146
Sequential distribution (or step-down) method, p. 160
Service department, p. 158
Step-down method, p. 160
Step variable cost, p. 147
Summary of factory overhead, p. 158
Under- and Overapplied Factory Overhead, p. 173
Underapplied or underabsorbed factory overhead, p. 173
Variable costs, p. 146

SELF-STUDY PROBLEM

JOB COST SHEETS; JOURNAL ENTRIES

WATER POWER COMPANY

Water Power Company, makers of custom-made Jet Skis, completed Job 500 on March 31, and there were no jobs in process in the plant. Prior to April 1, the predetermined overhead application rate for April was computed from the following data, based on an estimate of 40,000 direct labor hours:

Estimated variable factory overhead	$10,000
Estimated fixed factory overhead	20,000
Total estimated factory overhead	$30,000
Estimated variable factory overhead per hour	$ 0.25
Estimated fixed factory overhead per hour	0.50
Predetermined overhead rate per direct labor hour	$ 0.75

The factory has one production department, and the direct labor hour method is used to apply factory overhead.

Three jobs are started during the month, and postings are made daily to the job cost sheets from the materials requisitions and time tickets. The following schedule shows the jobs and the amounts posted to the job cost sheets:

Job	Date Started	Direct Materials	Direct Labor	Direct Labor Hours
401	April 1	$10,000	$20,000	12,000
402	April 12	20,000	25,000	18,000
403	April 15	8,000	14,000	8,000
		$38,000	$59,000	38,000

The factory overhead control account was debited during the month for actual factory overhead expenses of $32,500. On April 11, Job 401 was completed and delivered to the customer at a markup of 50% on manufacturing cost. On April 24, Job 402 was completed and transferred to Finished Goods. On April 30, Job 403 was still in process.

Required:

1. Prepare job cost sheets for Jobs 401, 402, and 403, including factory overhead applied when the job was completed or at the end of the month for partially completed jobs.
2. Prepare journal entries as of April 30 for the following:
   a. Applying factory overhead to production.
   b. Closing the applied factory overhead account.
   c. Closing the factory overhead account.
   d. Transferring the cost of the completed jobs to Finished Goods.
   e. Recording the cost of the sale and the sale of Job 401.

Suggestions:

1. When completing the job cost sheets, you must first determine how much overhead should be applied to each job.
2. When closing the factory overhead account, the balance will represent the under- or overapplied factory overhead.

SOLUTION TO SELF-STUDY PROBLEM

Preparing the job cost sheets:

1. On April 11, Job 401 was completed and factory overhead was applied as follows:

Job 401

Direct materials	$10,000
Direct labor	20,000
Applied factory overhead (12,000 hours × $0.75)	9,000
Total cost	$39,000

On April 24, Job 402 was completed and factory overhead was applied as follows:

Job 402

Direct materials	$20,000
Direct labor	25,000
Applied factory overhead (18,000 hours × $0.75)	13,500
Total cost	$58,500

On April 30, Job 403 is not completed; however, factory overhead is applied to the partially completed job to estimate the total cost incurred during the month of April, as follows:

Job 403

Direct materials	$ 8,000
Direct labor	14,000
Applied factory overhead (8,000 hours × $0.75)	6,000
Total cost (for month of April)	$28,000

Preparing the journal entries:

2. a. The total factory overhead applied to the three jobs during April was $28,500. The general journal entry made on April 30 to apply factory overhead to production follows:

April 30	Work in Process	28,500
	Applied Factory Overhead		28,500

The applied factory overhead of $28,500 has already been recorded on the job cost sheets. The above general journal entry brings the work in process control account into agreement with the subsidiary job cost ledger.

b. & c. The next procedure is to close the applied factory overhead account to Factory Overhead. Then, transfer any remaining balance to the under- and overapplied factory overhead account.

April 30	Applied Factory Overhead	28,500
	Factory Overhead		28,500
April 30	Under- and Overapplied Factory Overhead . .	4,000
	Factory Overhead		4,000
	Closed factory overhead ($32,500 actual – $28,500 applied).	

d. & e. During April, the following entries were made to transfer the cost of completed Jobs 401 and 402 to Finished Goods, and to record the cost of the sales and the sale of Job 401:

Finished Goods	97,500
Work in Process		97,500
Completed Jobs 401 ($39,000) and 402 ($58,500) and transferred to finished goods.		

Accounts Receivable	58,500
Sales		58,500
Delivered Job 401 to customer and billed at 50% markup ($39,000 × 150%).		

Cost of Goods Sold   39,000
Finished Goods   39,000
Recorded cost of Job 401 delivered to customer.

(Note: Problem 4-12 is similar to this problem.)

QUESTIONS

1. What are factory overhead expenses and what distinguishes them from other manufacturing costs? What other terms are used to describe factory overhead expenses?

2. What are three categories of factory overhead expenses? Give examples of each.

3. What are the distinguishing characteristics of variable, fixed, and semivariable factory overhead costs?

4. When a product's cost is composed of both fixed and variable costs, what effect does the increase or decrease in production have on total unit cost?

5. What effect does a change in volume have on total variable, fixed, and semivariable costs?

6. What is the basic premise underlying the high-low method of analyzing semivariable costs?

7. What are the advantages and disadvantages of the scattergraph method as compared to the high-low method?

8. How does accounting for factory overhead differ in small enterprises versus large enterprises?

9. What is the function and use of each of the two types of factory overhead analysis sheets?

10. What are two types of departments found in a factory? What is the function or purpose of each?

11. What are the two most frequently used methods of distributing service department costs to production departments?

12. What are the shortcomings of waiting until the actual factory overhead expenses are known before recording such costs on the job cost sheets?

13. What are the two types of budget data needed to compute predetermined overhead rates?

14. What are three methods traditionally used for applying factory overhead to jobs? Discuss the application of each method.

15. What factory operating conditions and data are required for each of the traditionally used methods for applying factory overhead to products? Discuss the strengths and weaknesses of each method.

16. Under what conditions would it be desirable for a company to use more than one method to apply factory overhead to jobs or products?

17. How does activity-based costing differ from traditional methods of applying overhead to products?

18. What steps must a company take to successfully employ activity-based costing?

19. If the factory overhead control account has a debit balance of $1,000 at the end of the first month of the fiscal year, has the overhead been under- or overapplied for the month? What are some probable causes for the debit balance?

20. What are two ways that an under- or overapplied factory overhead balance can be disposed of at the end of a fiscal period?

E X E R C I S E S

E4-1
Classifying fixed and variable costs
Objective 1

Classify each of the following items of factory overhead as either a fixed or a variable cost. (Include any costs that you consider to be semivariable within the variable category.)

a. Indirect labor
b. Indirect materials
c. Insurance on building
d. Overtime premium pay
e. Depreciation on building (straight-line)
f. Polishing compounds
g. Depreciation on machinery (based on hours used)
h. Employer's payroll taxes
i. Property taxes
j. Machine lubricants
k. Employees' hospital insurance (paid by employer)
l. Labor for machine repairs
m. Vacation pay
n. Patent amortization
o. Janitor's wages
p. Rent
q. Small tools
r. Plant manager's salary
s. Factory electricity
t. Product inspector's wages

E4-2
High-low methods
Objective 2

Derby Company has accumulated the following data over a six-month period:

	Indirect Labor Hours	Indirect Labor Costs
January	400	$ 6,000
February	500	7,000
March	600	8,000
April	700	9,000
May	800	10,000
June	900	11,000
	3,900	$51,000

Separate the indirect labor into its fixed and variable components, using the high-low method.

E4-3
Scattergraph method
Objective 2

Using the data in E4-2 and a piece of graph paper:

1. Plot the data points on the graph and draw a line by visual inspection, indicating the trend shown by the data points.

2. Determine the variable cost per unit and the total fixed cost from the information on the graph.

E4-4
Computing unit costs at different levels of production
Objective 3

Madison Manufacturing Company budgeted for 12,000 units of product XYLON during the month of May. The unit cost of product XYLON was $20, consisting of direct materials, $7; direct labor, $8; and factory overhead, $5 (fixed, $3; variable, $2).

a. What would be the unit cost if 8,000 units were manufactured? (Hint: You must first determine the total fixed costs.)
b. What would be the unit cost if 15,000 units were manufactured?
c. Explain why a difference occurs in the unit costs.

E4-5
Identifying basis for distribution of service department costs
Objective 5

What would be the appropriate basis for distributing the costs of each of the following service departments?

a. Building maintenance
b. Inspection and packing
c. Machine shop
d. Personnel
e. Purchasing
f. Shipping
g. Stores
h. Tool Room

E4-6
Sequential distribution of service department costs
Objective 5

A manufacturing company has two service and two production departments. Building maintenance and factory office are the service departments.

The production departments are assembly and machining. The following data have been estimated for next year's operations:

Direct labor hours: Assembly, 80,000; Machining, 40,000
Floor space occupied: Factory Office, 10%; Assembly, 50%; Machining, 40%

The direct charges expected to be made to the departments are as follows:

Building maintenance . . . . $ 90,000
Factory office 171,000
Assembly 378,000
Machining 328,000

The building maintenance department services all departments of the company and its costs are allocated using floor space occupied, while factory office costs are allocable to assembly and machining on the basis of direct labor hours. The sequential distribution method is used, with the department servicing the greatest number of other departments distributed first.

1. Distribute the service department costs, using the direct method.
2. Distribute the service department costs, using the sequential distribution method.

E4-7
Determining job cost, using direct labor cost, direct labor hour, and machine hour methods
Objective 6

a. If the direct labor cost method is used in applying factory overhead and the predetermined rate is 150%, what amount should be charged to Job 1776 for factory overhead? Assume that direct materials used totaled $5,000 and that the direct labor cost totaled $3,200.

b. If the direct labor hour method is used in applying factory overhead and the predetermined rate is $2 an hour, what amount should be charged to Job 1776 for factory overhead? Assume that the direct materials used totaled $5,000, the direct labor cost totaled $3,200, and the number of direct labor hours totaled 2,500.

c. If the machine hour method is used in applying factory overhead and the predetermined rate is $15 an hour, what amount should be charged to Job 1776 for factory overhead? Assume that the direct materials used totaled $5,000, the direct labor cost totaled $3,200, and the number of machine hours totaled 295.

E4-8
Determining job costs, using ABC method
Objective 6

Job 1107 required $5,000 for direct materials, $2,000 for direct labor, 200 direct labor hours, 100 machine hours, two setups, and three design changes. The cost pools and overhead rates for each pool follow:

Cost Pool	Overhead Rate
Direct labor usage	$5/direct labor hour
Machine usage	$10/machine hour
Machine setups	$250/setup
Design changes	$500/design change

Determine the cost of Job 1107.

E4-9
Determining actual factory overhead
Objectives 6, 7

The books of Prestige Products Company revealed that the following general journal entry had been made at the end of the current accounting period:

Factory Overhead	2,000	
Under- and Overapplied Factory Overhead		2,000

The total direct materials cost for the period was $40,000. The total direct labor cost, at an average rate of $10 per hour for direct labor, was one and one-half times the direct materials cost. Factory overhead was applied on the basis of $4 per direct labor hour. What was the total actual factory overhead incurred for the period? (Hint: First solve for direct labor cost and then for direct labor hours.)

E4-10
Determining labor and factory overhead costs
Objectives 6, 7

The general ledger of Joker Manufacturing Company contains the following control account:

Work in Process			
Materials	15,000	Finished goods	30,000
Labor	16,000		
Factory overhead	8,000		

If the materials charged to the one uncompleted job still in process amounted to $3,400, what amount of labor and factory overhead must have been charged to the job if the factory overhead rate is 50% of direct labor cost?

E4-11
General ledger
account analysis
Objective 7

The following form represents an account taken from the general ledger of Java Manufacturing Company:

Indirect materials	500	Work in Process	8,200
Supervisor's salary	1,200	(50% of $16,400 direct labor)	
Power	5,000		
Building expenses	1,000		
Miscellaneous overhead	1,400		
Bal. 900	9,100		

Answer the following questions:

a. What is the title of the account?
b. Is this a departmentalized factory?
c. What does the balance of the account represent?
d. How was the 50% rate determined?
e. What disposition should be made of the balance, assuming that this is the end of the fiscal year?

E4-12
Computing under-
and overapplied
overhead
Objective 7

Roberts Company had a remaining debit balance of $20,000 in its under- and overapplied factory overhead account at year-end. The balance was deemed to be large and, therefore, should be closed to Work In Process, Finished Goods, and Cost of Goods Sold. The year-end balances of these accounts, before adjustment, showed the following:

Work in Process	$ 25,000
Finished Goods	50,000
Cost of Goods Sold	125,000
Totals	200,000

a. Determine the prorated amount of the underapplied factory overhead that is chargeable to each of the accounts.
b. Prepare the journal entry to close the debit balance in Under- and Overapplied Factory Overhead.

PROBLEMS

P4-1
Variable and fixed
cost pattern analysis
Objective 1

The cost behavior patterns on the next page are lettered A through H. The vertical axes of the graphs represent total dollars of expense, and the horizontal axes represent production. In each case, the zero point is at the intersection of the two axes. Each graph may be used more than once or not used at all.

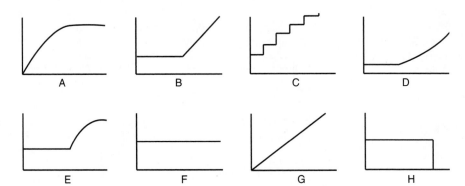

A   B   C   D

E   F   G   H

Required:

Select the graph that matches the lettered cost described below.

a. Depreciation of equipment—the amount of depreciation charged is computed by the machine hour method.
b. Electricity bill—flat fixed charge, plus a variable cost after a certain number of kilowatt hours are used.
c. City water bill—computed as follows:

First 1,000,000 gallons or less	$1,000 flat fee
Next 10,000 gallons	0.003 per gallon used
Next 10,000 gallons	0.006 per gallon used
Next 10,000 gallons	0.009 per gallon used
	and so on.

d. Depreciation of equipment—the amount is computed by the straight-line method.
e. Rent on a factory building donated by the city—the agreement calls for a fixed fee payment, unless 200,000 labor hours are worked, in which case no rent need be paid.
f. Salaries of repair workers—one repair worker is needed for every 1,000 machine hours or less (i.e., 0 to 1,000 hours requires one repair worker, 1,001 to 2,000 hours requires two repair workers, etc.).
g. Cost of raw materials used.

P4-2
Variable and fixed cost analysis; high-low method
Objective 2

Cavalier Company manufactures a product that requires the use of a considerable amount of natural gas to heat it to a desired temperature. The process requires a constant level of heat, so the furnaces are maintained at a set temperature for 24 hours a day. Although units are not continuously processed, management desires that the variable cost be charged directly to the product and the fixed cost to the factory overhead. The following data have been collected for the year:

	Units	Cost		Units	Cost
January . . .	2,400	$4,400	July	2,200	$4,400
February . . .	2,300	4,300	August	2,100	4,100
March	2,200	4,200	September	2,000	3,800
April	2,000	4,000	October	1,400	3,400
May	1,800	3,800	November	1,900	3,700
June	1,900	3,900	December	1,800	4,050

Required:

1. Separate the variable and fixed elements, using the high-low method.
2. Determine the cost to be charged to the product for the year. (Hint: First determine the number of annual units produced.)
3. Determine the cost to be charged to factory overhead for the year.

P4-3
Scattergraph method
Objective 2

Using the data in P4-2 and a piece of graph paper:

1. Plot the data points on the graph and draw a line by visual inspection, indicating the trend shown by the data points.
2. Determine the variable cost per unit and the total fixed cost from the information on the graph.
3. Determine the cost to be charged to the product for the year.
4. Determine the cost to be charged to factory overhead for the year.

P4-4
Distribution of service department costs to production departments
Objective 5

Marvin Manufacturing Company is divided into five departments, A, B, C, D, and E. The first three departments are engaged in production work. Departments D and E are service departments. During the month of June, the following factory overhead was incurred for the various departments:

Department A	$21,000	Department D	$9,000
Department B	18,000	Department E	6,400
Department C	25,000		

The bases for distributing service department expenses to the other departments follow:

Department E—On the basis of floor space occupied by the other departments as follows: Department A, 10,000 sq. ft.; Department B, 4,500 sq. ft.; Department C, 10,500 sq. ft.; and Department D, 7,000 sq. ft.

Department D—Divided: Department A—30%; Department B—20%; Department C—50%.

Required:

Prepare schedules showing the distribution of the service departments' expenses for the following:

1. The direct distribution method.
2. The sequential distribution method in the order of number of other departments served.

P4-5
Determining total job
costs, using
predetermined
overhead rate
Objective 6

Elizabeth Manufacturing Company uses the job order cost system of accounting. Shown below is a list of the jobs completed during the month of March, showing the charges for materials requisitioned and for direct labor.

Job	Materials Requisitioned	Direct Labor
007	$ 300.00	$ 600.00
008	1,080.00	940.00
009	720.00	1,400.00
010	4,200.00	5,120.00

Assume that factory overhead is applied on the basis of direct labor costs and that the predetermined rate is 200%.

Required:

1. Compute the amount of overhead to be added to the cost of each job completed during the month.
2. Compute the total cost of each job completed during the month.
3. Compute the total cost of producing all the jobs finished during the month.

P4-6
Determining job
cost—calculation of
predetermined rate
for applying overhead
by direct labor cost
and direct labor hour
methods
Objective 6

Hans Manufacturing Company has its factory divided into three departments, with individual factory overhead rates for each department. In each department, all the operations are sufficiently alike for the department to be regarded as a cost center. The estimated monthly factory overhead for the departments are as follows: Department A, $64,000; Department B, $36,000; and Department C, $10,080. The estimated production data include the following:

	Dept. A	Dept. B	Dept. C
Materials used	$20,000	$10,000	$10,000
Direct labor cost	$16,000	$15,000	$ 8,400
Direct labor hours	8,000	5,000	3,500

The job cost ledger shows the following data for Job 2525, which was completed during the month:

	Dept. A	Dept. B	Dept. C
Materials used	$12.00	$14.00	$12.00
Direct labor cost	$13.00	$13.50	$12.50
Direct labor hours	11	9	10

Required:

Determine the cost of Job 2525. Assume that the factory overhead is applied to production orders based on the following:
1. Direct labor cost
2. Direct labor hours

P4-7
Determining job costs,
using activity-based
costing
Objective 6

Modem Manufacturing Company uses activity-based costing. The factory overhead budget for the coming period is $500,000, consisting of the following:

Cost Pool	Budgeted Amount
Direct labor usage	$150,000
Machine usage	200,000
Machine setups	100,000
Design changes	50,000
Totals	$500,000

The potential allocation bases and their estimated amounts were as follows:

Allocation Base	Budgeted Amount
Number of design changes	50
Number of setups	200
Machine hours	10,000
Direct labor hours	20,000

Required:

1. Determine the overhead rate for each cost pool, using the most appropriate allocation base for each pool.
2. Job 1267 required $25,000 for direct materials, $10,000 for direct labor, 1,000 direct labor hours, 500 machine hours, five setups, and three design changes. Determine the cost of Job 1267.

P4-8
General journal entries for factory overhead
Objectives 4, 6, 7

Lyndon Company uses a job order cost system. Selected transactions dealing with factory items for the month follow:

a. Requisitioned indirect materials from storeroom, $3,200.
b. Purchased, on account, factory supplies for future needs, $4,400.
c. Purchased parts, on account, for repairing a machine, $1,400.
d. Requisitioned factory supplies from storeroom, $900.
e. Returned defective factory supplies to vendor, $700.
f. Factory rent accrued for the month, $2,400.
g. Returned previously requisitioned factory supplies to storeroom, $350.
h. Depreciation of machinery and equipment, $2,800.
i. Payroll taxes liability for month, $3,200.
j. Heat, light, and power charges payable for the month, $6,400.
k. Expired insurance on inventories, $1,350.
l. Factory overhead applied to production, $36,400.
m. Indirect labor for the month, $2,600.
n. Goods completed and transferred to finished goods: materials, $14,400; labor, $40,400; factory overhead, $30,400.

Required:

Record the above transactions. Assume that the records include a control account and a subsidiary ledger for factory overhead, to which the entries will be posted at some later date.

P4-9
Determining overhead
rates, using direct
labor cost, direct labor
hour, and machine
hour methods;
determining job cost;
computing
underapplied and
overapplied overhead
Objectives 6, 7

Moses Manufacturing Company is studying the results of applying factory overhead to production. The following data have been used: estimated factory overhead, $60,000; estimated materials costs, $50,000; estimated labor costs,
$60,000; estimated direct labor hours, 40,000; estimated machine hours, 25,000;
work in process at the beginning of the month, none.

The actual factory overhead incurred for the month of November was
$55,000, and the production statistics on November 30 are as follows:

Job	Materials Costs	Direct Labor Costs	Direct Labor Hours	Machine Hours	Date Jobs Completed
101	$ 5,000	$ 7,200	5,000	3,000	Nov. 10
102	7,000	10,000	6,000	3,200	Nov. 14
103	8,000	11,000	6,500	4,000	Nov. 20
104	9,000	9,000	5,600	3,400	In process
105	10,000	15,000	10,500	6,500	Nov. 26
106	11,000	4,200	3,000	1,500	In process
Total	$50,000	$56,400	36,600	21,600	

Required:

1. Compute the predetermined rate based on the following:
   a. Direct labor cost
   b. Direct labor hours
   c. Machine hours
2. Using each of the methods, compute the estimated total cost of each job at
   the end of the month.
3. Determine the under- or overapplied factory overhead, in total, at the end of
   the month under each of the methods.
4. Which method would you recommend? Why?

P4-10
Determining overhead
rate, using direct labor
cost, direct labor hour,
and machine hour
methods
Objectives 6, 7

The following information, taken from the books of Michael Company, represents the operations for the month of January:

	Dept. A	Dept. B	Dept. C
Materials used	$20,000	$10,000	$10,000
Direct labor cost	$ 8,000	$ 5,000	$ 9,000
Direct labor hours	20,000	10,000	27,000
Machine hours	4,000	5,000	2,025
Factory overhead	$20,000	$10,000	$16,200

The job cost system is used, and the February cost sheet for Job 1812 shows
the following:

	Dept. A	Dept. B	Dept. C
Materials	$2.00	$4.00	$2.00
Direct labor	$3.60	$3.00	$2.10
Direct labor hours	8	6	6
Machine hours	2	3	1

The following information was accumulated during February:

	Dept. A	Dept. B	Dept. C
Direct labor hours	15,000	9,800	20,000
Factory overhead	$14,000	$10,000	$11,800

Required:

1. Using the January data, ascertain the factory overhead application rates to be used during February, based on the following:
   a. Direct labor cost
   b. Direct labor hours
   c. Machine hours
2. Prepare a schedule showing the total production cost of Job 1812 under each method of applying factory overhead.
3. Prepare the entries to record the following for February operations:
   a. Payment of total factory overhead.
   b. Distribution of factory overhead to the departments.
   c. Application of factory overhead to the jobs, using direct labor hours. (Use the predetermined rate calculated in 1 above and separate accounts for each department.)
   d. Closing of the applied factory overhead accounts.
   e. Recording under- and overapplied factory overhead and closing the actual factory overhead accounts.

P4-11
Determining the under- and overapplied overhead
Objectives 5, 6, 7

Pluto Corporation has four departmental accounts: Building Maintenance, General Factory Overhead, Department A, and Department B. The direct labor hours method is used to apply factory overhead to the jobs being worked on in Departments A and B. The company expects each production department to use 30,000 direct labor hours during the year. The estimated overhead rates for the year include the following:

	Dept. A	Dept. B
Variable cost per hour	$1.30	$1.50
Fixed cost per hour	2.70	3.00
	$4.00	$4.50

During the year, both Departments A and B used 28,000 direct labor hours. Factory overhead costs incurred during the year follow:

Building maintenance	$30,000
General factory overhead	75,400
Department A	45,800
Department B	68,800

In determining application rates at the beginning of the year, cost allocations were made as follows, using the sequential distribution method:

Building Maintenance to General Factory Overhead, 10%; to Department A, 50%; to Department B, 40%.

General factory overhead was distributed according to direct labor hours.

Required:

Determine the under- or overapplied overhead for each production department.

P4-12
Job cost sheets,
journal entries.
Similar to Self-study
problem
Objectives 6, 7

Xian Manufacturing Company completed Job 2525 on May 31, and there were no jobs in process in the plant. Prior to June 1, the predetermined overhead application rate for June was computed from the following data, based on an estimate of 5,000 direct labor hours:

Estimated variable factory overhead	$20,000
Estimated fixed factory overhead	10,000
Total estimated factory overhead	$30,000
Estimated variable factory overhead per hour	$4
Estimated fixed factory overhead per hour	2
Predetermined overhead rate per direct labor hour	$6

The factory has one production department and uses the direct labor hour method to apply factory overhead.

Three jobs are started during the month, and postings are made daily to the job cost sheets from the materials requisitions and time tickets. The following schedule shows the jobs and amounts posted to the job cost sheets:

Job	Date Started	Direct Materials	Direct Labor	Direct Labor Hours
2526	June 1	$ 5,000	$10,000	1,600
2527	June 12	10,000	15,000	1,900
2528	June 15	4,000	7,000	1,300
		$19,000	$32,000	4,800

The factory overhead control account was debited during the month for actual factory overhead expenses of $25,500. On June 11, Job 2526 was completed and delivered to the customer at a markup of 50% on manufacturing cost. On June 24, Job 2527 was completed and transferred to Finished Goods. On June 30, Job 2528 was still in process.

Required:

1. Prepare job cost sheets for Jobs 2526, 2527, and 2528, including factory overhead applied when the job was completed or at the end of the month for partially completed jobs.
2. Prepare journal entries as of June 30 for the following:
   a. Applying factory overhead to production.
   b. Closing the applied factory overhead account.
   c. Closing the factory overhead account.
   d. Transferring the cost of the completed jobs to finished goods.
   e. Recording the cost of the sale and the sale of Job 2526.

P4-13
Closing under- and
overapplied overhead
at year-end
Objective 7

Eastwood Company had a remaining credit balance of $10,000 in its under- and overapplied factory overhead account at year-end. It also had year-end balances in the following accounts:

Work in Process	$ 25,000
Finished Goods	15,000
Cost of Goods Sold	85,000
Totals	$125,000

Required:

1. Prepare the closing entry for the $10,000 of overapplied overhead, assuming that the balance is not considered to be material.
2. Prepare the closing entry for the $10,000 of overapplied overhead, assuming that the balance is considered to be material.

P4-14
Comprehensive review of job order procedures
Chapters 1–4

Kooy Chrome Company manufactures special chromed parts made to the order and specifications of the customer. It has two production departments, stamping and plating, and two service departments, power and maintenance. In any production department, the job in process is wholly completed before the next job is started.

The company operates on a fiscal year, which ends September 30. Following is the post-closing trial balance as of September 30:

Kooy Chrome
Post-Closing Trial Balance
September 30, 20—

Cash	$ 22,500	
Accounts Receivable	21,700	
Finished Goods	8,750	
Work in Process	3,600	
Materials	15,000	
Prepaid Insurance	4,320	
Factory Building	64,000	
Accum. Depr.—Factory Building		22,500
Machinery and Equipment	38,000	
Accum. Depr.—Machinery		
and Equipment		16,000
Office Equipment	10,500	
Accum. Depr.—Office Equipment		7,500
Accounts Payable		2,500
FICA Tax Payable		3,120
Federal Unemployment Tax Payable		364
State Unemployment Tax Payable		1,404
Employees Income Tax Payable		5,200
Capital Stock		75,000
Retained Earnings		54,782
	188,370	188,370

Additional information:

1. The balance of the materials account represents the following:

Materials	Units	Unit Cost	Total
A	120	$25	$ 3,000
B	320	15	4,800
C	180	30	5,400
Factory Supplies			1,800
			$15,000

The company uses the FIFO method of accounting for all inventories. Material A is used in the stamping department and materials B and C in the plating department.

2. The balance of the work in process account represents the following costs that are applicable to Job 905. (The customer's order is for 1,000 units of the finished product.)

Direct materials	$1,500
Direct labor	1,200
Factory overhead	900
	$3,600

3. The finished goods account reflects the cost of Job 803, which was finished at the end of the preceding month and is awaiting delivery orders from the customer.

4. At the beginning of the year, factory overhead application rates were based on the following data:

	Stamping Dept.	Plating Dept.
Estimated factory overhead for the year	$145,000	$115,000
Estimated direct labor hours for the year	29,000	6,000

In October, the following transactions were recorded:
a. Purchased the following materials and supplies on account:

Material A	1,100 units @ $26
Material B	900 units @ $17
Material C	800 units @ $28
Factory Supplies	$3,200

b. The following materials were issued to the factory:

	Job 905	Job 1001	Job 1002
Material A		600 units	400 units
Material B		400 units	200 units
Material C	200 units	400 units	
Factory Supplies—$2,450			

Customers' orders covered by Jobs 1001 and 1002 are for 1,000 and 500 units of finished product, respectively.

c. Factory wages and office, sales, and administrative salaries are paid at the end of each month. The following data, provided from an analysis of labor time tickets and salary schedules, will be sufficient for the preparation of the entries to record the payroll. (Assume FICA and federal income tax rates of 8% and 10%, respectively.) Record the company's liability for state and federal unemployment taxes. (Assume rates of 4% and 1%, respectively.) Record the payroll distribution for the month of October.

	Stamping Dept.	Plating Dept.
Job 905	100 hrs. @ $9	300 hrs. @ $11
Job 1001	1,200 hrs. @ $9	300 hrs. @ $11
Job 1002	800 hrs. @ $9	

Wages of the supervisors, custodial personnel, etc., totaled $9,500; administrative salaries were $18,300.

d. Miscellaneous factory overhead incurred during the month totaled $4,230. Miscellaneous selling and administrative expenses were $1,500. These items as well as the FICA tax and federal income tax withheld for September were paid. (See account balances on the post-closing trial balance for September 30.)

e. Annual depreciation on plant assets is calculated using the following rates:

Factory buildings—5%
Machinery and equipment—20%
Office equipment—20%

f. The balance of the prepaid insurance account represents a three-year premium for a fire insurance policy covering the factory building and machinery. It was paid on the last day of the preceding month and became effective on October 1.

g. The summary of factory overhead prepared from the factory overhead ledger is reproduced below:

Summary of Factory Overhead for October

Trans-action	Account	Stamping	Plating	Power	Mainte-nance	Total
a.	Factory supplies	$ 940.00	$ 750.00	$ 260.00	$ 500.00	$ 2,450.00
b.	Indirect labor	3,780.00	2,860.00	970.00	1,890.00	9,500.00
c.	Payroll taxes	2,948.40	1,229.80	126.10	245.70	4,550.00
d.	Miscellaneous	1,692.00	1,410.00	752.00	376.00	4,230.00
e.	Depreciation	360.00	270.00	90.00	180.00	900.00
f.	Insurance	48.00	40.00	16.00	16.00	120.00
	Total	$9,768.40	$6,559.80	$2,214.10	$3,207.70	$21,750.00

h. The total expenses of the maintenance department are distributed on the basis of floor space occupied by the power department (8,820 sq. ft.), stamping department (19,500 sq. ft.), and plating department (7,875 sq. ft.). The power department expenses are then allocated equally to the stamping and plating departments.

i. After the actual factory overhead expenses have been distributed to the departmental accounts and the applied factory overhead has been recorded and posted, any balances in the departmental accounts are transferred to Under- and Overapplied Overhead.

j. Jobs 905 and 1001 were finished during the month. Job 1002 is still in process at the end of the month.

k. During the month, Jobs 803 and 905 were sold at a markup of 150% on cost.

l. Received $55,500 from customers in payment of their accounts.

m. Checks were issued in the amount of $43,706 for payment of the payroll.

Required:

1. Set up the beginning trial balance in T-accounts.
2. Prepare materials inventory ledger cards and enter October 1 balances.
3. Set up job cost sheets as needed.
4. Record all transactions and related entries for the month of October and post to T-accounts.
5. Prepare a service department expense distribution work sheet for October.
6. At the end of the month:
   a. Analyze the balance in the materials account, the work in process account, and the finished goods account.
   b. Prepare the statement of cost of goods manufactured, income statement, and balance sheet for October 31.

5

Cost Accounting
for Service Businesses

LEARNING OBJECTIVES

After studying this chapter you should be able to:

1. Perform job order costing for service businesses.
2. Prepare budgets for service businesses.
3. Apply activity-based costing for a service firm.
4. Compare the results of cost allocations using simplified costing versus activity-based costing.

A service is an intangible benefit, such as consulting, designing, grooming, transporting, and entertaining. It does not have physical properties and is consumed at the time that it is provided. It cannot be saved or stored and, therefore, is not inventoried. Examples of service businesses include accounting firms, airlines, hair stylists, plumbers, professional sports teams, and restaurants. Note that some service businesses have an associated raw material or product. While a restaurant, for example, is in the business of *serving* food, the food itself has tangible properties.

The main features of service businesses are that they have little or no inventory. Even the restaurant would not keep most food items for more than a day or two, and labor costs often comprise three-fourths or more of the total costs. Service businesses are important because roughly 70%

of U.S. workers are employed by service businesses, which account for more than 60% of the value of the total production of goods and services in this country. Approximately 90% of the jobs created in the U.S. in the last 20 years have been in service industries. Lack of growth in manufacturing, primarily due to imports and automation, account for most of the percentage increases in services' share of the job growth. Also, the automation of manufacturing has resulted in the production of many more goods with fewer workers, thus creating a need for more people to market, distribute, and service these additional products.

Historically, cost accountants spent most of their time developing product costs for manufactured goods and spent little time on costing services. Given the importance of services in our modern economy, the related cost issues can no longer be ignored. Knowing the cost of providing services is important to managers for such purposes as contract bidding and deciding what services to emphasize or de-emphasize in their line of offerings.

JOB ORDER COSTING FOR SERVICE BUSINESSES

LEARNING OBJECTIVE 1
Perform job order costing for service businesses.

The amount and complexity of services provided can vary substantially from customer to customer. When this is the case, a service firm should use job order costing, just as the manufacturers of differentiated products use such a system. Examples of service firms using job order costing include accounting firms whose cost of an audit would depend on the size and complexity of a client's operations and auto repairers whose charges are based on the parts, supplies, and labor time needed on each job. The basic document used to accumulate costs for a service business using job order costing is the job order cost sheet, which also was used in our manufacturing examples. Figure 5-1 is a job cost sheet used by an accounting firm for the audit of an automotive group with dealerships in a three-state area.

JOB COST SHEET FOR A SERVICE BUSINESS

Note that the cost per hour of partner, manager, and staff time includes both their compensation per hour and a share of the firm's overhead. Assume that a partner earns $100 per hour and it has been determined that for every $1 spent on direct labor (partner, manager, and staff time) the firm will spend $1.50 for overhead such as secretarial support, fringe benefits, depreciation on computers, rent, and utilities. Because direct labor cost is the single largest cost to the firm and the need for these direct laborers results in all the other costs the firm incurs, the amount of direct labor cost incurred on a job determines how much overhead will be charged to it. For example, the charge of $250 for each hour of partner

FIGURE 5-1   Job Cost Sheet for a Service Business

Devine, O'Clock, and Rooney CPAs
Summary of Engagement Account

Client Name: Superior Automotive, Inc.
Engagement Type: Audit
Engagement Number: 727
Date Contracted: 12/19/20—
Date Completed: 2/22/20—
Supervising Partner: Lueke

Partners' Time:

Period ending	Hours	Rate	Amount
1/31/20—	10	$250*	$2,500
2/28/20—	8	$250*	2,000
Subtotals:	18		$4,500

Managers' Time:

Period ending	Hours	Rate	Amount
1/31/20—	45	$125*	$5,625
2/28/20—	25	$125*	3,125
Subtotals:	70		$8,750

Staff Time:

Period ending	Hours	Rate	Amount
1/31/20—	120	$75*	$ 9,000
2/28/20—	80	$75*	6,000
Subtotals:	200		$15,000

Other:	Period ending 1/31/20—	Period ending 2/28/20—	Total Other
Travel	$2,970	$1,975	$ 4,945
Meals	1,430	795	2,225
Total Other:	$4,400	$2,770	$ 7,170

Total Engagement Costs: $35,420

*Includes direct labor plus overhead based on direct labor cost.

time consists of the $100 per hour wage rate and $150 of overhead. Therefore, the overhead rate is 150% ($150/$100) of direct labor cost.

The 150% overhead rate is a predetermined annual rate computed as follows:

Budgeted Overhead for 20—

Secretarial support	$1,500,000
Fringe benefits	1,250,000
Lease expense	500,000
Depreciation—equipment	750,000
Utilities	300,000
Telephone and fax	150,000
Photocopying	50,000
Total	$4,500,000

Budgeted Direct Labor for 20—

Partners	$ 800,000
Managers	1,200,000
Staff	1,000,000
Total	$3,000,000

$$\text{Budgeted overhead rate} = \frac{\text{Budgeted overhead}}{\text{Budgeted direct labor}}$$

$$= \frac{\$4,500,000}{\$3,000,000}$$

$$= 150\%$$

CHOOSING THE COST ALLOCATION BASE

Note that the firm could have used direct labor hours instead of direct labor dollars to charge overhead to jobs. By choosing direct labor cost, the firm decided that its overhead was more related to the direct labor dollars charged to a job than to the direct labor hours worked on the job. This means that partners who earn higher wages than managers and staff accountants create more overhead costs. They have more secretarial help, nicer offices, and order more computer studies than managers and staff accountants. If all three categories of direct labor consumed the same amount of overhead per hour worked on a job, direct labor hours would be the more appropriate basis to use for charging overhead.

TRACING DIRECT COSTS TO THE JOB

There are costs other than direct labor that can be traced to a job. Note the travel and meal charges appearing in the "Other" category in Figure 5-1.

These are expenses that can be specifically identified with a job and do not have to be allocated to the job using an overhead rate. For example, the accountants can keep a log of the travel and meal expenses incurred in servicing clients with out-of-town locations.

COST PERFORMANCE REPORT

Once the job is completed and all of the costs have been charged to it, management can use the information in a number of ways. It can compare the costs charged to the job with the bid price accepted by the client to determine the profitability of the job. For example, if the bid price were $48,000 for the job in Figure 5-1, the profit would be computed as follows:

Bid price		$48,000
Costs:		
Total labor and overhead	$28,250	
Total other direct costs	7,170	35,420
Profit		$12,580

The profit was approximately 26% ($12,580/$48,000) of the bid price, and labor and overhead costs were approximately 80% ($28,250/$35,420) of the total costs. The firm can use such information in bidding on the Superior Automotive audit next year, in bidding on audits for similar businesses, and in comparing budgeted to actual costs on the audit for purposes of controlling future costs. Figure 5-2 illustrates a **cost performance report** for the Superior Automotive job. It compares the budgeted

FIGURE 5-2   Cost Performance Report

Cost Performance Report

Item	Actual Result	Budget	Variance
Partners' salaries and overhead	$ 4,500	$ 3,900	$ 600 U
Managers' salaries and overhead	8,750	8,500	250 U
Staff accountants' salaries and overhead	15,000	13,500	1,500 U
Travel	4,945	4,695	250 U
Meals	2,225	2,060	165 U
Total	$35,420	$32,655	$2,765 U

U = unfavorable
F = favorable

costs for the job to the actual costs incurred and indicates the **variance,** or difference, for each item.

The actual costs of the job were $2,765 over budget. The partners will want to determine what caused the job to come in over budget. Was it poor budgeting that resulted in an unrealistically low cost estimate, or was it an inefficient use of resources on the job? If the budget had been met on the job, the profit on the job would have been $15,345 instead of $12,580, and the profit as a percentage of bid price would have been 32% instead of 26%.

BUDGETING FOR SERVICE BUSINESSES

LEARNING OBJECTIVE 2
Prepare budgets for
service businesses.

The estimate of revenue and expenses from the Superior Automotive job would be a part of the budgeted figures appearing in the annual budget for Devine, O'Clock, and Rooney CPAs. The **revenue budget,** illustrated in Figure 5-3, is the starting point for the annual budget because the amount of client business must be projected before the amount of labor hours needed and overhead incurred can be estimated.

FIGURE 5-3 Revenue Budget

Schedule 1
Revenue Budget for the Year Ended December 31, 20—

Item	Professional Hours	Billing Rate	Total Revenues
Audit:			
Partners	2,000	$300	$ 600,000
Managers	8,000	175	1,400,000
Staff	30,000	100	3,000,000
Subtotal	40,000		$5,000,000
Consulting:			
Partners	750	$300	$ 225,000
Managers	2,500	175	437,500
Staff	10,000	100	1,000,000
Subtotal	13,250		$1,662,500
Tax:			
Partners	1,500	$300	$ 450,000
Managers	5,000	175	875,000
Staff	20,000	100	2,000,000
Subtotal	26,500		$3,325,000
Total	79,750		$9,987,500

THE REVENUE BUDGET

The revenue budget in Figure 5-3 is developed around the three major services that the firm provides: audit, consulting, and tax. The professional labor hours to be worked in each area are budgeted based on the firm's knowledge of time spent on continuing clients in the past, expected new business, and the expected mix of audit, consulting, and tax work and the mix of professional labor categories required. The **billing rates** reflect the firm's best estimate of what it will charge clients for the various categories of professional labor in the coming year. The total revenue from all client services is budgeted at $9,987,500.

THE LABOR BUDGET

Once the amount of professional labor hours required to meet client services is budgeted, a **professional labor budget**, such as Figure 5-4, may be prepared. The budgeted hours required in each client service area are

FIGURE 5-4   Professional Labor Budget

Schedule 2
Professional Labor Budget for the Year Ended December 31, 20—

Item	Professional Hours	Wage Rate	Total Labor Dollars
Audit:			
Partners	2,000	$100	$ 200,000
Managers	8,000	50	400,000
Staff	30,000	30	900,000
Subtotal	40,000		$1,500,000
Consulting:			
Partners	750	$100	$ 75,000
Managers	2,500	50	125,000
Staff	10,000	30	300,000
Subtotal	13,250		$ 500,000
Tax:			
Partners	1,500	$100	$ 150,000
Managers	5,000	50	250,000
Staff	20,000	30	600,000
Subtotal	26,500		$1,000,000
Total	79,750		$3,000,000

multiplied by the budgeted rate to obtain the wages expense for each category of professional labor.

The wage rates in Figure 5-4 differ from the rates appearing on the job cost sheet in Figure 5-1. This is because the job cost sheet includes labor and overhead in a single combined rate. For budgeting purposes, we want to budget for professional labor hours and overhead separately.

Although we usually think of professional employees such as accountants as earning a salary rather than an hourly wage, it is important to develop an hourly rate for budgeting and billing purposes. For example, the $100 per hour wage rate for a partner was developed as follows:

$$\text{Hourly rate} = \frac{\text{Annual salary}}{\text{Annual billable hours}}$$

$$= \frac{\$200,000}{2,000 \text{ hours}}$$

$$= \$100/\text{hour}$$

It is very important to budget with care the professional labor hours needed. If the firm overestimates the number of hours needed, it will be overstaffed and the additional labor costs will reduce profits. If the firm underestimates the number of labor hours needed, it will be understaffed, and the lack of enough professionals will cause it to pass up jobs that would increase revenues and profits.

THE OVERHEAD BUDGET

The firm must next prepare an overhead budget that includes all of the expense items that cannot be traced directly to jobs, but must be allocated to them by using an overhead rate. The overhead budget for Devine, O'Clock, and Rooney appears in Figure 5-5.

Do not confuse the use of the term "overhead" here with its use in Chapter 4. Chapter 4 illustrated the accounting for manufacturing overhead, which only consists of the indirect expenses incurred in the factory. In this example, *the overhead consists of the indirect expenses incurred to support the activities of a professional services firm.* The totals from the professional labor budget (Figure 5-4) and the overhead budget (Figure 5-5) were used to compute the overhead rate of 150% ($4,500,000/$3,000,000) of direct labor dollars.

THE OTHER EXPENSES BUDGET

The last of the individual budgets for this firm would be the Other Expenses budget, appearing in Figure 5-6, which consists of the direct expenses other than professional labor that can be traced to specific jobs.

FIGURE 5-5   Overhead Budget

Schedule 3
Overhead Budget for the Year Ended December 31, 20—

Secretarial support	$1,500,000
Fringe benefits	1,250,000
Lease expense	500,000
Depreciation—equipment	750,000
Utilities	300,000
Telephone and fax	150,000
Photocopying	50,000
Total	$4,500,000

FIGURE 5-6   Other Expenses

Schedule 4
Other Expenses Budget for the Year Ended December 31, 20—

Travel	$1,105,000
Meals	285,000
Total	$1,390,000

THE BUDGETED INCOME STATEMENT

Once all of the individual budgets have been prepared, the information they contain can be used to prepare the budgeted income statement, appearing in Figure 5-7. Note the differences between this income statement and the income statements illustrated earlier for a manufacturer. There is no line item for cost of goods sold because the firm sells a service rather than a product. All of the operating expenses are charged against income in the period incurred because there are no inventory accounts to which they can be attached. Whereas, in a manufacturing firm, any expense incurred in the factory would be allocated to the jobs produced during the period and remain as part of the asset accounts, Work in Progress and Finished Goods, until the jobs were completed and sold. At that time they would be charged against income as cost of goods sold expense.

The income statement in Figure 5-7 also may be used for planning purposes in advance of the calendar year. For example, operating income

Figure 5-7   Budgeted Income Statement

Budgeted Income Statement
Devine, O'Clock, and Rooney CPAs
For the Year Ended December 31, 20—

Revenues (Schedule 1)		$9,987,500
Operating costs:		
Professional labor (Schedule 2)	$3,000,000	
Overhead support (Schedule 3)	4,500,000	
Other expenses (Schedule 4)	1,390,000	8,890,000
Operating income		$1,097,500

---

is estimated to be 11% of revenue ($1,097,500/$9,987,500). If the partners expect operating income to be at least 15% of revenue, they should return to the individual budgets and determine how to increase operating income by $400,625 through some combination of increasing budgeted revenues and/or decreasing budgeted costs. The income statement may also be used for control purposes during and at the end of the calendar year. By comparing budgeted to actual revenues and expenses, the partners can determine how well the firm is meeting expectations and take corrective action where necessary.

You should now be able to work the following: Questions 1–11; Exercises 5-1 to 5-4; and Problems 5-1 to 5-4.

ACTIVITY-BASED COSTING IN A SERVICE FIRM

LEARNING OBJECTIVE 3
Apply activity-based costing in a service firm.

Recall that Devine, O'Clock, and Rooney CPAs had only two major categories of direct costs—professional labor, and meals and travel—and only a single overhead rate was used for indirect costs. In Chapter 4, we introduced the concept of activity-based costing for a manufacturing firm. In this chapter those same principles will be applied to a service firm. Firms that use **activity-based costing** (ABC) attempt to shift as many costs as possible out of the indirect cost pool that has to be allocated to jobs and into direct cost pools that can be specifically traced to the individual jobs that caused the costs to occur. The remaining costs that cannot be traced to individual jobs are separated into homogeneous cost pools and then allocated to individual jobs by using separate allocation bases for each cost pool. For example, if the amount of payroll department and personnel department costs is related to the number of persons employed, then they may be grouped in a single indirect cost pool and allocated to jobs on the basis of the number of employees.

CONVERTING INDIRECT COSTS TO DIRECT COSTS

Photocopying and fax/telephone charges are two overhead costs incurred by Devine, O'Clock, and Rooney CPAs that would be prime candidates to be traced directly to the individual jobs. A client code number can be entered prior to running each photocopying job to identify the client recipient of the job, and long-distance calls and faxes can be traced to individual clients via telephone bills or a log kept by the business. The increased sophistication and affordability of information processing technology enables such costs, which previously were classified as indirect and were included in the overhead rate, to be traced directly to specific jobs at minimal cost. For example, if telephone, fax, and photocopying charges were traced directly to the Superior Automotive, Inc. job, the Other section of the cost sheet now would appear as follows:

Other	Period Ending 1/31/20—	Period Ending 2/28/20—	Total
Travel	$2,970	$1,975	$4,945
Meals	1,430	795	2,225
Photocopying	280	175	455
Fax/telephone	370	220	590
Total	$5,050	$3,165	$8,215

Note that the billing rates used in Figure 5-1 should be slightly lower because the overhead component of the rate no longer includes fax/telephone and photocopying charges. These items, which had previously been "spread like peanut butter" over all the jobs, can now be specifically identified with the jobs that caused these costs to occur. **Peanut-butter costing** refers to the practice of assigning costs evenly to jobs using an overhead rate, when different jobs consume resources in different proportions.

MULTIPLE INDIRECT COST POOLS

The other main ingredient of activity-based costing is to take overhead costs that were previously in a single indirect cost pool and to separate them into a number of homogeneous cost pools with a separate cost driver, or cost allocation base, for each pool. For example, the single overhead cost pool of $4,500,000 that previously was allocated to jobs on the basis of direct labor dollars could be separated into three cost pools with a different cost driver for each pool, as follows:

Cost Pool	Cost Allocation Base
Secretarial support	Partner labor hours
Fringe benefits	Professional labor dollars
Audit support	Professional labor hours

Using the budgeted numbers from Figure 5-5, and the additional information that 6,000 partner labor-hours and 106,000 professional labor-hours were budgeted, the overhead rates for the individual cost pools would be computed as follows:

Cost Pool	Budgeted Costs	Budgeted Cost Drivers	Budgeted Rate
Secretarial support . . .	$1,500,000	4,250 hours	$353/partner labor hour
Fringe benefits	$1,250,000	$3,000,000	0.4167/professional labor dollar
Audit support	$1,550,000	79,750 hours	$19.44/professional labor hour

Note that the $1,550,000 amount in the audit support cost pool was determined from the overhead budget in Figure 5-5 as follows:

Lease expense	$ 500,000
Depreciation—equipment	750,000
Utilities expense	300,000
	$1,550,000

The budgeted amounts for secretarial support, $1,500,000, and fringe benefits, $1,250,000, were separate line items in the overhead budget. Using an activity-based costing system to charge overhead costs to the Superior Automotive, Inc. job, the amounts allocated, using the above rates, would be as follows:

Cost Pool	Budgeted Rate	Number of Cost Driver Units Consumed	Amount
Secretarial support . . .	$353/partner labor hour	18 hours	$ 6,354
Fringe benefits	0.4167/professional labor dollar	$11,300	4,709
Audit support	$19.44/professional labor hour	288 hours	5,599
Total			$16,662

The cost driver numbers came from Figure 5-1, where 18 partner hours and 288 total professional hours were worked on the Superior

Automotive, Inc. job. The hourly rates were determined from the professional labor budget in Figure 5-4.

The professional labor dollars incurred on the job were computed as follows:

Partners	18 hours @ $100	=	$ 1,800
Managers	70 hours @ $50	=	3,500
Staff	200 hours @ $30	=	6,000
Total			$11,300

JOB COST SHEET—ACTIVITY-BASED COSTING

The revised job cost sheet reflecting all charges to the Superior Automotive, Inc. job, using activity-based costing, appears in Figure 5-8.

ALLOCATIONS USING SIMPLIFIED COSTING VERSUS ACTIVITY-BASED COSTING

LEARNING OBJECTIVE 4
Compare the results of cost allocations using simplified costing versus activity-based costing.

In the examples in Figures 5-1 and 5-8, the total costs charged to the job using a simplified costing system ($35,420) vary less than 10% from the total costs using activity-based costing ($36,177). Such small differences are not always the case, as illustrated by the following example. Assume that a law firm has two categories of professional labor—partner and associate. It also has two types of indirect costs—legal support and secretarial support. Budgeted information for the year is as follows:

	Partner Labor	Associate Labor
Number of attorneys	10	40
Annual billage hours per attorney	2,000	2,000
Annual compensation per attorney	$200,000	$75,000

	Legal Support	Secretarial Support
Annual overhead estimate	$2,000,000	$500,000

The direct cost category includes all professional labor costs, which are traced to jobs on a per hour basis. The indirect cost category includes all overhead costs. These costs are included in a single indirect cost pool—namely, professional support—and allocated to jobs using professional labor hours as the allocation base. Using a simplified costing system with one direct cost category and one indirect cost category, the jobs would be costed as shown in Figure 5-9. Further, consider two clients: Bryant, who requires 50 hours of trial work; and Zimmerman, who requires 75 hours of tax work.

FIGURE 5-8   Job Cost Sheet with Activity-Based Costing

Devine, O'Clock, and Rooney CPAs
Summary of Engagement Account

Client Name: Superior Automotive, Inc.
Engagement Type: Audit
Engagement Number: 727
Date Contacted: 12/19/20—
Date Completed: 2/22/20—
Supervising Partner: Lueke

Partners' Time:

Period Ending	Hours	Rate	Amount
1/31/20—	10	$100	$1,000
2/28/20—	8	$100	800
Subtotals	18		$1,800

Managers' Time:

Period Ending	Hours	Rate	Amount
1/31/20—	45	$50	$2,250
2/28/20—	25	$50	1,250
Subtotals	70		$3,500

Staff Time:

Period Ending	Hours	Rate	Amount
1/31/20—	120	$30	$3,600
2/28/20—	80	$30	2,400
Subtotals	200		$6,000

Overhead:

Cost Pool	Budgeted Rate	Number of Cost Driver Units	Amount
Secretarial support	$353/partner labor hour	18 hours	$ 6,354
Fringe benefits	0.4167/professional labor dollar	$11,300	4,709
Audit support	$19.44/professional labor hour	288 hours	5,599
Subtotals			$16,662

Other Direct Costs:

	Period Ending 1/31/20—	Period Ending 2/28/20—	Total Other
Travel	$ 2,970	$1,975	$ 4,945
Meals	1,430	795	2,225
Photocopying	280	175	455
Fax/telephone	·370	220	590
Subtotals	$ 5,050	$3,165	$ 8,215
Total Engagement Costs			$36,177

FIGURE 5-9   Simplified Job Costing for a Law Firm

	Bryant	**Zimmerman**
Professional labor cost:		
50 hours × $50	$2,500	
75 hours × $50		$3,750
Professional support:		
50 hours × $25	1,250	
75 hours × $25		1,875
Total	$3,750	$5,625

The professional labor rate of $50 per hour was computed as follows:

$$\text{Professional labor rate} = \frac{\text{Annual professional labor dollars}}{\text{Annual professional labor hours}}$$

$$= \frac{(10 \times \$200,000) + (40 \times \$75,000)}{(10 \times 2,000 \text{ hours}) + (40 \times 2,000 \text{ hours})}$$

$$= \frac{\$5,000,000}{100,000 \text{ hours}}$$

$$= \$50 \text{ per hour}$$

The professional support indirect cost rate of $25 per hour was computed as follows:

$$\text{Professional support rate} = \frac{\text{Annual support cost}}{\text{Annual professional labor hours}}$$

$$= \frac{\$2,000,000 + \$500,000}{100,000 \text{ hours}}$$

$$= \frac{\$2,500,000}{100,000 \text{ hours}}$$

$$= \$25 \text{ per hour}$$

Now, let's assume that the firm decides to implement a more sophisticated costing system because it feels that many bids, such as the Zimmerman job, are being rejected as too high. The firm decides to have two direct cost categories—partner labor and associate labor—and two indirect cost categories—legal support and secretarial support. The cost allocation base for legal support is professional labor hours, and for secretarial support it is partner labor hours. Using the data on page 213, the rates for each cost category would be as follows:

Category	Rate	
Partner labor	$200,000/2,000 hours	= $100 per hour
Associate labor	$75,000/2,000 hours	= $37.50 per hour
Legal support	$2,000,000/100,000 hours	= $20 per hour
Secretarial support	$500,000/20,000 hours	= $25 per hour

Further assume that the Bryant job will require 40 partner hours and 10 associate hours, while the Zimmerman job will require 70 associate hours and five partner hours. Using an activity-based costing system with two direct cost categories and two indirect cost categories, the jobs would be costed as shown in Figure 5-10.

The cost of the two jobs under the two costing systems are summarized as follows:

	Bryant	Zimmerman
Cost using simplified system	$ 3,750	$5,625
Cost using activity-based system	6,375	4,750
Difference	$(2,625)	$ 875

Using the simplified costing system, the Bryant job was undercosted by $2,625 (a difference of 70%), and the Zimmerman job was overcosted

FIGURE 5-10   Activity-Based Costing for a Law Firm

	Bryant	Zimmerman
Partner labor cost:		
40 hours × $100	$4,000	
5 hours × $100		$500
Associate labor cost:		
10 hours × $37.50	375	
70 hours × $37.50		2,625
Legal support:		
50 hours × $20	1,000	
75 hours × $20		1,500
Secretarial support:		
40 hours × $25	1,000	
5 hours × $25		125
Total	$6,375	$4,750

by \$875 (almost 16%). This helps explain why the firm lost the bid on the Zimmerman job. Although it won the bid on the Bryant job, it is conceivable that it may have done the job at a loss. If the firm added 50% to the cost estimate in bidding on the Bryant job, the adjusted bid is undercosted by \$750 relative to the activity-based cost of the job. This amount is determined as follows:

Bid price using simplified cost system [\$3,750 + .50(\$3,750)] \$5,625
Activity-based cost of job 6,375

Loss on job . . . . \$ (750)

To summarize, activity-based costing is worthwhile to implement when different jobs use resources in different proportions. In the preceding example, due to the nature of trial work, the Bryant job predominately required partner time, which is more expensive and requires more support services. It should be a **cost/benefit decision** in determining whether to implement a more sophisticated costing system. Namely, does the benefit received from the more refined information exceed the cost of implementing and maintaining the more sophisticated system?

The following hypothetical Real-World Example describes the use of activity-based costing for selling and administrative expenses in a small service business.

REAL-WORLD EXAMPLE

USING ABC TO DETERMINE THE COST OF SERVICING CUSTOMERS

Although most case studies of ABC applications have been in manufacturing, ABC can be used in a small service business to isolate costs for decision making. We conducted an ABC cost study in a small, family-run welding supply business. The purposes of the study were to determine the cost of servicing customers and to identify feasible cost reduction opportunities.

The owner, who operates the business in a very conservative management style typical of small, family-run business owners, has financial goals limited to just staying in the black from year to year. Nonetheless, there is a growing concern that certain parts of the company have been subsidizing other parts and that profits from some customers are subsidizing losses from others.

Applying ABC principles to historical data (fiscal 1994 financials) was used to address these concerns so that the business owner actually could see the problems and evaluate ideas on how to correct them.

The next step was to identify possible causal relationships between the occurrence of costs and activities as well as the underlying drivers of the activities. Company functions were broken down into 15 activities . . . [The following table lists activities, the most appropriate allocation base or cost driver for each activity, and the allocation rate.]

Activities, Bases, and Rates

Activity	Base	Calculation
1. Sales	Time	See . . . Time Study [not shown]
2. Purchasing	Number of invoices	Time spent/Total number of invoices ($6,150/13,780) = $.4463 per invoice
3. Collections	Sales dollars	Time spent/Total sales = ($6,150/$1,400,000) = $.0044 per sales dollar
4. Auditing	Number of invoices	Time spent/Total number of invoices ($6,150/13,780) = $.4463 per invoice
5. Administration	Even distribution	Time spent/Sales employees ($3,075/5) = $615 per sales employee
6. Warehousing	Sales dollars	Time spent/Total sales = ($24,650/$1,400,000) = $.0176 per sales dollar
7. Order pulling	Time	See . . . Time Study [not shown]
8. Billing	Number of invoices	Time spent/Total number of invoices ($24,115/13,780) = $1.75 per invoice
9. AP/GL	Number of invoices	Time spent/Total number of invoices ($18,000/13,780) = $13.06 per invoice
10. Advertising	Sales dollars	Total cost/Total sales = ($3,780/$1,400,000) = $.0027 per sales dollar
11. Telephone	Sales dollars	Total cost/Total sales = ($4,620/$1,400,000) = $.0033 per sales dollar
12. Legal and accounting	Even distribution	Time spent/Sales employees ($2,500/5) = $500 per sales employee
13. Miscellaneous	Sales dollars	Total cost/Total sales = ($1,540/$1,400,000) = $.0011 per sales dollar
14. Insurance	Sales dollars	Total cost/Total sales = ($19,320/$1,400,000) = $.0138 per sales dollar
15. Rent and utilities	Sales dollars	Total cost/Total sales = ($18,200/$1,400,000) = $.013 per sales dollar

After identifying the activities, performing time studies, finding a causal link between activities and costs, computing allocation rates, and putting the data into a contribution margin format, the desired cost numbers were obtained. Even if this analysis were not refined and tried again, it still identified the costs of servicing different customers, which is the main reason the project was implemented.

Michael Krupnicki and Thomas Tyson, "Using ABC to Determine the Cost of Servicing Customers," *Management Accounting* (December 1997), pp. 40–46.

You should now be able to work the following: Questions 12–15; Exercises 5-5 to 5-7; and Problems 5-5 to 5-7.

KEY TERMS

Activity-based costing, p. 210
Billing rates, p. 207
Cost/benefit decision, p. 217
Cost performance report, p. 205

Peanut-butter costing, p. 211
Professional labor budget, p. 207
Revenue budget, p. 206
Service, p. 201

SELF-STUDY PROBLEM

ALLOCATIONS USING SIMPLIFIED COSTING VERSUS ACTIVITY-BASED COSTING

JOHNSON AND MARKS

Johnson and Marks, architects, have been using a simplified costing system in which all professional labor costs are included in a single direct cost category, professional labor; and all overhead costs are included in a single indirect cost category, professional support, and allocated to jobs by using professional labor hours as the allocation base. Consider two clients: Neon's Restaurant, which required 25 hours of design work for a new addition, and Linda Herold, who required plans for a new ultramodern home that took 40 hours to draw. The firm has two partners, who each earn a salary of $150,000 a year, and four associates, who each earn $60,000 per year. Each professional has 1,500 billable hours per year. The professional support is $1,080,000, which consists of $700,000 of design support and $380,000 of staff support. The Neon's job required five hours of partner time and 20 hours of associate time. Herold's job required 30 hours of partner time and 10 hours of associate time.

Required:

1. Prepare job cost sheets for Neon's Restaurant and Linda Herold, using a simplified costing system with one direct and one indirect cost pool.
2. Prepare job cost sheets for the two clients, using an activity-based costing system with two direct cost categories—partner labor and associate labor—and two indirect cost categories, design support and staff support. Use professional labor dollars as the cost allocation base for design support and professional labor hours for staff support.
3. Determine the amount by which each job was under- or overcosted, using the simplified costing system.

SOLUTION TO SELF-STUDY PROBLEM

Suggestions:

1. When computing the overhead rate using the simplified costing system, be sure to use professional labor dollars as the cost allocation base.
2. When computing the job cost using activity-based costing, be sure to distinguish between partner labor hours and associate labor hours worked on each job.

3. When computing the job cost using activity-based costing, be sure to use professional labor dollars as the cost allocation base for design support and professional labor hours as the cost allocation base for staff support.

Preparing the job cost sheets using a simplified costing system:

1. You first must compute the average hourly wage rate for professional labor:

$$\text{Average professional wage rate} = \frac{\text{Professional salaries}}{\text{Billable hours}}$$

$$= \frac{(2 \times \$150,000) + (4 \times \$60,000)}{6 \times 1,500 \text{ hours}}$$

$$= \frac{\$540,000}{9,000 \text{ Hours}}$$

$$= \$60 \text{ per hour}$$

Next you must compute the indirect cost rate:

$$\text{Indirect cost rate} = \frac{\text{Total indirect costs}}{\text{Professional labor hours}}$$

$$= \frac{\$1,080,000}{9,000 \text{ hours}}$$

$$= \$120 \text{ per hour}$$

Now you may prepare the cost sheets:

	Neon's Restaurant	Linda Herold
Professional labor cost:		
25 hours × $60	$1,500	
40 hours × $60		$2,400
Professional support:		
25 hours × $120	3,000	
40 hours × $120		4,800
Total	$4,500	$7,200

Preparing the job cost sheet using an activity-based costing system:

2. You must first compute the average hourly wage rate for each classification of professional labor:

$$\text{Partner wage rate} = \frac{\text{Partner salaries}}{\text{Partner billable hours}}$$

$$= \frac{\$300,000}{3,000 \text{ hours}}$$

$$= \$100 \text{ per hour}$$

$$\text{Associate wage rate} = \frac{\text{Associate salaries}}{\text{Associate billable hours}}$$

$$= \frac{4 \times \$60,000}{4 \times 1,500 \text{ hours}}$$

$$= \$40 \text{ per hour}$$

Next you must compute the indirect cost rates for design support and for staff support:

$$\text{Design support} = \frac{\text{Budgeted design costs}}{\text{Budgeted professional labor dollars}}$$

$$= \frac{\$700,000}{\$540,000}$$

$$= 1.30 \text{ per professional labor dollar}$$

$$\text{Staff support} = \frac{\text{Budgeted staff costs}}{\text{Budgeted professional labor hours}}$$

$$= \frac{\$380,000}{9,000 \text{ hours}}$$

$$= \$42.22 \text{ per professional labor hour}$$

Now you may prepare the cost sheets:

	Neon's Restaurant	Linda Herold
Partner labor cost:		
5 hours × $100	$500	
30 hours × $100		$3,000
Associate labor cost:		
20 hours × $40	800	
10 hours × $40		400
Design support:		
1.30 × $1,300	1,690	
1.30 × $3,400		4,420
Staff support:		
$42.22 × 25	1,056	
$42.22 × 40		1,689
Total	$4,046	$9,509

Determining the amount by which each job was under- or overcosted using a simplified costing system:

3.

	Neon's Restaurant	Linda Herold
Cost using simplified system	$4,500	$7,200
Cost using activity-based system	4,046	9,509
Difference	$454	($2,309)

The simplified costing system overcosted Neon's job by $454 and undercosted Herold's job by $2,309.

(Note: Problem 5-6 is similar to this problem.)

QUESTIONS

1. Give at least five examples of service businesses.
2. Name some distinguishing features of service businesses.
3. Why are service businesses important to the U.S. economy?
4. What type of costing system do most service businesses use and why do they use it?
5. What factors would you consider in deciding whether to use direct labor dollars or direct labor hours in charging overhead to jobs in a service firm?
6. Distinguish between a direct cost and an indirect cost when the cost object is the job.
7. What are the elements of a cost performance report?
8. Which of the various budgets is the starting point for preparing an annual budget?

9. Why is it important for professional labor hours to be budgeted with extreme care?
10. What is the difference between the accounting treatment of overhead for a service business and for a manufacturer?
11. Explain how a budgeted income statement for a service business may be used for both planning and control purposes.
12. What are the two main things that an activity-based costing system attempts to accomplish relative to direct and indirect costs?
13. Explain the concept of "peanut-butter costing."
14. When is it generally worthwhile to implement an activity-based costing system?
15. Explain the concept of a "cost/benefit decision" and how it relates to job costing systems.

EXERCISES

E5-1
Computing budgeted overhead rates
Objective 2

Clark and Jones have a professional service firm that has the following budgeted costs for the current year:

Associates' salaries	$250,000
Depreciation—equipment	25,000
Fringe benefits	75,000
Lease expense	110,000
Partners' salaries	200,000
Telephone and fax	15,000

Compute the budgeted overhead rate for the coming year, using direct labor dollars as the overhead allocation base.

E5-2
Computing profit or loss on a bid
Objective 2

Allen and Smith, electricians, successfully bid $24,000 for the electrical work on a new luxury home. Total direct labor cost on the job was $9,500, other direct costs were $2,500, and overhead is charged to jobs at 150% of direct labor cost.

1. Compute the profit or loss on the job in (a) dollars and (b) as a percentage of the bid price.
2. Express labor and overhead as a percentage of total costs.

E5-3
Preparing a revenue budget
Objective 2

Seymour and Klein, CPAs, budgeted for the following professional labor hours for the coming year: partners, 1,500; managers, 5,000; and staff, 20,000. Budgeted billing rates are: partners, $250 per hour; managers, $120 per hour, and staff accountants, $80 per hour.

Prepare a revenue budget for the year ending December 31, 20—.

E5-4
Preparing a budgeted income statement
Objective 2

Bell and Green, physicians, budgeted for the following revenue and expenses for the month of September:

Depreciation—equipment	$1,850
Fringe benefits	3,300
Lease expense	2,500
Nursing wages	4,500
Physicians' salaries	24,000
Patient revenue	48,500
Secretarial support	2,200
Utilities	650

Prepare a budgeted income statement for the month ending September 30, 20—.

E5-5
Computing activity-based costing rates
Objective 3

The partners of Bailey and Stevens, Attorneys-at-Law, decide to implement an activity-based costing system for their firm. They identify the following three cost pools and budgeted amounts for each for the coming year: fringe benefits, $350,000; paralegal support, $500,000; and research support, $650,000. It is determined that the best cost driver for fringe benefits is professional labor dollars ($400,000); for paralegal support it is partner labor hours (4,000); and for research support it is professional labor hours (50,000).

Compute the budgeted overhead rates for each of the three cost pools.

E5-6
Job cost for a client
Objective 3

A client, Steven Albright, requires 5 partner labor hours and 20 professional associate hours from Bailey and Stevens, the law firm in E5-5. Partners are paid $125 per hour and associates make $60 per hour.

Compute the job cost of servicing Steven Albright.

E5-7
Comparisons of a simplified costing system with an activity-based system
Objective 4

Prior to instituting an activity-based costing system, Bailey and Stevens, the attorneys in E5-5 and E5-6, utilized a simplified costing system with one direct cost category, professional labor, and one indirect cost category, professional support. The average wage rate for professional labor was $75 per hour, and the overhead rate for professional support was $27.78 per professional labor hour.

Compute the job cost for Steven Albright, the client in E5-6, using the simplified costing system, and determine the difference between it and the job cost using activity-based costing in E5-6.

PROBLEMS

P5-1
Job cost sheet for a service business
Objective 2

Braun and Crable, Attorneys-at-Law, provided legal representation to Torrey Toys, Inc. in a product liability suit. Twenty partner hours and 65 associate hours were worked in defending the company. The cost of each partner hour is $325, which includes partner wages plus overhead based on direct labor cost. The cost of each associate hour is $145, which also includes both wages and overhead. Other costs that can be directly identified with the job are travel ($2,800) and telephone/fax charges ($1,740). The date Torrey contracted with Braun and Crable was May 8 and the defense was successfully completed on December 21. The engagement number is 525.

Required:

Prepare a job order cost sheet, in good form, for Torrey Toys, Inc.

P5-2
Cost performance report for a service business
Objective 2

The budget for the Torrey Toys, Inc. job in P5-1 consisted of the following amounts:

Partners' salary and overhead	$6,300
Associates' salary and overhead	9,175
Travel	3,150
Telephone/fax	1,475

The successful bid price of the job was $24,900.

Required:

1. Prepare a cost performance report.
2. Compute the budgeted profit and the actual profit on the job.

P5-3
Preparing a revenue budget and a labor budget for a service business
Objective 2

Cagle and Johnson, partners in a financial planning firm, budgeted the following professional labor hours for the year ended December 31, 20—:

Partners	4,000
Associates	14,000
Staff	22,000

Partners have a billing rate of $225 per hour and actually earn $110 per hour. Associates bill out at $140 per hour and earn $85 per hour. Staff have a billing rate of $95 per hour and earn $55 per hour.

Required:

1. Prepare a revenue budget.
2. Prepare a professional labor budget.

P5-4
Preparing an
overhead budget, an
other expenses
budget, and a
budgeted income
statement
Objective 2

Cagle and Johnson, the financial planners in P5-3, budgeted overhead and other expenses as follows for the year ended December 31, 20—:

Overhead:

Depreciation—equipment	$ 60,000
Depreciating—building	135,000
Fringe benefits	385,000
Photocopying	95,000
Secretarial support	465,000
Telephone/fax	115,000
Utilities	193,000

Other expenses:

Travel	$123,000
Meals	37,000

Required:

1. Prepare an overhead budget.
2. Prepare an other expenses budget.
3. Prepare a budgeted income statement.

P5-5
Computing activity-
based costing rates
Objective 3

The partners of Hastings and Stevens, a security services firm, decide to implement an activity-based costing system. They identify the following three cost pools and budgeted amounts for each for the coming year: fringe benefits, $200,000; technology support, $100,000; and litigation support, $50,000. It is determined that the best cost driver for fringe benefits is professional labor dollars ($200,000); for technology support it is partner labor hours (2,000); and for research support it is professional labor hours (25,000).

Required:

Compute the budgeted overhead rate for each of the three cost pools.

P5-6
Allocations using
simplified costing
versus activity-based
costing. **Similar to
self-study problem.**
Objective 4

Glaseo and Webb, architects, have been using a simplified costing system in which all professional labor costs are included in a single direct cost category, professional labor; and all overhead costs are included in a single indirect cost pool, professional support, and allocated to jobs using professional labor hours as the allocation base. Consider two clients: Rhino Products, which required 50 hours of design work for a new addition, and Sylvia Martin, who required plans for a new home that took 20 hours to draw. The firm has two partners who each earn a salary of $150,000 a year and four associates who each earn $60,000 per year. Each professional has 1,500 billable hours per year. The professional support is $590,000, which consists of $350,000 of design support and $240,000 of staff support. Rhino's job required 10 hours of partner time and 40 hours of associate time. Martin's job required 15 hours of partner time and 5 hours of associate time.

Required:

1. Prepare job cost sheets for Rhino Products and Sylvia Martin, using a simplified costing system with one direct and one indirect cost pool.
2. Prepare job cost sheets for the two clients, using an activity-based costing system with two direct cost categories, partner labor and associate labor, and two indirect cost categories, design support and staff support. Use professional labor dollars as the cost allocation base for design support and professional labor hours for staff support.

P5-7
Comparing the results
of cost allocations,
using simplified
costing versus
activity-based costing
Objective 4

Required:

Referring to P5-6, compare the results of the cost allocations to the Rhino Products and Sylvia Martin jobs under the simplified costing system and the activity-based costing system. Label each difference as undercosted or overcosted relative to the simplified costing system.

6

Process Cost Accounting— General Procedures

LEARNING OBJECTIVES

After studying this chapter, you should be able to:

1. Recognize the differences between job order and process cost accounting systems.
2. Compute unit costs in a process cost system.
3. Assign costs to inventories, using equivalent units of production with the average cost method.
4. Prepare a cost of production summary and journal entries for one department with no beginning inventory.
5. Prepare a cost of production summary and journal entries for one department with beginning inventory.
6. Prepare a cost of production summary and journal entries for multiple departments with no beginning inventory.
7. Prepare a cost of production summary and journal entries for multiple departments with beginning inventory.
8. Prepare a cost of production summary with a change in the prior department's unit transfer cost.

Cost accounting provides management with accurate information about the cost of manufacturing a product. The type of cost accounting system a business uses depends on the nature of its manufacturing operations. The preceding chapters focused on the job order cost system. Chapters 6 and 7 focus on procedures applicable in a process cost system.

COMPARISON OF BASIC COST SYSTEMS

LEARNING OBJECTIVE 1
Recognize the differences between job order and process cost accounting systems.

As explained in Chapter 1, a **job order cost system** is appropriate when products are manufactured or services are provided on a special order basis. A **process cost system** is used when goods of a similar or homogeneous nature are manufactured or services are provided in a continuous operation.

The focal point of a job order cost system is the *job*, even in a departmentalized factory. The costs of materials, labor, and overhead are accumulated for each job and divided by the number of units produced to determine the unit cost for the job. The primary objective of the system is to determine the cost of producing each completed job during the accounting period and the cost that has been incurred on each unfinished job. Management uses this information for inventory valuation and also for planning, control, and measuring performance.

The focus of a process cost system is the **cost center** or unit within the factory to which costs are practically and equitably assigned. It is usually a department, but it could be a process or an operation. Costs accumulated by a cost center are divided by the number of units produced to compute the cost per unit. The primary objectives, like that of the job order cost system, are to compute the unit cost of the products manufactured and the cost to be assigned to the units in process at the end of the period.

Many of the procedures utilized for job order cost accounting also apply to process cost accounting. The main difference in the two methods is the manner in which costs are accumulated.

MATERIALS AND LABOR COSTS

Under the job order cost system, the costs of materials and labor, as determined from the summaries of materials requisitions and time tickets, are charged to specific jobs or orders. Under the process cost system, the costs of materials and labor are charged directly to the departments where they are incurred. However, the indirect materials and indirect labor costs that cannot be directly associated with a particular department are charged to Factory Overhead, such as custodial supplies for the factory and the salary of a supervisor responsible for several departments.

A process system requires less clerical effort than a job order cost system because costs are charged to a few departments rather than to many jobs. For example, in a process cost system, detailed time tickets might be eliminated completely. In a job order cost system, if a typical factory employee works on several different jobs, the total hours worked are tracked by job. In a process cost system, the worker's time is generally assigned to the department where the work occurred.

Other than these limited differences, the procedures for acquiring, controlling, accounting for, and paying for materials and labor are similar in both systems. At the end of each month, the materials requisitions summary provides the data for the journal entry debiting Work in Process and Factory Overhead and crediting Materials. Similarly, the labor cost summary provides the data for the journal entry debiting Work in Process and Factory Overhead and crediting Payroll.

FACTORY OVERHEAD COSTS

In a process cost system, overhead costs are accumulated from the various journals in the same manner as in a job order cost system. The actual costs for the period are collected in a general ledger control account to which postings are made from the appropriate journals. The control account is supported by a subsidiary ledger, which consists of factory overhead analysis sheets that show the detailed allocation of costs to the departments. At the end of the month, based on the data reflected in the analysis sheets, the total actual factory overhead is distributed to the departmentalized overhead accounts.

Service Departments. As with job order cost accounting, the applicable factory overhead is charged to the service departments. Service department expenses are distributed to the production departments. A distribution work sheet shows the allocation of each service department's expenses to other service departments and to the production departments. A journal entry records the distribution of the service departments' expenses to the production departments and thus closes the service departments' accounts for factory overhead. Service department costs will not be considered in the following discussion because the fundamentals were developed in Chapter 4.

Application of Factory Overhead. In the job order cost system, overhead is applied to the jobs through predetermined rates. The use of predetermined rates is also common in a process cost system, but overhead is applied to departments rather than jobs. As in the job order cost system, the amount of overhead applied is calculated by multiplying the

"BATCH OF ONE" PROCESSING

Process cost accounting is suitable in manufacturing situations where all units of the final product are substantially identical. This type of operation produces a continuous output of homogeneous products. Industries of this type include those manufacturing automobiles, tires, chemicals, canned goods, lumber, paper, candy, foodstuffs, flour, glass, soap, toothpaste, and many other products.

Customers today demand variety in products. Businesses are faced with the challenge of producing products quickly and effectively while meeting this demand. An article in *Management Accounting* explains how industries that have produced products in large batches over long production runs are changing some of their production processes:

A combination of programmable automation and workers empowered to make decisions—"smart" technologies and "smart" people—provides an opportunity to break out of the dilemma of traditional mass production. A new "simple idea" is emerging and displacing the traditional model of economies of scale. It is the "batch of one" or "mass customization"—the ability to produce a customized batch, as small as a lot of one, at mass production prices.

This idea may seem to be an oxymoron. How could small to medium batch runs be more economical than a continuous process?

The "economics of flexibility" are achieved through short cycle times, flexible automation, and the ability to do quick changeovers with little or no production stoppage or cost penalty. People are as important to the production as technology. Pushing down decision making to the line and empowering teams of employees allows the variety to be handled without cumbersome approvals and delays.

The result is variety at low cost. For example, different car models come down the line. The first may be a station wagon bound for Australia. The equipment reads a bar code and then locks into a certain pattern of steps. The next vehicle may be a sports car bound for North America. The bar code is read once again, and the software-driven equipment executes a different pattern. Changeover is instantaneous and virtually costless.

Gerald H. B. Ross, "Revolution in Management Control," *Management Accounting* (November 1990), pp. 23–27.

predetermined rate by the selected base. The base may be direct labor cost, direct labor hours, machine hours, or any other method that will equitably distribute overhead to the departments in proportion to the benefit received by that department. Under- or overapplied overhead is treated in the same manner as discussed in Chapter 4.

PRODUCT COST IN A PROCESS COST SYSTEM

LEARNING OBJECTIVE 2
Compute unit costs in a process cost system.

A basic principle established in comparing the two cost systems is that in a process cost system all costs of manufacturing are charged to production departments, either directly or indirectly. The unit cost in each department is calculated by dividing the total cost charged to the department by the number of units produced during the period. The total cost of each item finished equals the combined unit costs of all departments used in the manufacture of the product.

NONDEPARTMENTALIZED FACTORY

When the factory is operated as a single department producing a single product in a continuous output, the process cost system is relatively simple. The costs of operating the factory are summarized at the end of each accounting period. Then the total costs incurred are divided by the quantity of units produced to calculate the cost of each unit manufactured during the period.

The following cost of production summary illustrates this procedure:

Materials	$ 50,000
Labor	75,000
Factory overhead	35,000
Total cost of production	$160,000
Unit output for period	40,000 units
Unit cost for period	$4.00*

*$160,000 ÷ 40,000 units = $4

DEPARTMENTALIZED FACTORY

Generally, a company has several production and service departments. Products accumulate costs as they pass through each successive production department. Departments record costs according to the following procedure: (1) the costs of the service departments are allocated to the production departments; (2) the costs added by prior departments are carried over to successive departments; and (3) the costs of materials and labor directly identifiable with a department, as well as applied overhead, are charged to the department. The unit cost within a department is calculated by dividing the total costs by the number of units produced during the period.

WORK IN PROCESS INVENTORIES

LEARNING OBJECTIVE 3
Assign costs to
inventories, using
equivalent units of
production with the
average cost method.

If there is no work in process at the end of an accounting period, calculating the unit cost under the process cost system is a simple procedure: merely divide the total cost incurred for the period by the number of units produced. However, each department will usually have work in process at the end of an accounting period. The calculation of unfinished work in process presents one of the most important and difficult problems in process cost accounting.

Normally, a factory will have units in varying stages of completion:

1.   Units started and finished during the current period

2.   Units started in a prior period and completed during the current period

3.   Units started during the current period but not finished

Because materials, labor, and overhead may have been applied to each of the unfinished items, such charges cannot be ignored in computing the cost of all units. Therefore, consideration must be given to not only the number of items finished during the period but also the units in process at the beginning and at the end of the period. The primary problem is allocating total cost between (1) units finished during the period and (2) units still in process at the end of the period.

Two procedures are commonly used for assigning costs to the inventories: the **average cost method** and the **first-in, first-out (FIFO) method**. The average cost method is discussed and illustrated in the remainder of this chapter. Chapter 7 covers the first-in, first-out method.

Under the average cost method, the cost of the work in process at the beginning of the period is added to the production costs incurred in the current period. Average unit cost for the period is then calculated by dividing the total costs (beginning inventory plus current costs) by the total equivalent production. **Equivalent production** represents the number of units that could have been completed during a period, using the production costs incurred during the period. For example, if 1,000 units were 50% completed, they are considered in terms of "equivalents" as 500 units, 100% completed. Therefore, calculating equivalent production requires that the ending work in process be restated in terms of completed units. To illustrate, assume that the production costs of a department during a given period are as follows:

Materials	$12,000
Labor	18,000
Factory overhead	6,000
Total cost of production	$36,000

If 18,000 units are produced during the period and no work in process exists, either at the beginning or end of the period, the unit cost of production is easily calculated to be $2 ($36,000 ÷ 18,000), and $36,000 would be transferred to Finished Goods in the general ledger.

Assume, instead, that the production report for the period shows no beginning work in process, 17,000 units are completed during the period, and the ending inventory consists of 2,000 units. The problem is to allocate the production cost for the period, $36,000, between the goods completed and the goods still in process. What portion of the total production cost was incurred during the month by the remaining 2,000 units in process?

If the 2,000 units are almost finished, more cost should be assigned to these unfinished units than would have been incurred if they had just been started in process. To make an accurate measurement, the stage of completion of the units still in process must be considered. **Stage of completion** represents the fraction or percentage of materials, labor, and overhead costs of a completed unit that has been applied to goods that have not been completed. The department manager estimates the stage of completion. The possibility of error is minimized because the manager usually has the skills and the familiarity with the work to make reliable estimates.

At the end of the accounting period, the department manager submits a **production report** showing the following:

1. Number of units in the beginning work in process
2. Number of units completed
3. Number of units in the ending work in process and their estimated stage of completion

Assume that 2,000 units in process are one-half completed. If materials, labor, and overhead are applied evenly throughout the process, one-half of the total cost for completing 2,000 units can be applied to these units. Expressed in another way, the cost to bring these 2,000 units to the halfway point of completion is equivalent to the cost of fully completing 1,000 units. Therefore, in terms of equivalent production, 2,000 units one-half completed equal 1,000 units fully completed. The unit cost is calculated as follows:

Units finished during the period	17,000
Equivalent units of work in process at the end of the period (2,000 units one-half completed)	1,000
Equivalent production for the period	18,000 units

$36,000 ÷ 18,000 = $2 unit cost for the month.

The inventory cost can now be calculated as follows:

Transferred to finished goods (17,000 units at $2)	$34,000
Work in process (2,000 units × 1/2 × $2)	2,000
Total production costs accounted for	$36,000

COST OF PRODUCTION SUMMARY—ONE DEPARTMENT, NO BEGINNING INVENTORY

LEARNING OBJECTIVE 4
Prepare a cost of production summary and journal entries for one department with no beginning inventory.

In a process cost system, the reporting of production and related costs in each department involves the following:

1. Accumulating costs for which the department is accountable
2. Calculating equivalent production for the period
3. Computing the unit cost for the period
4. Summarizing the disposition of the production costs

These data are reported on a **cost of production summary**, which presents the necessary information for inventory valuation and serves as a source for summary journal entries. To illustrate, assume that Kidco manufactures "teeny babies" on a continuous basis for inventory stock. The small factory, which had no inventory on January 1, operates as a single department and places finished goods in stock to be withdrawn as orders are received. At the end of January, the first month of operation for the company, the factory supervisor submits the January **production report**, Figure 6-1. The estimate of the stage of completion indi-

FIGURE 6-1   Production Report, January 31

PRODUCTION REPORT

For Month Ending __January 31, 20--__

In process, beginning of month _____none_____
Finished during the month _____4,900 units_____
In process, end of month _____200 units_____
Estimated stage of completion of work in process, end of month _1/2_

Remarks

__R.L.B.__
Supervisor

cates that the units in process at the end of the month were, on the average, about one-half completed.

After receiving the production report, the accountant begins the following cost of production summary by collecting the period's production costs from summaries of materials requisitions, payroll, and factory overhead analysis sheets. The units in process are then converted to equivalent units. The estimate that the 200 units in process are one-half completed means that one-half the total cost of the materials, labor, and factory overhead needed to produce 200 units has been incurred. The equivalent of 200 units in process, one-half completed, is 100 units. Therefore, the costs incurred in partially completing 200 units is considered to be equivalent to the total cost of producing 100 units. The cost of producing 4,900 fully completed units and 200 units one-half completed during the month is equivalent to producing 5,000 fully completed units.

Kidco
Cost of Production Summary
For the Month Ended January 31, 20—

Cost of production for month:		
Materials		$ 5,000
Labor		3,000
Factory overhead		2,000
Total costs to be accounted for		$10,000
Unit output for month:		
Finished during month		4,900
Equivalent units of work in process, end		
of month (200 units, one-half completed)		100
Total equivalent production		5,000
Unit cost for month:		
Materials ($5,000 ÷ 5,000 units)		$1.00
Labor ($3,000 ÷ 5,000 units)		0.60
Factory overhead ($2,000 ÷ 5,000 units)		0.40
Total		$2.00
Inventory costs:		
Cost of goods finished during month (4,900 × $2)		$ 9,800
Cost of work in process, end of month:		
Materials (200 × 1/2 × $1)	$100	
Labor (200 × 1/2 × $0.60)	60	
Factory overhead (200 × 1/2 × $0.40)	40	200
Total production costs accounted for		$10,000

At the end of the month, the following journal entries record the factory operations for January:

Jan. 31	Work in Process	5,000	
	Materials		5,000
	Work in Process	3,000	
	Payroll		3,000
Jan. 31	Factory Overhead	2,000	
	Various accounts (Accumulated Depreciation, Prepaid Insurance, Accrued Taxes, Accounts Payable)		2,000
	Work in Process	2,000	
	Factory Overhead		2,000

After preparing the cost of production summary, the accountant can make the following entry:

Jan. 31	Finished Goods	9,800	
	Work in Process		9,800

After posting these entries, the work in process account has a debit balance of $200, representing the valuation of the work in process on January 31, shown as follows:

Work in Process			
Jan. 31	5,000	Jan. 31	9,800
	3,000		
	2,000		
	10,000		
200			

The January statement of the cost of goods manufactured can now be prepared as follows:

Kidco
Statement of Cost of Goods Manufactured
For the Month Ended January 31, 20—

Materials	$ 5,000
Labor	3,000
Factory overhead	2,000
Total	$10,000
Less work in process inventory, January 31	200
Cost of goods manufactured during the month	$ 9,800

COST OF PRODUCTION SUMMARY—ONE DEPARTMENT, BEGINNING INVENTORY

LEARNING OBJECTIVE 5
Prepare a cost of production summary and journal entries for one department with beginning inventory.

At the end of February, the second month of operations for Kidco, the factory supervisor submits the February production report shown in Figure 6-2.

The cost of production summary for February is prepared as follows:

Kidco
Cost of Production Summary
For the Month Ended February 28, 20—

Cost of work in process, beginning of month:*		
Materials	$ 100	
Labor	60	
Factory overhead	40	$ 200
Cost of production for month:		
Materials	$7,000	
Labor	4,200	
Factory overhead	2,800	14,000
Total costs to be accounted for		**$14,200**
Unit output for month:		
Finished during month		6,900
Equivalent units of work in process, end of month		
(600 units, one-third completed)		200
Total equivalent production		7,100
Unit cost for month:		
Materials [($100 + $7,000) ÷ 7,100]		$1.00
Labor [($60 + $4,200) ÷ 7,100]		0.60
Factory overhead [($40 + $2,800) ÷ 7,100]		0.40
Total		$2.00
Inventory costs:		
Cost of goods finished during month (6,900 × $2) .		$13,800
Cost of work in process, end of month:		
Materials (600 × 1/3 × $1)	$ 200	
Labor (600 × 1/3 × $0.60)	120	
Factory overhead (600 × 1/3 × $0.40)	80	400
Total production costs accounted for		**$14,200**

The beginning inventory in February was the ending work in process inventory for the month of January.

FIGURE 6-2   Production Report, February 28

PRODUCTION REPORT	
For Month Ending _February 28, 20--_	
In process, beginning of month _____ 200 units	
Finished during the month _____ 6,900 units	
In process, end of month _____ 600 units	
Estimated stage of completion of work in process, end of month _1/3_	

All costs incurred or assigned must be accounted for. Therefore, the cost of the ending work in process in January, which is the beginning inventory in February, is added to the total costs incurred during the month of February. The calculation of unit output for the month includes the units finished during the month and the equivalent units in process at the end of the current month. The fact that one-half of the work had been completed on 200 units in the prior month does not have to be considered in this calculation because the cost of that work is added to the current month's costs for the purpose of calculating unit costs. This procedure is the identifying characteristic of the average costing method.

From the data developed on the cost of production summary, the following entry can now be made:

```
Feb. 28  Finished Goods . . . . . . . . . . . . . . . .     13,800
              Work in Process . . . . . . . . . . . . .               13,800
```

After posting this entry and the entries for the month's production costs, the work in process account has a debit balance of $400, as shown:

Work in Process

Jan. 31	5,000	Jan. 31	9,800
	3,000		
	2,000		
	10,000		
200			
Feb. 28	7,000	Feb. 28	13,800
	4,200		
	2,800		
	24,000		23,600
400			

The following statement of the cost of goods manufactured can now be prepared:

Kidco
Statement of Cost of Goods Manufactured
For the Month Ended February 28, 20—

Materials	$ 7,000
Labor	4,200
Factory overhead	2,800
Total	$14,000
Add work in process inventory, February 1	200
Total	$14,200
Less work in process inventory, February 28	400
Cost of goods manufactured during the month	$13,800

You should now be able to work the following: Questions 1–11; Exercises 6-1 to 6-6; and Problems 6-1 and 6-2.

COST OF PRODUCTION SUMMARY—MULTIPLE DEPARTMENTS, NO BEGINNING INVENTORY

LEARNING OBJECTIVE 6
Prepare a cost of production summary and journal entries for multiple departments with no beginning inventory.

The business of Kidco continued to grow until management decided to departmentalize the factory and reorganize the cost records. Accordingly, on January 1 of the following year, the factory was divided into three departments as follows:

Dept. A—Mixing
Dept. B—Molding
Dept. C—Finishing

Separate control accounts are maintained in the general ledger to record the costs of operating each department. Departmental expense analysis sheets are used to record the manufacturing expenses incurred. Production reports are prepared for each department for January. There are no beginning inventories of work in process in any department. The production report for Dept. A is shown in Figure 6-3.

After receiving the production report from the manager of Department A, the accountant prepares the following cost of production summary. Journal entries are then made from the cost of production summary to record the operations of the department and to transfer costs.

FIGURE 6-3   Production Report, Dept. A—Mixing

PRODUCTION REPORT

For Month Ending _January 31, 20--_

Dept. _A—Mixing_

In process, beginning of period	none
Stage of completion	
Placed in process during period	3,700 units
Received from dept. _____ during period	
Transferred to dept. ___B___ during period	2,700 units
Transferred to stockroom during period	none
In process, end of period	1,000 units
Stage of completion	1/2

Kidco
Cost of Production Summary—Department A
For the Month Ended January 31, 20—

Cost of production for month:		
Materials		$16,000
Labor		8,640
Factory overhead		7,360
Total costs to be accounted for		$32,000
Unit output for month:		
Finished and transferred to Dept. B during month		2,700
Equivalent units of work in process, end of month		
(1,000 units, one-half completed)		500
Total equivalent production		3,200
Unit cost for month:		
Materials ($16,000 ÷ 3,200 units)		$ 5.00
Labor ($8,640 ÷ 3,200 units)		2.70
Factory overhead ($7,360 ÷ 3,200 units)		2.30
Total		$10.00
Inventory costs:		
Cost of goods finished and transferred to Dept. B during		
month (2,700 × $10.00)		$27,000
Cost of work in process, end of month:		
Materials (1,000 × 1/2 × $5.00)	$2,500	
Labor (1,000 × 1/2 × $2.70)	1,350	
Factory overhead (1,000 × 1/2 × $2.30)	1,150	5,000
Total production costs accounted for		$32,000

Note that the costs accumulated in the department are transferred to the next department along with the units completed during the period. Thus, costs follow the flow of goods through the process.

After posting the usual end-of-month entries, the work in process account for Dept. A has a debit balance of $5,000, as shown below. The balance represents the cost of the partially completed ending inventory.

Work in Process—Dept. A			
Jan. 31	16,000	Jan. 31	27,000
	8,640		
	7,360		
5,000	32,000		

The only difference in procedure between this example and the one for a single-department factory (see page 236) is that the goods completed in Dept. A are transferred to Dept. B for further processing rather than being transferred to the stockroom as finished goods.

The production report for Dept. B is shown in Figure 6-4. Note that as the goods flow through the manufacturing process, the units transferred and their related costs are treated as completed products in Dept. A, but the units transferred to Dept. B are considered by Dept. B as raw materials that will be added at the beginning of Dept. B's processing operation. The transferred cost of the units includes the costs of materials, labor, and factory overhead incurred in Dept. A. However, the individual cost elements are combined and transferred in total to Dept. B.

In reviewing the cost of production summary for Dept. B on the next two pages, note that the calculation of unit cost for the month in Dept. B

FIGURE 6-4   Production Report, Dept. B—Molding

PRODUCTION REPORT

For Month Ending _January 31, 20--_

Dept. _B—Molding_

In process, beginning of period	_none_
Stage of completion	
Placed in process during period	_none_
Received from dept. __A__ during period	_2,700 units_
Transferred to dept. __C__ during period	_2,200 units_
Transferred to stockroom during period	_none_
In process, end of period	_500 units_
Stage of completion	_2/5_

takes into consideration only those costs incurred for materials, labor, and factory overhead during the month and the equivalent units produced in the department. The **transferred-in costs** and **units from the prior department** are not included in the computation. However, in determining the cost transferred to Dept. C, the prior department costs, along with Dept. B's cost of work in process, must be considered. Also, in calculating the ending work in process valuation, the full cost of $10 per unit from Dept. A is attached to the 500 units still in process in Dept. B, because the transferred-in units have been fully completed by Dept. A, while only a fraction of the cost of additional work performed by Dept. B, based on the stage of completion, is considered.

After posting the end-of-month entries, the work in process account for Dept. B has a debit balance of $5,500.

Work in Process—Dept. B		
Jan. 31	1,200	Jan. 31
	3,000	
	1,800	
	27,000	
5,500	33,000	

Jan. 31 .... 27,500 (credit side)

Kidco
Cost of Production Summary—Department B
For the Month Ended January 31, 20—

Cost of goods received from Dept. A during month		
(2,700 units × $10.00)		$27,000
Cost of production for month—Dept. B:		
Materials	$ 1,200	
Labor	3,000	
Factory overhead	1,800	6,000
Total costs to be accounted for		$33,000
Unit output for month:		
Finished and transferred to Dept. C during month		2,200
Equivalent units of work in process, end of month		
(500 units, two-fifths completed)		200
Total equivalent production		2,400
Unit cost for month—Dept. B:		
Materials ($1,200 ÷ 2,400 units)		$0.50
Labor ($3,000 ÷ 2,400 units)		1.25
Factory overhead ($1,800 ÷ 2,400 units)		0.75
Total		$2.50

Inventory costs:
    Cost of goods finished and transferred to Dept. C
    during month:
        Cost in Dept. A (2,200 × $10.00) $22,000
        Cost in Dept. B (2,200 ×   2.50)   5,500
                          (2,200 × $12.50) $27,500

Cost of work in process, end of month:
    Cost in Dept. A (500 × $10.00)   . . . . $ 5,000
    Cost in Dept. B:
        Materials (500 × 2/5 × $0.50) $100
        Labor (500 × 2/5 × $1.25)   250
        Factory overhead (500 × 2/5 × $0.75) .   150   500   5,500

Total production costs accounted for **$33,000**

The production report for Dept. C is shown in Figure 6-5.

The following cost of production summary for Dept. C is prepared in a manner similar to the Dept. B summary. Note that the *inventory costs* section of the report shows the *cost of goods finished and transferred to finished goods during the month.* The $16.50 unit cost of goods finished and

FIGURE 6-5   Production Report, Dept. C—Finishing

PRODUCTION REPORT

For Month Ending January 31, 20--

Dept. C—Finishing

In process, beginning of period   none
Stage of completion
Placed in process during period   none
Received from dept. __B__ during period 2,200 units
Transferred to dept. _____ during period _____
Transferred to stockroom during period   2,000 units
In process, end of period   200 units
Stage of completion   1/2

transferred represents the total unit cost of the goods through Dept. C. The detailed unit cost of completed goods, department by department, shows the accumulation of the total unit cost.

Kidco
Cost of Production Summary—Department C
For the Month Ended January 31, 20—

Cost of goods received from Dept. B during month (2,200 units × $12.50)		$27,500
Cost of production for month—Dept. C:		
Materials	$ 3,150	
Labor	2,310	
Factory overhead	2,940	8,400
Total costs to be accounted for		**$35,900**

Unit output for month:	
Finished and transferred to finished goods during month	2,000
Equivalent units of work in process, end of month (200 units, one-half completed)	100
Total equivalent production	2,100

Unit cost for month—Dept. C:	
Materials ($3,150 ÷ 2,100 units)	$1.50
Labor ($2,310 ÷ 2,100 units)	1.10
Factory overhead ($2,940 ÷ 2,100 units)	1.40
Total	$4.00

Inventory costs:

Cost of goods finished and transferred to finished goods during month:			
Cost in Dept. A (2,000 × $10.00)		$20,000	
Cost in Dept. B (2,000 × 2.50)		5,000	
Cost in Dept. C (2,000 × 4.00)		8,000	
(2,000 × $16.50)			$33,000

Cost of work in process, end of month:			
Cost in Dept. A (200 × $10.00)		$ 2,000	
Cost in Dept. B (200 × $2.50)		500	
Cost in Dept. C:			
Materials (200 × 1/2 × $1.50)	$150		
Labor (200 × 1/2 × $1.10)	110		
Factory overhead (200 × 1/2 × $1.40) .	140	400	2,900
Total production costs accounted for . . .			**$35,900**

After posting the end-of-month entries, the work in process account for Dept. C has a debit balance of $2,900.

Work in Process—Dept. C			
Jan. 31	3,150	Jan. 31	33,000
	2,310		
	2,940		
	27,500		
	35,900		
2,900			

As a means of classifying and summarizing the factory operations for January, the work sheet in Figure 6-6 provides the information for the following statement of cost of goods manufactured:

Kidco
Statement of Cost of Goods Manufactured
For the Month Ended January 31, 20—

Materials	$20,350
Labor	13,950
Factory overhead	12,100
Total	$46,400
Less work in process inventories, January 31	13,400
Cost of goods manufactured during the month	$33,000

At the end of the month, the following journal entries are made:

Jan. 31	Work in Process—Dept. A	. . . .	16,000	
	Work in Process—Dept. B	. . . .	1,200	
	Work in Process—Dept. C	. . . .	3,150	
	Factory Overhead*	. . . .	1,000	
	Materials	. . . .		21,350

*The amount charged to Factory Overhead for the actual amount of indirect materials is an *arbitrary amount* chosen for this example to illustrate how the costs are collected and distributed. This amount represents the cost of various supplies issued that could not be charged directly to a department.

FIGURE 6-6   Work Sheet, January 31

Kidco
Departmental Cost Work Sheet
For the Month Ended January 31, 20—

Analysis	Cost per unit transferred	Units received in department	Units transferred or on hand	Amount charged to department	Amount credited to department
Dept. A—Mixing:					
Started in process		3,700			
Costs for month:					
Materials				16,000 00	
Labor				8,640 00	
Factory overhead				7,360 00	
Finished and transferred to Dept. B . . . . . :	10 00		2,700		27,000 00
Closing work in process			1,000		5,000 00
Total	10 00	3,700	3,700	32,000 00	32,000 00
Dept. B—Molding:					
Received during month from Dept. A		2,700		27,000 00	
Costs added during month:					
Materials				1,200 00	
Labor				3,000 00	
Factory overhead				1,800 00	
Finished and transferred to Dept. C	2 50		2,200		27,500 00
Closing work in process			500		5,500 00
Total	12 50	2,700	2,700	33,000 00	33,000 00
Dept. C—Finishing:					
Received during month from Dept. B		2,200		27,500 00	
Costs added during month:					
Materials				3,150 00	
Labor				2,310 00	
Factory overhead				2,940 00	
Finished and transferred to stock	4 00		2,000		33,000 00
Closing work in process			200		2,900 00
Total	16 50	2,200	2,200	35,900 00	35,900 00

Analysis				Amount	Total
Summary:					
Materials:					
Dept. A				16,000 00	
Dept. B				1,200 00	
Dept. C				3,150 00	20,350 00
Labor:					
Dept. A				8,640 00	
Dept. B				3,000 00	
Dept. C				2,310 00	13,950 00
Factory overhead:					
Dept. A				7,360 00	
Dept. B				1,800 00	
Dept. C				2,940 00	12,100 00
Total production costs for January					46,400 00
Deduct work in process inventory, end of month:					
Dept. A				5,000 00	
Dept. B				5,500 00	
Dept. C				2,900 00	13,400 00
Cost of production, goods fully manufactured during January					33,000 00

Jan. 31	Work in Process—Dept. A	8,640	
	Work in Process—Dept. B	3,000	
	Work in Process—Dept. C	2,310	
	Factory Overhead	1,500	
	Payroll		15,450

Again, the amount charged to the factory overhead control account is an arbitrary amount chosen to illustrate payroll costs, such as the plant manager's salary, that could not be charged directly to any given department.

Jan. 31	Factory Overhead	9,000	
	Various Accounts (Accumulated Depre-		
	ciation, Prepaid Insurance, Payroll Taxes)		9,000

The previous entry summarizes several entries made in the general journal and possibly other journals to reflect an assumed amount for the current month's provision for depreciation, insurance, payroll taxes, and other expenses.

Jan. 31	Factory Overhead—Dept. A	6,600	
	Factory Overhead—Dept. B	2,100	
	Factory Overhead—Dept. C	2,800	
	Factory Overhead		11,500

The previous entry distributes the actual overhead for the period to the departments. The basis for this entry would be the *factory overhead analysis sheets,* which show in detail the allocation or apportionment of the actual expenses to the various departments. Note that these actual amounts do not appear on the cost of production summaries, which contain the estimated amounts of factory overhead applied to production.

Jan. 31	Work in Process—Dept. A	7,360	
	Work in Process—Dept. B	1,800	
	Work in Process—Dept. C	2,940	
	Factory Overhead—Dept. A		7,360
	Factory Overhead—Dept. B		1,800
	Factory Overhead—Dept. C		2,940

The previous entry charges the applied factory overhead appearing on the cost of production summaries to the work in process control accounts. The amounts are calculated by multiplying a predetermined overhead application rate by the base used for applying overhead to each department, such as labor hours or machine hours. A different base might be used for different departments, so that overhead would be equitably applied according to the benefit each department has received.

The cost of production summary is used to develop the entries to record the transfer of costs from one department to another and to Finished Goods, as follows:

Jan. 31 Work in Process—Dept. B	27,000	
Work in Process—Dept. A		27,000
31 Work in Process—Dept. C	27,500	
Work in Process—Dept. B		27,500
31 Finished Goods	33,000	
Work in Process—Dept. C		33,000

These journal entries are reflected in the following T-accounts. The balances remaining in the work in process accounts are reflected in total on the statement of cost of goods manufactured. The balances in the departmental factory overhead accounts represent under- or overapplied overhead and would usually be carried forward to future months. However, these balances can be transferred to an under- and overapplied factory overhead account. As discussed in previous chapters, these amounts of under- and overapplied overhead would be analyzed to determine if they are expected normal or seasonal variances, or if they represent inefficiencies that should be corrected.

Work in Process—Dept. A

Jan. 31	16,000	Jan. 31	27,000
	8,640		
	7,360		
	32,000		
5,000			

Work in Process—Dept. B

Jan. 31	1,200	Jan. 31	27,500
	3,000		
	1,800		
	27,000		
	33,000		
5,500			

Work in Process—Dept. C

Jan. 31	3,150	Jan. 31	33,000
	2,310		
	2,940		
	27,500		
2,900			

Finished Goods

Jan. 31	33,000		

Factory Overhead			
Jan. 31	1,000	Jan. 31	11,500
	1,500		
	9,000		
	11,500		

Materials			
		Jan. 31	21,350

Payroll			
		Jan. 31	15,450

Factory Overhead—Dept. A			
Jan. 31	6,600	Jan. 31	7,360
		760	

Factory Overhead—Dept. B			
Jan. 31	2,100	Jan. 31	1,800
300			

Factory Overhead—Dept. C			
Jan. 31	2,800	Jan. 31	2,940
		140	

You should now be able to work the following: Questions 12–14; Exercises 6-7 and 6-8; and Problems 6-3 and 6-4.

COST OF PRODUCTION SUMMARY—MULTIPLE DEPARTMENTS, BEGINNING INVENTORY

LEARNING OBJECTIVE 7
Prepare a cost of production summary and journal entries for multiple departments with beginning inventory.

The February production reports submitted by the department supervisors for Kidco differ from the January production reports. There are now inventories for work in process in each department at the beginning of the month. After receiving the production reports for February, the accountant prepares a cost of production summary for each department and makes entries to record the operations of each department in the general ledger accounts.

The February production report for Dept. A is shown in Figure 6-7. Note that the number of units in process at the beginning of the period *plus* the units placed in process or received from another department during the period equal the *total number of units* to be accounted for by the department.

FIGURE 6-7   Production Report, Dept. A—Mixing, February 28

PRODUCTION REPORT

For Month Ending _February 28, 20--_

Dept. _A—Mixing_

In process, beginning of period	1,000 units
Stage of completion	1/2
Placed in process during period	3,400 units
Received from dept. _____ during period	none
Transferred to dept. __B__ during period	3,900 units
Transferred to stockroom during period	none
In process, end of period	500 units
Stage of completion	4/5

In the following cost of production summary, the unit cost is determined by adding the cost of beginning work in process from the prior month to the total costs incurred during the current month and dividing by the equivalent units. The prior month's cost of materials is added to the current month's cost of materials and the total materials cost is divided by the equivalent production for materials. The same procedure is followed for labor and factory overhead. The calculation of unit output for the month takes into consideration all units finished during the month, including those in process at the beginning and those in process at the end of the period.

Kidco
Cost of Production Summary—Department A
For the Month Ended February 28, 20—

Cost of work in process, beginning of month:

Materials	$ 2,500	
Labor	1,350	
Factory overhead	1,150	$ 5,000

Cost of production for month:

Materials	$19,000	
Labor	10,260	
Factory overhead	8,740	38,000
Total costs to be accounted for		**$43,000**

Unit output for month:

Finished and transferred to Dept. B during month	3,900
Equivalent units of work in process, end of month	
(500 units, four-fifths completed)	400
Total equivalent production	4,300

Unit cost for month:

Materials [($2,500 + $19,000) ÷ 4,300]	$ 5.00
Labor [($1,350 + $10,260) ÷ 4,300]	2.70
Factory overhead [($1,150 + $8,740) ÷ 4,300]	2.30
Total	$10.00

Inventory costs:

Cost of goods finished and transferred to Dept. B during month (3,900 × $10.00)		$39,000
Cost of work in process, end of month:		
Materials (500 × 4/5 × $5.00)	$ 2,000	
Labor (500 × 4/5 × $2.70)	1,080	
Factory overhead (500 × 4/5 × $2.30)	920	4,000
Total production costs accounted for		**$43,000**

At this time the following journal entry can be made:

Feb. 28 Work in Process—Dept. B	39,000	
Work in Process—Dept. A		39,000

The work in process account for this department now appears as follows:

Work in Process—Dept. A			
Jan. 31	16,000	Jan. 31	27,000
	8,640		
	7,360		
	32,000		
5,000			
Feb. 28	19,000	Feb. 28	39,000
	10,260		
	8,740		
	70,000		*66,000*
4,000			

The February production report for Dept. B is shown in Figure 6-8.

FIGURE 6-8   Production Report, Dept. B—Molding, February 28

PRODUCTION REPORT

For Month Ending _February 28, 20--_

Dept. _B—Molding_

In process, beginning of period	500 units
Stage of completion	2/5
Placed in process during period	none
Received from dept. __A__ during period	3,900 units
Transferred to dept. __C__ during period	4,100 units
Transferred to stockroom during period	none
In process, end of period	300 units
Stage of completion	1/3

The February cost of production summary for Dept. B is shown below. In calculating the unit cost in Dept. B at the end of February, the amounts considered include (a) the production costs incurred by the department during the month, *plus* (b) the departmental cost of work in process at the beginning of the month. The cost from Dept. A included in the beginning work in process valuation ($5,000) is *not used* in this calculation because it is a *prior department's cost*.

Kidco
Cost of Production Summary—Department B
For the Month Ended February 28, 20—

Cost of work in process, beginning of month—Dept. B:
  Cost in Dept. A . . . . $ 5,000*
  Cost in Dept. B:
    Materials $100
    Labor   250
    Factory overhead   150   500 $ 5,500

Cost of goods received from Dept. A during month . .   39,000
Cost of production for month—Dept. B:
  Materials . . . . $ 1,664
  Labor   5,000
  Factory overhead   3,336   10,000

   Total costs to be accounted for **$54,500**

Unit output for month:
  Finished and transferred to Dept. C during month .   4,100
  Equivalent units of work in process, end of month
    (300 units, one-third completed)   100

   Total equivalent production   4,200

Unit cost for month—Dept. B:
  Materials [($100 + $1,664) ÷ 4,200] $0.42
  Labor [($250 + $5,000) ÷ 4,200] 1.25
  Factory overhead [($150 + $3,336) ÷ 4,200] 0.83

   Total $2.50

Inventory costs:
  Costs of goods finished and transferred to Dept. C
    during month:
    Cost in Dept. A (4,100 × $10.00) $41,000
    Cost in Dept. B (4,100 ×   2.50)   10,250

      (4,100 × $12.50) $51,250

  Cost of work in process, end of month:
    Cost in Dept. A (300 × $10.00) . . . . $ 3,000
    Cost in Dept. B:
      Materials (300 × 1/3 × $0.42) . . . . $ 42
      Labor (300 × 1/3 × $1.25)   125
      Factory overhead (300 × 1/3 × $0.83) . .   83   250   3,250

Total production costs accounted for **$54,500**

Not to be considered in calculating February unit cost in Department B.

The following journal entry can now be made:

Feb. 28 Work in Process—Dept. C   51,250
            Work in Process—Dept. B   51,250

The general ledger account for work in process in Dept. B appears as follows:

Work in Process—Dept. B

Jan. 31	1,200	Jan. 31	27,500
	3,000		
	1,800		
	27,000		
	33,000		
5,500			
Feb. 28	1,664	Feb. 28	51,250
	5,000		
	3,336		
	39,000		
	82,000		*78,750*
3,250			

The February production report for Dept. C is shown in Figure 6-9.

FIGURE 6-9   Production Report, Dept. C—Finishing, February 28

PRODUCTION REPORT

For Month Ending February 28, 20--

Dept. C—Finishing

In process, beginning of period	200 units
Stage of completion	1/2
Placed in process during period	none
Received from dept. B during period	4,100 units
Transferred to dept. during period	
Transferred to stockroom during period	3,900 units
In process, end of period	400 units
Stage of completion	1/2

The February cost of production summary for Dept. C is shown below.

Kidco
Cost of Production Summary—Department C
For the Month Ended February 28, 20—

Cost of work in process, beginning of month—Dept. C:			
Cost in Dept. A		$ 2,000*	
Cost in Dept. B		500*	
Cost in Dept. C:			
Materials	$150		
Labor	110		
Factory overhead	140	400	$ 2,900
Cost of goods received from			
Dept. B during month			51,250
Cost of production for month—Dept. C:			
Materials		$ 5,713	
Labor		4,564	
Factory overhead		5,723	16,000
Total costs to be accounted for . . .			**$70,150**
Unit output for month:			
Finished and transferred to finished goods			
during month			3,900
Equivalent units of work in process, end of month			
(400 units, one-half completed)			200
Total equivalent production			4,100
Unit cost for month—Dept. C:			
Materials [($150 + $5,713) ÷ 4,100] . . .			$1.43
Labor [($110 + $4,564) ÷ 4,100]			1.14
Factory overhead [($140 + $5,723) ÷ 4,100]			1.43
Total			$4.00
Inventory costs:			
Cost of goods finished and transferred to finished			
goods during month:			
Cost in Dept. A (3,900 × $10.00) . . .		$39,000	
Cost in Dept. B (3,900 × 2.50) . . .		9,750	
Cost in Dept. C (3,900 × 4.00) . . .		15,600	
(3,900 × $16.50) . . .			$64,350
Cost of work in process, end of month:			
Cost in Dept. A (400 × $10.00)		$ 4,000	
Cost in Dept. B (400 × $ 2.50)		1,000	
Cost in Dept. C:			
Materials (400 × 1/2 × $1.43)	$286		
Labor (400 × 1/2 × $1.14)	228		
Factory overhead (400 × 1/2 × $1.43)	286	800	5,800
Total production costs accounted for . .			**$70,150**

Not to be considered in calculating February unit cost in Department C.

The following journal entry can now be made:

Feb. 28	Finished Goods	64,350	
	Work in Process—Dept. C		64,350

The general ledger account for work in process in Dept. C appears as follows:

Work in Process—Dept. C			
Jan. 31	3,150	Jan. 31	33,000
	2,310		
	2,940		
	27,500		
	35,900		
2,900			
Feb. 28	5,713	Feb. 28	64,350
	4,564		
	5,723		
	51,250		
	103,150		*97,350*
5,800			

The work sheet in Figure 6-10 can now be prepared. It summarizes the factory operations for February and provides the data needed for preparing the following statement of cost of goods manufactured:

Kidco Statement of Cost of Goods Manufactured For the Month Ended February 28, 20—	
Materials	$26,377
Labor	19,824
Factory overhead	17,799
Total	$64,000
Add work in process inventories, February 1	13,400
	$77,400
Less work in process inventories, February 28	13,050
Cost of goods manufactured during the month	$64,350

FIGURE 6-10   Work Sheet, February 28

Kidco
Departmental Cost Work Sheet
For the Month Ended February 28, 20—

Analysis	Cost per unit transferred	Units received in department	Units transferred or on hand	Amount charged to department	Amount credited to department
Dept. A—Mixing:					
Opening inventory in process		1,000		5,000 00	
Started in process		3,400			
Costs for month:					
Materials				19,000 00	
Labor				10,260 00	
Factory overhead				8,740 00	
Finished and transferred to Dept. B . . .	10 00		3,900		39,000 00
Closing work in process			500		4,000 00
Total	10 00	4,400	4,400	43,000 00	43,000 00
Dept. B—Molding:					
Opening inventory in process		500		5,500 00	
Received during month from Dept. A . .		3,900		39,000 00	
Costs added during month:					
Materials				1,664 00	
Labor				5,000 00	
Factory overhead				3,336 00	
Finished and transferred to Dept. C . . .	2 50		4,100		51,250 00
Closing work in process			300		3,250 00
Total	12 50	4,400	4,400	54,500 00	54,500 00
Dept. C—Finishing:					
Opening inventory in process		200		2,900 00	
Received during month from Dept. B . .		4,100		51,250 00	
Costs added during month:					
Materials				5,713 00	
Labor				4,564 00	
Factory overhead				5,723 00	
Finished and transferred to stock	4 00		3,900		64,350 00
Closing work in process			400		5,800 00
Total	16 50	4,300	4,300	70,150 00	70,150 00

Analysis				Amount	Total
Summary:					
Materials:					
Dept. A				19,000 00	
Dept. B				1,664 00	
Dept. C				5,713 00	26,377 00
Labor:					
Dept. A				10,260 00	
Dept. B				5,000 00	
Dept. C				4,564 00	19,824 00
Factory overhead:					
Dept. A				8,740 00	
Dept. B				3,336 00	
Dept. C				5,723 00	17,799 00
Total production costs for February . . .					64,000 00
Add work in process, beginning of month:					
Dept. A				5,000 00	
Dept. B				5,500 00	
Dept. C				2,900 00	13,400 00
Total					77,400 00
Deduct work in process, end of month:					
Dept. A				4,000 00	
Dept. B				3,250 00	
Dept. C				5,800 00	13,050 00
Cost of production, goods fully manufactured during February					64,350 00

Occasionally, finished goods in a department at the end of the month may not be transferred to the next department until the following month. Because these units are still on hand in the department at the end of the month, they cannot be considered transferred. They are accounted for as "goods completed and on hand" and their cost is shown at the full unit price. They are considered work in process for financial statement purposes. Although the goods are finished in the department, they are considered in process until they are officially transferred to finished goods.

CHANGES IN PRIOR DEPARTMENT'S UNIT TRANSFER COSTS

LEARNING OBJECTIVE 8
Prepare a cost of production summary with a change in the prior department's unit transfer cost.

In the preceding illustrations, it was assumed that this month's unit cost from prior departments was the same transferred-in unit cost as last month. This assumption permitted the prior department's unit cost to be used without determining a *new average unit cost* for the goods transferred in, even though the transfers came from two different periods of production. However, the prior department's transfers from two different periods will often have different unit costs each month. Therefore, these previous department costs must be *averaged as a separate grouping* so that these transferred-in costs can be properly allocated to the products being produced in the department. The method resembles that used for the cost of materials, labor, and factory overhead in the department when the cost of these elements represents two different periods of time.

To illustrate, assume that 2,000 units are in process in Dept. 2 at the beginning of the month with a transferred cost of $10,600 from Dept. 1. During the month, 10,000 units with a total cost of $50,000 are received from Dept. 1; 11,000 units are finished and transferred to Dept. 3; and 1,000 units are in process in Dept. 2 at the end of the month, one-half completed. Processing costs in Dept. 2 for the month are $23,000 ($2,000 + $21,000) for materials, $16,100 ($1,400 + $14,700) for labor, and $11,500 ($1,000 + $10,000) for overhead. Using these data, the unit costs are calculated on the following cost of production summary. Note that the unit cost from the prior department is adjusted to $5.05.

You should now be able to work the following: Questions 15 and 16; Exercise 6-9; and Problems 6-5 to 6-8.

Cost of Production Summary—Dept. 2

Cost of work in process, beginning of month:			
Cost in Dept. 1		$ 10,600	
Cost in Dept. 2:			
Materials	$ 2,000		
Labor	1,400		
Overhead	1,000	4,400	$ 15,000
Cost of goods received from Dept. 1			50,000
Cost in Dept. 2:			
Materials		$21,000	
Labor		14,700	
Overhead		10,500	46,200
Total costs to be accounted for			**$111,200**

Unit output for month:		
Finished and transferred to Dept. 3		11,000
Equivalent production of work in process		
(1,000 units, one-half completed)		500
Total equivalent production		11,500

Unit cost for month:			
Cost from prior department:			
Beginning inventory	(2,000 units) . .	$10,600	
Transferred in this month	(10,000 units) . .	50,000	
Average cost per unit	(12,000 units) . .	$60,600	$5.05
Cost in Dept. 2:			
Materials [($2,000 + $21,000) ÷ 11,500] . . .			$2.00
Labor [($1,400 + $14,700) ÷ 11,500]			1.40
Overhead [($1,000 + $10,500) ÷ 11,500] . . .			1.00
			$4.40

Inventory costs:			
Cost of goods finished and transferred:			
Cost in Dept. 1	(11,000 × $5.05)	$55,550	
Cost in Dept. 2	(11,000 × 4.40)	48,400	
Total finished and transferred (11,000 × $9.45)			$103,950
Cost of work in process, end of month:			
Cost in Dept. 1 (1,000 × $5.05)		$ 5,050	
Materials (1,000 × 1/2 × $2.00) .	$1,000		
Labor (1,000 × 1/2 × $1.40) . . .	700		
Overhead (1,000 × 1/2 × $1.00) .	500	2,200	7,250
Total production costs accounted for			**$111,200**

KEY TERMS

SELF-STUDY PROBLEM

COST OF PRODUCTION SUMMARY, TWO DEPARTMENTS

PRO CONCRETE, INC.

Pro Concrete, Inc., which manufactures products on a continuous basis, had 800 units in process in Dept. 1, one-half completed, at the beginning of May. The costs in April for processing these units were as follows: materials, $1,200; labor, $900; and factory overhead, $1,000. During May, Dept. 1 finished and transferred 10,000 units to Dept. 2 and had 400 units in process at the end of May, one-half completed.

Dept. 2 had 200 units in process at the beginning of the month, one-half completed. April costs for these units were as follows: cost transferred from Dept. 1, $1,550; materials, $200; labor, $175; and factory overhead, $225. During May, Dept. 2 completed 9,000 units and had 1,200 units in process at the end of the period, two-thirds completed.

Production costs incurred by the two departments during May were as follows:

	Dept. 1	Dept. 2
Materials	$29,400	$19,400
Labor	22,050	16,975
Factory overhead	24,500	21,825

REQUIRED:

Prepare a cost of production summary for each department.

SOLUTION TO DEMONSTRATION PROBLEM

Suggestions:

Read the entire problem through thoroughly, keeping in mind what you are required to do: *Prepare a cost of production summary for each department.*

The specifics in the problem highlight the following facts:

1. There are two departments: Dept. 1 and Dept. 2.
2. Dept. 1 had 800 units in process, one-half completed, at the beginning of May. *This statement indicates that materials, labor, and factory overhead are being added uniformly to production.*
3. To prepare a cost of production summary:
    a. The total cost to be accounted for in the department must be determined.
    b. The equivalent production should be calculated.

c. Using the beginning inventory costs and the costs incurred during the period, determine the total cost of materials, the total cost of labor, and the total cost of factory overhead. Then divide the total cost of materials by the equivalent production of materials to calculate the unit cost of materials for the period. Also, divide the total cost of labor and factory overhead by the equivalent production determined for them.

d. Using the calculated unit costs for materials, labor, and factory overhead, determine the following:
1. The cost of goods finished and transferred
2. The cost of the ending work in process inventory

Preparing the cost of production summaries:

Pro Concrete, Inc.
Cost of Production Summary—Dept. 1
For the Month Ended May 31, 20—

First—Account for the total cost charged to Dept. 1.

Cost of work in process, beginning of month:		
Materials	$ 1,200	
Labor	900	
Factory overhead	1,000	$ 3,100
Cost of production for month:		
Materials	$29,400	
Labor	22,050	
Factory overhead	24,500	75,950
Total costs to be accounted for		$79,050

Second—Determine equivalent production for the month. Materials, labor, and factory overhead are added uniformly. Method of costing—average cost.

Units of output for month:	
Finished and transferred to Dept. 2	10,000
Equivalent units of work in process, end of month:	
400 units, one-half completed	200
Total equivalent production	10,200

Third—Determine unit cost, by elements, for the month. The average cost method requires that the beginning inventory's element cost be added to the current month's element cost. The total cost for each element is then divided by the equivalent production for that element.

Unit cost for month:	
Materials ($1,200 + $29,400) ÷ 10,200	$3.00
Labor ($900 + $22,050) ÷ 10,200	2.25
Factory overhead ($1,000 + $24,500) ÷ 10,200	2.50
Total	$7.75

Fourth—Using the unit costs, calculate the cost of goods transferred and the cost of the ending work in process.

Inventory costs:
Cost of goods finished and transferred to
    Dept. 2 during the month (10,000 × $7.75) $77,500

Cost of work in process, end of month:		
Materials (400 × 1/2 × $3.00)	$600	
Labor (400 × 1/2 × $2.25)	450	
Factory overhead (400 × 1/2 × $2.50)	500	1,550
Total production costs accounted for		$79,050

Prepare the cost of production summary for Dept. 2:

Pro Concrete, Inc.
Cost of Production Summary—Dept. 2
For the Month Ended May 31, 20—

First—Account for all costs charged to Dept. 2.

Cost of work in process, beginning of month:			
Cost in Dept. 1 (preceding department) . . .		$ 1,550	
Cost in Dept. 2:			
Materials	$200		
Labor	175		
Factory overhead	225	600	$ 2,150
Cost of goods received from Dept. 1 during month			77,500
Cost of production for month:			
Materials	$19,400		
Labor	16,975		
Factory overhead	21,825	58,200	
Total costs to be accounted for			$137,850

Second—Determine the equivalent production.

Finished and transferred to finished goods during month	9,000
Equivalent units of work in process, end of month	
(1,200 units, two-thirds completed)	800
Total equivalent production	9,800

Third—Determine unit cost by element. Add beginning inventory element cost to current month element cost and divide total by the equivalent production for that element.

Unit cost for month:	
Materials ($200 + $19,400) ÷ 9,800	$2.00
Labor ($175 + $16,975) ÷ 9,800	1.75
Factory overhead ($225 + $21,825) ÷ 9,800	2.25
Total unit cost for Dept. 2	$6.00

Fourth—Using the unit costs from Dept. 1 and Dept. 2, calculate the cost of goods transferred and the cost of the ending work in process.

Inventory costs:

Cost of goods finished and transferred to finished goods during month:

Cost in Dept. 1 (9,000 × $ 7.75) ...	$69,750	
Cost in Dept. 2 (9,000 × $ 6.00) ...	54,000	
Total (9,000 × $13.75) ...		$123,750

Cost of work in process, end of month:

Cost in Dept. 1 (1,200 × $7.75)		$ 9,300	
Cost in Dept. 2:			
Materials (1,200 × 2/3 × $2.00) ...	$1,600		
Labor (1,200 × 2/3 × $1.75)	1,400		
Overhead (1,200 × 2/3 × $2.25) ...	1,800	4,800	14,100
Total production costs accounted for ...			$137,850

Note that, in the above ending work in process inventory, the unit cost from Dept. 1 is multiplied by the full 1,200 units because all of those units are complete as to Dept. 1 processing.

(Note: Problem 6-6 is similar to this problem.)

QUESTIONS

1. What are the two basic systems of cost accounting and under what conditions may each be used advantageously?

2. Following is a list of manufactured products. For each product, would a job order or a process cost system be used to account for the costs of production?

   a. lumber   e. cereal

   b. buildings   f. textbooks

   c. airplanes   g. paint

   d. gasoline   h. women's hats

3. What is the primary difference between the two cost accounting systems regarding the accumulation of costs and the calculation of unit costs?

4. What is the difference between the term "unit cost" as commonly used in the process cost system and the term "job cost" as commonly used in the job order system of cost accounting?

5. How do the two cost accounting systems differ in accounting for each of the following items?

   a. materials

   b. labor

   c. factory overhead

6. What is the primary objective in accumulating costs by departments?

7. What is meant by the term "equivalent production" as used in the process cost system?

8. Why is it necessary to estimate the stage or degree of completion of work in process at the end of the accounting period under the process cost system?

9. What would be the effect on the unit cost of finished goods if an inaccurate estimate of the stage of completion of work in process is made?

10. What information is reflected on a production report?

11. What are the four divisions of a cost of production summary?

12. What is the major difference between the disposition of units transferred out of a first department in a single-department factory versus a multiple-department factory?

13. Does the calculation of unit cost in a department subsequent to the first take into consideration the costs transferred in from the previous departments?

14. In determining the costs transferred to a third department from a second department, are the costs from a first department considered? Are they considered in the computation of the ending work in process in the second department?

15. If finished goods are still on hand in a department at the end of the month, how are they reported on the cost of production summary and on the balance sheet?

16. If the prior department's transfers from two different periods have different unit costs each month, how are they treated for purposes of the cost of production summary for the department to which they were transferred?

EXERCISES

E6-1
Computing equivalent production
Objective 3

Compute the equivalent production (unit output) for the month for each of the following situations:

	Units Completed During Month	Units in Process, End of Month	Stage of Completion
a.	10,000	2,000	1/2
b.	32,000	4,000	3/4
c.	8,000	1,000	3/4
		500	2/5
d.	20,000	5,000	1/2
		5,000	3/4
e.	48,000	1,500	1/5
		4,000	3/4

E6-2
Computing units in process, units completed, and equivalent production
Objective 3

Using the data presented below, determine which figures should be inserted in the blank spaces.

	Beginning Units in Process	Units Started in Production	Units Transferred to Finished Goods	Ending Units in Process	Equivalent Units
a.	600	8,000	8,600	—	—
b.	900	6,500	—	400—1/2 completed	—
c.	1,500	—	12,900	1,200—1/4 completed	—
d.	—	7,250	7,200	150—1/2 completed	—
e.	—	8,400	8,200	200—1/2 completed	—
f.	400	6,200	6,200	—	6,300

E6-3
Computing unit cost
Objective 4

During the month, a company with no departmentalization incurred costs of $45,000 for materials, $36,000 for labor, and $22,500 for factory overhead. There were no units in process at the beginning or at the end of the month, and 10,000 units were completed. Determine the unit cost for the month for materials, labor, and factory overhead.

E6-4
Computing unit cost
Objective 4

Newark Manufacturing Co. recorded costs for the month of $18,900 for materials, $44,100 for labor, and $26,250 for factory overhead. There was no beginning work in process, 9,000 units were finished, and 2,000 units were in process at the end of the period, one-half completed. Compute the month's unit cost for each element of manufacturing cost and the total per unit cost.

E6-5
Computing unit cost
Objective 5

The records of Brown, Inc., reflect the following data:
  Work in process, beginning of month—2,000 units one-half completed at a cost of $1,250 for materials, $675 for labor, and $950 for overhead.
  Production costs for the month—materials, $99,150; labor, $54,925; factory overhead, $75,050.
  Units completed and transferred to stock—38,500.
  Work in process, end of month—3,000 units, one-half completed.
Calculate the unit cost for the month for materials, labor, and factory overhead.

E6-6
Computing unit cost
Objective 5

Hamilton Manufacturing Co. had 500 units, three-fifths completed, in process at the beginning of the month. During the month 2,000 units were started in process and finished. There was no work in process at the end of the month. Unit cost of production for the month was $1.20. Costs for materials, labor, and factory overhead incurred in the current month totaled $2,655. Calculate the unit cost for the *prior* month. (Hint: You must first determine what the balance in work in process must have been at the beginning of the month.)

E6-7
Computing unit cost
for department and
for completed units
Objective 6

Northridge Company has two production departments. The nature of the process is such that no units remain in process in Dept. 2 at the end of the period. During the period, 8,000 units with a cost of $27,200 were transferred from Dept. 1 to Dept. 2. Dept. 2 incurred costs of $8,800 for materials, $7,200 for labor, and $8,800 for factory overhead, and finished 8,000 units during the month.
a.   Determine the unit cost for the month in Dept. 2.
b.   Determine the unit cost of the products transferred to finished goods.

E6-8
Identifying cost flows
in process cost
system
Objective 6

List in columnar form the transactions and the accounts debited and credited to reflect the flow of costs through a process cost accounting system for:
1.   the purchase of materials and supplies
2.   the issuance of materials and supplies to the factory
3.   factory labor costs incurred
4.   other factory cost incurred
5.   the distribution of actual factory overhead to the departments
6.   the application of factory overhead to the departments
7.   the transfer of units from one department to another
8.   the completion of units
9.   the sale of units

E6-9
Computing unit cost for department and for completed units with beginning inventory
Objective 7

Matz Company has two production departments. Department 2 had 1,000 units in process at the beginning of the period, 2/5 complete. During the period 7,800 units were received from Department 1, 8,200 units were transferred to Finished Goods, and 600 units were in process at the end of the period, 1/3 complete. The cost of the beginning work in process was:

Cost in Department 1	$10,000
Cost in Department 2:	
Materials	200
Labor	500
Factory overhead	300

The costs during the month were:

Cost of goods received from Department 1 . .	$78,000
Cost in Department 2:	
Materials	3,328
Labor	10,000
Factory overhead	6,672

a. Determine the unit cost for the month in Department 2.
b. Determine the total cost of the products transferred to finished goods.
c. Determine the total cost of the ending work in process inventory.

PROBLEMS

P6-1
Cost of production summary, one department; beginning work in process
Objective 5

Shea Products Co. produces a latex paint and uses the process cost system. Materials, labor, and overhead are added evenly throughout the process. The following information was obtained from the company's accounts at the end of February:

Production Costs

Costs incurred during month:		
Materials	$30,000	
Labor	20,000	
Factory overhead	40,000	90,000

Production Report	Units
Finished and transferred to stockroom during month	76,000
Work in process, end of period, one-fourth completed	16,000

Required:

Prepare a cost of production summary for February.

P6-2
Cost of production
summary, one
department;
beginning work in
process
Objective 5

Trebby Company uses the process cost system. The following data, taken from the organization's books, reflect the results of manufacturing operations during the month of October:

Production Costs

Work in process, beginning of period:

Materials	$ 2,600	
Labor	2,300	
Factory overhead	1,000	$ 5,900
Costs incurred during month:		
Materials	$10,000	
Labor	7,500	
Factory overhead	6,000	23,500
Total		$29,400

Production Report	Units
Finished and transferred to stockroom during month	13,000
Work in process, end of period, one-half completed	2,000

Required:

Prepare a cost of production summary for October.

P6-3
Departmental cost
work sheet analysis;
cost of production
summary, three
departments, no
beginning inventories
Objective 6

Marvel Manufacturing Co. has three departments and uses the process cost system of accounting. A portion of the departmental cost work sheet prepared by the cost accountant at the end of July is reproduced on the next page.

Required:

Prepare a cost of production summary for each department.

P6-4
Journal entries and
cost of goods
manufactured
statement
Objective 6

Required:

Using the data in P6-3:
1. Draft the necessary entries to record the manufacturing costs incurred during the month of July.
2. Prepare a statement of cost of goods manufactured for the month ended July 31.

Marvel Manufacturing Co.
Departmental Cost Work Sheet
For the Month Ended July 31, 20—

Analysis	Cost per unit transferred		Units received in department	Units transferred or on hand	Amount charged to department		Amount credited to department	
Cutting:								
Started in process			6,600					
Costs for month:								
Materials					30,000	00		
Labor					16,000	00		
Factory overhead					14,000	00		
Completed and transferred to Shaping	10	00		5,400			54,000	00
Closing inventory in process (1/2 completed) . .				1,200			6,000	00
Total	10	00	6,600	6,600	60,000	00	60,000	00
Shaping:								
Received during month from Cutting			5,400		54,000	00		
Costs added during month:								
Materials					1,200	00		
Labor					6,000	00		
Factory overhead					4,800	00		
Completed and transferred to Finishing	2	50		4,400			55,000	00
Closing inventory in process (2/5 completed) . .				1,000			11,000	00
Total	12	50	5,400	5,400	66,000	00	66,000	00
Finishing:								
Received during month from Shaping			4,400		55,000	00		
Costs added during month:								
Materials					6,300	00		
Labor					4,200	00		
Factory overhead					6,300	00		
Completed and transferred to stock	4	00		4,000			66,000	00
Closing inventory in process (1/2 completed) . .				400			5,800	00
Total	16	50	4,400	4,400	71,800	00	71,800	00

P6-5
Change in unit cost from prior department and valuation of inventory
Objective 7

Tino Products Co. has two departments: mixing and cooking. At the beginning of the month, the cooking department had 2,000 units in process with costs of $8,600 from the mixing department, and its own departmental costs of $500 for materials, $1,000 for labor, and $2,500 for factory overhead. During the month, 8,000 units were received from the mixing department with a cost of $36,400. The cooking department incurred costs of $4,250 for materials, $8,500 for labor, and $21,250 for factory overhead, and finished 9,000 units. At the end of the month, there were 1,000 units in process, one-half completed.

Required:

1. Determine the unit cost for the month in the cooking department.
2. Determine the new average unit cost for all units received from the mixing department.

3. Determine the unit cost of goods finished.
4. Determine the accumulated cost of the goods finished and of the ending work in process.

P6-6
Cost of production summary, two departments; beginning inventory.
Similar to self-study problem.
Objective 7

Homewood Corporation uses a process cost system. The records for the month of May show the following information:

Production Report	Dept. 1	Dept. 2
Units in process, May 1	5,000	10,000
Started during the month	20,000	—
Received from prior department	—	15,000
Finished and transferred	15,000	10,000
Finished and on hand	5,000	—
Units in process, May 31	5,000	15,000
Stage of completion	1/5	1/3

Production Costs

Work in process, May 1:		
Cost in Dept. 1		$ 50,000
Materials	$ 5,000	
Labor	6,450	
Factory overhead	3,550	
Cost in Dept. 2:		
Materials		5,000
Labor		5,500
Factory overhead		3,500
Costs incurred during the month:		
Materials	37,000	40,000
Labor	45,000	44,000
Factory overhead	50,000	37,000
Total	$147,000	$185,000

Required:

Prepare a cost of production summary for each department.

P6-7
Ledger account analysis; cost of production summary
Objective 7

Analyze the information presented in the following general ledger account of Cole Manufacturing Co.:

Work in Process—Dept. B			
Mar. 1	10,250	Mar. 31	50,000
31 Materials	4,000		
31 Labor	8,000		
31 Factory overhead	6,000		
31 Dept. A	36,000		

Additional facts:
a. 2,000 units were in process at the beginning of the month, one-half completed.

b. 9,000 units were received from Dept. A during the month.
c. 8,000 units were transferred to Dept. C during the month.
d. Unit costs in Depts. A and B were the same for March as for the prior month.
e. The ratio of materials, labor, and factory overhead costs for Dept. B in the beginning and ending balances of Work in Process was in the same ratio as the costs incurred in Dept. B during the current month.

Required:

Prepare a cost of production summary for March.

P6-8
Cost of production summary, three departments; change in unit cost from prior department; departmental cost work sheet; journal entries; manufacturing statement
Objectives 7, 8

Cristobel Manufacturing Co. uses the process cost system. The following information for the month of December was obtained from the company's books and from the production reports submitted by the department heads:

Production Report	Mixing	Blending	Bottling
Units in process, beginning of period	2,500	1,500	3,000
Started in process during month	12,500	—	—
Received from prior department	—	13,000	10,000
Finished and transferred	13,000	10,000	11,000
Finished and on hand	—	500	—
Units in process, end of period	2,000	4,000	2,000
Stage of completion	1/4	4/5	1/2

Production Costs

	Mixing	Blending	Bottling
Work in process, beginning of period:			
Cost in Mixing		$ 3,075	$ 6,150
Materials	$ 1,470		
Labor	650		
Factory overhead	565		
Cost in Blending			3,660
Materials		240	
Labor		905	
Factory overhead		750	
Cost in Bottling			
Materials			900
Labor			3,100
Factory overhead			3,080
Costs incurred during month:			
Materials	15,000	2,500	1,500
Labor	4,750	8,000	6,500
Factory overhead	5,240	6,100	7,000
Total	$27,675	$21,570	$31,890

Required:

1. Prepare cost of production summaries for the Mixing, Blending, and Bottling departments.
2. Prepare a departmental cost work sheet.
3. Draft the journal entries required to record the month's operations.
4. Prepare a statement of cost of goods manufactured for December.

7

Process Cost Accounting—
Additional Procedures

LEARNING OBJECTIVES

After studying this chapter, you should be able to:

1. Compute unit costs when materials are not added uniformly throughout the process.
2. Account for units lost in the production process.
3. Account for units gained in the production process.
4. Assign costs to inventories, using the first-in, first-out method.
5. Identify the methods used to apportion joint costs to joint products and account for by-products.

The illustrative problems presented in Chapter 6 were based on the assumption that materials, labor, and factory overhead were uniformly applied during the processing period. When the work in process at the end of the accounting period was considered to be one-half completed, it was assumed that one-half of the materials cost, one-half of the labor cost, and one-half of the factory overhead cost had been added. Before these additional details of process costing are discussed, read the following Real-World Example regarding a company that uses process costing and aims for continuous improvement in its production processes.

A PLANT MANAGER KEEPS REINVENTING HIS PRODUCTION LINE

Since 1995, Dana's Stockton plant has been making truck chassis for a single customer: Toyota Motor Corp. To win Toyota's business, Dana promised to shoot for a 2% price cut by 1997 and further decreases thereafter, something that automakers increasingly expect of their suppliers. "Every dollar has to come out of the process," says . . . Mark Schmink, the founding plant manager here. . . . "You can only work and sweat so much; it's finite,". . . says Mr. Schmink. "That leaves you with finding better ways to do things. To my knowledge, that's not finite at all."

. . . Mr. Schmink's only hope of improving this process was creating a culture of inventiveness, with no change too small. He began by choosing welders with zero experience, reasoning that unconditioned hands would be freer to explore new ways of welding. Early on he insisted that everyone learn every job in the plant (to know how each fit into the whole) and that no one receive a permanent assignment (thus maintaining a supply of fresh perspectives). . . .

. . . With wages and benefits gradually rising, the pressure for improvements accelerated. Worker teams questioned every routine of the plant, right down to the sequencing of individual welds.

Mr. Schmink demanded that everyone submit two ideas in writing each month, with an astonishing 81% proving sufficiently worthwhile to implement. . . .

Mr. Schmink provided continuous feedback by displaying minute-by-minute productivity figures on electronic signs that looked like gymnasium scoreboards. He celebrated the conquest of every goal with an occasion—a rib-eye lunch, a family barbecue. . . .

By this time last year the plant had passed a long-sought threshold of 33 frames an hour. Immediately Mr. Schmink set a new goal of 36 frames per hour, toward which the plant is still reaching. . . .

Tom Petzinger, Jr., "A Plant Manager Keeps Reinventing His Production Line," *The Wall Street Journal*, September 19, 1997, page B1.

EQUIVALENT PRODUCTION—MATERIALS NOT UNIFORMLY APPLIED

LEARNING OBJECTIVE 1
Compute unit costs when materials are not added uniformly throughout the process.

In industries that use the process cost system, the materials may be put into production in varying quantities and at different points in the processing cycle. For example, before any manufacturing process can begin, materials must be introduced in the first production department. This material may be a sheet of metal that will be cut or trimmed to size, shaped, and formed through the application of labor and the use of machines. In this case, all of the material is added at the beginning of processing in the first department. Then, labor and factory overhead are used to convert the material into a finished product. The stage of completion of partially completed work at the end of a period is irrelevant to material because all material costs will have been added at the very beginning of production. Some labor and overhead costs will need to be applied to the unfinished units in the department during the next period.

In the second production department, this same material may be processed further through the application of other labor operations, such as buffing and polishing. At the end of the process in the second department, several coats of enamel are to be applied. In this case, the units uncompleted in the department at the end of the period would have had a part of the departmental labor and overhead costs applied to them, but no materials cost would have been added because the enamel is applied at the very end of production in the second department.

In the third department, other materials, such as a knob, a handle, or pads, are added to the unit at the start of production. Then, a final polish is applied, involving labor and equipment. After it is polished, the unit is placed in a plastic container, which is an added material, and the package is sealed, incurring more labor and overhead cost.

In the third department, the uncompleted units may have had the first items of material and some labor and overhead applied, or they may have had the first material, some labor and overhead, and the additional materials added. In any event, the stage of completion must be carefully determined to measure accurately how much of each element of cost to apply to these unfinished units.

Compared with the principles and procedures developed in the preceding chapter, the only new procedure presented here is that equivalent production must be computed for each element of production cost, rather than only one equivalent production quantity used for materials, labor, and overhead. In addition, the allocation of cost for each element must be carefully considered when valuing the ending work in process.

To illustrate the problems involved in calculating unit costs under these conditions, three problems using the average cost method are presented. In these examples, materials are added at different stages in the process. Labor and factory overhead are assumed to be applied evenly throughout the process. This situation is typical in that overhead is usually so closely related to labor costs or labor hours that overhead is generally thought of as being incurred or applied in the same ratio as labor expense.

ILLUSTRATIVE PROBLEM NO. 1

Computing the unit cost in department A where all the materials are added at the beginning of processing—average cost method. The production report for the month submitted by the department head, Figure 7-1, resembles those studied in the previous chapter. The illustration continues for Kidco, which has the following departments: Dept. A–Mixing; Dept. B–Molding; Dept. C–Finishing.

The cost of production summary, Figure 7-2, is similar to the ones previously discussed, but it has the added feature of determining equivalent production for materials separately from that of labor and factory overhead.

In Dept. A, because all materials are added at the start of processing, it is easy to determine the equivalent units for materials. The production report from the factory indicates that 500 units were in process at the beginning of the month with all materials added, and 2,500 units were started in process. Therefore, the equivalent production for materials is 3,000 units. Another way to calculate the figure by the method used in this chapter is as follows: the 2,600 units finished during the month plus the 400 units in process at the end of the month have all of the materials added. The total equivalent production for materials, therefore, is 3,000 units (2,600 + 400).

The unit output for labor and factory overhead is calculated as shown in the preceding chapter: 2,600 completed units, plus the equivalent of

FIGURE 7-1   Production Report, Dept. A

PRODUCTION REPORT

For Month Ending __April 30, 20—__

Dept. __A–Mixing__

In process, beginning of period	500 units
Stage of completion	2/5
Placed in process during period	2,500 units
Received from dept. _____ during period	
Transferred to dept. ___B___ during period	2,600 units
Transferred to stockroom during period	
In process, end of period	400 units
Stage of completion	3/4

FIGURE 7-2   Cost of Production Summary, Dept. A

Kidco
Cost of Production Summary—Dept. A
For the Month Ended April 30, 20—

Cost of work in process, beginning of month:

Materials	$1,500	
Labor	250	
Factory overhead	150	$ 1,900

Cost of production for month:

Materials	$7,500	
Labor	3,375	
Factory overhead	2,025	12,900
Total costs to be accounted for		**$14,800**

Unit output for month:
Materials:

Finished and transferred to Dept. B during month	2,600
Equivalent units of work in process, end of month	
(400 units, three-fourths completed, all materials)	400
Total equivalent production	3,000

Labor and factory overhead:

Finished and transferred to Dept. B during month	2,600
Equivalent units of work in process, end of month	
(400 units, three-fourths completed)	300
Total equivalent production	2,900

Unit cost for month:

Materials ($1,500 + $7,500) ÷ 3,000	$3.00
Labor ($250 + $3,375) ÷ 2,900	1.25
Factory overhead ($150 + $2,025) ÷ 2,900	0.75
Total	$5.00

Inventory costs:

Cost of goods finished and transferred to Dept. B		
during month (2,600 × $5)		$13,000
Cost of work in process, end of month:		
Materials (400 × $3)	$1,200	
Labor (400 × 3/4 × $1.25)	375	
Factory overhead (400 × 3/4 × $0.75)	225	1,800
Total production costs accounted for		**$14,800**

300 completed units (400 units three-fourths completed), gives a total of 2,900 for the unit output for the month for labor and factory overhead.

With the equivalent production figures calculated for materials, labor, and overhead, the unit cost for the month can now be calculated. The cost of each element in the beginning work in process is added to the cost for that element incurred in the current month. This total cost for the element is then divided by the appropriate equivalent production figure to determine the unit cost for each element. In this example, the unit cost of materials is $3.00, for labor $1.25, and for overhead $0.75, giving a total unit cost of $5.00.

The 2,600 units transferred to Dept. B are costed at $5.00 each and amount to a total cost of $13,000. In costing the ending work in process, the stage of completion and the point at which materials were added must be considered. In this instance, because materials were put into production at the beginning of the manufacturing cycle, the 400 units in process at the end of the period have had all materials added and are, therefore, costed at the full unit cost of $3.00 for materials. Because the goods are three-fourths completed, and labor and factory overhead are added evenly throughout the process, the 400 units are costed at three-fourths of the month's unit cost for labor and overhead.

ILLUSTRATIVE PROBLEM NO. 2

Computing the unit cost in Dept. B where all the materials are added at the close of processing—average cost method. Figure 7-3 shows the production report for Dept. B. In Dept. B, because the materials are added at the end of the process, materials cost will be applied only to those units finished. Therefore, the equivalent production for the month for materials in Dept. B is 2,500 units. The labor and factory overhead adds the 2,500 finished units to the equivalent production of the ending work in process, 350 units two-fifths completed, or 140, giving a total of 2,640 units as the equivalent output for the month. Figure 7-4 shows the cost of production summary.

As in Dept. A, the unit cost for each element is determined by adding the cost in the beginning work in process to the cost for that element incurred during the month and dividing this total by the unit output for the month. For Dept. B, these unit costs for materials, labor, and factory overhead are $4, $3, and $3, respectively.

The units finished and transferred to Dept. C are valued at the full unit cost of $5 (from Dept. A), plus the unit cost of $10 added in Dept. B, amounting to a total cost transferred of $37,500 (2,500 units × $15).

The cost of the units in process at the end of the period includes the full cost of $5 from Dept. A. There is no materials cost for Dept. B ending

FIGURE 7-3   Production Report, Dept. B

PRODUCTION REPORT

For Month Ending _April 30, 20—_

Dept. _B—Molding_

In process, beginning of period _____ 250 units

Stage of completion _____ 1/2

Placed in process during period _____

Received from dept. ___A___ during period _2,600 units_

Transferred to dept. ___B___ during period _2,500 units_

Transferred to stockroom during period _____

In process, end of period _____ 350 units

Stage of completion _____ 2/5

---

work in process because no materials were added. Because the units are two-fifths completed, two-fifths of the current unit costs for labor and factory overhead is used in costing the units. The combination of these items results in a cost of $2,590 for the ending work in process.

ILLUSTRATIVE PROBLEM NO. 3

Computing the unit cost in Dept. C where 60 percent of the materials cost is added to production at the beginning of processing and 40 percent of the materials when the processing is one-half completed—average cost method. In Dept. C, the calculation of equivalent production is more difficult because materials are added at different points throughout the process. The stage of completion of units in process cannot be averaged but must be reported in separate groups of units at various points in the manufacturing operation as shown in the production report, Figure 7-5. In calculating the units of output for the period, as shown in Figure 7-6, the stage of completion of each element group must be carefully examined.

The equivalent production for materials for the month is calculated as follows: 2,400 units were finished, which includes all the materials, and 200 units are one-fourth completed at the end of the period. Because they are not yet at the halfway point of the process, only 60 percent of the materials have been added to the uncompleted units, an equivalent of 120 units. The 400 units that are three-fourths completed have passed the halfway stage and have had all materials added, a total of 400 equivalent

FIGURE 7-4   Cost of Production Summary, Dept. B

Kidco
Cost of Production Summary—Dept. B
For the Month Ended April 30, 20—

Cost of work in process, beginning of month—Dept. B:

Cost in Dept. A		$ 1,250	
Cost in Dept. B:			
Materials	-0-		
Labor	$375		
Factory overhead	375	750	$ 2,000
Cost of goods received from Dept. A during month			13,000
Cost of production for month:			
Materials	$10,000		
Labor	7,545		
Factory overhead	7,545	25,090	
Total costs to be accounted for			**$40,090**

Unit output for month:

Materials:	
Finished and transferred to Dept. C during month	2,500
Equivalent units of work in process, end of month	-0-
Total equivalent production	2,500

Labor and factory overhead:	
Finished and transferred to Dept. C during month	2,500
Equivalent units of work in process, end of month	
(350 units, two-fifths completed)	140
Total equivalent production	2,640

Unit cost for month—Dept. B:

Materials ($10,000 ÷ 2,500)	$4.00
Labor ($375 + $7,545) ÷ 2,640	3.00
Factory overhead ($375 + $7,545) ÷ 2,640	3.00
Total	$10.00

Inventory costs:

Cost of goods finished and transferred to Dept. C during month:			
Cost in Dept. A (2,500 × $ 5)	$12,500		
Cost in Dept. B (2,500 × $10)	25,000		
(2,500 × $15)		$37,500	
Cost of work in process, end of month:			
Cost in Dept. A (350 × $5)	$ 1,750		
Cost in Dept. B:			
Materials	-0-		
Labor (350 × 2/5 × $3)	$420		
Factory overhead (350 × 2/5 × $3)	420	840	2,590
Total production costs accounted for			**$40,090**

FIGURE 7-5   Production Report, Dept. C

PRODUCTION REPORT

For Month Ending __April 30, 20—__

Dept. __C—Finishing__

In process, beginning of period _____ 500 units
Stage of completion   200 units 3/4 completed;300 units
                                        1/3 completed
Placed in process during period _____
Received from dept. ___B___ during period __2,500 units__
Transferred to dept. _____ during period _____
Transferred to stockroom during period _____ 2,400 units
In process, end of period _____ 600 units
Stage of completion ___ 200 units 1/4 completed;400 units
                        3/4 completed

units. Combining these figures—2,400, 120, and 400—results in the equivalent output for materials of 2,920 units.

It is simpler to calculate the equivalency for labor and factory overhead: 2,400 completed units, plus the equivalent of 50 completed units (200 units one-fourth completed), plus the equivalent of 300 completed units (400 units three-fourths completed) equals a total equivalent production for labor and overhead of 2,750 units.

The unit costs for the month are calculated as previously illustrated and are determined to be $1.75, $1.20, and $0.60 for materials, labor, and factory overhead, respectively, for a total unit cost in Dept. C of $3.55. The cost of the units finished and transferred to the stockroom includes the unit costs from Dept. A of $5, from Dept. B of $10, and from Dept. C of $3.55, a total cost of $18.55.

In calculating the cost to be assigned to the ending work in process, the stage of completion must be considered. The 200 units that are one-fourth completed will have all the costs from Depts. A and B assigned to them because they were 100% completed by those departments. The costs in Dept. C are determined as follows: 60 percent of the materials cost has been added to the 200 units, an equivalent of 120 units. The cost of the materials will be as follows: 200 units × 60% × $1.75 = $210. The costs allocated for labor and overhead are one-fourth of this month's unit cost for each, or 200 units × 25% × $1.20 = $60 for labor and 200 units × 25% × $0.60 = $30 for overhead.

FIGURE 7-6   Cost of Production Summary, Dept. C

Kidco
Cost of Production Summary—Dept. C
For the Month Ended April 30, 20—

Cost of work in process, beginning of month—Dept. C:			
Cost in Dept. A		$ 2,500	
Cost in Dept. B		5,000	
Cost in Dept. C:			
Materials	$665		
Labor	300		
Factory overhead	150	1,115	$ 8,615
Cost of goods received from Dept. B during month			$37,500
Cost of production for month:			
Materials		$ 4,445	
Labor		3,000	
Factory overhead		1,500	8,945
Total costs to be accounted for			**$55,060**
Unit output for month:			
Materials:			
Finished and transferred to finished goods during month			2,400
Equivalent units of work in process, end of month:			
200 units, one-fourth completed (60% of materials)			120
400 units, three-fourths completed (all materials)			400
Total equivalent production			2,920
Labor and overhead:			
Finished and transferred to finished goods during month			2,400
Equivalent units of work in process, end of month:			
200 units, one-fourth completed			50
400 units, three-fourths completed			300
Total equivalent production			2,750
Unit cost for month—Dept. C:			
Materials ($665 + $4,445) ÷ 2,920			$1.75
Labor ($300 + $3,000) ÷ 2,750			1.20
Factory overhead ($150 + $1,500) ÷ 2,750			0.60
Total			$3.55

FIGURE 7-6   (Concluded)

Inventory costs:
  Cost of goods finished and transferred to finished goods
  during month:
    Cost in Dept. A (2,400 × $ 5.00) $12,000
    Cost in Dept. B (2,400 × $10.00)   24,000
    Cost in Dept. C (2,400 × $ 3.55)   8,520
                                                          _____
                     (2,400 × $18.55) $44,520
                                                          ========

  Cost of work in process, end of month:
    200 units, one-fourth completed:
      Cost in Dept. A (200 × $5) . . . . $ 1,000
      Cost in Dept. B (200 × $10)   2,000
      Cost in Dept. C:
        Materials (200 × 60% × $1.75) . . . . . $ 210
        Labor (200 × 25% × $1.20)   60
        Factory overhead (200 × 25% × $0.60) . .   30   300

    400 units, three-fourths completed:
      Cost in Dept. A (400 × $5)   2,000
      Cost in Dept. B (400 × $10)   4,000
      Cost in Dept. C:
        Materials (400 × $1.75) . . . . $ 700
        Labor (400 × 75% × $1.20)   360
        Factory overhead (400 × 75% × $0.60) . .   180   1,240   10,540

  Total production costs accounted for $55,060
                                                                             ========

The 400 units that are three-fourths completed are assigned all of the unit costs from Depts. A ($5) and B ($10). Although these units are still in process, all materials required by department C have been added. Therefore, they are charged for the full cost of materials in Dept. C, $700 (400 units × $1.75). Three-fourths of the cost for labor and factory overhead would also be included in the cost of these units: $360 for labor (400 units × 75% × $1.20), and $180 for overhead (400 units × 75% × $0.60).

After the cost of production summaries have been prepared for each department, the journal entries can be made as illustrated in Chapter 6. Entries would be made to transfer costs from one department to the next department and so on, ending at Finished Goods. The actual costs incurred during the month for materials, labor, and factory overhead would be recorded in the journals and ledgers. After all entries have been made, the work in process accounts in the general ledger should have balances that equal the cost assigned to work in process on the cost of production summaries. If desired, a departmental cost work sheet can be prepared as illustrated in Chapter 6.

> You should now be able to work the following: Questions 1–4; Exercises 7-1 to 7-6; and Problems 7-1 to 7-4.

UNITS LOST IN PRODUCTION

LEARNING OBJECTIVE 2
Account for units lost in the production process.

In many industries that have a process manufacturing operation, the process is of a nature that some units will always be lost due to evaporation, shrinkage, spillage, or other factors. The effect of such losses is that when the number of units completed in a given period is added to the number of units still in process at the end of the period, the total units calculated will be less than the number of units that should be accounted for.

Normal losses are expected in the manufacturing process and cannot be avoided. They represent a necessary cost of producing the marketable units. Usually, normal losses are treated as **product costs**; that is, the cost of the lost units are included as a part of the cost of all units finished or still in process. In other words, the good units absorb the cost of the units lost. The effect is that the unit cost of the remaining units is greater than if no losses had been incurred, because of the smaller number of units over which to spread the production costs for the period. The following is a basic example to illustrate the concept.

Assume that materials, labor, and factory overhead are applied evenly throughout the process; units are lost throughout the process, but inspection does not occur until the end of the process. The monthly production report for the Refining Department of Zyon Oil Corporation reports the following data:

Units started in process		12,000
Units finished and transferred to the next department . . .	9,000	
Units still in process, one-half completed		
(materials, labor, and overhead)	2,000	11,000
Units lost in production		1,000

This report is significant to factory managers, who review these figures to determine whether they represent normal unavoidable losses or abnormal losses that will require a different type of action. From the production statistics and costs of production data for the month, a cost of production summary as shown in Figure 7-7 can be prepared.

FIGURE 7-7   Zyon Oil Cost of Production Summary, Refining Dept.

Zyon Oil Corporation
Cost of Production Summary—Refining Dept.
For the Month Ended July 31, 20—

Cost of production for month:

Materials	$20,000
Labor	10,000
Factory overhead	5,000
Total costs to be accounted for	**$35,000**

Unit output for month:

Finished and transferred to Dept. B during month	9,000
Equivalent units of work in process, end of month	
(2,000 units, one-half completed)	1,000
Total equivalent production	10,000

Unit cost for month:

Materials ($20,000 ÷ 10,000)	$2.00
Labor ($10,000 ÷ 10,000)	1.00
Factory overhead ($5,000 ÷ 10,000)	0.50
Total	$3.50

Inventory costs:

Cost of goods finished and transferred to Dept. B during month (9,000 × $3.50)		$31,500
Cost of work in process, end of month:		
Materials (2,000 × 1/2 × $2)	$2,000	
Labor (2,000 × 1/2 × $1)	1,000	
Factory overhead (2,000 × 1/2 × $0.50)	500	3,500
Total production costs accounted for		**$35,000**

Notice on the cost of production summary that the lost units have not been considered. They have been ignored in the calculation of equivalent production and in the determination of inventory costs. If the units had not been spoiled but had been completed according to specifications, equivalent production would have been 11,000 units, and the unit costs for materials, labor, and factory overhead would have been lower. In the case illustrated, there is a loss of units that have already incurred some costs, which will be absorbed by the good units produced during the month.

The preceding discussion has considered only normal losses, with the cost of lost units being treated as product cost—that is, charged to the remaining good units. But abnormal losses may also occur. Such losses are not expected in the manufacturing process and should not happen under normal, efficient operating conditions. Units lost under abnormal circumstances are included in the calculation of equivalent production, and unit costs are determined as if the units were lost at the end of the process. However, abnormal losses are not included as part of the cost of transferred or finished goods, but are treated as a period cost—that is, they are charged to a separate account, such as Loss from Abnormal Spoilage, and shown as a separate item of expense on the current income statement and not as a part of the manufacturing costs.

UNITS GAINED IN PRODUCTION

LEARNING OBJECTIVE 3
Account for units gained in the production process.

For some products, the addition of materials in any department after the first department may increase the number of units being processed. For example, assume that a liquid product is being produced. In the first department, 1,000 gallons of various materials are put into production. In the next department, an additional 500 gallons of a different material are added, increasing the number of units being manufactured to 1,500. This increase in units has the opposite effect of lost units and requires an adjustment to the unit cost. The calculation of this adjusted unit cost is similar to that made when units are lost, except that the total cost for the original units must now be spread over a greater number of units in the subsequent department, thereby reducing the unit cost.

To illustrate, assume that a concentrated detergent, Mor-Glean, is manufactured. During the month, 10,000 gallons of the partially processed product are transferred to the Blending Dept. at a cost of $15,000, with a unit cost of $1.50. In the Blending Dept., 5,000 gallons of additional materials are added to these units in process. As these materials are added, the mixing and refining of the liquid involves the equal application of materials, labor, and overhead. A production report shows that 13,000 gallons were completed and transferred to finished goods, leaving 2,000 gallons in process, one-half completed. The cost of production summary, Figure 7-8, shows that the cost transferred from the Mixing Dept. for 10,000 gallons was $15,000, at a unit cost of $1.50. The addition of 5,000 gallons in the Blending Dept. increases the liquid in process to 15,000 units. The $15,000 cost from the Mixing Dept. must now be spread over these 15,000 units, resulting in an adjusted unit cost of $1.00.

FIGURE 7-8   Mor-Glean Cost of Production Summary, Dept. B

Mor-Glean Manufacturing Company
Cost of Production Summary—Blending Dept.
For the Month Ended May 31, 20—

Cost of goods received from Mixing Dept. during month (10,000 gallons × $1.50)		$15,000
Cost of production for month:		
Materials	$15,400	
Labor	3,500	
Factory overhead	2,800	21,700
Total costs to be accounted for		**$36,700**

Unit output for month:	
Finished and transferred to finished goods	13,000
Equivalent units of work in process, end of month (2,000 gallons, one-half completed)	1,000
Total equivalent production	14,000

Unit cost for month:	
Materials ($15,400 ÷ 14,000)	$1.10
Labor ($3,500 ÷ 14,000)	0.25
Factory overhead ($2,800 ÷ 14,000)	0.20
Total	$1.55

Inventory costs:		
Cost of goods finished and transferred to finished goods:		
Cost in Dept. A (13,000 × $1.00*, adjusted unit cost)	$13,000	
Cost in Dept. B (13,000 × $1.55)	20,150	
(13,000 × $2.55)		$33,150

Cost of work in process, end of month: Cost in Mixing Dept. (2,000 × $1.00, adjusted unit cost)		$2,000	
Cost in Blending Dept.:			
Materials (2,000 × 1/2 × $1.10)	$1,100		
Labor (2,000 × 1/2 × $0.25)	250		
Factory overhead (2,000 × 1/2 × $0.20) .	200	1,550	3,550
Total production costs accounted for			**$36,700**

$15,000 ÷ 15,000 gal. = $1 per gal.

EQUIVALENT PRODUCTION—-FIRST-IN, FIRST-OUT METHOD

LEARNING OBJECTIVE 4
Assign costs to
inventories, using
the first-in, first-out
method.

The previous discussion and illustrations have used the average method of costing. As mentioned in Chapter 6, another method commonly used is the **first-in, first-out (FIFO) method**. This procedure assumes that the unit costs calculated for the current period are applied for a variety of reasons: first, to complete the beginning units of work in process; second, to start and fully complete an additional number of units; and finally, to start other units that will remain unfinished at the end of the period.

The two problems that follow illustrate the FIFO method and compare it to the average costing method for Brunner Manufacturing Company, which has the following two departments: Dept. 1–Machining and Dept. 2–Assembly. When studying these examples, note that FIFO costing differs from average costing only if there are units in process at the start of the period. If no beginning work in process exists, both methods will produce the same results.

Whether using the FIFO or the average cost method, the first step in preparing the cost of production summary is to list the costs that must be accounted for: the beginning balance of work in process, the current period's costs of production, and the cost of units transferred from a prior department, if any. With the FIFO method, it is not necessary to break down the cost of the beginning work in process into its cost elements as the average cost method requires.

The second step under the FIFO method, as with the average cost procedure, is to determine the unit output for the month. If there were units in process at the start of the period, the total equivalent production figures for the FIFO method will differ from those for the average cost method because the unit output required to complete the beginning work in process must be calculated in the FIFO method.

ILLUSTRATIVE PROBLEM NO. 1

FIFO cost method compared with average cost method—materials added at start of process. Assume that in Dept. 1, materials are added at the start of processing. Labor and factory overhead are applied evenly throughout the process. The production report for March reflects the following data:

Units in process, beginning of month, two-thirds completed . . .	3,000
Units started in process	9,000
Units finished and transferred to Dept. 2	8,000
Units in process, end of month, one-half completed	4,000

Cost data are as follows:
Beginning work in process, prior month's cost:

Materials	$ 9,600
Labor	3,600
Factory overhead	2,800
Total	$16,000

Current month's production costs:

Materials	$27,000
Labor	16,000
Factory overhead	8,000
Total	$51,000

Using the FIFO method, a cost of production summary is prepared as presented in Figure 7-9. For comparative purposes, Figure 7-10 shows a cost of production summary using the average cost method.

There were 3,000 units in process at the beginning of the month. These units were complete as to materials and two-thirds complete as to labor and factory overhead.

In the current month, no materials had to be added to the beginning inventory. However, the equivalent of 1,000 units (3,000 × 1/3) of labor and overhead had to be applied to finish the units in Dept. 1.

Of the 8,000 units finished and transferred to Dept. 2 during the month, 3,000 were from the beginning units in process. Therefore, 5,000 units were started and fully completed during the month. Under the FIFO cost method, the beginning units in process *are not merged* with the units started and finished during the month.

The calculation of equivalent production for the *ending work in process* is the *same* under FIFO and the average cost method. These 4,000 units in ending inventory have had all materials added and only one-half of the labor and overhead. Thus, the ending inventory equivalent production for materials is 4,000 units and for labor and overhead, 2,000 units (4,000 × 1/2).

The calculation of unit costs with the FIFO method takes into consideration only the current period's cost data. The total cost of each element—materials, labor, and factory overhead—is divided by the equivalent production for the period to determine the unit cost for each element. The cost elements of the beginning work in process is not merged with current cost elements under the FIFO method, as it is in the average cost method.

FIGURE 7-9   Cost of Production Summary, Dept. 1, FIFO Method

FIFO METHOD

Brunner Manufacturing Company
Cost of Production Summary—Dept. 1 (Machining)
For the Month Ended March 31, 20—

Cost of work in process, beginning of month		$16,000
Cost of production for month:		
Materials	$27,000	
Labor	16,000	
Factory overhead	8,000	51,000
Total costs to be accounted for		**$67,000**

Unit output for month:

	Materials	Labor and Factory Overhead
To complete beginning units in process	-0-	1,000
Units started and finished during month	5,000	5,000
Ending units in process	4,000	2,000
Total equivalent production	9,000	8,000

Unit cost for month:		
Materials ($27,000 ÷ 9,000)		$3.00
Labor ($16,000 ÷ 8,000)		2.00
Factory overhead ($8,000 ÷ 8,000)		1.00
Total		$6.00

Inventory costs:		
Cost of goods finished and transferred to Dept. 2 during month:		
Beginning units in process:		
Prior month's cost	$16,000	
Current cost to complete:		
Materials	-0-	
Labor (3,000 × 1/3 × $2)	2,000	
Factory overhead (3,000 × 1/3 × $1)	1,000	$19,000
Units started and finished during month		
(5,000 × $6.00)		30,000
Total cost transferred (8,000 × $6.125*) . . .		$49,000
Cost of work in process, end of month:		
Materials (4,000 × $3)	$12,000	
Labor (4,000 × 1/2 × $2)	4,000	
Factory overhead (4,000 × 1/2 × $1)	2,000	18,000
Total production costs accounted for		**$67,000**

*$49,000 ÷ 8,000 = $6.125

FIGURE 7-10   Cost of Production Summary, Dept. 1, Average Cost Method

---

AVERAGE COST METHOD

Brunner Manufacturing Company
Cost of Production Summary—Dept. 1 (Machining)
For the Month Ended March 31, 20—

Cost of work in process, beginning of month:		
Materials	$ 9,600	
Labor	3,600	
Factory overhead	2,800	$16,000
Cost of production for month:		
Materials	$27,000	
Labor	16,000	
Factory overhead	8,000	51,000
Total costs to be accounted for		**$67,000**
Unit output for month:		
Materials:		
Finished and transferred to Dept. 2 during month		8,000
Work in process, end of month		4,000
Total equivalent production		12,000
Labor and factory overhead:		
Finished and transferred to Dept. 2 during month		8,000
Work in process, end of month (4,000 units,		
1/2 completed)		2,000
Total equivalent production		10,000
Unit cost for month:		
Materials ($9,600 + $27,000) ÷ 12,000		$3.05
Labor ($3,600 + $16,000) ÷ 10,000		1.96
Factory overhead ($2,800 + $8,000) ÷ 10,000		1.08
Total		$6.09
Inventory costs:		
Cost of goods finished and transferred to Dept. 2		
during month (8,000 × $6.09)		$48,720
Cost of work in process, end of month:		
Materials (4,000 × $3.05)	$12,200	
Labor (4,000 × 1/2 × $1.96)	3,920	
Factory overhead (4,000 × 1/2 × $1.08)	2,160	18,280
Total production costs accounted for		**$67,000**

When assigning costs to the units finished and transferred, the average cost approach charges the 8,000 units transferred with the total unit cost of $6.09. Under the FIFO method, however, two calculations are necessary to determine the cost assigned to units transferred. First, the 3,000 units in process at the beginning of the month were previously completed as to materials; therefore, no cost for materials is added. However, the units had been only two-thirds completed as to labor and overhead during the previous month and must be one-third completed this month. Thus, one-third of the current period's unit cost for labor and overhead is assigned to each of the 3,000 units. The cost to complete the beginning inventory then is added to the $16,000 beginning inventory cost carried over from the prior period to arrive at a completed cost for the beginning inventory of $19,000.

Second, the 5,000 units started and fully manufactured during the month are priced at the unit cost of $6 for the period. The total accumulated cost of the 3,000 units in process at the beginning of the month ($19,000) plus the cost of the 5,000 units started and finished during the month ($30,000) is then transferred to Dept. 2 ($49,000). Note that when making this transfer of cost, the cost and unit cost related to the beginning inventory units lose their identity because they are merged with the cost of units started and finished during the current period. Thus, the $49,000 of the total cost transferred to Dept. 2 is divided by the 8,000 units transferred to Dept. 2 to arrive at a single unit cost of $6.125. The costs assigned to the ending work in process inventory are determined in the same manner under the FIFO method and the average cost approach. The 4,000 units are complete as to materials and are charged with the full cost of materials. They are one-half complete as to labor and overhead and are allocated one-half of the labor and overhead cost. Although the method of calculation is the same, the total costs charged to the ending units in process differ between the FIFO and average cost methods because of the difference in unit costs determined by the two procedures.

ILLUSTRATIVE PROBLEM NO. 2

FIFO cost method compared with average cost method—materials added at end of process. Assume that in Dept. 2, materials are added at the end of the process and labor and factory overhead are applied evenly throughout the process. The production for March reflects the following information:

Units in process, beginning of month, three-fourths completed .	2,000
Units received from Dept. 1	8,000
Units finished	8,000
Units in process, end of month, one-half completed	2,000

Cost data are as follows:
Beginning work in process, prior month's cost:

Prior department cost	$12,000
Materials	-0-
Labor	4,160
Factory overhead	3,000
Total	$19,160

Cost of units received from Dept. 1	$49,000

Current month's production costs:

Materials	$16,000
Labor	21,000
Factory overhead	13,875
Total	$50,875

Figure 7-11 shows the cost of production summary for Dept. 2, using the FIFO method, and Figure 7-12 shows the summary using the average cost method. In the cost of production summary using the FIFO method, the costs to be accounted for are listed and then the unit output for the period is determined. In this department, materials are added at the end of the process. Therefore, in order to finish the 2,000 units in process at the beginning of the period, all materials have to be added—a total of 2,000 units. Three-fourths of the labor and factory overhead were applied to these beginning inventory units in the previous period, so one-fourth of the labor and overhead need to be applied in the current month to finish the 2,000 units—an equivalent of 500 units.

Of the 8,000 units completed during the period, 2,000 were from the beginning inventory; therefore, 6,000 new units were started and fully manufactured during the current month. The 2,000 units in process at the end of the month have had no materials added but are one-half complete as to labor and overhead—an equivalent of 1,000 units.

As in Dept. 1, unit cost for FIFO is calculated by dividing the current period's cost of each element by the equivalent production for that element. Under the average cost method, unit cost is calculated by dividing the merged element costs of the current period and work in process by the equivalent production for each element.

In FIFO, to calculate the total completed cost of the beginning inventory, the total cost balance of the beginning work in process from the previous period is added to the costs incurred to complete these units in the current period. The 2,000 units are charged for the full cost of materials and with one-fourth of the current costs for labor and overhead. The average cost method does not require a separate computation to complete the beginning inventory.

FIGURE 7-11   Cost of Production Summary, Dept. 2, FIFO Method

FIFO METHOD

Brunner Manufacturing Company
Cost of Production Summary—Dept. 2 (Assembly)
For the Month Ended March 31, 20—

Cost of work in process, beginning of month . . .		$ 19,160
Cost of goods received from Dept. 1 during month		49,000
Cost of production for month:		
Materials	$16,000	
Labor	21,000	
Factory overhead	13,875	50,875
Total costs to be accounted for		**$119,035**

Unit output for month:

	Materials	Labor and Factory Overhead
To complete beginning units in process	2,000	500
Units started and finished during month	6,000	6,000
Ending units in process	-0-	1,000
Total equivalent production	8,000	7,500

Unit cost for month:	
Materials ($16,000 ÷ 8,000)	$2.00
Labor ($21,000 ÷ 7,500)	2.80
Factory overhead ($13,875 ÷ 7,500)	1.85
Total	$6.65

Under the FIFO method, the cost transferred from Dept. 1 during the period, $49,000, is divided by the 8,000 units transferred, which results in an adjusted unit cost of $6.125 for the goods received from Dept. 1. The 6,000 units started and finished during the month are charged with the $6.125 adjusted unit cost from the prior department *plus* the $6.65 current unit cost generated by Dept.2.

Under the average cost method, all of the units from Dept. 1, whether this month's or last month's units, must be considered in determining the unit cost. The 2,000 units in process at the beginning of the period and the 8,000 units received during the month are included in the calculation. The prior department cost of $12,000, carried over from the previous month, is added to the current month's cost ($49,000) transferred

FIGURE 7-11   Concluded

Inventory costs:
  Cost of goods finished:
    Beginning units in process:
      Prior month's cost $19,160
      Current cost to complete:
        Materials (2,000 × $2)   4,000
        Labor (2,000 × 1/4 × $2.80)   1,400
        Factory overhead (2,000 × 1/4 × $1.85) . .   925 $25,485

    Units started and finished during month:
      Cost in Dept. 1 (6,000 × $ 6.125) $36,750
      Cost in Dept. 2 (6,000 × $ 6.65)   39,900   76,650

      Total [(2,000 units + 6,000 units) × $12.7669]* $102,135
  Cost of work in process, end of month:
    Cost in Dept. 1 (2,000 × $6.125) $12,250
    Cost in Dept. 2:
      Materials . . . .   -0-
      Labor (2,000 × 1/2 × $2.80)   2,800
      Factory overhead (2,000 × 1/2 × $1.85) . . .   1,850   16,900

Total production costs accounted for **$119,035**

*$102,135 ÷ 8,000 units = $12.7669

from Dept. 1. The total prior department cost of $61,000 is then divided by 10,000 units to produce a unit cost of $6.10. The 8,000 units completed during the period have a total unit cost for the period of $12.7706, which consists of the transferred-in cost of $6.10 plus the cost added by the Dept. 2 operations of $6.6706.

The costs to be charged to the units in process at the end of the month are different, although both FIFO and average cost use the same mathematical methods. The values of the ending work in process differ because of the procedures used to derive the prior department and current month unit costs.

In comparing the FIFO and the average cost methods, FIFO provides that units started within the current period are valued at the current

FIGURE 7-12   Cost of Production Summary, Dept. 2, Average Cost Method

AVERAGE COST METHOD

Brunner Manufacturing Company
Cost of Production Summary—Dept. 2 (Assembly)
For the Month Ended March 31, 20—

Cost of work process, beginning of month:			
Cost in Dept. 1		$12,000	
Cost in Dept. 2:			
Materials	-0-		
Labor	$4,160		
Factory overhead	3,000	7,160	$ 19,160
Cost of goods received from Dept. 1 during month			49,000
Cost of production for month:			
Materials		$16,000	
Labor		21,000	
Factory overhead		13,875	50,875
Total costs to be accounted for			**$119,035**
Unit output for month:			
Materials finished during month			8,000
Labor and overhead:			
Finished during month		8,000	
Work in process, end of month . . .		1,000	9,000
Unit cost for month:			
Materials ($16,000 ÷ 8,000)			$2.0000
Labor [($4,160 + $21,000) ÷ 9,000]			2.7956
Factory overhead [($3,000 + $13,875) ÷ 9,000] . .			1.8750
Total			$6.6706
Inventory costs:			
Cost of goods finished:			
Cost in Dept. 1 (8,000 × $ 6.1000)	$48,800.00		
Cost in Dept. 2 (8,000 × $ 6.6706)	53,364.80		
(8,000 × $12.7706)			$102,164.80
Cost of work in process, end of month:			
Cost in Dept. 1 (2,000 × $6.10) . . .		$12,200.00	
Cost in Dept. 2:			
Materials		-0-	
Labor (2,000 × 1/2 × $2.7956) . .		2,795.60	
Factory overhead (2,000 × 1/2 × $1.8750). . .		1,875.00	16,870.60
Total production costs accounted for			**$119,035.40***

*Rounding difference

period's costs and are not distorted by the merging of the current costs with costs from the preceding period, which could be considerably different. The units and costs in the beginning inventory in a processing department maintain their separate identity. This helps to control costs by having purely current unit costs each month to compare when analyzing month-to-month costs for deviations. Use of the FIFO method, however, means that the units in the beginning inventory are valued when completed at a cost that represents neither the prior period's cost nor the current period's cost, but a combination of the two. Also, the identity of the beginning units in process is typically not maintained when these units are transferred to the next department. The cost of these units is usually combined with the cost of units fully manufactured during the month at the time of transfer.

The average cost method has an advantage when compared to FIFO in that all units completed during the period will be assigned the same unit cost. This cost assignment procedure makes average cost a simpler method to use. In the final analysis, however, a manufacturer should choose the method that not only minimizes the clerical cost of application but also most accurately gauges its cost of production so that its products can successfully compete in the marketplace.

> **You should now be able to work the following: Questions 5–11; Exercises 7-7 to 7-10; and Problems 7-5 to 7-8, and 7-11.**

JOINT PRODUCTS AND BY-PRODUCTS

LEARNING OBJECTIVE 5
Identify the methods used to apportion joint costs to joint products and account for by-products.

In many industries, the manufacturing process originates with one or more raw materials started in process, from which two or more distinct products are derived. Examples of these industries are petroleum refineries, lumber mills, and meat packing plants. Petroleum yields gasoline, heating oils, and lubricants. Lumber mills produce various grades of lumber and salable sawdust. Meat packing processes result in a variety of different cuts of meat and other products. The several items obtained from a common process are divided into two categories: those that are the primary objectives of the process, called **joint products**, and secondary products with relatively little value, called **by-products**.

ACCOUNTING FOR JOINT PRODUCTS

The costs of materials, labor, and overhead incurred during the joint process are called **joint costs**. The separate products become identifiable at the **split-off point**. The manufacturing costs incurred up to this point usually cannot be specifically identified with any one of the individual products. A joint process may have one or more split-off points, depending on the types of output produced. If a market exists for the product, it may be sold at the split-off point. However, some method must be adopted to equitably allocate the joint costs to each identifiable product. If further processing of any of the products is required after the split-off point, these additional costs will be applied directly to the specific products.

Typical bases for apportionment of joint costs to joint products follow:

1. Relative sales value of each product (or adjusted sales value).

2. A physical unit of measure such as volume, weight, size, or grade.

3. Chemical, engineering, or other types of analyses.

The assignment of costs in proportion to **relative sales value** of each product is most commonly used and is the only method that will be illustrated here. This method assumes a direct relationship between selling prices and joint costs. It follows the logic that the greatest share of joint cost should be assigned to the product that has the highest sales value.

To illustrate, assume that the Chem-alene Co. produces two liquid products from one process. In the manufacturing process, various materials are mixed in a huge vat and allowed to settle, so that a light liquid rises to the top and a heavier liquid settles to the bottom of the vat. The products, A and B, are drawn off separately and piped directly into tank cars for shipment. The costs of materials, labor, and overhead total $200,000, producing 30,000 gallons of A and 20,000 gallons of B.

Product A sells for $10.00 a gallon and Product B for $25.00 a gallon. Using the relative sales value method, the joint costs of $200,000 would be allocated as follows:

Product	Units Produced		Unit Selling Price		Total Sales Value	Percent of Sales Value	Assignment of Joint Costs
A	30,000	×	$10.00	=	$300,000	37.5%	$ 75,000
B	20,000	×	25.00	=	500,000	62.5	125,000
Total	50,000				$800,000	100.0%	$200,000

Some companies further refine this method by subtracting each product's estimated selling expenses from its sales value to determine the net realizable value of the product. If a product is to be processed further after the point of separation, costs should not be assigned on the basis of ultimate sales value because the additional processing adds value to the product. In a case such as this, an **adjusted sales value** is used that takes into consideration the cost of the processing after split-off.

Assume that Chem-alene Co. market researchers determine that Product B would have a better market if it were sold in powder form in individual packages. After studying this proposition, the company decides to pipe Product B into ovens to dehydrate it. The resulting powder is divided into one-pound packages that will sell for $80 each.

During the month of October, when the new process began, the costs of materials, labor, and factory overhead in the mixing and settling department were $127,500, $42,500, and $30,000, respectively, and 30,000 gallons of Product A were transferred to tank cars. In the baking department, costs totaled $100,000 for baking and packaging the 20,000 gallons of Product B received from mixing and settling, and 10,000 one-pound packages were produced.

The assignment of costs of $200,000 in the mixing and settling department, using the adjusted sales value method, follows:

Units Produced	Unit Selling Price		Ultimate Sales Value	Less Cost after Split-Off	Sales Value at Split-Off	Percent Sales Value	Assignment of Joint Costs
A—30,000 gals. ×	$10.00	=	$ 300,000	-0-	$ 300,000	30%	$ 60,000
B—10,000 lbs.* ×	80.00	=	800,000	$100,000	700,000	70	140,000
Total			$1,100,000	$100,000	$1,000,000	100%	$200,000

*20,000 gallons of liquid is further processed into 10,000 lbs. of powder.

The allocated cost of Product A is transferred to a finished goods inventory account. The assigned cost of Product B is transferred to a work in process account to which the additional costs of processing are charged. The total cost of Product B is then transferred to a finished goods inventory account.

ACCOUNTING FOR BY-PRODUCTS

In accounting for by-products, the common practice is to make no allocation of the processing costs up to the split-off point. Costs incurred up to that point are chargeable to the main products. If no further processing is required to make the by-products marketable, they may be accounted for by debiting an inventory account, By-Products, and crediting Work in Process for the estimated sales value of the by-products recovered. Under this procedure, the estimated sales value of the by-products reduces the cost of the main products. The reduction in costs, due to the by-product, is shown in the inventory costs section of the cost of production summary. If the by-products are sold for more or less than the estimated sales value, the difference may be credited or debited to Gain and Loss on Sales of By-Products.

Principles of Cost Accounting

Assume that the production management of the Chem-alene Co. finds that nonusable residue at the bottom of the vat can be sold for $10,000 without further processing. Also assume that other data for the month of November are the same as for October. The cost of production summary in Figure 7-13 reflects the assignment of joint costs under the

FIGURE 7-13   Cost of Production Summary, Joint Products and By-Products

---

Chem-alene Co.
Cost of Production Summary—Mixing and Settling Department
For the Month Ended November 30, 20—

Cost of production for month:

Materials	$127,500
Labor	42,500
Factory overhead	30,000
Total costs to be accounted for	**$200,000**

Unit output for month:

Finished and transferred to finished goods (Product A)	30,000
Finished and transferred to baking department (Product B)	20,000
Total	50,000

Unit cost for month:

Materials ($127,500 ÷ 50,000)	$2.55
Labor ($42,500 ÷ 50,000)	0.85
Factory overhead ($30,000 ÷ 50,000)	0.60
Total	$4.00

Total costs to split-off point	$200,000
Less market value of by-product	10,000
Total cost to be assigned to joint products finished and transferred	$190,000

Inventory costs:

Cost of goods finished (Product A) and transferred to finished goods (30% × $190,000)	$ 57,000
Cost of goods finished (Product B) and transferred to baking department (70% × $190,000)	133,000
Cost of by-product finished and transferred to by-product inventory	10,000
Total production costs accounted for	**$200,000**

adjusted sales value method and uses the by-product value as a reduction in the cost of the joint products and as the cost assigned to the by-product.

In some instances, an unstable market will make the sales value of the by-product so insignificant or so uncertain that the cost of the main products will not be reduced. In this case, no entry for the by-product is made at the point of separation. When the by-product is sold, the transaction is recorded by debiting Cash or Accounts Receivable and crediting By-Product Sales or Miscellaneous Income. The revenue account will usually be treated as "other income" on the income statement. However, some companies, if the amount is significant, will show this revenue as sales income, as a deduction from the cost of the main products sold, or as a reduction in the total cost of the main products manufactured.

If further processing is required to make the by-product salable, an account entitled By-Products in Process may be opened, and all subsequent processing costs are charged to that account. As with other products, when the processing is completed, an entry is made to transfer the costs from the in-process account to an inventory account.

> **You should now be able to work the following: Questions 12–15; Exercises 7-11 to 7-14; and Problems 7-9 and 7-10.**

K E Y   T E R M S

Adjusted sales value, p. 296
By-products, p. 295
First-in, first-out (FIFO) method, p. 286
Joint costs, p. 295
Joint products, p. 295

Normal losses, p. 282
Product costs, p. 282
Relative sales value, p. 296
Split-off point, p. 295

S E L F - S T U D Y   P R O B L E M

AVERAGE AND FIFO COST METHODS; LOSSES AT THE BEGINNING AND END OF PROCESSING

MERCURY PRODUCTION COMPANY

Mercury Production Company uses a process cost system. Its manufacturing operation is carried on in two departments: Machining and Finishing. The Machining Department uses the average cost method and the Finishing Department uses the FIFO cost method. Materials are added in both departments at the beginning of operations, and the added materials do not increase the number of units being processed. Units are lost in the Machining Department throughout the production process, and inspection occurs at the end of the process. The lost units have no scrap value and are considered to be a normal loss.

Production statistics for May show the following data:

	Machining	Finishing
Units in process, May 1 (all material, 20% of labor and overhead)	10,000	
Units in process, May 1 (all material, 60% of labor and overhead)		20,000
Units started in production	70,000	
Units completed and transferred	50,000	
Units transferred from Machining		50,000
Units completed and transferred to finished goods		50,000
Units in process, May 31 (all material, 40% of labor and overhead)	20,000	
Units in process, May 31 (all material, 20% of labor and overhead)		20,000
Units lost in production	10,000	

Production Costs	Machining	Finishing
Work in process, May 1:		
Materials	$20,000	$55,000
Labor	12,000	30,000
Factory overhead	4,000	20,000
Costs in machining department		120,000
Costs incurred during month:		
Materials	139,600	120,000
Labor	89,500	80,220
Factory overhead	30,220	39,900
Total	$295,300	$696,120

Required: Prepare a cost of production summary for each department.

SOLUTION TO SELF-STUDY PROBLEM

Suggestions: Read the entire problem thoroughly, keeping in mind that you will *prepare a cost of production summary for each department.*
Highlight the following facts:

1. The company has two departments.
2. The Machining Department uses the average cost method, while the Finishing Department uses the FIFO cost method.
3. Units are lost throughout the process, but inspection doesn't occur until the end of the process.
4. The lost units have no scrap value and the losses are considered normal.
5. The materials are added at the beginning of operations in both departments, but the labor and overhead are added evenly. Therefore, the equivalent production for materials will differ from the labor and overhead equivalent production in each department.

Preparing a cost of production summary for the Machining Department:

1. Account for the total cost charged to the department.
2. Calculate the equivalent production, using the average cost procedures for (a) materials and (b) labor and factory overhead.
3. Calculate the unit costs for materials, labor, and overhead. (Note that the good units which make it to the end of the production process will bear all of the production costs, including the costs incurred up until the time the units were lost.)
4. Using the calculated unit costs, determine the following:
   a. Cost of goods finished and transferred.
   b. The cost of the ending work in process.

Mercury Production Company
Cost of Production Summary—Machining Department
For the Month Ended May 31, 20—

First—Account for the total cost charged to the department.

Cost in work in process, beginning of month:

Materials	$ 20,000	
Labor	12,000	
Factory overhead	4,000	$ 36,000

Cost of production for month:

Materials	$139,600	
Labor	89,500	
Factory overhead	30,220	259,320
Total costs to be accounted for		**$295,320**

Second—Calculate the unit output (equivalent production).

Unit output for month:
Materials:

Finished and transferred during month	50,000
Equivalent units of work in process, end of month (20,000, 100% completed)	20,000
Total equivalent production	70,000

Labor and factory overhead:

Finished and transferred during month	50,000
Equivalent units of work in process, end of month (20,000, 40% completed)	8,000
Total equivalent production	58,000

Third—Calculate unit costs.

Materials ($20,000 + $139,600) ÷ 70,000	$2.28
Labor ($12,000 + $89,500) ÷ 58,000	1.75
Factory overhead ($4,000 + $30,220) ÷ 58,000	0.59
Total	$4.62

Fourth—Determine inventory costs using calculated unit costs.

Inventory costs:		
Cost of goods finished and transferred		
(50,000 × $4.62)		$231,000
Cost of work in process, end of month:		
Materials (20,000 × $2.28)	$ 45,600	
Labor (20,000 × 40% × $1.75)	14,000	
Factory overhead (20,000 × 40% × $0.59)	4,720	64,320
Total production costs accounted for		**$295,320**

Preparing a cost of production summary for the Finishing Department:

Note: Use the same sequence of instructions as were given for the Machining Department.

Mercury Production Company
Cost of Production Summary—Finishing Department
For the Month Ended May 31, 20—

Cost of work in process, beginning of month:			
Cost in Machining Department		$120,000	
Cost in Finishing Department:			
Materials	$55,000		
Labor	30,000		
Factory overhead	20,000	105,000	$225,000
Cost of goods received from Machining during month			231,000
Cost of production for month:			
Materials		$120,000	
Labor		80,220	
Factory overhead		39,900	240,120
Total costs to be accounted for			**$696,120**

Unit output for month:	
Materials:	
To complete beginning units in process	-0-
Units started and fully manufactured	
during month (50,000 – 20,000)	30,000
Ending units in process (20,000, all materials)	20,000
Total equivalent production	50,000
Labor and factory overhead:	
To complete beginning units in process	
(20,000, 40% completed)	8,000
Units started and fully manufactured during month	30,000
Ending units in process (20,000, 20% completed)	4,000
Total equivalent production	42,000

Unit cost for month:

Materials ($120,000 ÷ 50,000)	$2.40
Labor ($80,220 ÷ 42,000)	1.91
Factory overhead ($39,900 ÷ 42,000)	0.95
Total	$5.26

Inventory costs:

Cost of goods finished and transferred to finished goods during month:

Beginning units in process:

Prior month's cost	$225,000	
Current cost to complete:		
Labor (20,000 × 40% × $1.91)	15,280	
Overhead (20,000 × 40% × $0.95)	7,600	$247,880

Units started and finished during month:

Cost in prior dept. (30,000 × $4.62) . . .	$138,600	
Cost in Finishing Dept. (30,000 × $5.26) . . .	157,800	
Total cost transferred (30,000 × $9.88) . . .		296,400

Cost of work in process, end of month:

Cost in prior dept. (20,000 units × $4.62)	$ 92,400	
Materials (20,000 units × $2.40)	48,000	
Labor (20,000 units × 20% × $1.91)	7,640	
Factory overhead (20,000 units × 20% × $0.95)	3,800	151,840
Total production costs accounted for		$696,120

(Note: Problem 7-11 is similar to this problem.)

QUESTIONS

1. Under what conditions may the unit costs of materials, labor, and overhead be computed by using only one equivalent production figure?

2. When is it necessary to use separate equivalent production figures in computing the unit costs of materials, labor, and overhead?

3. If materials are not put into process uniformly, what must be considered when determining the cost of the ending work in process?

4. In what way does the cost of production summary, Figure 7-2, differ from the cost of production summaries presented in Chapter 6? What is the reason for this difference in treatment?

5. Why might the total number of units completed during a month plus the number of units in process at the end of a month be less than the total number of units in process at the beginning of the month plus the number of units placed in process during the month?

6. What is the usual method of handling the cost of losses that occur normally during processing?

7. If some units are normally lost during the manufacturing process and all units absorb the cost, what effect does this have on the unit cost of goods finished during the period and to the cost of the work in process at the end of the period?

8. How is the cost of units normally lost in manufacturing absorbed by the unit cost for the period?

9. How would you describe the method used to treat the cost of abnormal processing losses?

10. What computations must be made if materials added in a department increase the number of units being processed in that department?

11. What is the difference between the average cost method and the first-in, first-out cost method?

12. How would you define each of the following?
    a. joint products
    b. by-products
    c. joint costs
    d. split-off point
13. What are three methods of allocating joint costs?

14. How would you describe accounting for by-products for which no further processing is required?
15. Explain the refinement that some companies make to the relative sales value method of accounting for joint products.

EXERCISES

E7-1
Computing equivalent units of production for materials, labor, and overhead
Objective 1

Using the data given for Cases 1–3 and the average cost method, compute the separate equivalent units of production—one for materials and one for labor and overhead—under each of the following assumptions (labor and factory overhead are applied evenly during the process in each assumption):

a. All materials go into production at the beginning of the process.
b. All materials go into production at the end of the process.
c. At the beginning of the process, 75% of the materials go into production and 25% go into production when the process is one-half completed.

Case 1— Started in process 5,000 units; finished 3,000 units; work in process, end of period 2,000 units, three-fourths completed.
Case 2— Opening inventory 5,000 units, three-fifths completed; started in process 40,000 units; finished 39,000 units; work in process, end of period 6,000 units, one-fourth completed.
Case 3— Opening inventory 1,000 units, one-half completed, and 8,000 units, one-fourth completed; started in process 30,000 units; finished 29,000 units; closing inventory work in process 5,000 units, one-fourth completed, and 5,000 units, one-half completed.

E7-2
Computing equivalent production, unit costs, and costs for completed units and ending inventory
Objective 1

Precision Company manufactures wristwatches on an assembly line. The work in process inventory as of May 1 consisted of 5,000 watches that were complete as to materials and 50% complete as to labor and overhead. The May 1 work in process costs were as follows:

Materials	$ 5,000
Labor	5,000
Overhead	8,000
Total	$18,000

During the month, 10,000 units were started and 9,500 units were completed. The 1,500 units of ending inventory were complete as to materials and one-third complete as to labor and overhead.
The costs for May were as follows:

Materials	$ 61,000
Labor	40,000
Overhead	97,000
Total	$198,000

Calculate:

a. Equivalent units for material, labor, and overhead, using the average cost method
b. Units costs for materials, labor, and overhead
c. Cost of the units completed and transferred
d. Detailed cost of the ending inventory
e. Total all costs accounted for

E7-3
Computing unit costs; cost of units finished; cost of units in process
Objective 1

The following data appeared in the accounting records of Martinez Manufacturing Company, which uses an average cost production system:

Started in process	12,000 units
Finished and transferred	10,500 units
Work in process, end of month	1,500 units (2/5 completed)
Materials	$36,000
Labor	$44,400
Factory overhead	$22,200

Case 1— All materials are added at the beginning of the process and labor and factory overhead are added evenly throughout the process.
Case 2— One-half of the materials are added at the start of the manufacturing process and the balance of the materials are added when the units are one-half completed. Labor and factory overhead are applied evenly during the process.

Make the following computations for each case:

a. Unit cost of materials, labor, and factory overhead for the month
b. Cost of the units finished during the month
c. Cost of the units in process at the end of the month

E7-4
Calculating equivalent units
Objective 1

Mayo Manufacturing Company uses an average cost processing system. All materials are added at the start of the production process. Labor and overhead are added evenly at the same rate throughout the process. Mayo Manufacturing's records indicate the following data for May:

Beginning work in process, May 1 (60% completed)	1,000 units
Started in May	5,000 units
Completed and transferred	4,000 units

Ending work in process, May 31, is 20% completed as to labor and factory overhead. Make the following calculations:

a. Equivalent units for direct materials
b. Equivalent units for labor and overhead

E7-5
Computing costs and
units
Objective 1

Assuming that all materials are added at the beginning of the process and the labor and factory overhead are applied evenly during the process, compute the figures to be inserted in the blank spaces of the following data, using the average cost method.

	Case 1	Case 2	Case 3
Units in process, beginning of period	300	None	—
Materials cost in process, beginning of period	$ 915	None	$ 568
Labor cost in process, beginning of period	$ 351	None	$ 200
Overhead cost in process, beginning of period	$ 300	None	$ 188
Units started in process	—	—	19,200
Units transferred	1,300	8,000	—
Units in process, end of period	200	—	1,400
Stage of completion	1/4	—	1/5
Equivalent units—materials	—	—	—
Equivalent units—labor and factory overhead	—	—	18,440
Materials cost, current month	$3,660	$13,120	$ —
Labor and factory overhead cost, current month	$5,100	$16,200	$ —
Materials unit cost for period	$ —	$ 1.60	$ 0.30
Labor and factory overhead unit cost for period	$ —	$ 2.00	$ 0.20

E7-6
Computing average
unit costs
Objective 1

Raef Company manufactures shaving cream and uses an average cost system. In November, production is 14,800 equivalent units for materials and 13,300 units for labor and overhead. During the month, materials, labor, and overhead costs were as follows:

Materials	$ 73,000
Labor	68,134
Overhead	77,200

Beginning work in process for November had a cost of $11,360 for materials, $11,666 for labor, and $9,250 for overhead.

Compute the following:

a. Average cost per unit for materials
b. Average cost per unit for labor
c. Average cost per unit for overhead
d. Total unit cost for the month

E7-7
Calculating unit costs;
cost of units
transferred and in
process
Objective 2

Thomas Products Company manufactures a liquid product in one department. Due to the nature of the product and the process, units are regularly lost at the beginning of production. Materials and conversion costs are added evenly throughout the process. The following summaries were prepared for the month of January.

Production Summary	Units
Started in process	10,000
Finished and transferred to the stockroom	8,000
In process, end of the month	1,000
Stage of completion	1/4
Lost in process	1,000

Cost Summary	
Materials	$132,000
Labor	33,000
Factory overhead	20,625

Calculate the unit cost for materials, labor, and factory overhead for January and show the costs of units transferred and in process.

E7-8
Calculating unit costs; costs of units transferred and in process
Objective 3

A company manufactures a liquid product called Day-Glo. The basic ingredients are put into process in Dept. 1. In Dept. 2, other materials are added that increase the number of units being processed by 50%. The factory has only two departments.

	Units	
Production Summary	Dept. 1	Dept. 2
Started in process	18,000	
Received from prior department		14,000
Added to units in process		7,000
Finished and transferred	14,000	15,000
In process, end of month	4,000	6,000
Stage of completion—materials, labor		
factory overhead	1/4	1/2

Cost Summary		
Materials	$90,000	$36,000
Labor	30,000	13,500
Factory overhead	15,000	4,500

Calculate the following for each department: (a) unit cost for the month for materials, labor, and factory overhead, (b) cost of the units transferred, and (c) cost of the work in process.

E7-9
Computing equivalent units, FIFO method
Objective 4

Using the data given below for Cases 1–3 and the FIFO cost method, compute the separate equivalent units of production, one for materials and one for labor and overhead, under each of the following assumptions (labor and factory overhead are applied evenly during the process in each assumption):

a. All materials go into production at the beginning of the process.
b. All materials go into production at the end of the process.
c. At the beginning of the process, 75% of the materials go into production and 25% go into production when the process is one-half completed.

Case 1— Started in process 5,000 units; finished 3,000 units; work in process, end of period 2,000 units, three-fourths completed.

Case 2— Opening inventory 5,000 units, three-fifths completed; started in process 40,000 units; finished 39,000 units; work in process, end of period 6,000 units, one-fourth completed.

Case 3— Opening inventory 1,000 units, one-half completed, and 8,000 units, one-fourth completed; started in process 30,000 units; finished 29,000 units; closing inventory work in process 5,000 units, one-fourth completed, and 5,000 units, one-half completed.

Compare your answers with those from E7-1 on the average cost basis.

E7-10
Computing equivalent units, FIFO and average cost methods
Objectives 1, 4

Assume each of the following conditions concerning the data given:

1. All materials are added at the beginning of the process.
2. All materials are added at the end of the process.
3. Half of the materials are added at the beginning of the process and the balance of the materials are added when the units are three-fourths completed.

In all cases, labor and factory overhead are added evenly throughout the process.

Production Summary	Dept. 1	Dept. 2	Dept. 3
		Units	
Work in process, beginning of month	3,000	1,500	1,200
Stage of completion	1/2	3/5	4/5
Started in process	18,000	16,000	21,000
Finished and transferred	19,000	15,500	21,000
Work in process, end of month	2,000	2,000	1,200
Stage of completion	1/4	4/5	1/5

Compute separate equivalent units of production, one for materials and one for labor and factory overhead, for each of the conditions listed, using (a) the average cost method and (b) the FIFO cost method.

E7-11
Making a journal entry—joint products
Objective 5

Lacey Lumber Co. processes rough timber to obtain three grades of finished lumber, A, B, and C. The company allocates costs to the joint products on the basis of market value. During the month of May, Lacey incurred total production costs of $208,000 in producing the following:

Grade	Thousand Board Feet	Selling Price per 1,000 Board Feet
A	100	$200
B	300	100
C	500	160

Make the journal entry to transfer the finished lumber to separate inventory accounts for each product.

E7-12
Computing joint
costs—relative sales
value method
Objective 5

Warren Company's joint cost of producing 1,000 units of Product A, 500 units of Product B, and 500 units of Product C is $200,000. The unit sales values of the three products at the split-off point are Product A—$20, Product B—$200, and Product C—$160. Ending inventories include 100 units of Product A, 200 units of Product B, and 300 units of Product C.

Compute the amount of joint cost that would be included in the ending inventory valuation of the three products on the basis of their relative sales values.

E7-13
Making a journal
entry—by-product
Objective 5

Parlor City Chemical Co. manufactures Product X. During the process, a by-product, AX, is obtained and placed in stock. The estimated sales value of AX produced during the month of April is $1,020. Assume that the value of the by-product reduces production cost.

Make the journal entry for April to record the following:

a. Placing of AX in stock
b. Sale of three-fourths of the AX for $800

E7-14
Making journal
entries—by-product
Objective 5

Williams Manufacturing Co. makes one main product, X, and a by-product, Z, which splits off from the main product when the work is three-fourths completed. Product Z is sold without further processing and without being placed in stock. During June, $1,200 is realized from the sale of the by-product.

Make the entries to record the recovery and sale of the by-product on the assumption that the recovery is treated as one of the following:

a. A reduction in the cost of the main product
b. Other income

PROBLEMS

P7-1
Cost of production
summaries, one
department, two
months; journal
entries
Objective 1

Manufacturing data for the months of January and February in the Mixing Dept. of Cougar Manufacturing Co. follow:

	January	February
Materials used	$20,000	$28,400
Labor	$15,200	$23,000
Factory overhead	$11,400	$19,800
Finished and transferred to Blending Dept.	3,600	3,200
Work in process, end of month	400	600
Stage of completion	1/2	1/3

All materials are added at the start of the process. Labor and factory overhead are added evenly throughout the process. No units were in process at the beginning of January. Goods finished in Mixing are transferred to Blending for further processing.

Required:

1. From an analysis of this information, prepare a cost of production summary for each month, using the average cost method.
2. Make the journal entries necessary to record each month's transactions. (Hint: See Chapter 6 to review.)

P7-2
Journal entries for a manufacturer
Objective 1

On December 1, Monty Production Company had a work in process inventory of 1,200 units that were complete as to materials and one-third complete as to labor and overhead. December 1 costs follow:

Materials	$6,000
Labor	2,000
Overhead	2,000

During December the following transactions occurred:

a. Purchased materials costing $50,000 on account.
b. Placed direct materials costing $49,000 into production.
c. Incurred production wages totaling $50,500.
d. Incurred overhead costs for December:

Depreciation	$20,000
Utilities	28,000 (Cash payment)
Salaries	11,000 (Cash payment)
Supplies	2,000 (From inventory)

e. Applied overhead to work in process at a predetermined rate of 100% of direct labor cost.
f. Completed and transferred 10,000 units to Finished Goods. (Hint: You should first compute equivalent units and unit costs.)

Monty Company uses an average cost system. The ending inventory of work in process consisted of 1,000 units that were completed as to materials and 50% complete as to labor and overhead.

Required:

Prepare the journal entries to record the above information for the month of December.

P7-3
Cost of production summaries, three departments; departmental cost work sheet; journal entries; statement of cost of goods manufactured
Objective 1

Capitol Manufacturing Company manufactures a cement sealing compound called Plugit. The process requires that the product pass through three departments. In Dept. 1, all materials are put into production at the beginning of the process; in Dept. 2, materials are put into production evenly throughout the process; and in Dept. 3, all materials are put into production at the end of the process. In each department, it is assumed that the labor and factory overhead are applied evenly throughout the process.

At the end of January, the production reports for the month show the following:

	Dept. 1	Dept. 2	Dept. 3
Started in process	50,000	—	—
Received from prior department	—	40,000	30,000
Finished and transferred	40,000	30,000	28,000
Finished and on hand	—	5,000	—
Work in process, end of month	10,000	5,000	2,000
Stage of completion	1/2	1/4	3/4

The cost summary for January shows the following:

	Dept. 1	Dept. 2	Dept. 3
Materials	$22,500	$23,200	$19,600
Labor	7,200	14,500	11,800
Factory overhead	10,800	14,500	8,850
	$40,500	$52,200	$40,250

Required:

1. Prepare a cost of production summary for each department for January, using the average cost method.
2. Prepare a departmental cost work sheet for January. (Hint: See Chapter 6 to review.)
3. Make the required journal entries to record the January operations.
4. Prepare a statement of cost of goods manufactured for the month ended January 31.

P7-4
Cost of completed units and ending inventory
Objective 1

Giant Company cans corn and uses an average cost system. For the month of November the company showed the following:

Corn completed and canned	245,000 pounds
Corn in process at the end of November:	
100% complete as to corn, 50% complete as to labor and overhead, 0% complete as to cans	16,500 pounds

Cost data:
Corn	$0.05 per equivalent pound
Labor	$0.25 per equivalent pound
Overhead	$0.15 per equivalent pound
Cans	$0.07 per can

Each can contains 16 oz. or one pound of Corn

Required:

1. Calculate the cost of the completed production for November.
2. Show the detailed cost of the ending inventory for November.

P7-5
Lost units; cost of production summaries
Objective 2

Apex Products Co. uses the process cost system. A record of the factory operations for the month of October follows:

Production Summary	Units
Started in process	12,500
Finished and transferred to stockroom	9,500
In process, end of month, one-half completed as to materials, labor, and overhead	1,000

Cost Summary	
Materials	$30,000
Labor	12,000
Factory overhead	18,000

Required:

Prepare a cost of production summary, assuming that the cost of lost units is absorbed by the good units completed.

P7-6
Units gained; cost of production summaries
Objective 3

Bravo Manufacturing Co., which uses the process cost system, has two departments: A and B. In both departments, all of the materials are put into production at the beginning of the process. The materials added in Dept. B increase the number of units being processed by 25%. Labor and factory overhead are incurred uniformly throughout the process in all departments.

A record of the factory operations for May follows:

Cost Summary	Dept. A	Dept. B
Materials	$25,000	$ 7,500
Labor	10,800	10,140
Factory overhead	8,100	7,215

Production Summary	Units	
	Dept. A	Dept. B
Started in process	10,000	
Received from prior department		8,500
Added to units in process		1,500
Finished and transferred	8,500	9,500
Units in process, end of month	1,500	500
Stage of completion	1/3	1/2

Required:

Prepare a cost of production summary for each department for the month of May.

P7-7
FIFO cost method; cost of production summary
Objective 4

Jackyl Products Co. uses the FIFO cost method and adds all materials, labor, and factory overhead evenly to production. A record of the factory operations for the month of October follows:

Production Summary	Units
Work in process, beginning of month, one-fourth completed	5,000
Started in process	13,000
Finished and transferred to stockroom	11,000
Work in process, end of month, three-fourths completed	7,000

Cost Summary	
Work in process, beginning of month	$10,000
Materials	45,000
Labor	30,000
Factory overhead	15,000

Required:

Prepare a cost of production summary for the month.

P7-8
Cost of units completed and ending inventory
Objective 4

Plain Center Company had a cost per equivalent unit for the month of $4.56 for materials, $1.75 for labor, and $1.00 for overhead. During the period, 10,250 units were completed and transferred to finished goods. The 3,200 units in ending work in process were 100% complete as to materials and 60% complete as to labor and overhead. At the beginning of the month, 1,500 units were in process, 100% complete as to materials and 50% complete as to labor and overhead. The beginning inventory had a cost of $8,775. Plain Center uses FIFO costing.

Required:

1. Calculate the cost of the units completed and transferred.
2. Calculate the cost of ending work in process.

P7-9
Joint cost allocations
Objective 5

Tie-Sun Corporation specializes in chicken farming. Chickens are grown, packaged, and sold mostly to grocery chains. Chickens are accounted for in batches of 50,000. At the end of each growing period, the chickens are separated and sold by grades. Grades AA and A are sold to large grocery chains, and B and C are sold to other buyers. For costing purposes, Tie-Sun treats each batch of chicks as a joint product. The cost data for a batch of 50,000 chicks follows:

Grade	Number of Chickens	Average Pounds per Chicken	Selling Price per Pound
AA	25,000	5	$0.70
A	15,000	4	0.50
B	6,000	2	0.40
C	4,000	1	0.30

Total joint costs for the batch were $50,000.

Required:

Compute the cost allocations for each product, using the relative sales value method.

P7-10
Allocation of joint costs
Objective 5

Moto Manufacturing Company buys zeon for $0.80 a gallon. At the end of processing in Dept. 1, zeon splits off into products A, B, and C. Product A is sold at the split-off point with no further processing. Products B and C require further processing before they can be sold. Product B is processed in Dept. 2, and Product C is processed in Dept. 3. Following is a summary of costs and other related data for the year ended December 31:

	Dept. 1	Dept. 2	Dept. 3
Cost of zeon	$ 76,000	—	—
Direct labor	14,000	$45,000	$ 65,000
Factory overhead	10,000	21,000	49,000
Total	$100,000	$66,000	$114,000

	Product A	Product B	Product C
Gallons sold	20,000	30,000	45,000
Gallons on hand at December 31	10,000	—	15,000
Sales in dollars	$30,000	$96,000	$141,750

No inventories were on hand at the beginning of the year, and no zeon was on hand at the end of the year. All gallons on hand at the end of the year were complete as to processing. Moto uses the relative sales value method of allocating joint costs.

Required:

1. Calculate the allocation of joint costs.
2. Calculate the cost of Product B sold.

P7-11
Average and FIFO cost methods; losses at the beginning and end of processing.
Similar to self-study problem.
Objectives 2, 4

Pluto Production Company uses a process cost system. Its manufacturing operation is carried on in two departments: Machining and Finishing. The Machining Department uses the average cost method and the Finishing Department uses the FIFO cost method. Materials are added in both departments at the beginning of operations, and the added materials do not increase the number of units being processed. Units are lost in the Machining Department throughout the production process, and inspection occurs at the end of the process. The lost units have no scrap value and are considered to be a normal loss.

Production statistics for July show the following data:

	Machining	Finishing
Units in process, July 1 (all material, 40% of labor and overhead)	20,000	
Units in process, July 1 (all material, 80% of labor and overhead)		40,000
Units started in production	140,000	
Units completed and transferred	100,000	
Units transferred from Machining		100,000
Units completed and transferred to finished goods		100,000
Units in process, July 31 (all material, 60% of labor and overhead)	40,000	
Units in process, July 31 (all material, 40% of labor and overhead)		40,000
Units lost in production	20,000	

Production Costs	Machining	Finishing
Work in process, July 1:		
Materials	$ 40,000	$110,000
Labor	24,000	60,000
Factory overhead	8,000	40,000
Costs in Machining Department		240,000
Costs incurred during month:		
Materials	$280,000	$240,000
Labor	180,000	160,000
Factory overhead	60,000	80,000
Total	$592,000	$690,000

Required:

Prepare a cost of production summary for each department. (Round to three decimal places.)

8

Standard Cost Accounting— Materials and Labor

LEARNING OBJECTIVES

After studying this chapter, you should be able to:

1. Describe the different standards used in determining standard costs.
2. Use the proper procedures for recording standard costs for materials and labor.
3. Explain the meaning of variances and how they are analyzed.
4. Prepare journal entries to record and dispose of variances.
5. Perform an in-depth variance analysis.
6. Recognize the specific features of a standard cost system.
7. Account for standard costs in a departmentalized factory.

T he discussions of cost control in previous chapters emphasized the comparison of current costs with historical costs—costs of yesterday, last week, last month, or last year. When current costs differed unfavorably from earlier costs, it was suggested that management immediately investigate the cause of the deviation and try to eliminate it before the change became too costly. Management was also advised not only to watch for these fluctuations and attempt to correct them but to consider all possible ways to control costs.

While these previous methods of cost control are useful, management may tend to become complacent if the costs of manufacturing do not differ significantly from period to period. Managers may feel that the manufacturing operation is efficient because unit and overall costs have stabilized at a certain level. But stability of costs does not necessarily indicate efficiency when the earlier costs with which current costs are being compared may have built-in inefficiencies. Also, it may be possible to utilize current costs more effectively.

The purpose of **standard cost accounting** is to control costs and promote efficiency. This system is not another cost accounting method for accumulating manufacturing costs but is used in conjunction with such methods as job order, process, or backflush costing. Standard cost accounting is based on a predetermination of what it should cost to manufacture a product and a subsequent comparison of the actual costs with the established standard. Any deviation from the standards set can be quickly detected and responsibility pinpointed so that the company can take appropriate action to eliminate inefficiencies or take advantage of efficiencies. This is known as **management by exception**, where both significant unfavorable and favorable differences from standard are the focal point of management attention.

Standard costs are usually determined for a period of one year and should be revised annually. However, if cost analyses during the year indicate that a standard is incorrect, or if a significant change has occurred in costs or other related factors, management should not hesitate to adjust the standard to remedy an adverse situation.

TYPES OF STANDARDS

LEARNING OBJECTIVE 1
Describe the different standards used in determining standard costs.

A **standard** is a norm against which the actual performance can be measured. The objective of setting standards is to measure efficiency and to monitor costs by assigning responsibility for deviations from the standards. Also, a standard can motivate employees by providing a goal for achievement. But a question that often arises is "What is the proper standard to use?" A company can estimate materials, labor, and factory overhead usage and costs, but what about the unforeseen costs, such as spoilage, lost time, and equipment breakdowns? Should these items be considered in determining the standard cost to manufacture a product?

Some companies set their standards at the maximum degree of efficiency. Using such an **ideal standard**, costs are determined by considering estimated materials, labor, and overhead costs, the condition of the factory and machinery, and time for rest periods, holidays, and vacations; but no allowances are made for inefficient conditions such as lost time, waste, or spoilage. This ideal standard can be achieved only under the most efficient operating conditions; therefore, it is practically unattainable, generally giving rise to unfavorable variances. Companies using this type of standard feel that it provides a maximum objective for which to strive in the attempt to improve efficiency. There is, however, a psychological disadvantage—the factory personnel may become discouraged and lose their incentive to meet standards that are usually impossible to attain except under perfect operating conditions.

Recognizing this potential problem, most companies set attainable standards that include such factors as lost time, spoilage, or waste. These companies realize that some inefficiencies cannot be completely eliminated, and so they design a standard that can be met or even bettered in efficient production situations. The primary concern of the manufacturer should be to set a standard that is high enough to provide motivation and promote efficiency, yet not so high that it is unreasonable and thus unattainable.

STANDARD COST PROCEDURES

LEARNING OBJECTIVE 2
Use the proper procedures for recording standard costs for materials and labor.

Standard cost accounting is based on the following procedures:

1. Standard costs are determined for the three elements of cost—direct materials, direct labor, and factory overhead.

2. The standard costs, the actual costs, and the variances between the actual and standard costs are recorded in appropriate accounts.

3. All variances are analyzed and investigated and appropriate action taken.

DETERMINATION OF STANDARD COSTS FOR MATERIALS AND LABOR

The first step, the determination of standard costs for a product, is a complex task that requires considerable experience and familiarity with manufacturing operations as well as the cooperation of the departmental employees. The accounting department is often consulted to help determine historical costs, to point out prevalent trends, and to assist in establishing the standards. A materials cost standard is based on estimates of the *quantity of materials required* for a unit of product and the *unit cost* of the materials used. In setting a materials cost standard, management may consult the production engineering department to determine the amounts and types of materials needed, and the purchasing agent should supply knowledge of suppliers' prices to calculate the cost of these materials.

A labor cost standard is based on estimates of the *labor hours required* to produce a unit of product and the *cost of labor per unit*. In establishing a labor cost standard, the heads of various departments contribute their knowledge of the processing operations. The manufacturer may use services of time-study engineers to establish the time necessary to perform each operation, and the personnel manager should be consulted regarding prevailing wage rates for the various types of labor needed.

Historical costs and processes are studied to gain familiarity with these items, but the individuals who set the standards should also consider the prevailing trends that may cause changes in the company's future operations. In setting standards for materials and labor, a variety of factors may be considered:

1. The trend of prices for raw materials.
2. The use of different types of materials due to new processing or market developments.
3. The effect of negotiations with labor unions on labor rates.
4. The possible saving of labor time due to the use of more modern machinery and equipment.

The following table illustrates a simple standard cost summary for a product:

Fine Products, Inc.
Standard Cost Summary
Product X

Materials—1 lb. @ $4 per lb.	$ 4.00
Labor —1/2 hr. @ $10 per hr.	5.00
Factory overhead—40% of direct labor cost	2.00
Standard cost per unit	$11.00

The development of factory overhead standards will be discussed in the following chapter.

RECORDING STANDARD COSTS FOR MATERIALS AND LABOR

Once the standard cost for manufacturing a product has been determined, the second phase of the system can be put into effect: the standard costs, the actual costs, and the variances are recorded in journals and transferred to the general ledger. The journalizing and posting may occur weekly or monthly depending on the needs of management for current information.

DETERMINATION OF VARIANCES

LEARNING OBJECTIVE 3
Explain the meaning of variances and how they are analyzed.

A **variance** represents the difference between the actual and the standard costs of materials, labor, and overhead. The variances measure efficiencies or inefficiencies in **usage** (quantity of materials used or number of labor hours worked) and **price** (cost of materials and wage rates). Note that although the variances computed here are for a manufacturer, they could just as well be computed for a service business, such as food cost and labor cost variances for a Burger King outlet. Also, a manufacturer can compute variances for nonmanufacturing items such as marketing costs that would explain, for example, the reasons why the actual wages of distribution employees differed from budgeted wages.

Assume that the production report of Fine Products, Inc., whose standard cost summary is shown on the previous page, indicates that equivalent production for the month, calculated as discussed in previous chapters, was 10,000 units. The standard cost of this production is computed as follows:

Materials cost (10,000 units × $4.00)	$ 40,000
Labor cost (10,000 units × $5.00)	50,000
Factory overhead cost (10,000 units × $2.00)	20,000
Total standard cost of manufacturing 10,000 units	$110,000

Assume that the materials requisitions, the time tickets or payroll records, and the factory overhead records indicate the following actual costs of manufacturing these units:

Cost of direct materials used (11,000 lbs. @ $3.80)	$ 41,800
Cost of direct labor (4,500 hrs. @ $11.00)	49,500
Factory overhead	20,000
Total actual cost of manufacturing 10,000 units	$111,300

The standards can now be compared to the actual costs to determine whether any variances exist. This analysis is performed as follows:

	Standard Cost	Actual Cost	Net Variances—Favorable or (Unfavorable)
Materials	$ 40,000	$ 41,800	$(1,800)
Labor	50,000	49,500	500
Factory Overhead	20,000	20,000	—
Total	$110,000	$111,300	$(1,300)

The information presented by these comparative figures is significant because it shows that the total actual manufacturing costs have exceeded the standards previously established. The variances indicate that the cost of materials was $1,800 higher than it should have been and that the cost of labor was $500 less than the established standards, resulting in an overall unfavorable variance of $1,300. These figures can be of more value to cost control, however, if a further breakdown of the variances is made. The accounts used to indicate the materials and labor variances follow:

1. **Materials price variance** reflects the actual unit cost of materials above or below the standard unit cost, multiplied by the actual quantity of materials used.

    (Actual unit cost of materials – standard unit cost) ×
    actual quantity of materials used = Materials Price Variance

2. **Materials quantity (usage) variance** represents the actual quantity of direct materials used above or below the standard quantity allowed for the actual level of production at standard price.

    (Actual quantity used – standard quantity allowed) ×
    standard price of material = Materials Quantity Variance

3. **Labor rate (price) variance** represents the average of the actual hourly rates paid above or below the standard hourly rate, multiplied by the actual number of hours worked.

    (Actual labor rate per hour – standard labor rate per hour) ×
    actual number of labor hours worked = Labor Rate Variance

4. **Labor efficiency (usage) variance** indicates the number of actual direct labor hours worked above or below the standard hours allowed for the actual level of production at standard price.

    (Actual number of labor hours worked – standard number of labor hours
    allowed) × standard cost per labor hour = Labor Efficiency Variance

The standard quantity for the actual level of production used for the materials quantity variance and the labor efficiency variance represents the equivalent production determined for each of these elements. The equivalent production is calculated in exactly the same way as was used to determine the equivalent units in process costing. However, an additional calculation may be necessary when *each equivalent unit* requires *several pieces of material* or *several hours* to complete. For example, assume that a calculation of the materials equivalent production determines that 1,000 units were produced during the period. The standard set for the material allows five pieces of material for each completed unit; therefore, the standard quantity allowed for the actual production would be 5,000 units of material (1,000 units × 5 pieces).

A *debit balance* in a variance account indicates an **unfavorable** variance; that is, actual costs have exceeded the established standard cost. A *credit balance* reflects a **favorable variance,** indicating that actual costs were less than the standard cost. In management terminology, an unfavorable variance means that a charge (debit) has been added that increases the cost beyond the standard established, thereby reducing the expected profitability of the product. A favorable variance (credit) would add to a product's anticipated profitability because it reduces the standard cost set for the product. When a company uses a standard cost system, it usually considers the product's standard cost to be the cost for setting its selling price. Therefore, any movement of cost above or below the standard will have a direct effect on the revenue earned.

Figure 8-1 shows the formulas commonly used to calculate the materials and labor variances, using the data previously presented for materials and labor.

FIGURE 8-1   Formulas for Calculating Variances

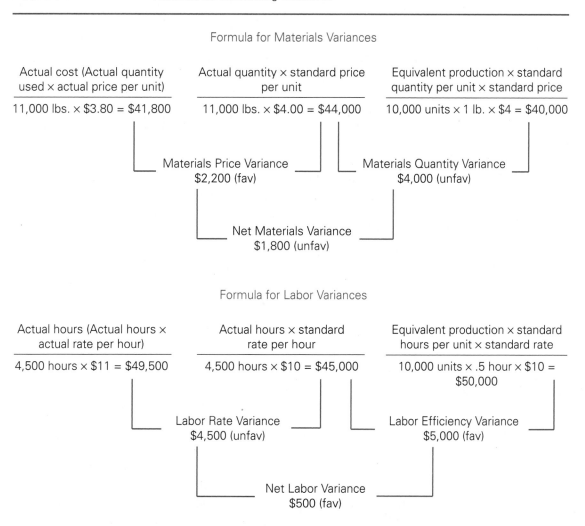

Formula for Materials Variances

Actual cost (Actual quantity used × actual price per unit)	Actual quantity × standard price per unit	Equivalent production × standard quantity per unit × standard price
11,000 lbs. × $3.80 = $41,800	11,000 lbs. × $4.00 = $44,000	10,000 units × 1 lb. × $4 = $40,000

Materials Price Variance
$2,200 (fav)

Materials Quantity Variance
$4,000 (unfav)

Net Materials Variance
$1,800 (unfav)

Formula for Labor Variances

Actual hours (Actual hours × actual rate per hour)	Actual hours × standard rate per hour	Equivalent production × standard hours per unit × standard rate
4,500 hours × $11 = $49,500	4,500 hours × $10 = $45,000	10,000 units × .5 hour × $10 = $50,000

Labor Rate Variance
$4,500 (unfav)

Labor Efficiency Variance
$5,000 (fav)

Net Labor Variance
$500 (fav)

This analysis shows the specific variances as quantity and price deviations from the established standards. The manufacturing effort exceeded the established materials standard for 10,000 units, which, at a standard price of $4.00 per pound, created an unfavorable materials quantity variance of $4,000 (1,000 pounds used in excess of standard allowed × $4.00). This variance was partially offset by the fact that the 11,000 pounds of materials used were obtained at a below-standard cost of $3.80 per pound, thereby creating a favorable price variance of $2,200 (11,000 pounds used at a saving of $0.20 per pound).

The calculation of labor variances indicates a favorable labor efficiency variance of $5,000 because the number of hours worked was 500 hours below the standard allowed for the production of 10,000 units (500 hours × the standard rate of $10.00). However, during the period, the company paid a labor rate of $11.00 per hour, which was higher than standard, creating an unfavorable rate variance of $4,500 (4,500 hours at a rate of $1.00 over standard).

It is important to understand that the terms *favorable* and *unfavorable* indicate only a deviation of the actual cost below or above standard. Further analysis and investigation may indicate that the unfavorable variance is not necessarily reflecting an inefficiency, nor is the favorable variance always indicating a desirable situation. An apparently unfavorable condition may be offset completely by a favorable situation. For example, a favorable materials price variance that results from buying less expensive materials than the standards call for may more than offset an unfavorable materials quantity variance that results from additional spoilage due to the use of cheaper materials. In any event, all variances, favorable or unfavorable, should be analyzed to determine the cause for and the effect of the deviations. Appropriate action should then be taken to improve the problem areas.

ACCOUNTING FOR VARIANCES

LEARNING OBJECTIVE 4
Prepare journal entries to record and dispose of variances.

The work in process account is always debited with the standard cost (standard quantity × standard price) determined for the period's equivalent production. The materials inventory account is credited for the actual cost of materials issued to the factory as indicated by materials requisitions and inventory ledger cards if an alternate method of recording materials cost is not used. The payroll account is credited with the actual cost of labor incurred for the period. The differences between the debits (at standard costs) and the credits (at actual costs) are debited (unfavorable variances) or credited (favorable variances) to the variance accounts. The standard cost of units finished is transferred from Work in Process to Finished Goods.

To illustrate, use the figures previously presented for materials and labor costs.

1. To record the entry for direct materials cost:

Work in Process	40,000	
Materials Quantity Variance	4,000	
Materials Price Variance		2,200
Materials		41,800

2. To record the entry for direct labor cost:

Work in Process	50,000	
Labor Rate Variance	4,500	
Labor Efficiency Variance		5,000
Payroll		49,500

3. To record the entry applying factory overhead to work in process (assuming no variances):

Work in Process	20,000	
Applied Factory Overhead		20,000

4. To record the entry for finished goods at standard cost (assuming no beginning or ending inventory of work in process, 10,000 units @ $11.00):

Finished Goods	110,000	
Work in Process		110,000

The balance sheet of Fine Products, Inc., using a standard cost system, would reflect inventories for work in process and finished goods at standard cost, while the materials inventory account would be shown at actual cost. This procedure will be followed in this text. The materials inventory account, however, may also be shown at standard cost, as explained in the following section.

ALTERNATIVE METHOD OF RECORDING MATERIALS COST

Some companies recognize materials price variances at the time materials are purchased, rather than waiting until they are used, by recording a **purchase price variance**, which represents the deviation of the purchase cost above or below the standard cost. The rationale for recording this variance at the time of purchase is that the difference between actual and standard cost is known at this time, so there is no reason for delaying the recognition of this variance until the materials are used.

Using the previous price figures and assuming that 12,000 pounds are purchased, the purchase entry under this method is as follows:

Materials (12,000 lbs. @ $4.00 standard price)   48,000
   Materials Purchase Price Variance   2,400
   Accounts Payable (12,000 lbs. @ $3.80 actual price)   45,600

Under these conditions, the materials inventory account on the balance sheet would reflect standard cost. At the time the materials are used, there would be no price variance to record, and the quantity variance would be recorded as follows:

Work in Process (10,000 lbs. @ $4.00 standard price) .   40,000
Materials Quantity Variance   4,000
   Materials (11,000 lbs. @ $4.00)   44,000

Another benefit of using the purchase price variance method is that the individual materials inventory accounts are maintained at standard cost. This saves record-keeping expense because it is only necessary to keep track of the quantities purchased, issued, and on hand. It is not necessary to post individual materials costs or to calculate continuously dollar amounts on the inventory ledger cards. Because the materials inventory account is kept at standard cost, the balance, in dollars, can be determined at any time by multiplying the standard price by the quantity on hand.

DISPOSITION OF STANDARD COST VARIANCES

At the end of the accounting period, the variances of actual cost from standard must be reflected in some appropriate manner on the financial statements. Different approaches for handling these items exist:

1. Some companies prorate these variances to Cost of Goods Sold, Work in Process, and Finished Goods. With the increased affordability of computer hardware and software, this method is gaining in popularity. The net effect of this method is that these accounts are adjusted to actual or historical cost. The rationale is that standard costs are important for management's evaluation of operations but are not proper for external financial reports. Therefore, the variances, being a part of actual manufacturing cost, should be included in inventory costs. When this method is followed, the allocation of materials, labor, and overhead variances will be in proportion to the standard materials, labor, and overhead costs included in cost of goods sold, work in process, and finished goods.

2. A more common approach is to show the unfavorable net variance as an addition to the cost of goods sold for the period and the favorable net variance as a deduction. This is shown in the partial income statement that follows. This approach is based on the fact that these

variances result from favorable or unfavorable conditions or inefficiencies during the period. Therefore, they should be charged or credited to the period. These items should not be charged to future periods by including them in inventory costs.

Sales		$100,000
Cost of goods sold at standard	$80,000	
Add unfavorable variance:		
Materials quantity variance	800	
	$80,800	
Less favorable variances:		
Materials price variance $410		
Labor efficiency variance 100		
Labor rate variance 105	615	
Cost of goods sold (actual cost)		80,185
Gross margin on sales (actual cost)		$ 19,815

3. If the variances are significant or have been caused by the use of an incorrect standard, the variances should be allocated to Inventory and to Cost of Goods Sold, and the standard cost adjusted accordingly.

4. If production is seasonal, with extreme peaks and valleys during the year, variances should be shown as deferred charges or credits on interim balance sheets, using the logic that they would be mostly offset in future periods. At the end of the year, however, some disposition of these variances, as described previously, must be made and the variance accounts closed.

5. If the variances are due to abnormal or unusual circumstances, such as strikes, fires, storms, or floods, there is justification for charging off these items as extraordinary losses on the income statement.

This text will, unless indicated otherwise, use the more common approach of reflecting the materials and labor variances as adjustments to the standard cost of goods sold, as illustrated in Item 2 above. Variances of factory overhead costs, to be discussed in the next chapter, would also be reflected in the statements in a similar manner. Figure 8-2 provides an aid to understanding cost flow through a standard cost system.

ANALYSES OF VARIANCES

LEARNING OBJECTIVE 5
Perform an in-depth variance analysis.

In analyzing materials and labor variances, two components are investigated: usage (quantity) and price. The analyst looks closely at the quantity of materials used, the cost per unit of each type of material, the number of direct labor hours worked, and the cost of each labor hour. When

Principles of Cost Accounting

FIGURE 8-2   Cost Flow Through a Standard Cost System

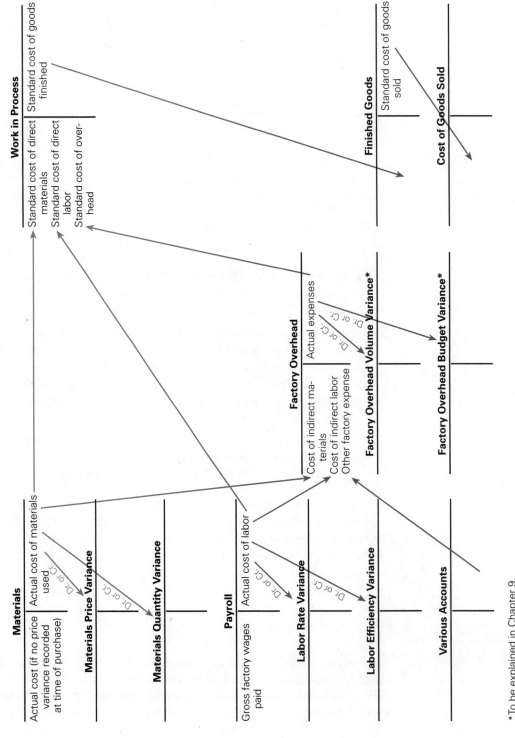

*To be explained in Chapter 9.

the usage and/or price differ from the established standards, the analyst examines the reason for the variance and considers whatever action can be taken to correct any deficiency before the loss becomes significant and is inventoried.

In analyzing the materials cost variance, the usage of materials may be above, below, or at standard, or the cost per unit of the materials used might be above, below, or at standard. Management requires this analyzed data to make corrective decisions if deemed necessary. Consider the following three possibilities in the manufacture of 10,000 units:

Example 1:

Standard cost, 10,000 lbs. of materials @ $4.00	$40,000
Actual cost, 10,000 lbs. of materials @ $4.18	41,800
Unfavorable materials price variance (10,000 × $0.18)	$ (1,800)

This analysis shows that the factory usage of materials is at standard, but the price set for the materials has been exceeded. The variance is caused by the fact that the company used materials costing $0.18 more than the standard price. With 10,000 pounds used, this $0.18 per unit variance causes a total variance of $1,800.

Management now has the data with which to investigate why the materials cost per unit is higher than the standard of $4.00 per pound. Several possibilities exist, including the following:

1. Inefficient purchasing methods
2. Use of a slightly different material as an experiment
3. Increase in market price

Inefficient purchasing can be corrected by better planning and by careful selection of suppliers. If different material, which will be higher priced, is selected for use in manufacturing operations, the standard cost per unit of materials will have to be increased. The standard cost would also have to be increased if there is an increase in market price that is considered to be permanent.

The example illustrates the principle that management should carefully investigate any variance, favorable or unfavorable, so that corrective action can be taken. Such a decision may involve eliminating inefficiencies or changing the standard cost of the product.

Example 2:

Standard cost, 10,000 lbs. of materials @ $4.00	$40,000
Actual cost, 10,450 lbs. of materials @ $4.00	41,800
Unfavorable materials quantity variance (450 × $4.00)	$ (1,800)

In this case, the cost of the materials is at standard but the materials usage is excessive. The manufacturing operation used 450 pounds of materials more than it should have, as indicated by the standard. This additional 450 pounds at a cost of $4.00 per pound created the variance of $1,800 over standard cost.

As with the previous example, management must now determine why the extra materials were used. Again, various circumstances might have created this situation:

1. Materials were spoiled or wasted. This loss could have been due to a different type of material being used, careless workers, or lax supervisory personnel. If possible, the cause of the loss should be eliminated.
2. More materials were deliberately used per manufactured unit as an experiment to determine if the product's quality could be increased. If management decides to continue this usage, the standard cost per unit must be changed.

An analysis of the cause of this variance might also result in the elimination of inefficiencies or in a change in the standard cost.

Example 3:

Standard cost, 10,000 lbs. of materials @ $4.00	$40,000
Actual cost, 11,000 lbs. of materials @ $3.80	41,800
Unfavorable net materials variance	$ (1,800)

In this example, a combination of usage and price variances causes the overall unfavorable variance. The factory has used 1,000 pounds of materials over standard but has purchased these materials at a cost that is $0.20 below standard. Once again, management should know why the additional materials were used and take appropriate action. It is important to recognize that the price variance of $0.20 will also require investigation. The fact that this variance is favorable, below standard cost, is no reason for production personnel to be complacent and ignore it. This "better" price may have been created by more efficient buying techniques, a bargain purchase, or a general price reduction. On the other hand, materials of a lesser quality could have been purchased, thereby reducing the quality of the product and possibly causing an unfavorable effect on marketing.

It is also possible that the greater usage of materials may be related to the lower price. Waste and spoilage might be created by (1) the use of cheaper materials or (2) the production workers' unfamiliarity in the use of a different material. Further investigation may reveal that the standard was not properly determined and should be revised.

The following important points have been illustrated by the three examples with identical net variances:

1. The total variance between standard and actual cost must be broken down by usage and price.

2. The variances in usage and price, whether unfavorable or favorable, must be analyzed as to cause and effect. Variances may be stated in dollar amounts or in terms of units such as pounds or hours. The method chosen should be that which provides the greatest benefit in determining the cause of the variances.

3. Appropriate action must be taken. This action may include a change in methods of manufacturing, supervision, or purchasing, or a change in the standard cost of the product. It may involve taking advantage of efficient operations or functions. If the standard cost is changed, the units in inventory are often revalued at the new figure.

The same principles of analysis apply to the labor cost variances. Three similar examples are presented below.

Example 1:

Standard cost, 5,000 hrs. @ $10.00 per hr.	$50,000
Actual cost, 5,000 hrs. @ $9.90 per hr.	49,500
Favorable labor rate variance (5,000 × $0.10)	$ 500

Example 2:

Standard cost, 5,000 hrs. @ $10.00 per hr.	$50,000
Actual cost, 4,950 hrs. @ $10.00 per hr.	49,500
Favorable labor efficiency variance (50 × $10.00)	$ 500

Example 3:

Standard cost, 5,000 hrs. @ $10.00 per hr.	$50,000
Actual cost, 4,500 hrs. @ $11.00 per hr.	49,500
Favorable net labor variance	$ 500

In the first example, it is apparent that the number of actual labor hours was at standard, but the cost per hour was lower than the standard of $10.00. Although this result appears to be favorable, the reason and the possible effect should still be determined. It may be that the personnel department is doing a more efficient job in hiring qualified employees and should be commended; or it may be that less-than-qualified workers are being hired at a lower rate, possibly reducing the quality of the work on the product. This second condition would not be acceptable.

The second example indicates that the labor rate is at standard, but the time required was 50 hours below standard. Again, the question is, why? It is possible that the speed of production has been increased, and the employees are working too fast to do top-quality work. This situation could have an adverse effect on sales. Again, of course, the possibility exists that the manufacturing and/or supervisory functions have become more efficient so that more work is done in less time.

In the third example, a saving of 500 hours is indicated, but there has been a payment per hour of $1.00 in excess of standard. These two factors could be related. The hiring of more highly skilled and higher-paid personnel quite often results in a reduction in the number of hours worked. But, as with the other examples, management should investigate to determine the cause and the effect of the variances in usage and price. If the labor efficiency variance is unfavorable, it may have been caused by the use of unskilled workers or it may be due to time lost because of machine breakdowns, improper production scheduling, or an inefficient flow of materials to the production line.

The analyses of materials and labor variances are not isolated from each other. It is very possible that a difference above or below the standard of one is directly related to a variance of the other. For example, the hiring of more highly skilled personnel at a higher labor rate does not always reduce the number of hours worked, but it may reduce the amount of materials lost through spoilage. Conversely, the use of less skilled workers at a lower rate may cause greater materials loss. In examining any variance, management should look closely at the relationship of that variance to other variances.

FEATURES OF STANDARD COST ACCOUNTING

LEARNING OBJECTIVE 6
Recognize the specific features of a standard cost system.

Some features of standard cost accounting must be emphasized. First, the company does not determine the actual unit cost of manufacturing a product. Only the total actual costs and the total standard costs are gathered.

Second, the fact that standards are based on estimates does not make them unreliable. A close examination and analysis of variances will quickly indicate whether the manufacturing operation is inefficient or whether the standards are reasonable.

Third, standards will change as conditions change. Permanent changes in prices, processes, or methods of operating may indicate the need for the standards to be adjusted.

Fourth, the purpose of using a standard cost accounting system is to provide continual incentive for factory personnel to keep costs and performance in line with predetermined management objectives. As mentioned earlier in the chapter, comparisons between actual costs and the predetermined standards are much more effective than comparisons between current actual costs and actual costs of prior periods.

Fifth, a standard cost accounting system, through the recording and analysis of manufacturing cost variances, helps focus management's attention on these questions:

1. Were materials purchased at prices above or below standard?
2. Were materials used in quantities above or below standard?
3. Is labor being paid at rates above or below standard?
4. Is labor being used in amounts above or below standard?

Finally, although the discussion in this text suggests that variances are determined at the end of the month, most manufacturing companies calculate variances on a weekly, or even daily, basis to allow for more timely action in correcting inefficiencies or taking advantage of efficiencies. The variances for the month, however, are still recorded in the accounts at the end of the month.

You should now be able to work the following: Questions 1–16; Exercises 8-1 to 8-12; and Problems 8-1 to 8-9.

ILLUSTRATION OF STANDARD COST IN A DEPARTMENTALIZED FACTORY

LEARNING OBJECTIVE 7
Account for standard costs in a departmentalized factory.

The following example demonstrates standard cost accounting procedures in a factory having two departments.

Standard Cost Summary

	Dept. A	Dept. B	Total
Materials: 5 lbs. @ $1.00 lb.	$ 5		
1 lb. @ $2.00 lb.		$ 2	$ 7
Labor:			
1 hour @ $8.00	8		
2 hours @ $10.00		20	28
Factory overhead:			
Per unit	1	2	3
Standard costs per unit	$14	$24	$38

Production Report for the Month

	Dept. A	Dept. B
Beginning units in process	None	None
Units finished and transferred	2,200	1,800
Ending units in process	None	400
Stage of completion		1/2

Units pass through Dept. A to Dept. B. In both departments, materials, labor, and overhead are added evenly throughout the process. Actual costs for the month, as determined from materials requisitions, payroll records, and factory overhead records, follow:

	Dept. A		Dept. B		Total
Direct materials:					
12,000 lbs. @ $0.95		$11,400			
1,900 lbs. @ $2.10				$ 3,990	$15,390
Direct labor:					
2,000 hrs. @ $8.10		16,200			
4,100 hrs. @ $9.90				40,590	56,790
Factory overhead:					
Indirect materials .	$ 400		$1,000		
Indirect labor . . .	600		1,000		
Other items	1,200	2,200	2,000	4,000	6,200
		$29,800		$48,580	$78,380

From the data given on the standard cost summary, the standard costs of production can be determined. To facilitate the comparison of these figures with actual costs and the determination of variances, a form similar to Figure 8-3 can be used.

Using the data given in Figure 8-3, the specific variances for materials can be computed as follows:

Materials—Dept. A

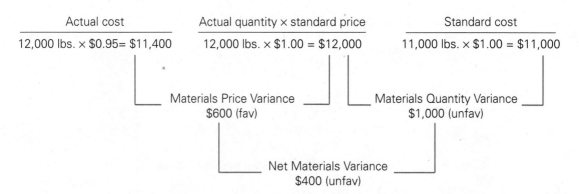

Actual cost	Actual quantity × standard price	Standard cost
12,000 lbs. × $0.95= $11,400	12,000 lbs. × $1.00 = $12,000	11,000 lbs. × $1.00 = $11,000

Materials Price Variance
$600 (fav)

Materials Quantity Variance
$1,000 (unfav)

Net Materials Variance
$400 (unfav)

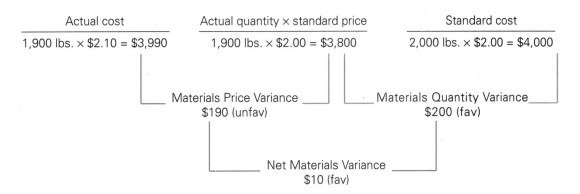

Materials—Dept. B

Actual cost	Actual quantity × standard price	Standard cost
1,900 lbs. × $2.10 = $3,990	1,900 lbs. × $2.00 = $3,800	2,000 lbs. × $2.00 = $4,000

Materials Price Variance
$190 (unfav)

Materials Quantity Variance
$200 (fav)

Net Materials Variance
$10 (fav)

One thousand pounds of materials in excess of standard were used in Dept. A, which, at the standard cost of $1.00, caused an unfavorable variance of $1,000. If prices had not changed, there would have been no other variances. But price did change—12,000 pounds of materials at a cost of $0.05 below standard resulted in a favorable price variance of $600. The combined variances resulted in a net unfavorable materials cost variance of $400 in Dept. A.

Dept. B used 100 pounds of materials less than standard. At a standard cost of $2.00 per pound, the favorable quantity variance was $200. But this variance was partially offset by the unfavorable price variance created by the increase in the cost per unit of the materials of $0.10. With 1,900 pounds being used, the price variance was $190 above standard. The two variances resulted in a net favorable materials cost variance of $10 in Dept. B.

The journal entry for the issuance of direct and indirect materials into production and to record the materials variances is as follows:

Work in Process—Dept. A	11,000	
Work in Process—Dept. B	4,000	
Materials Quantity Variance—Dept. A	1,000	
Materials Price Variance—Dept. B	190	
Factory Overhead (Indirect Materials)	1,400	
Materials Price Variance—Dept. A		600
Materials Quantity Variance—Dept. B		200
Materials		16,790

Note that the accounts for work in process are charged for the standard cost of direct materials, the factory overhead account is debited for the actual cost of indirect materials used, the materials account is credited at actual cost for all direct and indirect materials used, and the variance

FIGURE 8-3   Calculation of Variances

	Dept. A — Equivalent Production of 2,200 Units			Dept. B — Equivalent Production of 2,000 Units			Total		
	Standard Cost	Actual Cost	Net Favorable (Unfavorable) Variance	Standard Cost	Actual Cost	Net Favorable (Unfavorable) Variance	Standard Cost	Actual Cost	Net Favorable (Unfavorable) Variance
Materials:									
11,000 lbs. @ $1.00	$11,000								
12,000 lbs. @ $0.95		$11,400	$(400)	$4,000	$3,990	$10	$15,000	$15,390	$(390)
2,000 lbs. @ $2.00									
1,900 lbs. @ $2.10									
Labor:									
2,200 hrs. @ $8.00	17,600								
2,000 hrs. @ $8.10		16,200	1,400	40,000	40,590	(590)	57,600	56,790	810
4,000 hrs. @ $10.00									
4,100 hrs. @ $9.90									
Factory overhead:									
Standard cost per unit, $1.00	2,200								
Actual cost		2,200	—	4,000	4,000	—	6,200	6,200	—
Standard cost per unit, $2.00									
Actual cost									
Total	$30,800	$29,800	$1,000	$48,000	$48,580	$(580)	$78,800	$78,380	$420

accounts are debited if the variance is unfavorable and credited if it is favorable. (If this company followed the practice of recording the materials price variance at the time of purchase, no price variances would be recorded at this time because the materials purchase price variance would have been determined when the goods were received.)

Based on the data in Figure 8-3, the specific variances for labor can be computed as follows:

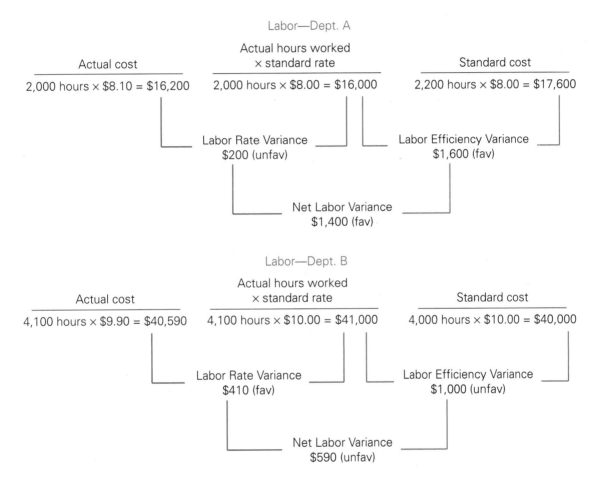

During the month, Dept. A saved 200 hours by working fewer hours than the number established as a standard for the number of units produced. At a standard cost of $8.00 per hour, a favorable efficiency variance of $1,600 was realized. The average hourly rate of pay, however, was $0.10 above standard so there was also an unfavorable rate variance. The company paid $0.10 more per hour than the standard rate for 2,000 hours of work, or a total of $200.

Dept. B used 100 hours more than the standard. Therefore, at the standard rate of $10.00, it had an unfavorable efficiency variance of $1,000. Because the actual rate was $0.10 below standard, a favorable rate variance of $410 resulted, determined by multiplying the 4,100 hours worked by the $0.10 rate differential. (For the purposes of discussion in this chapter, no variances have been shown for factory overhead. This variance will be discussed in the next chapter.)

The journal entry to record the direct and indirect labor used in production and the labor variances is as follows:

Work in Process—Dept. A	17,600	
Work in Process—Dept. B	40,000	
Labor Rate Variance—Dept. A	200	
Labor Efficiency Variance—Dept. B	1,000	
Factory Overhead (Indirect Labor)	1,600	
Labor Efficiency Variance—Dept. A		1,600
Labor Rate Variance—Dept. B		410
Payroll		58,390

As with materials, only standard costs for direct labor are charged to Work in Process. The factory overhead account is debited for the actual cost of the indirect labor used, the payroll account is credited for the actual cost of direct and indirect labor during the month, and the variances are debited or credited to the appropriate accounts.

During the month and at the end of the month, there would be the usual entries in the journals to record the factory overhead other than indirect materials and indirect labor. These entries are summarized as follows:

Factory Overhead	3,200	
Various credits (Accounts Payable, Accumulated		
Depr., Prepaid Insurance)		3,200

Factory overhead would be applied to work in process by the following entry:

Work in Process—Dept. A (2,200 units × $1)	2,200	
Work in Process—Dept. B (2,000 units × $2)	4,000	
Applied Factory Overhead		6,200

The entries are then made to transfer the standard cost of units finished in Dept. A to Dept. B and from Dept. B to finished goods.

Work in Process—Dept. B	. . . .	30,800	
Work in Process—Dept. A			30,800
(2,200 units @ $14)			
Finished Goods		68,400	
Work in Process—Dept. B			68,400
(1,800 units @ $38)			

After these entries have been posted, the general ledger accounts would reflect the data as shown in T-account form. (Note that the postings assume that entries were previously made for the purchase of materials and to record the payroll.)

Materials		Work in Process—Dept. A	
16,790	16,790	11,000	30,800
		17,600	
		2,200	
		30,800	

Work in Process—Dept. B		Finished Goods	
4,000	68,400	68,400	
40,000			
4,000			
30,800			
78,800			
10,400			

Materials Quantity Variance—Dept. A		Materials Quantity Variance—Dept. B	
1,000			200

Materials Price Variance—Dept. A		Materials Price Variance—Dept. B	
	600	190	

Labor Efficiency Variance—Dept. A		Labor Efficiency Variance—Dept. B	
	1,600	1,000	

Labor Rate Variance—Dept. A		Labor Rate Variance—Dept. B	
200			410

Payroll		Factory Overhead	
58,390	58,390	1,400	
		1,600	
		3,200	
		6,200	

Applied Factory Overhead	
	6,200

The work in process account for Dept. A has no balance because all work has been completed and transferred to Dept. B. The work in process account for Dept. B has a balance of $10,400 accounted for as follows:

Cost in Dept. A—400 units @ $14	$ 5,600
Cost in Dept. B—400 units @ $12 (one-half completed)	4,800
. . . .	$10,400

> **You should now be able to work the following: Question 17; Exercise 8-13; and Problem 8-10. Note that any of the material of this chapter not worked previously may be worked at this time.**

KEY TERMS

Attainable standard, p. 317
Favorable variance, p. 320
Ideal standard, p. 316
Labor cost standard, p. 317
Labor efficiency (usage) variance, p. 320
Labor rate (price) variance, p. 320
Management by exception, p. 316
Materials cost standard, p. 317
Materials price variance, p. 320

Materials quantity (usage) variance, p. 320
Price, p. 318
Purchase price variance, p. 323
Standard, p. 316
Standard cost accounting, p. 316
Unfavorable variance, p. 320
Usage, p. 318
Variance, p. 318

SELF-STUDY PROBLEM

MATERIALS AND LABOR VARIANCE ANALYSES

ADIRONDACK COMPANY

Adirondack Company manufactures one product and uses a standard cost system. The established standards for materials and labor follow:

Material A: 3 lbs. @ $6 per lb.	$18
Labor: 4 hours @ $7.50 per hour	$30

The operating data for the month of May follow:

Work in process, May 1: 200 units, all materials, 20% complete as to labor.
Work in process, May 31: 600 units, all materials, 80% complete as to labor.
Completed during the month: 6,400 units.
All materials are added at the beginning of processing in the department.
   20,900 pounds of materials were used in production during the month, at a total cost of $123,310. Direct labor amounted to $208,670, which was at a rate of $7.70 per hour.

Required:

Using the FIFO method of costing, calculate the following variances:
1. Materials quantity variance
2. Materials price variance
3. Labor efficiency variance
4. Labor rate variance

SOLUTION TO DEMONSTRATION PROBLEM

The specifics in the problem highlight the following facts:

In addition to the usual procedures used to solve standard cost problems, equivalent production (FIFO) must be calculated. The equivalent production determined by the FIFO method will be used to calculate the standard materials and standard labor allowed. Two variances (price and quantity) must be determined for materials, and two variances (rate and efficiency) must be determined for labor.

Calculating equivalent production for materials and labor by the FIFO method:

	Units
Materials:	
Work in process, May 1: 200 units (all materials added last period)	-0-
Units started and finished during May (6,400 – 200)	6,200
Work in process, May 31: 600 units (all materials added)	600
Total equivalent production—materials	6,800
Labor:	
Work in process, May 1: 200 units (80% of labor required)	160
Units started and finished during May	6,200
Work in process, May 31: 600 units (80% labor added)	480
Total equivalent production—labor	6,840

Determining the materials and labor variances:

Materials Variances

Actual cost	Actual pounds × standard price	Equivalent units × pounds per unit × standard price
20,900 lbs. × $5.90* = $123,310	20,900 lbs. × $6.00 = $125,400	6,800 units × 3 lbs. × $6.00 = $122,400

Materials Price Variance
$2,090 (fav)

Materials Quantity Variance
$3,000 (unfav)

Net Materials Variance
$910 (unfav)

*$123,310/20,900 = $5.90 per pound

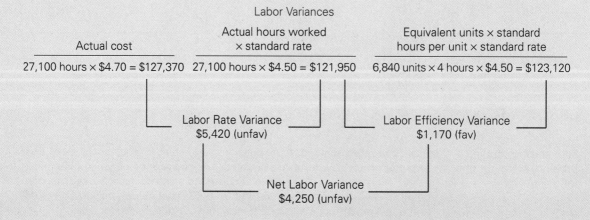

Labor Variances

	Actual hours worked	Equivalent units × standard
Actual cost	× standard rate	hours per unit × standard rate

27,100 hours × $4.70 = $127,370   27,100 hours × $4.50 = $121,950   6,840 units × 4 hours × $4.50 = $123,120

Labor Rate Variance
$5,420 (unfav)

Labor Efficiency Variance
$1,170 (fav)

Net Labor Variance
$4,250 (unfav)

(Note: Problem 8-7 is similar to this problem.)

QUESTIONS

1. What are the function and objectives of standard cost accounting?

2. What is the difference between standard cost and actual cost of production?

3. What is a "standard"?

4. What are the specific procedures upon which a standard cost accounting system is based?

5. How are standards for materials and labor costs determined?

6. What is a "variance"?

7. When are variances usually recorded in the journals?

8. How do price and quantity variances relate to materials costs?

9. How do rate and efficiency variances relate to labor costs?

10. Is a favorable variance "good" or an unfavorable variance "bad"? Explain.

11. Are actual costs or standard costs charged to Work in Process?

12. When a company uses a standard cost system, are the inventory accounts—Finished Goods, Work in Process, and Materials—valued at actual cost or standard cost?

13. What two factors must be considered when breaking down a variance into its components? Explain.

14. What might cause the following variances?
    a. An unfavorable materials price variance.
    b. A favorable materials price variance.
    c. An unfavorable materials quantity variance.
    d. A favorable materials quantity variance.
    e. An unfavorable labor rate variance.
    f. A favorable labor rate variance.
    g. An unfavorable labor efficiency variance.
    h. A favorable labor efficiency variance.

15. Is it possible that a variance of one type might be partially or fully offset by another variance? Explain.

16. If, in a given period, the total actual cost of all materials used is exactly the same as the standard cost so that no net variance results, should the data be further analyzed? Explain.

17. At what amount is the entry made to transfer the cost of finished goods from the first department to a subsequent department in a standard cost system?

EXERCISES

E8-1 through E8-5 use the following data:
The standard operating capacity of the Ultima Manufacturing Co. is 1,000 units. A detailed study of the manufacturing data relating to the production of one product revealed the following:

1. Two pounds of materials are needed to produce one unit.
2. Standard unit cost of materials is $8 per pound.
3. It takes one hour of labor to produce one unit.
4. Standard labor rate is $10 per hour.
5. Standard overhead for this volume is $4,000.

Each case in E8-1 through E8-5 requires the following:

a. Set up a standard cost summary showing the standard unit cost.
b. Analyze the variances and make journal entries to record the transfer to Work in Process of
   (1) materials costs
   (2) labor costs
   (3) overhead costs

When making these entries, indicate the types of variances, and state whether each variance is favorable or unfavorable.

c. Prepare the journal entry to record the transfer of costs to the finished goods account.

E8-1
Standard unit cost; variance analysis; journal entries
Objectives 2, 3, 4

1,000 units were started and finished.
Case 1. All prices and quantities for the cost elements are standard, except for materials cost, which is $7.70 per pound.
Case 2. All prices and quantities for the cost elements are standard, except that 2,100 pounds of materials were used.

E8-2
Standard unit cost; variance analysis; journal entries
Objectives 2, 3, 4

1,000 units were started and finished.
Case 1. All prices and quantities are standard, except for the labor rate, which is $10.20 per hour.
Case 2. All prices and quantities are standard with the exception of labor hours, which totaled 900.

E8-3
Computing standard unit cost; variance analysis; journal entries
Objectives 2, 3, 4

All of the deviations listed in E8-1 and E8-2 took place, and 1,000 units were started and finished. (Note that the quantities used will affect the rate variances for both materials and labor.)

E8-4
Standard unit cost; variance analysis; journal entries
Objectives 2, 3, 4

All of the deviations listed in E8-1 and E8-2 took place, and 950 units were started and finished.

E8-5
Standard unit cost;
variance analysis;
journal entries
Objectives 2, 3, 4

All of the deviations listed in E8-1 and E8-2 took place, and 1,050 units were started and finished.

E8-6
Computing materials
variances
Objective 3

Panoramic Calendar Company specializes in manufacturing calendars that depict landscape pictures from around the world. The company uses a standard cost system to control its costs. During one month of operations, the direct materials costs and the quantities of paper used showed the following:

Actual purchase price	$0.165 per page
Standard quantity allowed production	170,000 pages
Actual quantity purchased during month	200,000 pages
Actual quantity used during month	185,000 pages
Standard price per page	$0.17 per page

Calculate the following:

1. Total cost of purchases for the month
2. Materials price variance
3. Materials quantity variance
4. Net materials variance (Note: Use the diagram format shown in Figure 8-1 to compute variances.)

E8-7
Computing labor
variances
Objective 3

The Overhead Door Company manufactures garage doors for homes. The standard quantity of direct labor to manufacture a door is 4.5 hours. The standard hourly wage in this department is $12.50 per hour. During August, 6,100 doors were produced. The payroll records indicate that 31,110 hours were worked at a total cost for payroll of $405,985.50.
    Calculate the following:

1. Labor rate variance
2. Labor efficiency variance
3. Net labor variance (Note: Use the diagram format shown in Figure 8-1 to compute the variances.)

E8-8
Standard cost
summary; materials
and labor cost
variances
Objectives 2, 3

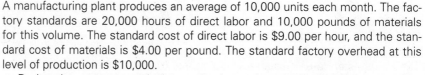

A manufacturing plant produces an average of 10,000 units each month. The factory standards are 20,000 hours of direct labor and 10,000 pounds of materials for this volume. The standard cost of direct labor is $9.00 per hour, and the standard cost of materials is $4.00 per pound. The standard factory overhead at this level of production is $10,000.
    During the current month the production and cost reports reflected the following information:

Beginning units in process	None
Units finished	9,500
Units in process, end of month	None
Direct labor hours worked	20,000
Pounds of materials used	9,400
Cost of direct labor	$178,000
Cost of materials used	$ 39,480

On the basis of the above information:

1. Prepare a standard cost summary.
2. Calculate the materials and labor cost variances and indicate whether they are favorable or unfavorable, using the formulas in Figure 8-1.

E8-9
Computing labor
variances
Objective 3

Fill in the missing figures for each of the following independent cases:

	Case 1	Case 2
Units produced	1,200	?
Standard hours per unit	2	0.6
Standard hours allowed	?	1,200
Standard rate per hour	$5	?
Actual hours used	2,460	1,160
Actual labor cost	?	?
Labor rate variance	$123 U	$290 U
Labor efficiency variance	?	$80 F

E8-10
Preparing a standard
cost summary and
making journal entries
Objectives 2, 3, 4

The normal capacity of a manufacturing plant is 40,000 direct labor hours and 20,000 units per month. A finished unit requires 6 pounds of materials at an esti-mated cost of $2 per pound. The estimated cost of labor is $10.00 per hour. The plant estimates that overhead for a month will be $40,000.

During the month of March, the plant totaled 34,800 direct labor hours at an average rate of $9.50 an hour. The plant produced 18,000 units, using 105,000 pounds of materials at a cost of $2.04 per pound.

1. Prepare a standard cost summary showing the standard unit cost.
2. Make journal entries to charge materials and labor to Work in Process. Indicate variances as favorable or unfavorable.

E8-11
Making journal entries
Objectives 3, 4

Assume that during the month of April the production report of the company in E8-10 revealed the following information:

Units produced during the month	21,000
Direct labor hours for the month	41,000
Materials used (in pounds)	130,000
Labor rate per hour	$10.04
Materials cost per pound	$1.98

Make journal entries to charge materials and labor to Work in Process. Indicate variances as favorable or unfavorable. (Remember to retrieve the standard costs from E8-10 before solving this exercise.)

E8-12
Using variance
analysis and
interpretation
Objectives 3, 5

Last year Junction Corporation adopted a standard cost system. Labor standards were set on the basis of time studies and prevailing wage rates. Materials stan-dards were determined from materials specifications and the prices then in effect.

On June 30, the end of the current fiscal year, a partial trial balance revealed the following:

	Debit	Credit
Materials Price Variance		25,000
Materials Quantity Variance	9,000	
Labor Rate Variance	30,000	
Labor Efficiency Variance	7,500	

Standards set at the beginning of the year have remained unchanged. All inventories are priced at standard cost. What conclusions can be drawn from each of the four variances shown in Junction's trial balance?

E8-13
Journalizing standard costs in two departments
Objective 7

Hoosier Manufacturing, Inc. has two departments, Mixing and Blending. When goods are completed in Mixing they are transferred to Blending and then to the finished goods storeroom. There was no beginning or ending work in process in either department. Listed below is information to be used in preparing journal entries at the end of October:

Standard cost of direct materials for actual production—Mixing	$185,000
Actual cost of direct materials used in production—Mixing	193,000
Materials price variance—Mixing.	10,000 unfav
Materials quantity variance—Mixing	2,000 fav
Standard cost of direct materials for actual production—Blending.	130,000
Actual cost of direct materials used in production—Blending	124,000
Materials price variance—Blending	4,000 fav
Materials quantity variance—Blending	2,000 fav
Standard cost of direct labor for actual production—Mixing	110,000
Actual cost of direct labor used in production—Mixing	117,000
Labor rate variance—Mixing	10,000 unfav
Labor efficiency variance—Mixing.	3,000 fav
Standard cost of direct labor for actual production—Blending.	95,000
Actual cost of direct labor used in production—Blending	80,000
Labor rate variance—Blending.	8,000 fav .
Labor efficiency variance—Blending	7,000 fav
Actual factory overhead.	145,000
Factory overhead applied—Mixing	85,000
Factory overhead applied—Blending	70,000

Prepare journal entries for the following:

1. The issuance of direct materials into production and the recording of the materials variances.

2. The use of direct labor in production and the recording of the labor variances.
3. The entries to record the actual and applied factory overhead.
4. The entries to transfer the production costs from Mixing to Blending and from Blending to finished goods.

PROBLEMS

P8-1
Materials and labor variances
Objective 3

A housing inspection company specializes in determining whether a building or house's drain pipes are properly tied into the city's sewer system. The company pours colored chemical through the pipes and collects an inspection sample from each outlet, which is then analyzed. Each job should take 15 hours for each of 4 inspectors who are paid $18 per hour. Each job uses 5 gallons of Pruff (a colored chemical), which costs $25 per gallon. Data from the company's most recent job (a building) follow:

5 men worked a total of 80 hours and were paid $20 per hour	$1,600.00
4.5 gallons of Pruff were used and cost $27.50 per gallon	123.75
Total cost of the job	$1,723.75

Required:

1. Compute the materials price and quantity variances.
2. Compute the labor rate and efficiency variances.

P8-2
Materials and labor variances analyses
Objective 3

Acceleration, Inc. manufactures a fuel additive, Zippy, that has a stable selling price of $44 per drum. The company has been producing and selling 80,000 drums per month.

In connection with your examination of Acceleration's financial statements for the year ended September 30, management has asked you to review some computations made by Acceleration's cost accountant. Your working papers disclose the following about the company's operations:

Standard costs per drum of product manufactured:

Materials:		
8 gallons of Zippy @ $2	$16	
1 empty drum	1	$17
Direct labor—1 hour		$ 8
Factory overhead		$ 6

Costs and expenses during September:

Zippy : 600,000 gallons purchased at a cost of $1,140,000; 645,000 gallons used
Empty drums: 94,000 purchased at a cost of $94,000; 80,000 used
Direct labor: 81,000 hours worked at a cost of $654,480
Factory overhead: $768,000

Required:

Calculate the following variances for September:

1. Materials quantity variance
2. Materials price variance (determined at time of purchase)
3. Labor efficiency variance
4. Labor rate variance

P8-3
Calculation of materials and labor variances
Objective 3

Odus Corporation manufactures and sells a single product. The company uses a standard cost system. The standard cost per unit of product follows:

Materials—one pound of plastic @ $3.00	$ 3.00
Direct labor—1.6 hours @ $10.00	16.00
Factory overhead	4.45
Total	$23.45

The charges to the manufacturing department for November, when 5,000 units were produced, follow:

Materials—5,300 pounds @ $3.00	$ 15,900
Direct labor—8,200 hours @ $9.80	80,360
Factory overhead	23,815
Total	$120,075

The purchasing department normally buys about the same quantity as is used in production during a month. In November, 5,200 pounds were purchased at a price of $2.90 per pound.

Required:

Calculate the following variances from standard costs for the data given:

1. Materials quantity
2. Materials price (at time of purchase)
3. Labor efficiency
4. Labor rate

P8-4
Analysis of materials and labor variances
Objective 3

Jacoby Manufacturing Company uses a standard cost system in accounting for the cost of production of its only product, product A. The standards for the production of one unit of product A follow:

Direct materials: 10 feet of Prolax at $0.75 per foot and 3 feet of Laxpro at $1.00 per foot.
Direct labor: 4 hours at $8.00 per hour.
Factory overhead: applied at 150% of standard direct labor costs.

There was no beginning inventory on hand at July 1. Following is a summary of costs and related data for the production of product A during the following year ended June 30:

100,000 feet of Prolax were purchased at $0.78 per foot.
30,000 feet of Laxpro were purchased at $0.90 per foot.
8,000 units of product A were produced that required 78,000 feet of Prolax; 26,000 feet of Laxpro; and 31,000 hours of direct labor at $8.20 per hour.
6,000 units of product A were sold.

On June 30, there are 22,000 feet of Prolax, 4,000 feet of Laxpro, and 2,000 completed units of product A on hand. All purchases and transfers are "charged in" at standard.

Required:

Calculate the following:

1. Materials quantity variance for Prolax
2. Materials quantity variance for Laxpro
3. Materials price variance for Prolax (recorded at purchase)
4. Materials price variance for Laxpro (recorded at purchase)
5. Labor efficiency variance
6. Labor rate variance

P8-5
Materials and labor variances
Objective 3

Chase Company uses a standard cost to account for its single product. The standards established for the product include the following:

Materials . . . . 8 lbs. @ $0.05 per lb.
Labor . . . . 6 hours @ $5.60 per hour

The following operating data came from the records for the month:

In process, beginning inventory, none.
In process, ending inventory, 800 units, 80% complete as to labor; material is issued at the beginning of processing.
Completed during the month, 5,600 units.

Materials issued to production were 51,680 pounds @ $0.045 per pound.
Direct labor was $215,840 at the rate of $5.68 per hour.

Required:

Calculate the following variances:

1. Materials price
2. Materials quantity
3. Net materials variance
4. Labor rate
5. Labor efficiency
6. Net labor variance

(Hint: Before determining the standard quantity for materials and labor, you must first compute the equivalent units for materials and labor.)

P8-6
Analysis of materials and labor variances
Objective 3

Home Products Company manufactures a variety of products made of plastic and aluminum components. During the winter months, substantially all of the production capacity is devoted to the production of lawn sprinklers for the following spring and summer seasons. Other products are manufactured during the remainder of the year.

The company has developed standard costs for its several products. Standard costs for each year are set in the preceding October. The standard cost of a sprinkler for the current year is $3.70, computed as follows:

Direct materials:
   Aluminum—0.2 lb. @ $0.40 per lb. $0.08
   Plastic—1.0 lb. @ $0.38 per lb. 38
Production labor—0.3 hr. @ $8.00 per hr. 2.40
Factory overhead 84

Total $3.70

During February, Home Products manufactured 8,500 good sprinklers. The company incurred the following costs, which it charged to production:

Materials requisitioned for production:
   Aluminum—1,900 lbs. @ $0.40 per lb. . . . . $ 760
   Plastic—Regular grade—6,000 lbs. @ $0.38 per lb.   2,280
             Low grade—3,500 lbs. @ $0.38 per lb.   1,330
Production labor—2,700 hrs.   23,220
Factory overhead   7,140

Costs charged to production $34,730

Materials price variations are not determined by usage but are charged to a materials price variation account at the time the invoice is entered. All materials are carried in inventory at standard prices. Materials purchases for February were as follows:

Aluminum—1,800 lbs. @ $0.48 per lb. . . . . $ 864
Plastic—Regular grade—3,000 lbs. @ $0.50 per lb.   1,500
         Low grade*—6,000 lbs. @ $0.29 per lb.   1,740

Due to plastic shortages, the company was forced to purchase lower grade plastic than called for in the standards. This increased the number of sprinklers rejected on inspection.

Required:

Calculate price and usage variances for each type of material and for labor.

**P8-7
Materials and labor
variance analyses.
Similar to self-study
problem.
Objectives 3, 5**

The standard cost summary of Corey Manufacturing Company is shown below, together with production and cost data for the period.

Standard Cost Summary

Materials:
  2 gallons of A @ $2.00 . . . . $4.00
  2 gallons of B @ $3.00 . . . .   6.00 $10.00

Labor:
  1 hour @ $12.00 . . . .   12.00
Factory overhead:
  $1.00 per direct labor hour 1.00

Total standard unit cost $23.00

Production and Cost Summary

Units completed during the month	9,000
Ending units in process (one-fourth completed)	2,000
Gallons of material A used	21,000
Gallons of material B used	20,000
Direct labor hours worked	10,000
Cost of material A used	$ 41,160
Cost of material B used	$ 60,000
Cost of direct labor	$117,000

One gallon each of materials A and B are added at the start of processing. The balance of the materials are added when the process is two-thirds complete. Labor and overhead are added evenly throughout the process.

Required:

1. Calculate equivalent production. (Be sure to refer to the standard cost summary to help determine the percent of materials in ending work in process.)
2. Calculate materials and labor variances and indicate whether they are favorable or unfavorable, using the formulas shown in Figure 8-1.
3. Determine the cost of materials and labor in the work in process account at the end of the month.
4. Prove that all materials and labor costs have been accounted for. (Hint: Don't forget the net variances in reconciling the costs accounted for with the costs to be accounted for.)

P8-8
Journal entries for materials and labor variances
Objective 4

Lin-Mar Corporation has established the following standard cost per unit:

Materials—6 lbs. @ $2 per lb.	$12
Labor—2 hours @ $6.00 per hour	12

Although 10,000 units were budgeted, only 8,800 units were produced.

The purchasing department bought 55,000 pounds of materials at a cost of $123,750. Actual pounds of materials used were 54,305. Direct labor cost was $127,400 for 18,200 hours worked.

Required:

1. Make journal entries to record the materials transactions, assuming that the materials price variances were taken at the time of purchase.
2. Make journal entries to record the labor variances.

P8-9
Allocation of variances
Objectives 4, 5

Myrna Manufacturing Corporation uses a standard cost system that records raw materials at actual cost, records materials price variances at the time that raw materials are issued to work in process, and prorates all variances at year-end. Variances associated with direct materials are prorated based on the direct materials balances in the appropriate accounts, and variances associated with direct labor are prorated based on the direct labor balances in the appropriate accounts. The following information is available for Myrna for the year ended December 31.

Raw materials inventory at December 31	$ 65,000
Finished goods inventory at December 31:	
Direct materials	87,000
Direct labor	130,500
Applied factory overhead	104,400
Cost of goods sold for the year ended December 31:	
Direct materials	348,000
Direct labor	739,500
Applied factory overhead	591,600
Materials quantity variance (favorable)	15,000
Materials price variance (unfavorable)	10,000
Labor efficiency variance (favorable)	5,000
Labor rate variance (unfavorable)	20,000
Factory overhead applied	696,000

There were no beginning inventories and no ending work in process inventory.

Required:

Calculate the following:

1. Amount of materials price variance to be prorated to finished goods inventory at December 31. (Hint: You must first determine the ratio of direct materials cost in the ending finished goods inventory.)
2. Total amount of direct materials cost in the finished goods inventory at December 31, after all variances have been prorated.
3. Total amount of direct labor cost in the finished goods inventory at December 31, after all variances have been prorated.
4. Total cost of goods sold for the year ended December 31, after all variances have been prorated.

P8-10
Variance analysis, journal entries, other analyses for multiple departments
Objectives 3, 4, 5, 7

Cost and production data for the Bell Products Company are presented below.

Standard Cost Summary

	Dept. I	Dept. II	Total
Materials:			
4 lbs. @ $0.50	$ 2		
1 gal. @ $1.00		$ 1	$ 3
Labor:			
1 hour @ $ 8.00	8		
1 hour @ $10.00		10	18
Factory overhead:			
Per unit	1	2	3
	$11	$13	$24

Production Report

	Dept. I	Dept. II
Beginning units in process	None	None
Units finished and transferred	6,000	5,000
Ending units in process	2,000	1,000
Stage of completion	1/2	1/2

Cost Data

	Dept. I		Dept. II	
Direct materials:				
30,000 lbs. @ $0.52	$15,600			
5,500 gal. @ $0.95			$ 5,225	
Direct labor:				
6,800 hours @ $ 8.00	54,400			
5,600 hours @ $10.20			57,120	
Factory overhead:				
Indirect materials	$ 500		$1,000	
Indirect labor	2,000		5,000	
Other	4,500	7,000	5,000	11,000

Required:

1. Calculate net variances for materials, labor, and factory overhead.
2. Calculate specific materials and labor variances by department.
3. Make all journal entries to record production costs in Work in Process and Finished Goods.
4. Prove balances of Work in Process for both departments.
5. Prove that all costs have been accounted for. *Note:* Assume that materials, labor, and overhead are added evenly throughout the process.
6. Assume that 4,000 units were sold at $40 each.
   a. Calculate the gross margin based on standard cost. (Hint: Recall that Gross margin = Sales – Cost of Goods Sold.)
   b. Calculate the gross margin based on actual cost.

9

Budgeting and Standard Cost Accounting for Factory Overhead

LEARNING OBJECTIVES

After studying this chapter, you should be able to:

1. Explain the general principles involved in the budgeting process.
2. Recognize the different types of budgets prepared by businesses.
3. Explain the appropriate procedures to determine standard amounts of factory overhead at different levels of production.
4. Recognize the difference between actual and applied factory overhead.
5. Compute the controllable variance and the volume variance for the two-variance method of analysis.
6. Compute the spending, efficiency, budget, and volume variances for the four-variance method of analysis.
7. Compute the budget, capacity, and efficiency variance for the three-variance method of analysis.

A standard cost system is a good control procedure because it provides a method of data comparison essential for precision planning and control. Also, the study of changing volumes is an important factor in controlling factory overhead costs because certain costs vary with changes in activity, while other costs do not.

To determine proper standards for the comparison of predetermined costs with actual costs at different activity levels, factory overhead must be accumulated in a manner that allows the relationship of cost to the volume of activity to be readily determined. Therefore, in addition to being classified by function, costs must be further classified as to behavior when an associated activity changes. **Cost behavior** is determined through the process of distinguishing whether a cost remains fixed or varies with changes that occur in activities.

Factory overhead costs are first grouped by department and then by behavior, fixed or variable. Then, overhead costs are further reduced to a predetermined or standard cost basis for each unit of product—either units of product, per direct labor hour, per machine hour, or per direct labor cost dollar. Because factory overhead cost per unit will increase as volume or activity decreases and vice versa, control of factory overhead costs can best be established by using a sliding or flexible budget. The development and use of *flexible budgets* facilitate more effective cost control and improved management planning.

PRINCIPLES OF BUDGETING

LEARNING OBJECTIVE 1
Explain the general principles involved in the budgeting process.

Most successful companies today use operating budgets to help them in their constant effort to analyze and control operations, keep costs in line, and reduce expenses. A **budget** is a planning device that helps a company set goals and that serves as a gauge against which actual results can be measured. Many heads of households are familiar with the basic aspects of budgeting whereby they estimate their income for the following year, determine what their living expenses will be, and then, depending on the figures, reduce unnecessary spending, set up a savings plan, or possibly determine additional ways to supplement their income. During the year, they compare their budget with their actual income and expenditures to be sure that expenses do not exceed income and cause financial difficulties. The Real-World Example discusses the difficulties of budgeting for a household and then looks at the budgeting problems for a university.

Budgeting in business and industry is a formal method of detailed financial planning. It encompasses the coordination and control of every significant item in the balance sheet and income statement. Budgeting is used to help the company reach its long-term and short-term objectives. If the principles of budgeting are carried out in a proper manner, the company can be assured that it will efficiently use all of its resources and achieve the most favorable results possible in the long run.

Basically, the primary objective of any company is to maximize its net income or attain the highest volume of sales at the lowest possible cost.

MY HOUSEHOLD BUDGET

Our family consists of two adults (Jim and Kathy), four children, and two cats. We have limited income and have the normal bills of most families, including a house payment, car payments, insurance, food, utilities, clothes, medical and dental bills, education expenses, and savings commitments.

Let's assume that next year we will have $1,000 of discretionary income after taxes and no desire to go further in debt. How shall we spend this money? Kathy would like to spend $500 on clothes for the kids, who are quickly outgrowing their wardrobe. In addition, she would like to spend the other $500 on piano lessons for the children. On the other hand, Jim would like to spend $500 to replace the garage door, which is falling down, and another $500 to fix the car's transmission, which is starting to slip. Jim and Kathy are having trouble making a decision on how their money should be spent. How shall this family allocate these scarce resources and finalize their budget for next year?

This example illustrates on a small scale the roots of many issues and problems any organization faces in allocating scarce resources. These problems tend to arise during the budget process because that is where resources typically get allocated. The real problems may lie elsewhere, with the "budget" process getting blamed for the discomfort.

This example shows that there seems to be a difference of opinion regarding the goals and strategies of this family and a difference in what each person feels is important. You can determine a person's priorities by watching how he or she spends money.

There doesn't seem to be a traditional way to make spending decisions. Also, there is apparently no framework to evaluate proposed expenditures, especially those involving qualitative factors.

THE LOCAL UNIVERSITY

During the annual budgeting process, proposals regarding program and departmental funding are discussed. The administration wants to hold the line on spending and keep tuition competitive, but the department chairs raise a number of questions.

"Shouldn't the Arts and Humanities Department get more money this year to help emphasize the importance of the liberal arts curriculum? What about the Business School? Shouldn't the B-school receive more operating funding because its classes have the highest demand? Shouldn't more money be put into diversity programs to help make students more aware of the differences between cultures, races, and sexes for greater understanding? How about the building and grounds: the roofs need replacing, and the sidewalks are cracking. Don't we need to make repairs? What's more, how can we have a winning basketball team without a new basketball arena?"

How would you like to be responsible for resolving these questions? Finally a decision is made that solves all these competing requests for funds—of course, raise tuition! What are the problems and issues here? Many competing constituencies greatly magnify the challenge of resource allocation as compared to the household example. Each department within the university has its own sense of mission, priorities, goals, objectives, and agendas. There may not be a good alignment at the university level. It is difficult to prioritize the proposed funding requests because there may not be clear agreed-upon criteria in which to compare the benefits of one department's request over another. The intangible nature of the benefits for each program makes it even more challenging.

James C. Horsch, "Redesigning the Resource Allocation Process," *Management Accounting* (July 1995), pp. 55–59.

Planning and control are absolutely essential in achieving this goal, and budgeting produces the framework within which the organization can reach this objective. The budget then becomes a road map that guides managers along the way and lets them know when the company is straying from its planned route. It is a chart of the course of operations, and in addition to forecasting costs and profits as a means of controlling costs, it requires those in authority in all areas of the business to analyze carefully all aspects of their responsibility for costs and also to analyze company strengths and weaknesses.

The general principles of budgeting have several requirements:

1. Management must clearly define its objectives.

2. Goals must be realistic and possible to attain.

3. Because the budgeting process involves looking to the future, the budget must carefully consider economic developments, the general business climate, and the condition of the industry, as well as changes and trends that may influence sales and costs. Historical data should be used only as a stepping-off point for projections into the future.

4. There must be a plan, which is consistently followed, to constantly analyze the actual results as compared with the budget.

5. The budget must be flexible enough so that it can be modified in the light of changing conditions; it must not be so restrictive that changes cannot be made where more favorable results are foreseeable.

6. Responsibility for forecasting costs must be clearly defined, and accountability for actual results must be enforced. This principle encourages careful analysis and precise evaluation.

PREPARING AND USING BUDGETS

LEARNING OBJECTIVE 2
Recognize the different types of budgets prepared by businesses.

The following discussion is not intended to be an exhaustive survey of budgeting but is principally concerned with the preparation of the production plan and the manufacturing expense budget. However, a brief presentation of other budgets is appropriate, so that you can see how all budgets are interrelated and how the budget for the factory is influenced by the other budgets. Although this example is for a manufacturing business, budgeting is equally important for merchandising and service businesses.

FORECAST OF SALES

In preparing a budget, management must consider all the items of income and expense. The usual starting point in the budgeting process is a **forecast of sales**, followed by a determination of inventory policy, a production plan, a budget of manufacturing costs, and a budget for all administrative and selling expenses. The final product is the amount of net income budgeted for the year. A balance sheet forecast should also be prepared, concerned primarily with cash, receivables, and capital additions.

Although all of the aforementioned budgets are important, the forecast of sales is especially significant, because management must use this information as a basis for preparing all other budgets. This forecast is concerned with projecting the volume of sales both in units and dollars. In estimating the sales for the forthcoming year, the sales department must take into consideration present and future economic situations. It should research and carefully analyze market prospects for its products and give consideration to the development of new products and the discontinuance of old products. It should make these analyses by territory, by type of product, and possibly by type of customer. Marketing researchers should also carefully survey and evaluate consumer demand. After this detailed examination, the mix of the products to be sold as well as the volume and the sales price can be determined.

INVENTORY AND PRODUCTION PLANNING

After the sales mix and volume plans have been made, the factory can proceed with the determination of production requirements. In a simple situation, assuming one product, stable production throughout the year, and an ending inventory 2,000 units greater than the beginning inventory, the number of units to be produced can be calculated as follows:

Units to be sold	100,000
Ending inventory required	4,500
Total	104,500
Beginning inventory	2,500
Units to be manufactured	102,000
Units per month (102,000 / 12)	8,500

In actual practice, this computation is more complex. Management must try to achieve a satisfactory balance between production, inventory, and the timely availability of goods to be sold. For example, if the company's sales are seasonal rather than evenly distributed throughout the year, stable production might produce the following situation:

	Number of Units		
	Produced	Sold	On Hand
Beginning balance			2,500
January	8,500	1,000	10,000
February	8,500	2,000	16,500
March	8,500	3,000	22,000
April	8,500	10,000	20,500
May	8,500	15,000	14,000
June	8,500	15,000	7,500
July	8,500	12,000	4,000
August	8,500	9,000	3,500
September	8,500	9,000	3,000
October	8,500	8,000	3,500
November	8,500	8,000	4,000
December	8,500	8,000	4,500
Total	102,000	100,000	

The company must have enough storage facility to handle as many as 22,000 units. However, most of this space would be unused during several months of the year, resulting in a waste of invested capital for inventory and storage facilities and expenditures for upkeep, insurance, and taxes that provide no direct benefit. In this situation, a manufacturing concern might lease some storage facilities during the peak months, thereby requiring a much smaller company-owned facility. However, leasing may present problems of inconvenience, expense, and unavailability of the facilities at the right time and in the right place. In addition, during some months the company would have a considerable amount of capital tied up in finished goods that could be threatened by obsolescence.

Another solution is for management to schedule different levels of production each month in order to maintain a stable inventory and to minimize the number of units stored. The following table shows this approach:

	Number of Units Produced	Sold	On Hand
Beginning balance			2,500
January	1,500	1,000	3,000
February	2,500	2,000	3,500
March	3,000	3,000	3,500
April	10,000	10,000	3,500
May	15,000	15,000	3,500
June	15,000	15,000	3,500
July	12,000	12,000	3,500
August	9,500	9,000	4,000
September	9,500	9,000	4,500
October	8,000	8,000	4,500
November	8,000	8,000	4,500
December	8,000	8,000	4,500
Total	102,000	100,000	

This alternative requires minimum storage space and related expenses, but it creates a new problem. The factory must have enough facilities to handle the peak production of 15,000 units, but these facilities would be from 50 percent to 90 percent idle during some months. A possible solution is to establish a smaller facility and to engage two or three shifts of employees during the busier months. Although the facility investment problem is reduced, a bigger problem is created because the working force can vary by 1,000 percent from the slowest period to the most active. This condition would require hiring new employees in the earlier months as production is climbing, with the problem of the high cost of recruiting and training as well as the problem of quality production with new, possibly inexperienced employees. In the later months, as production drops, many workers would be laid off, creating considerable additional expense for unemployment compensation as well as hardship for the employees and a feeling of ill-will toward the company.

Management is often faced with the problem of determining which course to follow—whether to maintain stable production, with the necessity of providing for storage capacity, the tie-up of capital funds in inventory, and the possibility of obsolescence; or to maintain a stable inventory, with all of the ensuing expenses of personnel and facilities. Most companies will carefully analyze the alternatives and arrive at a plan that represents a reasonable compromise between the two alternatives. As has been discussed previously, just-in-time manufacturing represents a third alternative that many companies have adopted.

BUDGETS FOR MANUFACTURING COSTS
AND ADMINISTRATIVE AND SELLING EXPENSES

Once the production schedule has been determined, the budget for manufacturing costs can be prepared, which involves determining the costs of materials, labor, and factory overhead for each month (or week, or day) of the coming year. After standard costs have been determined, this calculation, whether for one or for several products, is relatively simple for direct materials and direct labor—the number of units to be produced multiplied by the standard cost per unit. However, the forecast of the factory overhead is more involved and will be considered in detail later in this section. When a company has determined its level of activity for sales and production, it can prepare its budgets for administrative, selling, and other expenses. As with other forecasts, the planners should take into consideration not only the planned volume for the company but also economic conditions, trends for local and national wages and salaries, and other expenses.

OTHER BUDGETS

Completing these budgets permits the company to determine its budgeted income statement for the year. Keep in mind that, although this discussion has centered around units and dollars, these forecasts could also be used to plan the hiring (or laying off) of personnel, to schedule the purchases of materials, to arrange for necessary facilities, to develop sales promotion, and other appropriate functions.

The company can now prepare its balance sheet budgets. The cash budget shows the anticipated flow of cash and the timing of receipts and disbursements based on projected revenues, the production schedule, and expenses. Using this budget, management can plan for necessary financing or for temporary investment of surplus funds. The budget for receivables, based on anticipated sales, credit terms, the economy, and other relevant factors, will influence the cash budget by showing when cash can be expected from the turnover of inventory and receivables. A liabilities budget is also necessary, reflecting how the company's cash position will be affected by paying these items.

The company may prepare a capital expenditures budget, which is a plan for the timing of acquisitions of buildings, equipment, or other significant assets during the year. This plan ties in with the sales and production plans and may influence the cash budget for expenditures to the extent that additional financing may be necessary.

Teamwork and cooperation in preparing the budgets are absolutely essential. The sales, engineering, manufacturing, and accounting divisions of the company must work together to produce meaningful forecasts, because many of the estimates depend on the plans of other departments. Also, a considerable amount of coordination is required. For example, the sales goal must be compatible with the production that can be attained with the facilities available. At the same time, the amount and scheduling of production relies heavily on the needs of the marketing department. As mentioned previously, some budgets can be prepared only after certain others have been completed, and they will be influenced by these other plans.

An important factor in the budgeting process is that the budgets are not necessarily prepared sequentially. After the sales forecast in units is made, the manufacturing division can begin working on the production schedule and the manufacturing expense budget, the sales department can start preparing its budget for selling expenses, and the administrative expense forecast can begin. The receivables turnover schedule can also be made at this point, and possibly the capital expenditures budget can be prepared. The cash budget and the schedule of liabilities and payments cannot be considered until all of the aforementioned items are completed.

EVALUATING BUDGET PERFORMANCE

If a budget is to be used successfully as a management tool for control, the actual results should be periodically compared with the budgeted figures and the differences thoroughly analyzed. Without this constant follow-up and analysis, the budget is a useless item. This principle has been discussed previously in connection with standard costs, and it also applies to the other planned amounts, both by unit and by dollar volume. If variances are found to exist in the number of units sold or manufactured, or in the dollar amounts of sales or expenses, or in other budgeted items, the planners must carefully evaluate the variances and determine responsibility.

Typically, performance reports are prepared and distributed to the people who are accountable for the actual results. For example, all supervisors and department heads receive reports for their respective departments. The vice president in charge of production receives information on all elements of manufacturing involving the production and service departments. The president of the company receives reports on all functions of the business—manufacturing, sales, and administrative. These reports should clearly reflect the variances from the budget in all areas so that appropriate action can be taken.

FLEXIBLE BUDGETING

The comparison of actual results with the budget to see if the planned objectives are being met leads to the use of **flexible budgeting**. This concept, introduced in Chapter 4, will be discussed from the standpoint of the factory overhead budget, but the principles are applicable to any item of expense that involves fixed and variable elements.

To implement a flexible budget, a company must plan how it will respond to varying sets of conditions—for example, the sale of 10,000 units per month rather than 9,000, the production of 15,000 units per month rather than 17,000, the addition or replacement of a machine in a department, or the development of new products or the discontinuance of the old. In other words, the company plans in advance what the effect will be on revenue, expense, and profit if sales or production differ from the budget. To illustrate, if budgeted sales for a month are $100,000 and the budgeted selling expense is $25,000, it is reasonable to assume that if actual sales are $80,000, the actual selling expense would be less than $25,000. If production volume was 10,000 units rather than the budgeted 9,000 units, the cost of production should logically be greater than the amount budgeted for the 9,000 units.

The flexible budget is influenced by the presence of fixed and variable costs as discussed in Chapter 4. **Fixed costs** have been previously defined as those costs that do not change as production changes over a given range. They are a function of time and generally will be incurred regardless of the level of production. These expenses, such as straight-line depreciation, insurance, taxes, supervisory salaries, and others, will remain the same in dollar total, except in the extreme case of a major change in production that requires more or fewer machines, facilities, and supervisory personnel.

Many costs do vary in total dollar amount in proportion to any change in production. These **variable costs**, which are a function of activity, include direct labor, direct materials, indirect labor, and maintenance costs. It is because of these variable elements that the total cost differs from amounts originally budgeted when the level of production is different. If the manufacturer has budgeted production of 5,000 units for the month at a cost of $50,000 and the actual production is more or less than 5,000 units, there would be little value in comparing the actual cost of production with the items making up the $50,000 of a **static budget**—that is, a budget where the costs are shown for only one level of activity. Under such operating conditions, however, a flexible budget is useful because it shows the planned expenses at various levels of production. Thus, management can quickly determine variances by comparing the actual costs with what the costs of production should have been at the actual level of production.

PREPARING THE FLEXIBLE BUDGET FOR FACTORY OVERHEAD

Determining the standard overhead cost per unit and preparing the flexible budget for factory overhead follow the basic principles suggested for determining standards for materials and labor costs. All costs that might be incurred should be carefully considered. Prior costs, as adjusted, must be studied as well as the effect of new costs, future economic conditions, changes in processes, and trends. As with other standards, the individuals responsible for setting factory overhead standards should have considerable experience and familiarity with manufacturing operations.

Because costs are affected by the level of production, the first step is to determine what should be the standard volume of production. **Standard production** is the volume on which the initial calculation of costs is based. Several approaches are used to determine this figure and there are several related definitions of manufacturing capacity. These types of capacity include the following:

1. **Theoretical capacity** represents the maximum number of units that can be produced with the completely efficient use of all available facilities and personnel. Generally, this production level is impossible to attain. It represents a rigid standard for the factory because it requires maximum production with no allowance for inefficiencies of any kind.

2. **Practical capacity** is the level of production that provides complete utilization of all facilities and personnel, but allows for some idle capacity due to operating interruptions, such as machinery breakdowns, idle time, and other inescapable inefficiencies.

3. **Normal capacity** is the level of production that will meet the normal requirements of ordinary sales demand over a period of years. Although it conceivably can be equal to or greater than practical capacity, normal capacity usually does not involve a plan for maximum usage of manufacturing facilities but allows for some unavoidable idle capacity and some inefficiencies in operations. Most manufacturing firms use this level of capacity for budget development because it represents a logical balance between maximum production capacity and the capacity that is demanded by actual sales volume. Furthermore, over a period of years, all factory overhead expense will normally be absorbed by production. The following discussion will assume the use of normal capacity for planning purposes.

To illustrate the flexible budget, the following figures were determined to be the factory overhead costs at the normal or standard volume of 1,000 units. (To simplify the illustration, only a few overhead classifications are used. In actual practice, many types of expenses would be broken down into fixed and variable categories.)

```
Standard production—1,000 units
Standard direct labor hours—2,000
Fixed cost:
    Depreciation of building and equipment  . . . . . . .   $4,000
    Property tax and insurance  . . . . . . . . . . . . .    1,000
    Supervisory salaries   . . . . . . . . . . . . . . .    4,000
        Total fixed cost  . . . . . . . . . . . . . . . . . . .           $ 9,000
Variable cost:
    Maintenance   . . . . . . . . . . . . . . . . . . . .   $2,000
    Supplies . . . . . . . . . . . . . . . . . . . . . .     1,000
        Total variable cost   . . . . . . . . . . . . . . . .             3,000
Total factory overhead cost  . . . . . . . . . . . . . . .                $12,000

Standard factory overhead application rate per direct labor hour:
    Fixed cost ($9,000 ÷ 2,000 hours)   . . . . . . . . . . .              $ 4.50
    Variable cost ($3,000 ÷ 2,000 hours)  . . . . . . . . .                 1.50
Total factory overhead rate ($12,000 ÷ 2,000 hours)   . . .               $ 6.00

Standard overhead cost per unit ($12,000 ÷ 1,000 units)  .                $12.00
```

As discussed in Chapter 4, factory overhead can be applied to work in process using different bases, such as direct labor hours, direct labor cost, or machine hours. One of the most commonly used bases—direct labor hours—applies overhead in relation to the standard number of direct labor hours allowed for the current actual production.

In the preceding schedule, both standard units and standard hours are given, because production may be expressed in terms of units or the standard number of direct labor hours allowed for the actual production. Whichever base for measuring production is chosen, the results are not affected. Based on the preceding budget, if 900 units are manufactured, Work in Process would be charged with $10,800 (900 units × $12) for factory overhead. If production is expressed in terms of standard direct labor hours of 1,800 (900 units × 2 hours), Work in Process would still be charged with $10,800 (1,800 hours × $6).

Figure 9-1 shows the flexible budget for this illustration. The individuals responsible for the work have determined what the fixed and variable costs will be at various levels of production. Notice that the factory overhead per direct labor hour decreases as volume increases, because

FIGURE 9-1   Factory Overhead Cost Budget

Percent of Normal Capacity	80%	90%	100%	110%	120%
Number of units	800	900	1,000	1,100	1,200
Number of standard direct labor hours	1,600	1,800	2,000	2,200	2,400
Budgeted factory overhead:					
Fixed cost:					
Depreciation of building and equipment	$ 4,000	$ 4,000	$ 4,000	$ 4,000	$ 4,000
Property taxes and insurance	1,000	1,000	1,000	1,000	1,000
Supervisory salaries	4,000	4,000	4,000	4,000	4,000
Total fixed cost	$ 9,000	$ 9,000	$ 9,000	$ 9,000	$ 9,000
Variable cost:					
Maintenance	$ 1,600	$ 1,800	$ 2,000	$ 2,200	$ 2,400
Supplies	800	900	1,000	1,100	1,200
Total variable cost	$ 2,400	$ 2,700	$ 3,000	$ 3,300	$ 3,600
Total factory overhead cost	$11,400	$11,700	$12,000	$12,300	$12,600
Factory overhead per direct labor hour	$7.125	$6.50	$6.00	$5.59	$5.25

the fixed factory overhead is being spread over more production. Also, notice that the standard volume of production is expressed as being 100% of capacity. This production level is not necessarily the maximum capacity of the manufacturing facility. It does represent, considering sales demand, the most efficient use of the present facilities under normal operating conditions, with some allowance for operating interruptions. A factory can always produce more than the normal volume by working overtime, adding a shift, or squeezing in more machinery and workers; but these conditions are not normal. Because it is not uncommon to operate above or below normal, the flexible budget shows expense amounts for production above and below normal capacity of 100%.

USING THE FLEXIBLE BUDGET

If actual production for a given period is exactly 1,000 units, a comparison of total or individual factory overhead costs incurred with these budgeted figures can be made and variances determined as follows:

Factory Overhead Cost Variances

Normal production . . . .   1,000 units (or 2,000 direct labor hours)
Actual production . . . .   1,000 units (or 2,000 direct labor hours)

	Budget	Actual	Variances Favorable (Unfavorable)
Fixed cost:			
Depreciation of building and equipment	$ 4,000	$ 4,000	
Property taxes and insurance	1,000	1,000	
Supervisory salaries	4,000	4,000	
Total fixed cost	$ 9,000	$ 9,000	
Variable cost:			
Maintenance	$ 2,000	$ 2,500	$(500)
Supplies	1,000	900	100
Total variable cost	$ 3,000	$ 3,400	$(400)
Total factory overhead cost	$12,000	$12,400	$(400)

The net unfavorable variance is considered a budget variance or controllable variance because production was at normal capacity, eliminating the possibility of a volume variance, which would result from a volume differing from the normal capacity. Usually, however, factory activity will not be exactly at the normal level. The volume of production invariably fluctuates to a certain extent from the standard level because it is affected by such factors as vacations, holidays, absentee employees, work interruptions, and equipment breakdowns. If a seasonal factor is involved, the fluctuation from one month to the next could be significant. Under these circumstances, the flexible budget provides the budgeted figures for the actual levels of production rather than the established normal level.

Upon receiving the report on actual volume for the period, the factory overhead costs that should have been incurred at that volume can be compared with the actual costs to determine variances. If the volume of production falls between two of the amounts shown in the budget, an approximation of budgeted cost can be interpolated.

Actual production 850 units (85%):
Budgeted cost at 90% $11,700
Budgeted cost at 80%   11,400
Difference . . . . $ 300

Range between volume levels 10%

Dividing the difference of $300 by 10 determines an additional cost of $30 for each percentage point increase.

Next lower budgeted volume	80%
Costs at 80% volume	$11,400
Additional costs at 85% volume (5 × $30)	150
Budgeted costs at 85% volume	$11,550

SEMIFIXED AND SEMIVARIABLE COSTS

The preceding method of determining the budgeted amount of factory overhead at a level of production different from that given in the budget is satisfactory if the overhead increases evenly throughout each range of activity, as would be the case if all costs were either fixed or variable. However, if significant semifixed or semivariable costs exist, then this method would not always be accurate enough for a meaningful evaluation.

Semifixed costs, or **step costs,** are those that tend to remain the same in dollar amount through a certain range of activity, but increase when production exceeds certain limits. For example, the salary of a department head is generally considered a fixed cost, because no other department head will be employed through a given range of activity, and the salary cost will not change as the volume fluctuates. But if the production level exceeds a given number of units, an assistant department head might have to be employed to aid in supervising the greater number of workers that would be necessary. In this case, the fixed expense for supervisory personnel would increase, as illustrated in the following table.

Percent of Normal Capacity	80%	90%	100%	110%	120%	130%
Fixed cost	$20,000	$20,000	$20,000	$20,000	$28,000	$28,000
Variable cost	24,000	27,000	30,000	33,000	36,000	39,000
Total factory overhead	$44,000	$47,000	$50,000	$53,000	$64,000	$67,000

In this case, if the actual volume of production falls into the range between 110% and 120%, the use of interpolation to determine budgeted expense would probably not be satisfactory. A careful analysis of the expenses would need to be made, without the use of interpolation, to determine whether more supervisory personnel would be needed at 119% of capacity or 111% of capacity, for example.

Semivariable costs are those that may change with production but not necessarily in direct proportion. For example, if a company incurs expense to train new employees before they go into the factory, this expense will increase as production increases and new employees are hired. But if the volume of production decreases and no new employees are hired, no training expense will be incurred.

The existence of semifixed or semivariable costs indicates an even greater need for careful analysis and evaluation of the costs at each level of production. Semivariable expenses were discussed in Chapter 4. The approach in this chapter, however, assumes that fixed costs remain constant and variable costs vary evenly throughout the ranges of activity given, unless stated otherwise.

SERVICE DEPARTMENT BUDGETS AND VARIANCES

Preparing a budget for a service department follows the same procedure as that for production departments. Expenses at different levels of production are estimated, and a standard rate for application of service department expenses to production departments is determined based on the type of service provided and the estimated usage by the production departments. The production departments will take these expenses into consideration in setting up their budgets.

During the period, the production departments are charged with service department expenses at the standard rate using their actual activity base, such as kilowatt hours or hours of maintenance labor. At the end of the period, the service department's actual expenses are compared with the amount charged to the production departments to determine the variances.

SUMMARY OF THE BUDGETING PROCESS

Figure 9-2 summarizes the budgeting process for the factory and the determination of standard costs.

You should now be able to work the following: Questions 1–14; Exercises 9-1 and 9-2; and Problems 9-1 to 9-3.

ANALYSIS OF FACTORY OVERHEAD STANDARD COST VARIANCES

LEARNING OBJECTIVE 4
Recognize the difference between actual and applied factory overhead.

Determining the **standard unit cost for factory overhead** involves estimating factory overhead cost at the standard, or normal, level of production, considering historical data (adjusted for distorting items in the past such as strikes or fire losses), and future changes and trends. The estimated factory overhead cost is divided by the standard number of hours expected for the planned units to be produced. For example, assume that the budgeted production is 1,000 units, which will require 2,000 direct labor hours. At this level of activity, the standard factory overhead is determined, as shown on the next page.

FIGURE 9-2   Summarization of the Budgeting Process

1 **A Sales Forecast** in units, considering the

2 **Inventory Policy**, minimum-maximum and stable or fluctuating, helps in developing the

3 **Production Plan** in units and by periods.

This information aids in developing the

4(a)	4(b)	4(c)
Requirements for Direct Materials	Requirements for Direct Labor	Requirements for Indirect Costs, Facilities, and Supplies
(quantities and prices)	(hours and rates)	(fixed and variable costs)

From this information is developed the

5(a)	5(b)	5(c)
Direct Materials Budget	Direct Labor Budget	Factory Overhead Budget

From these budgets are developed the

6(a)	6(b)	6(c)
Standard Unit Cost for Direct Materials	Standard Unit Cost for Direct Labor	Standard Unit Cost for Factory Overhead

(These combined figures determine the **Standard Unit Cost for the Product.**)

Depreciation on building and machinery	$ 4,000
Taxes and insurance on building and machinery	1,000
Supervisory salaries	4,000
Maintenance costs	2,000
Supplies	1,000
Total standard factory overhead	$12,000

Dividing the standard factory overhead cost of $12,000 by the 2,000 direct labor hours results in a standard per direct labor hour cost of $6 per hour, and because each unit requires two direct labor hours, the standard cost per unit is $12. If equivalent production during the period is exactly 1,000 units, which used 2,000 direct labor hours, Work in Process will be charged with $12,000 of estimated factory overhead (1,000 units × 2 hours per unit × $6 per hour). As illustrated in the following journal entry and T-accounts, if the actual factory overhead were $12,000, all of this cost would be applied to the work in process account, and no over- or underapplied factory overhead would exist.

Work in Process   12,000

    Factory Overhead   12,000

        Applied factory overhead to work in process.

Work in Process		Factory Overhead	
12,000		12,000	12,000
		(actual costs	(standard cost
		recorded from	applied to Work
		various journals)	in Process)

If the actual factory overhead was greater than $12,000, Factory Overhead would have a debit balance after $12,000 of standard cost had been applied to Work in Process. This balance would reflect the amount of factory overhead cost not charged to the goods produced. An underapplied (unabsorbed) cost represents the amount of overhead incurred over and above the standard cost allowed for the attained level of production. The balance in the account would be considered an unfavorable variance. Note that a single account for factory overhead is used in this example to highlight the difference between actual and applied overhead.

The following section of this chapter and the appendix analyze, in detail, what could cause an overhead variance. Although the two-variance method of factory overhead analysis is favored by many companies, the three-variance method is also used. The four-variance method, which is actually a derivative of the two-variance method, is often encountered in managerial-type textbooks because it more clearly indicates the cost behavior patterns of factory overhead costs. Because the four-variance method is somewhat related to the two-variance method, it is discussed sequentially after the two-variance method.

TWO-VARIANCE METHOD OF ANALYSIS

LEARNING OBJECTIVE 5
Compute the controllable variance and the volume variance for the two-variance method of analysis.

The method a company chooses to analyze factory overhead variances depends on the benefits the company derives from the detailed analysis. The cost incurred in applying the standard factory overhead to production, maintaining the necessary accounts, and analyzing the results also plays a part in the process of selecting a method. Textbooks may give extensive coverage to the four-variance method (discussed in the appendix) but ignore the added cost of maintaining the method if it were used in actual practice.

The four-variance method requires separating the variable and fixed cost elements as does the two-variance method. However, when the four-variance method is used, the separated elements are recorded in individual accounts established for overhead variable costs and overhead fixed costs. The two-variance method combines the variable and fixed elements into one rate for factory overhead application and records all actual factory overhead costs in one factory overhead control account.

In **controllable variance** analysis, the actual factory overhead and the standard amount of overhead allowed for the actual (equivalent) production for the period are compared. The difference results from the behavior of the fixed and variable cost items. As discussed previously, fixed cost items tend to remain the same in total dollars despite normal fluctuations in production volume, while total variable costs tend to vary proportionately with changes in production. In the previous example, depreciation, taxes, insurance, and supervisory salaries are common items of fixed expense, while maintenance costs and supplies are usually listed in the category of variable cost.

Assume that the actual level of production given previously was 900 units—or 90% of the planned production of 1,000 units—and the 900 units are allowed 1,800 standard direct labor hours (900 units × 2 hours per unit). The actual amount of factory overhead for this period follows:

Depreciation on building and machinery (fixed)	$ 4,000
Taxes and insurance on the above (fixed)	1,000
Supervisory salaries (fixed)	4,000
Maintenance costs (variable)	1,800
Supplies (variable)	1,000
	$11,800

The fixed cost remains the same as budgeted at 1,000 units of production, but the variable costs are lower. Because 900 units were produced and each unit is allowed 2 direct labor hours at $6 per hour, the work in process was debited and factory overhead credited for $10,800. The factory overhead account shows a $1,000 underapplied (debit) balance.

Factory Overhead	
11,800	10,800
(actual cost)	(applied 900 units
	× 2 standard hours per unit
	× $6)
(1,000 underapplied)	

Using the variable and fixed cost rates per unit calculated previously at $1.50 for variable cost and $4.50 for fixed cost, the calculation of the controllable variance follows:

Standard factory overhead budgeted for *actual* level of production:
Variable cost:
    900 units × 2 hours per unit × $1.50 . . . . $ 2,700
Fixed cost:
    As budgeted (total from budget)   9,000
Flexible budget at *actual* production level $11,700
Actual factory overhead incurred   11,800
    Controllable variance (unfavorable) . . . . $ 100

The **volume variance** calculation uses the same flexible budget amount as determined in the previous calculation ($11,700) and compares the budget amount to the overhead applied to the production for the period.

Flexible budget at *actual* production level $11,700
Factory overhead applied:
    900 units × 2 hours per unit × $6   10,800
    Volume variance (unfavorable) . . . . $ 900

In summary, the controllable and volume variances explain the underapplied $1,000 in the factory overhead account as follows:

Controllable variance (unfavorable) . . . . $ 100
Volume variance (unfavorable)   900
Underapplied factory overhead $1,000

The budget for the year anticipated that the fixed cost of $9,000 would be spread over 2,000 direct labor hours and would be used to produce 1,000 units of product. Because only 900 units were produced, only $8,100 (1,800 direct labor hours × $4.50 fixed cost per hour) was applied. The result was an unfavorable variance of $900. The following illustration shows this effect:

Actual Level of Production—900 units

	Budget	Applied	Volume Variance
Fixed cost applied:			
900 units × 2 hours × $4.50	$ 9,000	$ 8,100	$900
Variable cost applied:			
900 units × 2 hours × $1.50	2,700	2,700	-0-
Total applied (900 × 2 hours × $6)	$11,700	$10,800	$900

The volume variance is a significant factor because it indicates the degree that production was below the established standard. If management feels that 1,000 units should have been produced during the period, it will be concerned that only 900 units were produced and will investigate to determine the cause. This reduced production may result from inefficiencies in labor or supervision, machine breakdowns due to faulty maintenance, or from any number of unfavorable conditions. On the other hand, this level of production may indicate a normal seasonal fluctuation that will be offset by higher than normal production in other periods. If the reduction in production is not seasonal, it may have occurred because sales were not as high as predicted, in which case the marketing department could then be held accountable.

Whatever the circumstances, a factory that is producing below its normal capacity has idle and possibly wasted excess capacity. If it is producing above its normal capacity, the higher volume may create inefficient operating conditions and excessive costs. Such situations should be scrutinized by management, who is ultimately responsible for planning and implementing the most efficient production methods and schedules.

The formula for calculating factory overhead variances using the **two-variance method** is illustrated in the following example.

Formula for Calculating Factory Overhead Variances Using the Two-Variance Method

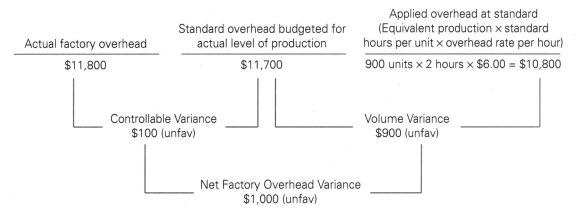

Actual factory overhead	Standard overhead budgeted for actual level of production	Applied overhead at standard (Equivalent production × standard hours per unit × overhead rate per hour)
$11,800	$11,700	900 units × 2 hours × $6.00 = $10,800

Controllable Variance
$100 (unfav)

Volume Variance
$900 (unfav)

Net Factory Overhead Variance
$1,000 (unfav)

The factory overhead account would have a debit balance of $1,000, as shown in the following T-account. The debit balance represents a net unfavorable variance.

Factory Overhead	
11,800	10,800
(actual costs recorded	(standard cost applied to
from various journals)	Work in Process)
Balance *1,000*	

The amount of overhead applied to production is $900 less than the factory overhead calculated for the actual level of production by the flexible budget. This variance is unfavorable because the fixed overhead budgeted at the beginning of the period was not completely charged to production due to an insufficient number of units produced. It is referred to as a *volume variance* because it is created by the excess or lack of actual units produced compared to the planned production quantity.

The *controllable variance* originated because the actual factory overhead for the period exceeded the amount of overhead allowed for the level of production. The controllable variance is favorable when the actual expenditures are less than the flexible dollar amount calculated for the attained level of production. It is unfavorable when the actual factory overhead costs exceed the calculated budget.

After the variance analysis, the following journal entry can be made. This entry closes out the account for factory overhead and records the variances in individual accounts.

Factory Overhead—Volume Variance	900	
Factory Overhead—Controllable Variance	100	
Factory Overhead		1,000

The journal entries to apply overhead and to record the variances may be combined in the following manner:

Work in Process	10,800	
Factory Overhead—Volume Variance	900	
Factory Overhead—Controllable Variance	100	
Factory Overhead		11,800

Production below the standard number of units will always cause an unfavorable volume variance. Conversely, production greater than the standard number of units will always produce a favorable volume variance. Assume the following facts for the period:

Standard overhead cost per unit (2 direct labor hours × $6)	$	12
Number of units actually produced		1,200
Number of units expected to be produced (budgeted)		1,000
Actual factory overhead		$15,000

Standard factory overhead budgeted for actual level of production:

Fixed costs: (as budgeted)	$ 9,000
Variable costs:	
1,200 units × 2 hours per unit × $1.50	3,600
Flexible budget for actual production level	$12,600

Under these circumstances, the work in process account would be charged with $14,400 applied factory overhead (1,200 units × 2 hours per unit × $6). The factory overhead account would have a debit balance of $600. The debit balance represents a net unfavorable variance.

The breakdown of the net variance shows a favorable volume variance because factory overhead was overabsorbed when the actual volume of production was higher than the established standard. The unfavorable controllable variance indicates that the actual overhead costs exceeded the amount allowed for the actual level of production.

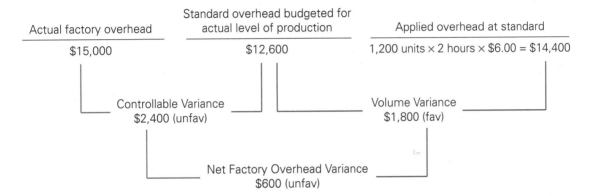

Both variances should be investigated for cause and effect. The *favorable volume variance* may be due to an anticipated seasonal fluctuation, and it may offset all or part of the previous unfavorable volume variances that arose during periods of low production. However, this level of production may have occurred because the company received more orders for goods than it had anticipated. From the standpoint of increased profits, this factor is favorable. However, if the factory worked beyond an established efficient capacity of production, the quality of the product may have suffered.

The *unfavorable controllable variance* should be examined to determine why the costs were higher than expected, where the responsibility for this condition lies, and what steps can be taken to keep these costs under control in the future. This variance could result from several factors, such as laxity in purchasing, inefficiency in supervision, or weak control of expenditures. However, some portion of the controllable variance may result from additional machine maintenance and repair costs, which are attributable to the increased use of facilities at the higher level of production.

On the financial statements, the overhead variances can be treated as additions to or deductions from the standard cost of goods sold. If the variances are material (sizable) in amount, seasonal, or due to unusual circumstances, they will be treated as discussed in Chapter 8.

> **You should now be able to work the following: Questions 15–20; Exercises 9-3 to 9-6; and Problems 9-4 to 9-7.**

APPENDIX: FOUR-VARIANCE AND THREE-VARIANCE METHODS OF ANALYSIS

FOUR-VARIANCE METHOD OF ANALYSIS

LEARNING OBJECTIVE 6
Compute the spending, efficiency, budget, and volume variances for the four-variance method of analysis.

A refined management view of the two-variance method isolates the fixed and variable components that comprise the factory overhead cost and calculates separate variances for the variable costs and the fixed costs. The **four-variance method** recognizes *two* variable cost variances and *two* fixed cost variances. The cost variances are identified as a *variable overhead spending variance*, a *variable overhead efficiency variance*, a *fixed overhead budget variance*, and a *fixed overhead volume variance*.

The *variable overhead spending variance* measures the effect of differences in the actual variable overhead rate and the standard variable overhead rate. The *variable overhead efficiency variance* measures the change in the variable overhead consumption that occurs because of efficient or inefficient use of the cost allocation base, such as direct labor hours. The *fixed overhead budget variance* measures the difference between the actual fixed overhead and the budgeted fixed overhead. The *fixed overhead volume variance* is the difference between budgeted fixed overhead and applied fixed overhead.

The four-variance method has two important aspects: (1) separate actual factory overhead accounts must be maintained for variable costs and fixed costs and (2) actual direct labor hours worked must be known. Using the same data for factory overhead as shown in the previous illustration (except recognizing that the actual factory overhead of $15,000 was composed of $8,000 of variable overhead costs and $7,000 of fixed overhead costs and that 3,000 direct labor hours were used in production), the four-variance calculations would be as follows:

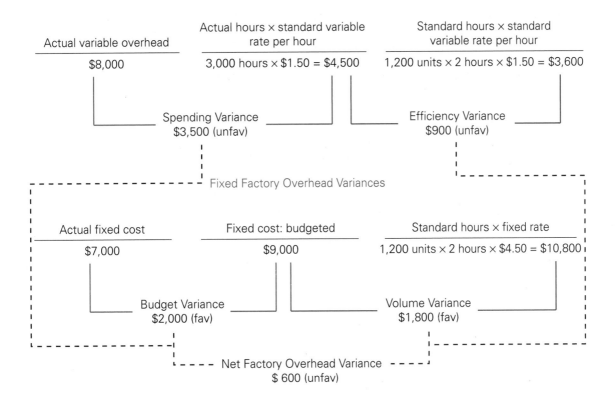

Variable Factory Overhead Variances

Actual variable overhead	Actual hours × standard variable rate per hour	Standard hours × standard variable rate per hour
$8,000	3,000 hours × $1.50 = $4,500	1,200 units × 2 hours × $1.50 = $3,600

Spending Variance
$3,500 (unfav)

Efficiency Variance
$900 (unfav)

Fixed Factory Overhead Variances

Actual fixed cost	Fixed cost: budgeted	Standard hours × fixed rate
$7,000	$9,000	1,200 units × 2 hours × $4.50 = $10,800

Budget Variance
$2,000 (fav)

Volume Variance
$1,800 (fav)

Net Factory Overhead Variance
$ 600 (unfav)

After analyzing the variances, the following journal entry can be made:

Factory Overhead—Spending Variance	3,500	
Factory Overhead—Efficiency Variance	900	
Factory Overhead—Budget Variance		2,000
Factory Overhead—Volume Variance		1,800
Factory Overhead		600

To close the factory overhead account and record variances.

The four-variance method and the two-variance method result in the same net factory overhead variance—$600 unfavorable—as shown below. Although the four-variance method identifies the fixed cost budget variance as originating from the differences between actual fixed cost expenditures and the amount of fixed cost budgeted, the controllable variance (two-variance method) considers the budget variance to be a variable cost and includes it as part of the total controllable variance. The controllable variance encompasses the spending, efficiency, and budget variances in one total variance. The volume variance amount is shown as a single, separate item by both methods.

Four-Variance Method		Two-Variance Method	
Variable cost:			
Spending variance—unfavorable	$3,500 ⎤		
Efficiency variance—unfavorable	900 ⎬→ Controllable variance—unfavorable		$2,400
Fixed cost:			
Budget variance—favorable	2,000 ⎦		
Volume variance—favorable	1,800	Volume variance—favorable	1,800
Net variance (unf.)	$ 600		$ 600

Historically most companies have used the two-variance method of analysis for factory overhead and applied the factory overhead to production using a single rate that combines both the fixed and variable components. These companies consider it too costly from a clerical standpoint to apply separate fixed and variable rates to completed products and also maintain separate factory overhead accounts for fixed and variable elements. However, the most valuable use of the four-variance method is that it demonstrates the cost behavior patterns of fixed and variable costs when production volumes fluctuate. It is an excellent exercise in the study of cost behavior because it demonstrates the behavior patterns important in making management cost decisions that affect profitability. For companies that consider this additional information important, the computer age has made this type of data analysis much more cost effective.

THREE-VARIANCE METHOD OF ANALYSIS

LEARNING OBJECTIVE 7
Compute the budget, capacity, and efficiency variances for the three-variance method of analysis.

The **three-variance method** of factory overhead analysis, although not as common as the two-variance method, is frequently used by manufacturers. This method separates actual and applied overhead into three variances: (1) budget (spending), (2) capacity, and (3) efficiency.

The **budget variance,** or **spending variance,** reflects the difference between the actual costs of overhead and the budgeted amount calculated for the actual hours worked. The saving or overspending is chargeable to the manager or a departmental supervisor responsible for the costs.

These budget variances should not be confused with those for the two-variance method. The calculations are different and result in a sharper distinction in variances. The primary difference between the two methods of variance analysis is that the three-variance method determines the budget allowances based on actual hours worked rather than on the standard number of hours allowed for the units produced.

The **capacity variance** indicates that the volume of production was more or less than normal. It reflects an under- or overabsorption of fixed costs and measures the difference between actual hours worked, multiplied by the standard overhead rate, and the budget allowance based on actual hours worked. This variance is considered the responsibility of management and can be due to expected seasonal variations or changes in the volume of production (caused by poor scheduling, improper use of labor, strikes, or other factors).

The **efficiency variance** measures the difference between the overhead applied (standard hours at the standard rate) and the actual hours worked multiplied by the standard rate. It shows the effect on fixed and variable overhead costs when the actual hours worked are more or less than standard hours allowed for the production volume. Unfavorable variances may be caused by inefficiencies in the use of labor or an excessive use of labor hours. Favorable efficiency variances indicate a more effective use of labor than was anticipated by the standards.

Many accountants feel that the budget allowance for overhead is more appropriate when the base used reflects actual labor hours rather than standard labor hours. They believe that a more definitive relationship exists between actual hours worked and factory expense involved and that the three-variance method provides a more precise analysis of overhead costs.

Whether the two-, three-, or four-variance method is used, the overhead applied to production is the same because the application is based on the standard number of labor hours allowed for the actual production, multiplied by the standard rates established for overhead. Also, the actual overhead incurred would be similar in all cases. Therefore, the calculated net factory overhead variance would also be the same in all methods.

In the following illustration, the budget variance is unfavorable because the actual overhead exceeded the budget allowance. Again, the amount differs from the two-variance method because actual rather than standard hours are used to determine the budget amount. Note that a budget variance is calculated for the four-variance method, but it is specifically used to compare the fixed costs actually incurred for the period to the previously budgeted fixed cost. It is unfortunate that these variances have similar designations. The designations were not changed because both are widely accepted by accountants. These terms are rarely confused because they refer to different types of factory overhead analyses.

Formula for Calculating Factory Overhead Variances

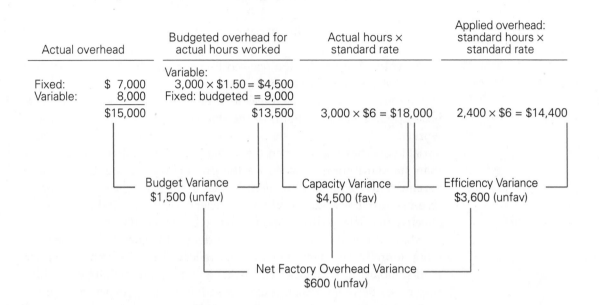

The efficiency variance, as illustrated, is unfavorable because the labor hours worked were more than the standard hours allowed for the level of production. In this case, the excess 600 hours, multiplied by the standard overhead application rate of $6, equals the variance of $3,600 and reflects the underabsorption of fixed and variable costs.

The new budget for overhead, based on the actual hours worked, is calculated by multiplying the actual hours worked by the variable rate for overhead (3,000 hours × $1.50 per hour), amounting to $4,500, and adding the expected fixed cost of $9,000 for the period. The new budget, for the hours worked, totals $13,500. The capacity variance theoretically reflects the cost of unused plant facilities and involves mostly fixed costs. At 3,000 actual labor hours worked, $13,500 (3,000 × $4.50) of fixed cost was absorbed in Work in Process, $4,500 more than was budgeted. This variance is similar to the volume variance under the two-variance method, but the amount differs because it is based on actual hours worked rather than on the standard hours allowed for 1,200 units.

For comparison purposes, the two-variance method would produce the following results:

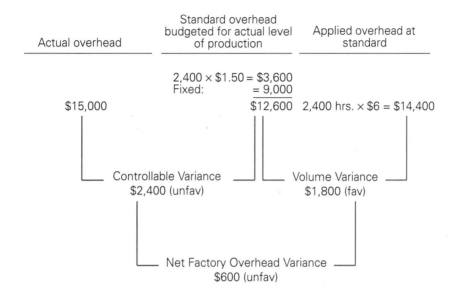

Actual overhead	Standard overhead budgeted for actual level of production	Applied overhead at standard
	2,400 × $1.50 = $3,600 Fixed: = 9,000	
$15,000	$12,600	2,400 hrs. × $6 = $14,400

Controllable Variance
$2,400 (unfav)

Volume Variance
$1,800 (fav)

Net Factory Overhead Variance
$600 (unfav)

> **You should now be able to work the following: Questions 21 and 22; Exercises 9-7 and 9-8; and Problems 9-8 to 9-13.**

K E Y   T E R M S

Budget, p. 354
Budget for manufacturing costs, p. 360
Budget for receivables, p. 360
Budget variance, p. 378
Budgeted income statement, p. 360
Budgets for administrative, selling, and other expenses, p. 360
Capacity variance, p. 379
Capital expenditures budget, p. 360
Cash budget, p. 360
Controllable variance, p. 371
Cost behavior, p. 354
Efficiency variance, p. 379
Fixed costs, p. 362
Flexible budgeting, p. 361
Forecast of sales, p. 357

Four-variance method, p. 376
Liabilities budget, p. 360
Normal capacity, p. 363
Practical capacity, p. 363
Semifixed costs, p. 367
Semivariable costs, p. 367
Spending variance, p. 378
Standard production, p. 363
Standard unit cost for factory overhead, p. 368
Static budget, p. 362
Step costs, p. 367
Theoretical capacity, p. 363
Three-variance method, p. 378
Two-variance method, p. 373
Variable costs, p. 362
Volume variance, p. 372

S E L F - S T U D Y   P R O B L E M

FLEXIBLE BUDGETS; TWO-, THREE-, AND FOUR-VARIANCE METHODS OF FACTORY OVERHEAD ANALYSIS

SHAMROCK COMPANY

Shamrock Company manufactures a single product and uses a standard cost system. The factory overhead is applied on a basis of direct labor hours. A condensed version of the company's flexible budget follows:

Direct labor hours	20,000	25,000	40,000
Cost per hour $2			
Factory overhead costs:			
Variable costs	$ 40,000	$ 50,000	$ 80,000
Fixed costs	200,000	200,000	200,000
Total	$240,000	$250,000	$280,000

The product requires 3 pounds of materials at a standard cost per pound of $7 and 2 hours of direct labor at a standard cost of $6 per hour.

For the current year, the company planned to operate at 25,000 direct labor hours and to produce 12,500 units of product. Actual production and costs for the year follow:

Number of units produced	14,000
Actual direct labor hours worked	30,000
Actual variable overhead costs incurred	$ 52,000
Actual fixed overhead costs incurred	$208,000

Required:

1. Compute the factory overhead rate that will be used for production for the current year. Show the variable and fixed components that make up the total predetermined rate to be used.
2. Prepare a standard cost card for the product. Show the individual elements of the overhead rate as well as the total rate.
3. Compute (a) standard hours allowed for production and (b) under- or overapplied factory overhead for the year.
4. Determine the reason for any under- or overapplied factory overhead for the year by computing all variances, using each of the following methods:
   a. two-variance method
   b. three-variance method (appendix)
   c. four-variance method (appendix)

SOLUTION TO SELF-STUDY PROBLEM

Compute the factory overhead rate by variable and fixed elements:

1. Show the total predetermined rate that will be used during the current year.

			Per DLH
Variable rate:			
Variable costs	$50,000	=	$2.00
Direct labor hours	25,000		
Fixed rate:			
Fixed costs	$200,000	=	$8.00
Direct labor hours	25,000		
Total rate:			
Variable costs	$ 50,000		
Fixed costs	200,000		
Total costs	$250,000	=	$10.00
Direct labor hours	25,000		

2. Prepare a standard cost card for each unit of product.

Direct materials: 3 lbs. @ $7 per lb.		$21.00
Direct labor: 2 hours @ $6 per hour		12.00
Factory overhead:		
Variable cost: 2 hrs. @ $2	$ 4.00	
Fixed cost: 2 hrs. @ $8	16.00	20.00
Standard cost per unit		$53.00

3. (a) Compute the standard hours allowed for production for the year.

Actual units produced	14,000
Number of hours allowed by standard established for each unit of product	× 2
Total standard hours allowed	28,000

(b) Compute the under- or overapplied factory overhead for the year.

Actual factory overhead incurred:	
Variable costs	$ 52,000
Fixed costs	208,000
Total actual overhead costs	$260,000
Factory overhead costs applied:	
Standard hours allowed × standard rate:	
28,000 hours × $10.00	280,000
Overapplied factory overhead	$ 20,000

4. Calculate the reason for the overapplied factory overhead by:
a. Two-variance method:

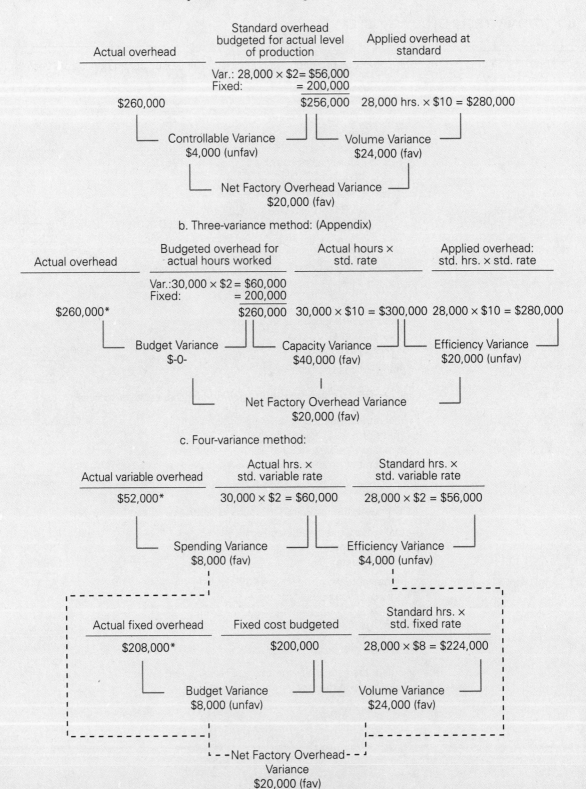

These total costs represent actual hours × actual rates per hour. When the total cost is given, it is not necessary to determine the specific components which make up the total cost unless you do it to understand the formulas being used.

(Note: Problem 9-13 is similar to this problem.)

QUESTIONS

1. How is the standard cost per unit for factory overhead determined?

2. How is factory overhead cost applied to work in process in a standard cost accounting system?

3. What is the difference between fixed and variable costs? Give examples of each.

4. What is a budget?

5. What is the advantage of using budgets for business and industry?

6. What are the six principles of good budgeting?

7. Which budget must be prepared before the others? Why?

8. If the sales forecast estimates that 50,000 units of product will be sold during the following year, should the factory plan on manufacturing 50,000 units in the coming year? Explain.

9. What are the advantages and disadvantages of each of the following?
   a. A stable production policy
   b. A stable inventory policy for a company that has greatly fluctuating sales during the year

10. After budgets have been prepared in units and dollars, what other activities can be planned?

11. What is a flexible budget?

12. How would you define the following?
   a. Theoretical capacity
   b. Practical capacity
   c. Normal capacity

13. Is it possible for a factory to operate at more than 100% of capacity?

14. If a factory operates at 100% of capacity one month, 90% of capacity the next month, and 105% of capacity the next month, will a different cost per unit be charged to Work in Process each month for factory overhead?

15. What is a controllable variance?

16. Why is it important to determine controllable variances?

17. What is a volume variance?

18. What is the significance of a volume variance?

19. If production is more or less than the standard volume, is it possible that no controllable or volume variances would exist? Explain.

20. At the end of the current fiscal year, the trial balance of King Corporation revealed the following debit balances:

    Controllable Variance—$2,000

    Volume Variance—$75,000

    What conclusions can be drawn from these two variances?

21. What variances from the four-variance method are included in the controllable variance from the two-variance method?

22. What is the primary difference between the two-variance and three-variance methods of calculation?

EXERCISES

E9-1
Preparing production budget and materials budget
Objective 2

The sales department of your company has forecast sales in March to be 20,000 units. Additional information follows:

Finished goods inventory, March 1 . . . .   3,000 units
Finished goods inventory required, March 31 . . . .   1,000 units

Materials used in production:

	Inventory March 1	Required Inventory March 31	Standard Cost
A (one gallon per unit)	500 gal.	1,000 gal.	$2 per gal.
B (one pound per unit)	1,000 lbs.	1,000 lbs.	$1 per lb.

Prepare the following:

a.   A production budget for March (in units)
b.   A materials budget for the month (in units and dollars)

E9-2
Calculating factory overhead
Objective 3

The normal capacity of a manufacturing plant is 5,000 units per month. Fixed overhead at this volume is $2,500, and variable overhead is $7,500. Additional data follow:

	Month 1	Month 2
Actual production (units)	5,200	4,500
Actual factory overhead	$9,900	$9,400

Calculate the amount of factory overhead allowed for the actual levels of production and the overhead application rate per unit at the various levels of production. (Round to two decimal places.)

E9-3
Calculating factory overhead
Objectives 3, 4

The standard capacity of a factory is 8,000 units per month. Cost and production data follow:

Standard application rate for fixed overhead . . . . $0.50 per unit
Standard application rate for variable overhead . . . . $1.50 per unit
Production—Month 1 . . . .   7,200 units
Production—Month 2 . . . .   8,400 units
Actual factory overhead—Month 1 . . . . $14,500
Actual factory overhead—Month 2 . . . . $17,600

Calculate the amount of factory overhead allowed for the actual volume of production each month and the variance between budgeted and actual overhead for each month.

E9-4
Calculating factory overhead: two-variances
Objectives 4, 5

Victor Manufacturing Company normally produces 10,000 units of product X each month. Each unit requires 2 hours of direct labor, and factory overhead is applied on a direct labor hour basis. Fixed costs and variable costs in factory overhead at the normal capacity are $5 and $3 per unit, respectively. Cost and production data for May follow:

Production for the month	9,000 units
Direct labor hours used	18,500 hours
Factory overhead incurred for:	
Variable costs	$28,500
Fixed costs	$52,000

a. Calculate the controllable variance.
b. Calculate the volume variance.
c. Was the total factory overhead under- or overapplied? By what amount?

E9-5
Making journal entries for factory overhead and variances; analysis of variances
Objectives 4, 5

The normal capacity of a manufacturing plant is 30,000 direct labor hours or 20,000 units per month. Standard fixed costs are $6,000 and variable costs are $12,000. Data for two months follow:

	June	July
Units produced	18,000	21,000
Factory overhead incurred	$16,500	$19,000

For each month, make journal entries to charge overhead to Work in Process and to record variances. Indicate the types of variances and state whether each is favorable or unfavorable. (Hint: You must first compute the controllable and volume variances.)

E9-6
Calculating amount of factory overhead applied to work in process
Objectives 4, 5

The overhead application rate for a company is $2.50 per unit, made up of $1.00 for fixed overhead and $1.50 for variable overhead. Normal capacity is 10,000 units. In one month, there was an unfavorable controllable variance of $200. Actual overhead for the month was $27,000. What was the amount of the budget for the actual level of production?

E9-7 (Appendix)
Calculating factory overhead: four-variance
Objective 6

Gyro Gasket Company budgets 8,000 direct labor hours for the year. The total overhead budget is expected to amount to $20,000. The standard cost for a unit of the company's product estimates the variable overhead as follows:

Variable factory overhead (3 hours @ $2) . . . . $6 per unit

The actual data for the period follow:

Actual completed units	2,500
Actual direct labor hours	7,640
Actual variable overhead	$16,100
Actual fixed overhead	3,920

Using the four-variance method, calculate the overhead variances. (Hint: First compute the budgeted fixed overhead.)

E9-8 (Appendix)
Calculating factory overhead: three-variances
Objective 7

Using the data shown in E9-4, calculate the following overhead variances:

a. Budget variance
b. Capacity variance
c. Efficiency variance
d. Was the factory overhead under- or overapplied? By what amount?

P R O B L E M S

P9-1
Flexible budget;
overhead variance
analysis
Objective 2

Presented below are the monthly factory overhead cost budget (at normal capacity of 5,000 units or 20,000 direct labor hours) and the production and cost data for a month.

Factory Overhead Cost Budget

Fixed cost:			
	Depreciation on building and machinery	$1,200	
	Taxes on building and machinery	500	
	Insurance on building and machinery	500	
	Superintendent's salary	1,500	
	Supervisors' salaries	2,300	
	Maintenance wages	1,000	$7,000
Variable cost:			
	Repairs	$ 400	
	Maintenance supplies	300	
	Other supplies	200	
	Payroll taxes	800	
	Small tools	300	2,000
Total standard factory overhead			$9,000

Production and Cost Data

Number of units produced	4,000
Factory overhead:	
Depreciation on building and machinery	$1,200
Supervisors' salaries	2,300
Insurance on building and machinery	480
Maintenance supplies	200
Maintenance wages	1,050
Other supplies	150
Payroll taxes	650
Repairs	275
Small tools	170
Superintendent's salary	1,500
Taxes on building and machinery	525

Required:

1. Assuming that variable costs will vary in direct proportion to the change in volume, prepare a flexible budget for production levels of 80%, 90%, and 110%. Also determine the rate for application of factory overhead to work in process at each level of volume.

2. Prepare a flexible budget for production levels of 80%, 90%, and 110%, assuming that variable costs will vary in direct proportion to the change in volume, but with the following exceptions: (Hint: Set up a third category for semifixed expenses.)

   a. At 110% of capacity, an assistant department head will be needed at a salary of $10,500 annually.

   b. At 80% of capacity, the repairs expense will drop to one-half of the amount at 100% capacity.
   c. Maintenance supplies expense will remain constant at all levels of production.
   d. At 80% of capacity, one part-time maintenance worker, earning $6,000 a year, will be laid off.
   e. At 110% of capacity, a machine not normally in use and on which no depreciation is normally recorded will be used in production. Its cost was $12,000 and it has a ten-year life.
3. Using the flexible budget prepared in (1), determine the budgeted cost at 96% of capacity, using interpolation.
4. Using the flexible budget prepared in (1), determine the budgeted cost at 104% of capacity using a method other than interpolation.

P9-2
Overhead application rate
Objective 3

Clinton Manufacturing Company uses a job order cost system and standard costs. It manufactures one product, whose standard cost follows:

Materials, 20 yards @ $0.90 per yard	$18
Direct labor, 4 hours @ $9.00 per hour	36
Total factory overhead (the ratio of variable costs to fixed costs is 3 to 1)	32
Total unit cost	$86

The standards are based on normal activity of 2,400 direct labor hours. Actual activity for October follows:

Materials purchased, 18,000 yards @ $0.92	$16,560
Materials used, 9,500 yards	
Direct labor, 2,100 hours @ $9.15	19,215
Total factory overhead, 500 units actually produced	17,760

Required:

Compute the variable and fixed factory overhead rates per direct labor hour and the total fixed factory overhead based on normal activity.

P9-3
Analyses
Objective 3 and review of Chapter 8

SS

On May 1, Collegiate Company began the manufacture of a new mechanical device known as Preppy. The company installed a standard cost system in accounting for manufacturing costs. The standard costs for a unit of Preppy follow:

Raw materials (5 lbs. @ $1 per lb.)	$ 5
Direct labor (1 hour @ $8 per hour)	8
Overhead (50% of direct labor costs)	4
	$17

The following data came from Collegiate's records for the month of May:

	Units
Actual production	4,000
Units sold	2,500

	Debit	Credit
Sales		$50,000
Purchases (22,000 pounds)	$23,300	
Materials price variance	1,300	
Materials quantity variance	1,000	
Direct labor rate variance	770	
Direct labor efficiency variance		1,200
Manufacturing overhead total variance	500	

The amount shown above for the materials price variance is applicable to raw materials purchased during May.

Required:

Compute each of the following items for Collegiate for the month of May. Show computations in good form.

1. Standard quantity of raw materials allowed (in pounds) for actual production
2. Actual quantity of raw materials used (in pounds) (Hint: Be sure to consider the materials quantity variance.)
3. Standard direct labor hours allowed
4. Actual direct labor hours worked
5. Actual direct labor rate
6. Actual total overhead

P9-4
Materials, labor, and overhead variances; two-variance overhead analysis
Objectives 4, 5

The standard specifications for an electric motor manufactured by the DHL Motor Corporation follow:

DHL

Standard cost per unit:

Materials (2 lbs. × $5 per lb.) $10.00
Labor (4 hours × $6 per hour) 24.00
Factory overhead (4 hours × $3.38* per hour) 13.52

Total standard cost $47.52

*$1.00 variable + $2.38 fixed = $3.38

Factory overhead rates are based on a normal 70% capacity and use the following flexible budget:

		Normal	
	70%	85%	100%
Motors to be produced	2,100	2,550	3,000
Variable overhead	$ 8,400	$10,200	$12,000
Fixed overhead	20,000	20,000	20,000

The actual production was 2,500 motors, and factory overhead costs totaled $30,305.

Required:

Calculate the factory overhead variances using the two-variance method.

P9-5
Journal entries;
variance analysis;
other analyses
Objectives 4, 5 and
review of Chapter 8

Cost and production data for the Johnny Products Company follow:

Standard Cost Sheet
(Normal capacity—1,000 units)

	Dept. A	Dept. B	Total
Materials:			
I—2 lbs.@ $2	$ 4		
II—2 lbs.@ $1		$ 2	$ 6
Labor:			
2 hours @ $5	10		
1 hour @ $6		6	16
Factory overhead (per standard labor hour):			
Fixed Variable			
$2 $1	6		
1 3		4	10
Total	$20	$12	$32

Production Report

	Dept. A	Dept. B
Beginning units in process	None	None
Units finished and transferred	1,000	900
Ending units in process	200	100
Stage of completion	1/2	1/2

Actual Cost Data

	Dept. A		Dept. B	
Direct materials used:				
I—2,300 lbs	$ 4,715			
II—1,850 lbs				$1,813
Direct labor:				
2,150 hours	10,965			
1,000 hours				5,900
Factory overhead:				
Indirect materials	$ 1,000		$ 500	
Indirect labor	1,300		1,000	
Other (fixed costs)	4,400	6,700	2,250	3,750
Total		$22,380		$11,463

During the month, 850 units were sold at $50 each.

Note: Materials, labor, and overhead are added evenly throughout the process.

Required:

1. Make general journal entries to record all transactions and variances. (Use the two-variance method for overhead variance analysis.) (Hint: You must first compute equivalent units and the variances for materials, labor, and factory overhead.)
2. Prove balances of Work in Process in both departments.
3. Prove that all costs have been accounted for.

P9-6
Variance analysis
Objectives 3, 5 and
review of Chapter 8

Lopo Shirts, Inc., manufactures men's sport shirts for large stores. Lopo produces a single quality shirt in lots of a dozen according to each customer's order and attaches the store's label. The standard costs for a dozen shirts include the following:

Direct materials	24 yards @ $0.55	$13.20
Direct labor	3 hours @ $7.35	22.05
Factory overhead	3 hours @ $2.00	6.00
Standard cost per dozen		$41.25

During October, Lopo worked on three orders for shirts. Job cost records for the month disclose the following:

Lot	Units in Lot	Materials Used	Hours Worked
30	1,000 dozen	24,100 yards	2,980
31	1,700 dozen	40,440 yards	5,130
32	1,200 dozen	28,825 yards	2,890

The following information is also available:

a. Lopo purchased 95,000 yards of materials during October at a cost of $53,200. The materials price variance is recorded when goods are purchased and all inventories are carried at standard cost.
b. Direct labor incurred amounted to $81,400 during October. According to payroll records, production employees were paid $7.40 per hour.
c. Overhead is applied on the basis of direct labor hours. Factory overhead totaling $22,800 was incurred during October.
d. A total of $288,000 was budgeted for overhead for the year, based on estimated production at the plant's normal capacity of 48,000 dozen shirts per year. Overhead is 40% fixed and 60% variable at this level of production.
e. There was no work in process at October 1. During October, Lots 30 and 31 were completed, and all materials were issued for Lot 32, which was 80% completed as to labor and overhead.

Required:

1. Prepare a schedule computing the October standard cost of Lots 30, 31, and 32.
2. Prepare a schedule computing the materials price variance for October and indicate whether it is favorable or unfavorable.
3. For each lot produced during October, prepare schedules computing the following (indicate whether favorable or unfavorable):
   a. Materials quantity variance in yards
   b. Labor efficiency variance in hours (Hint: Don't forget the percentage of completion.)
   c. Labor rate variance in dollars

4. Prepare a schedule computing the total controllable and volume overhead variances for October and indicate whether they are favorable or unfavorable.

P9-7
Materials, labor, and
overhead variances—
two-variance method
Objectives 4, 5 and
review of Chapter 8

Ollie Company manufactures products in batches of 100 units per batch. The company uses a standard cost system and prepares budgets that call for 500 of these batches per period. Fixed overhead is $60,000 per period. The standard costs per batch follow:

Material (80 gallons)	$ 32
Labor (60 hours)	216
Factory overhead	252
Standard cost per batch	$500

During the period, 503 batches were manufactured and the following costs were incurred:

Materials used (40,743 gallons)	$ 15,482.34
Labor (29,677 hours at $3.65 per hour)	108,321.05
Actual variable overhead	67,080.00
Actual fixed overhead	60,500.00

Required

Calculate the variances for materials, labor, and overhead. For overhead use the two-variance method.

P9-8 (Appendix)
All variances;
four-variances for
factory overhead
Objective 6

Brady Manufacturing Company manufactures a small electric motor that is a replacement part for the more popular gas furnaces. The standard cost card shows the product requirements as follows:

Direct materials—2 lbs. @ $4 per lb.	$ 8.00
Direct labor—5 hours @ $8 per hour	40.00
Factory overhead:	
Variable cost—5 hours @ $2 per hour	10.00
Fixed cost—5 hours @ $4 per hour	20.00
Total standard cost per unit	$78.00

Factory overhead rates are based on normal 100% capacity and the following flexible budgets:

	90%	Normal 100%	110%
Units produced	2,500	3,000	3,500
Factory overhead—variable	$25,000	$30,000	$35,000
Factory overhead—fixed	60,000	60,000	60,000

The company produced 3,500 units and incurred the following overhead costs:

Factory overhead—fixed	$61,950
Factory overhead—variable	33,710

Required:

1. Calculate the factory overhead, spending, efficiency, budget, and volume variances.
2. Does the net variance represent under- or overapplied factory overhead?

P9-9 (Appendix)
Materials, labor, and overhead variances—four-variance method
Objective 6 and review of Chapter 8

Magic Corporation uses a standard cost system and manufactures one product. The variable costs per product follow:

Materials (4 parts)	$ 2
Labor (2 hours)	6
Overhead	3
	$11

Budgeted fixed costs for the month are $4,000, and Magic expected to manufacture 2,000 units. Actual production, however, was only 1,800 units. Materials prices were 5% over standard, and labor rates were 10% over standard. Of the factory overhead expense, only 80% was used and fixed overhead was $100 over the budgeted amount. In materials usage, 8% more parts were used than were allowed for actual production by the standard and 6% more labor hours were used than were allowed.

Required:

1. Calculate the materials and labor variances.
2. Calculate the variances for overhead by the four-variance method.

P9-10 (Appendix)
Labor variances and four-variance overhead analysis
Objective 6 and review of Chapter 8

Modern Manufacturing Company estimates the following labor and overhead costs for the period:

Variable overhead	$44,200
Fixed overhead	50,050
Total estimated overhead	$94,250
Estimated direct labor cost	$65,000
Standard direct labor rate per hour	$5

Each unit will require 26 hours of labor.
Estimated production for the period . . . . . 500 units

Production statistics for the period:
Actual production	510 units	
Actual direct labor hours used	13,015 hours	
Actual direct labor cost		$66,116.20
Actual overhead costs:		
Variable costs		$45,009
Fixed costs		50,125

Required:

Use the four-variance method for overhead analysis. Calculate the variances for direct labor and overhead. Prove that the overhead variances equal over- or underapplied factory overhead for the period.

**P9-11 (Appendix)
Three-variance
overhead analysis
Objective 7**

Using the data provided in P9-5, calculate the overhead cost variances under the three-variance method.

**P9-12 (Appendix)
Variance analysis
using the three-
variance method for
overhead costs
Objective 7**

Foxworthy Furniture Company uses a standard cost system in accounting for its production costs. The standard cost of a unit of furniture follows:

Lumber, 100 feet @ $150 per 1,000 feet		$15.00
Direct labor, 4 hours @ $10 per hour		40.00
Factory overhead:		
Fixed (15% of direct labor)	$ 6.00	
Variable (30% of direct labor)	12.00	18.00
Total unit cost		$73.00

The following flexible monthly overhead budget applies:

Direct Labor Hours	Estimated Overhead
5,200	$21,600
4,800	20,400
4,400	19,200
4,000 (normal capacity)	18,000
3,600	16,800

The actual unit costs for the month of December follow:

Lumber used (110 feet @ $120 per 1,000 feet)		$13.20
Direct labor (4 1/4 hours @ $10.24 per hour)		43.52
Factory overhead:		
Variable costs	$ 7,400	
Fixed costs	13,720	
	$21,120 ÷ 1,200 units	17.60
Total actual unit cost		$74.32

Required:

Compute the variances for materials, labor, and factory overhead, using the three-variance method for overhead costs.

**P9-13 (Appendix)
Flexible budgets;
two-, three-, and four-
variance methods of
factory overhead
analysis. Similar to
self-study problem.
Objectives 5, 6, 7**

Moses Company manufactures a single product and uses a standard cost system. The factory overhead is applied on a basis of direct labor hours. A condensed version of the company's flexible budget follows:

	5,000	6,250	10,000
Direct labor hours @ $2/hour . .	5,000	6,250	10,000
Factory overhead costs:			
Variable costs	$10,000	$12,500	$20,000
Fixed costs	50,000	50,000	50,000
Total	$60,000	$62,500	$70,000

The product requires 3 pounds of materials at a standard cost of $5 per pound and 2 hours of direct labor at a standard cost of $10 per hour.

For the current year, the company planned to operate at the level of 6,250 direct labor hours and to produce 3,125 units of product. Actual production and costs for the year follow:

Number of units produced	3,500
Actual direct labor hours worked	7,000
Actual variable overhead costs incurred	$14,000
Actual fixed overhead costs incurred	$52,000

Required:

1. For the current year, compute the factory overhead rate that will be used for production. Show the variable and fixed components that make up the total predetermined rate to be used.
2. Prepare a standard cost card for the product. Show the individual elements of the overhead rate as well as the total rate.
3. Compute (a) standard hours allowed for production and (b) under- or overapplied factory overhead for the year.
4. Determine the reason for any under- or overapplied factory overhead for the year by computing all variances, using each of the following methods:
   a. two-variance method
   b. three-variance method (appendix)
   c. four-variance method (appendix)

10

Cost Analysis for Management Decision Making

LEARNING OBJECTIVES

After studying this chapter, you should be able to:

1. Compute net income under the direct costing and absorption costing methods.
2. Discuss the merits and limitations of direct costing.
3. Define the concept of segment profitability analysis and explain the distinction between direct and indirect costs.
4. Compute the break-even point and the target volume needed to earn a certain profit.
5. Calculate the contribution margin ratio and the margin of safety ratio.
6. Use differential cost analysis techniques to make special decisions.
7. Identify the appropriate techniques to analyze and control the distribution costs incurred in selling and delivering products.

The features that distinguish cost accounting from managerial accounting are not easy to detect. To a degree, the differences between the two areas are subjective. Most cost accounting textbooks (including this one) give considerable attention to the managerial uses of cost data by interweaving the data uses and management needs with the discussions of cost systems. Most managerial accounting textbooks include some discussion of cost systems and the accumulation and processing of cost data. However, a more comprehensive coverage of cost accounting systems (job order, process, and standard), which are the major thrust of cost accounting texts, increases an individual's analytical ability to resolve the special problems encountered internally by manufacturing firms.

Many studies that generate special reports for management use the regularly accumulated cost data. Often, however, the system's regularly compiled data must be altered and enhanced to create additional reports because of economic occurrences that were not predicted. These reports, which are prepared for internal use and are not distributed to external parties, require that the user understand terminology not commonly used in operational cost accounting systems. In this chapter, several new terms relating to the special-purpose reports for internal management decision making are introduced and defined.

DIRECT COSTING AND ABSORPTION COSTING

LEARNING OBJECTIVE 1
Compute net income under direct costing and absorption costing.

Under **direct costing**, the cost of a manufactured product includes only the costs that vary directly with volume: direct materials, direct labor, and variable factory overhead. This method is also referred to as **variable costing**, because only variable manufacturing costs are assigned to the product, while fixed factory overhead is classified as a period cost and charged totally to the period in which the fixed costs were incurred.

The alternative to direct costing is **absorption costing** or **full costing** (the method used in the preceding nine chapters). Under this method, both fixed and variable manufacturing costs are assigned to the product and no particular attention is given to classifying the costs as either fixed or variable.

PRODUCT COSTS VERSUS PERIOD COSTS

All costs, both manufacturing and nonmanufacturing, can be classified as either product costs or period costs. As discussed in previous chapters, a **product cost** (or inventory cost) is assigned to Work in Process and subsequently to Finished Goods. When inventory is sold, product costs are recognized as expense (cost of goods sold) and matched with the related revenues. In contrast, **period costs** are not assigned to the product but are recognized as expenses, totally in the period incurred. All nonmanufacturing costs are period costs. These include selling expenses and general and administrative expenses.

The only difference between direct costing and absorption costing is the classification of fixed factory overhead. Under direct costing, fixed overhead costs are classified as period costs. Under absorption costing, they are treated as product costs.

ILLUSTRATION OF DIRECT AND ABSORPTION COSTING METHODS

To illustrate the differences between direct costing and absorption costing, assume the following conditions for a 3-month period:

Selling price per unit	$11
Variable cost per unit:	
Direct materials	$ 2
Direct labor	2
Variable factory overhead	1
Variable cost per unit	$ 5
Fixed cost per unit:	
Fixed factory overhead for the year	$108,000
Normal production for the year in units	36,000
Fixed cost per unit ($108,000 ÷ 36,000)	$3

	Units Produced	Units Sold
January	3,000	1,500
February	500	2,000
March	4,000	2,000

January has no beginning inventories.

The comparative production report in Figure 10-1 shows the costs charged to the product under each costing method. Note that under absorption costing, the goods manufactured in January are charged with

FIGURE 10-1   Comparison of Product Costs for Absorption Costing and Direct Costing

Comparative Production Report

	January (3,000 units)		February (500 units)		March (4,000 units)	
	Absorption Costing	Direct Costing	Absorption Costing	Direct Costing	Absorption Costing	Direct Costing
Direct materials	$ 6,000	$ 6,000	$1,000	$1,000	$ 8,000	$ 8,000
Direct labor	6,000	6,000	1,000	1,000	8,000	8,000
Variable factory overhead	3,000	3,000	500	500	4,000	4,000
Fixed factory overhead	9,000	—	1,500	—	12,000	—
Total cost	$24,000	$15,000	$4,000	$2,500	$32,000	$20,000
Unit cost	$8	$5	$8	$5	$8	$5

the standard costs of the direct materials, direct labor, and both fixed and variable factory overhead, totaling $8 per unit. Under direct costing, the fixed factory overhead is not charged to the product, resulting in a unit cost of $5.

Figure 10-2 uses absorption costing to compare the average fixed factory overhead of $9,000 ($108,000 ÷ 12) per month with the amount applied to production each month. In January, 3,000 units are manufactured, and the manufacturing costs under absorption costing include $9,000 ($3 × 3,000) in fixed factory overhead. February manufacturing costs covering the 500 units produced include fixed factory overhead of $1,500, and the manufacturing costs for March covering the 4,000 units produced include $12,000 of fixed factory overhead. As a result of the unevenness of production, $7,500 of fixed expense in February is not included in manufacturing costs; but in March, the fixed overhead is overapplied by $3,000. These variances of underapplied and overapplied factory overhead are reflected in the income statements for February and March as an addition to and a deduction from cost of goods sold, respectively. Under direct costing, no fixed factory overhead expenses are charged to production in any month. These fixed costs appear as an expense on each month's income statement, along with selling and administrative expenses.

Figure 10-3 compares the effects of direct costing and absorption costing on income. Each month, the cost of goods sold reflects a cost of $8 per unit under absorption costing, compared to $5 per unit under direct costing. Under absorption costing, the difference between sales revenue and cost of goods sold is termed the **gross margin** or **gross profit**. The term commonly used in direct costing to designate the difference between sales and cost of goods sold is **contribution margin**. Because cost of goods sold determined under absorption costing includes both fixed and variable overhead, but includes only variable overhead under direct costing, the gross margin under absorption costing is always lower than the contribution margin under direct costing.

FIGURE 10-2   Schedule of Fixed Overhead Applied under Absorption Costing

Fixed Overhead Applied—Absorption Costing

	January	February	March
Monthly fixed factory overhead	$9,000	$9,000	$ 9,000
Fixed factory overhead applied	9,000	1,500	12,000
Under (over)applied overhead	-0-	$7,500	$ (3,000)

FIGURE 10-3   Comparison of Net Income for Absorption Costing and Direct Costing

COMPARATIVE INCOME STATEMENTS
For Three Months Ended March 31, 20—

	January (1,500 units sold)		February (2,000 units sold)		March (2,000 units sold)	
	Absorption Costing	Direct Costing	Absorption Costing	Direct Costing	Absorption Costing	Direct Costing
Sales	$16,500	$16,500	$22,000	$22,000	$22,000	$22,000
Cost of goods sold (see schedule below)	(12,000)	(7,500)	(16,000)	(10,000)	(16,000)	(10,000)
(Under)/overapplied factory overhead	—	—	(7,500)	—	3,000	—
Gross margin (loss)	$ 4,500		$ (1,500)		$ 9,000	
Contribution margin		$ 9,000		$12,000		$12,000
Less:						
Fixed factory overhead		(9,000)		(9,000)		(9,000)
Selling and administrative expenses	(2,000)	(2,000)	(2,000)	(2,000)	(2,000)	(2,000)
Net income (loss)	$ 2,500	$ (2,000)	$ (3,500)	$ 1,000	$ 7,000	$ 1,000

COMPARATIVE SCHEDULE OF COST OF GOODS SOLD
For Three Months Ended March 31, 20—

Finished goods inventory, January 1	—	—	$12,000	$ 7,500	—	—
Cost of goods manufactured	$24,000	$15,000	4,000	2,500	$32,000	$20,000
Goods available for sale	$24,000	$15,000	$16,000	$10,000	$32,000	$20,000
Less finished goods inventory, March 31	12,000	7,500	—	—	16,000	$10,000
Cost of goods sold	$12,000	$ 7,500	$16,000	$10,000	$16,000	$10,000

Under absorption costing, selling and administrative expenses are deducted from the gross margin to determine net income or loss. In the illustration, these costs are assumed to be $2,000 each month. Under direct costing, the total amount of monthly fixed overhead is deducted from the contribution margin, along with selling and administrative expenses. Thus, $9,000 of fixed overhead costs are charged against revenue each month regardless of the number of units produced or sold.

An examination of the comparative income statements in Figure 10-3 reveals the effect that fluctuating production has on reported income under absorption costing. Although February sales exceed January sales, the net income decreased from $2,500 in January to a net loss of $3,500 in February under absorption costing. This decrease is caused in part by adding $7,500 of underapplied overhead at the end of February to the cost of goods sold.

March sales are the same as February sales, but reported net income increased from a $3,500 net loss in February to a $7,000 net income in March. This increase is due to the increased production that caused more of the fixed factory overhead to be applied to production in March than in February. In fact, overhead is overapplied in March, and this overapplication is shown as a decrease in cost of goods sold on the March statement.

A study of the income statement under direct costing shows that as sales increase in February, income also increases. When sales remain the same in March as they were in February, income does not change.

With absorption costing, inventories have a higher cost than under direct costing because fixed costs are included in the cost of inventory in absorption costing. This element of fixed cost will not be reported as a charge against revenue until the goods are sold. Under direct costing, fixed costs are not included in inventory; they are charged against revenue in the period they are incurred.

MERITS AND LIMITATIONS OF DIRECT COSTING

LEARNING OBJECTIVE 2
Discuss the merits and limitations of direct costing.

The merits of direct costing may be viewed in terms of the usefulness of the data provided by its application. Some company managers believe that direct costing furnishes more understandable data regarding costs, volumes, revenues, and profits to members of management who are not formally trained in the field of accounting. It presents cost data in a manner that highlights the relationship between sales and variable production costs, which move in the same direction as sales. Furthermore, they believe direct costing helps management planning, because it presents a clearer picture of how changes in production volume affect costs and income. From the direct costing portion of the production report in Figure 10-1, management can determine that units produced and sold above normal production will cost only $5 each in out-of-pocket expenditures for variable costs, because the fixed manufacturing costs have been completely absorbed by the expected normal production. Therefore, the additional units will produce a marginal income of $6 each at a selling price of $11. Assume that a plant's capacity is not fully utilized and management has the opportunity to fill a special order at a selling price of $7 each. If management incorrectly used the absorption cost of $8 per unit in Figure 10-1, it would reject the special order. If it correctly compared the selling price of $7 to the additional variable costs of $5 to produce each unit, management would accept the special order and earn additional income of $2 per unit because the fixed overhead cost of $3 per unit had already been absorbed by the normal production and therefore should not be considered in making the decision. Only the additional variable costs are relevant to the decision.

Although direct costing may provide useful information for internal decision making, it is not a generally accepted method of inventory costing for external reporting purposes. The measurement of income, in traditional accounting theory, is based on the matching of revenues with associated costs. Under absorption costing, product costs include all variable and fixed manufacturing costs. These costs are matched with the sales revenue in the period in which the goods are sold. Direct costing, however, matches only the variable manufacturing costs with revenue. Absorption costing must be used for income tax purposes as well as for external financial statements. Regulations of the Internal Revenue Service specifically prohibit direct costing in computing taxable income.

Direct costing has other limitations and criticisms. Even when sophisticated statistical techniques are used to separate costs into variable and fixed components, the results may lead to erroneous conclusions. The procedures often use historical trends and data adjusted for future expectations in order to establish the components; but unforeseen occurrences may have a significant effect on such established cost categories. To avoid overlooking significant changes in cost behavior patterns, a systematic review of the costs and the statistical techniques should be included in the system. Any unexpected event related to previously established plans should trigger an analysis to determine its effect on the designated categories of costs so that faulty data are not used in decision making.

Direct costing is also criticized because no fixed factory overhead cost is included in work in process or finished goods inventories. In the opinion of direct costing opponents, both fixed and variable costs are incurred in manufacturing products. Because the inventory figures do not reflect the total cost of production, they do not present a realistic cost valuation.

Adjustments can be made to the inventory figures to reflect absorption cost on published financial reports while retaining the benefits of direct costing internally for income analysis purposes. In the example given, the unit cost was $5 under direct costing and $8 under absorption costing. Absorption costing reflects 60% more cost than direct costing; therefore, inventories could be adjusted as follows:

	Ending Inventory Under Direct Costing	Absorption-Direct Cost Ratio ($8 ÷ $5)	Ending Inventory Under Absorption Costing
January	$ 7,500	× 160%	$12,000
February	None		None
March	$10,000	× 160%	$16,000

> **You should now be able to work the following: Questions 1-3; Exercises 10-1 to 10-6; and Problem 10-1.**

SEGMENT REPORTING FOR PROFITABILITY ANALYSIS

LEARNING OBJECTIVE 3
Define the concept of segment profitability analysis and explain the distinction between direct and indirect costs.

Segment reporting provides data that management can use to evaluate the operations and profitability of individual segments within a company. A **segment** may be a division, a product line, a sales territory, or other identifiable organizational unit.

The results of a segment profitability analysis may be questioned as to its validity if it is based on absorption costing data. This is due to the fact that the measure of each company segment's profitability may be distorted by arbitrarily assigning indirect costs to the segments being examined. The contribution margin approach (as used in direct costing), which separates the fixed and variable elements that comprise cost, is often used to overcome these objections.

Segment profitability analysis requires that all costs be classified into one of two categories: direct or indirect. A **direct (traceable) cost** is a cost that can be traced to the segment being analyzed. Direct costs include both variable and fixed costs directly identifiable with a specific segment. An **indirect (nontraceable) cost** is a cost that cannot be identified directly with a specific segment. This cost is often referred to in segment analysis as a **common cost.** Under the contribution margin approach, only those costs directly traceable to a segment are assigned to the segment. The excess of segment revenue over direct costs assigned to the segment is called the **segment margin.** Indirect costs are excluded from the computation of the segment margin.

Although indirect costs cannot be directly identified with a specific segment, they are identifiable as common to all segments at a particular level of an organization. Often the differences between direct and indirect costs are not markedly distinctive; however, the costs that will disappear when the company eliminates the segment should be classified as direct costs. Costs difficult to classify should not be allocated to individual segments without a careful evaluation of the allocation method. For instance, if a company consists of two divisions, each division manager's salary would be a direct cost to the division. However, if each division manufactured two products, each division's product segment report would classify the manager's salary as an indirect cost. Arbitrarily allocating the manager's salary to a product would distort the profitability shown for each product.

The following table shows two segment reports, one listed by divisions and the other listed by products for one of the divisions. The company is divided into two divisions, and each division manufactures two products.

| | **Segment Report by Divisions** | | | **Segment Report by Product —Division One** | | |
	Total Company	Division One	Division Two	Total Division One	Product A	Product B
Sales	$1,000,000	$750,000	$250,000	$750,000	$500,000	$250,000
Less variable costs	800,000	675,000	125,000	675,000	450,000	225,000
Contribution margin	$ 200,000	$ 75,000	$125,000	$ 75,000	$ 50,000	$ 25,000
Less direct fixed costs:						
Production	$ 50,000	$ 25,000	$ 25,000	$ 20,000	$ 10,000	$ 10,000
Administration	75,000	40,000	35,000	15,000	10,000	5,000
Total direct fixed costs . . .	$ 125,000	$ 65,000	$ 60,000	$ 35,000	$ 20,000	$ 15,000
Segment margin	$ 75,000	$ 10,000	$ 65,000	$ 40,000	$ 30,000	$ 10,000
Less common fixed costs:						
Selling	$ 30,000					
Production				$ 5,000		
Administration	20,000			25,000		
Total common fixed costs .	$ 50,000			$ 30,000		
Segment margin				$ 10,000		
Net income	$ 25,000					

An analysis of the segment report by divisions reveals that the division segment margin was $75,000 for the total company. Division One contributed $10,000 to the margin and Division Two, $65,000. The direct fixed costs chargeable to the divisions totaled $125,000, and the nonallocated common fixed costs totaled $50,000.

When Division One is isolated and analyzed to determine how each product contributed to the segment margin of $10,000, the direct fixed costs chargeable to the individual products amount to $35,000. Product A is charged $20,000 and Product B, $15,000. Division One has nonallocated common fixed costs of $30,000, not directly chargeable to either product. For example, the $25,000 for Administration listed under common fixed costs may represent the salary of the manager of Division One who oversees the production of both products. These reports reveal how costs shift from one category to another depending on the segment under scrutiny. Each segment report prepared for a company isolates those costs, variable and fixed, that can be charged directly to the segment elements. As different segments are analyzed, these costs may be direct costs in one segment and indirect costs in another segment.

The divisions' contribution margins are determined by subtracting the variable costs from the sales. The contribution margin can be used as a guide in making management decisions in regard to short-run opportunities, such as pricing of special orders.

The direct fixed costs chargeable to each segment are subtracted from the contribution margin to determine the segment margin. The segment margin can be used as a guide relating to the segment's long-run profitability. In other words, it measures the ability of the division or product to recover not only the assigned variable costs but also the direct fixed costs that must be recovered to keep the company solvent in the long run. In the short run, if a segment margin is positive, the segment should be retained even if the company as a whole is operating at a loss. Because the common fixed costs will usually remain at the same level even if a segment is eliminated, deleting a segment with a positive segment margin will only increase the amount of the company's net loss. The remaining revenue, after direct variable and fixed costs have been deducted, is the amount left to be applied toward the unallocated common costs and the net income of the company as a whole. The segment margin analysis is particularly beneficial as an aid to making decisions that relate to a company's long-run requirements and performance, such as changing production capacities, product pricing policies, decisions to retain or eliminate specific segments, analyses of segment managers' performance, and selecting a segment's expected return on investment.

COST-VOLUME-PROFIT ANALYSIS

LEARNING OBJECTIVE 4
Compute the break-even point and the target volume needed to earn a certain profit.

A company's net income is a measure of management's success in attaining its goals. In planning, management must anticipate how selling prices, costs, expenses, and profits will react to changes in activity when the activity is measured in terms of capacity or volume. When the degree of variability in costs is known, the effect of volume changes can be predicted.

Cost-volume-profit (CVP) analysis is a technique that uses the degrees of cost variability to measure the effect of changes in volume on resulting profits. Such analysis assumes that the plant assets of the firm will remain the same in the short run; therefore, the established level of fixed cost will also remain unchanged during the period being studied.

BREAK-EVEN ANALYSIS

The usual starting point in CVP analysis is the determination of a firm's break-even point. The break-even point can be defined as the point at which sales revenue is adequate to cover all costs to manufacture and sell the product but no profit is earned. The equation can be stated as follows:

Sales revenue (to break even) = Cost to manufacture + Cost to sell

Break-even analysis relies on segregating costs according to their degree of variability. The established groupings are usually classed as variable and fixed (or nonvariable) costs, and the break-even equation is rewritten as follows:

Sales revenue (to break even) = Fixed costs + Variable costs

The annual income statement for McGrath Manufacturing Company in condensed form follows.

McGrath Manufacturing Company
Income Statement
For the Year Ended December 31, 20—

Net sales (10,000 units at $10)		$100,000
Cost of goods sold:		
Materials	$20,000	
Labor	25,000	
Factory overhead	15,000	60,000
Gross margin on sales		$ 40,000
Operating expenses:		
Selling expense	$15,000	
Administrative expense	10,000	25,000
Net income		$ 15,000

The costs and expenses of McGrath Manufacturing Company were analyzed and classified as follows. The analysis shows that variable costs are 70% of net sales ($70,000 ÷ $100,000).

Items	Total	Variable Costs	Fixed Costs
Materials	$20,000	$20,000	
Labor	25,000	25,000	
Factory overhead	15,000	10,000	$ 5,000
Selling expense	15,000	10,000	5,000
Administrative expense	10,000	5,000	5,000
	$85,000	$70,000	$15,000

The break-even equation in mathematical terms is as follows:

$$\text{Break-even sales volume} = \frac{\text{Total fixed costs}}{1 - (\text{Total variable costs} \div \text{Total sales volume})}$$

Using this equation, the break-even point in sales revenue for McGrath Manufacturing Company would be as follows:

$$\text{Break-even sales volume (dollars)} = \frac{\$15,000}{1 - (\$70,000 \div \$100,000)}$$

$$= \frac{\$15,000}{1 - .70}$$

$$= \frac{\$15,000}{.30}$$

$$= \$50,000$$

The break-even point can also be calculated in terms of units by using the following equation:

$$\text{Break-even sales volume (units)} = \frac{\text{Total fixed cost}}{\text{Sales price per unit} - \text{Variable cost per unit}}$$

Using this equation, the break-even point for McGrath Manufacturing Company would be as follows:

$$\text{Break-even sales volume} = \frac{\$15,000}{\$10 - \$7}$$

$$= \frac{\$15,000}{\$3}$$

$$= 5,000 \text{ units}$$

Note that 5,000 units multiplied by a selling price of $10 per unit equals the $50,000 break-even sales volume computed previously. The break-even point can be rechecked, if desired, as follows:

Sales at break-even point	$50,000
Less variable costs at break-even point (70% × $50,000)	35,000
Contribution margin	$15,000
Less fixed costs	15,000
Net income (loss)	-0-

BREAK-EVEN CHART

The break-even point can also be graphically depicted by a break-even chart as in Figure 10-4. The break-even chart is constructed and interpreted as follows:

1. A horizontal line, the x-axis, is drawn and divided into equal distances to represent the sales volume in dollars.

2. A vertical line, the y-axis, is drawn and spaced into equal parts representing costs and revenues in dollars.

FIGURE 10-4   Break-Even Chart

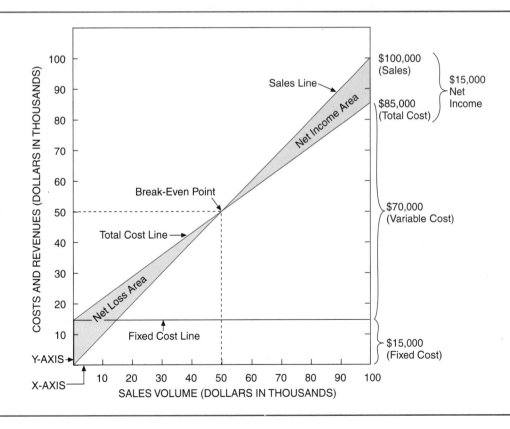

3. A fixed cost line is drawn parallel to the x-axis at the $15,000 point on the y-axis.

4. A total cost line is drawn from the $15,000 fixed cost point above the point where the x-axis and the y-axis intersect to the $85,000 total cost point on the right.

5. A sales line is drawn from the intersection of the x-axis and y-axis to the $100,000 total sales point on the right.

6. The sales line intersects the total cost line at the break-even point, representing $50,000 of sales.

7. The shaded area to the left of the break-even point is the net loss area, and the shaded area to the right of the break-even point is the net income area.

BREAK-EVEN ANALYSIS FOR MANAGEMENT DECISIONS

Break-even analysis can be used to help management select an action when several alternatives exist. This analysis is based on the conditions that variable costs will vary in constant proportion to the sales volume and that fixed costs will be fixed over a prescribed or relevant range of activity. If management, therefore, wishes to test new proposals that will change the percentage of variable costs to sales volume, or the total amount of fixed costs, or even a combination of these changes, it can use the basic break-even equation to calculate the results.

For example, assume that McGrath Manufacturing Company has established its break-even point in sales volume at $50,000 and now wishes to determine the amount of sales dollars needed to earn a net income of $18,000. The $18,000 net income is viewed as a nonvariable factor, and the sales volume would be calculated as follows, using a modified equation:

$$\text{Sales volume} = \frac{\text{Total fixed costs} + \text{Net income}}{1 - (\text{Total variable costs} \div \text{Total sales volume})}$$

$$= \frac{\$15,000 + \$18,000}{1 - (\$70,000 \div \$100,000)}$$

$$= \frac{\$33,000}{1 - .70}$$

$$= \frac{\$33,000}{.30}$$

$$= \$110,000$$

The new conditions can be checked, in income statement form, as follows:

Sales	$110,000
Less variable costs (70% × $110,000)	77,000
Contribution margin	$ 33,000
Less fixed costs	15,000
Net income	$ 18,000

Further assume that management of McGrath Manufacturing Company, fearing that changing economic conditions may make it difficult for the company to attain its present sales volume, wants to analyze the effect on the break-even point if it increases the percentage of variable costs to sales and lowers fixed costs. Management believes that fixed costs can be reduced to $5,000, with a corresponding increase in the percentage of variable costs to 80%.

The break-even sales volume calculated with these conditions is as follows:

$$\text{Break-even sales volume} = \frac{\$5,000}{1 - .80}$$

$$= \frac{\$5,000}{.20}$$

$$= \$25,000$$

If the proposed shift from fixed costs to variable costs is accomplished, the break-even point is reduced from $50,000 to $25,000. The higher the variable costs, the smaller the risk of not attaining the expected break-even point. On the other hand, if the sales volume exceeds expectations, a large portion of the sales revenue will be used to cover the variable costs. Therefore, a smaller net income must be anticipated.

To illustrate, assume that McGrath Manufacturing Company achieves a sales volume of $200,000. With a variable cost percentage of 70%, the net income would amount to $45,000. If the fixed costs were reduced to $5,000 and the variable cost percentage increased to 80%, the profit would be only $35,000, a reduction of $10,000 at the same sales volume.

	Variable Cost Rate	
	70%	80%
Sales	$200,000	$200,000
Variable costs	140,000	160,000
Contribution margin	$ 60,000	$ 40,000
Fixed costs	15,000	5,000
Net income	$ 45,000	$ 35,000

CONTRIBUTION MARGIN RATIO AND MARGIN OF SAFETY

LEARNING OBJECTIVE 5
Calculate the contribution margin ratio and the margin of safety ratio.

Two terms frequently used in cost-volume-profit relationships are *contribution margin* and *margin of safety*. The contribution margin, introduced in the discussion of direct costing, is the difference between sales revenue and total variable costs and expenses. When an income statement depicts the contribution margin, management can use it as a tool for studying the effects of changes in sales volume. The **contribution margin ratio**, also referred to as the **marginal income ratio**, is the relationship of contribution margin to sales.

The **margin of safety** indicates the amount that sales can decrease before the company will suffer a loss. The **margin of safety ratio** is a relationship computed by dividing margin of safety in dollars by the total sales. To illustrate, assume the following income statement:

Sales (10,000 units @ $100)	$1,000,000	100%
Variable costs	600,000	60
Contribution margin	$ 400,000	40%
Fixed costs	300,000	30
Net income	$ 100,000	10%

In this income statement, the contribution margin is $400,000. The contribution margin ratio is calculated as follows:

$$\text{Contribution margin ratio} = \frac{\text{Contribution Margin}}{\text{Sales}}$$

$$= \frac{\$400,000}{\$1,000,000}$$

$$= 40\%$$

Using the contribution margin ratio of 40%, the break-even point can be calculated as follows:

$$\text{Break-even sales volume} = \frac{\text{Fixed costs}}{\text{Contribution margin ratio}}$$

$$= \frac{\$300,000}{.40}$$

$$= \$750,000$$

The margin of safety is computed as follows:

Margin of safety = Sales – Break-even sales
                  = $1,000,000 – $750,000
                  = $250,000

The margin of safety ratio (M/S) is calculated as follows:

$$\text{Margin of safety ratio} = \frac{\text{Margin of safety}}{\text{Sales}}$$

$$= \frac{\$250,000}{\$1,000,000}$$

$$= 25\%$$

If the break-even sales equal $750,000 but the total expected sales are $1,000,000, the M/S ratio shows that the $1,000,000 in sales can decline by 25% before it reaches the firm's break-even level. Because the margin of safety is directly related to net income, the M/S ratio can be used to calculate net income as a percentage of sales and vice versa.

Net income percentage = Contribution margin ratio × Margin of safety ratio
                       = 40% × 25%
                       = 10% (*Note:* This figure agrees with the net income
                              as a percent of sales as shown in the
                              income statement on page 412.)

$$\text{Margin of safety ratio} = \frac{\text{Net income percentage}}{\text{Contribution margin ratio}}$$

$$= \frac{.10}{.40}$$

$$= 25\%$$

Cost-volume-profit analysis assumes that all factors used in the analysis except volume will remain constant (unchanged) for a given period of time. It is unrealistic to assume that the established relationship between sales and production will remain as forecast, or even that the sales mix, as established, will remain constant for any long period. Even price changes that have not been predicted can occur, and the outcome will be substantially affected. If a fairly stable set of relationships cannot be established, a series of analyses should be prepared that recognizes the changing sets of circumstances and their related outcomes.

DIFFERENTIAL COST ANALYSIS

LEARNING OBJECTIVE 6
Use differential cost
analysis techniques to
make special decisions.

All management requirements cannot be satisfied by one concept or combination of cost data. The designated purpose for which a cost measurement is made needs to be studied carefully to determine what items should be included in the cost analysis. This study should then provide a series of alternative solutions based on the comparison of the different sets of relevant cost data. A study that highlights the significant cost data of alternatives is referred to as **differential cost analysis**.

Assume that a company, now operating at 80% capacity, has been asked by a one-time purchaser to sell additional units at less than its established sales price. The company would make a study to determine the difference in costs at the two volume levels.

The company produces 30,000 units at 80% of its total capacity. Its fixed factory overhead costs are $20,000, and it sells each unit for $10. A new customer wishes to purchase 7,500 units for $4 per unit. Should the company agree to the terms or reject the offer?

The variable production costs per unit are as follows:

Direct materials	$2.00
Direct labor	1.00
Variable overhead	.75
Total variable cost per unit	$3.75

At the present level of operations, the total production cost per unit is $4.42 ([(30,000 units × $3.75) + $20,000] ÷ 30,000 units). If the additional units are produced, the total cost per unit would be $4.28 ([(37,500 units × $3.75) + $20,000] ÷ 37,500 units). Because the new customer is offering only $4 per unit, the company apparently should not accept such an offer.

However, when the total fixed factory overhead cost of $20,000 is not affected by producing the additional units, only the differential cost (in this case variable cost) will increase. Thus, each additional unit produced, and sold at $4, will increase the contribution margin by $0.25 ($4.00 selling price − $3.75 variable cost per unit). If the company accepts the offer, its total increase in the contribution margin would be $1,875 (7,500 units × $0.25). Because the fixed cost will not change, the gross margin would also increase by $1,875, shown as follows:

	Accept Order	Reject Order
Sales:		
30,000 units @ $10	$300,000	$300,000
7,500 units @ $4	30,000	-0-
Total revenues	$330,000	$300,000
Variable costs	140,625*	112,500**
Contribution margin	$189,375	$187,500
Fixed overhead costs	20,000	20,000
Gross margin on sales	$169,375	$167,500

*37,500 units × $3.75 (variable cost) $140,625

**30,000 units × $3.75 (variable cost) $112,500

The differential cost concept is applicable only when excess capacity exists that can be utilized at little or no increase in fixed cost. Also, in accepting additional orders at selling prices below the usual price levels, care should be exercised so that legislation barring sales to different customers at different prices is not violated or that regular customers will not expect the same price treatment for their purchases.

To illustrate another analysis of differential costs, assume that a company may buy a finished part that could perhaps be more economically manufactured in its own plant. For example, assume that 40,000 parts are purchased each month at a unit price of $1 per part. All the tools and necessary skills required for manufacturing this part are available in Dept. A of the company.

Dept. A has a total capacity of 30,000 direct labor hours per month. The present utilization is 24,000 direct labor hours, or 80% of plant capacity. Analyses of Dept. A's factory overhead costs include the following:

	Budgeted (80%) 24,000 Hours		Normal (100%) 30,000 Hours	
	Total Costs	Per Hour Costs	Total Costs	Per Hour Costs
Fixed costs	$ 72,000	$3.00	$ 72,000	$2.40
Variable costs	48,000	2.00	60,000	2.00
Total	$120,000	$5.00	$132,000	$4.40
Differential cost			$ 12,000	$0.60

The costs to manufacture 40,000 parts include the following:

Materials	$ 2,000
Labor, 6,000 hours @ $4	24,000
Total	$26,000
Add differential overhead cost of 6,000 labor hours	12,000
Total cost to manufacture parts	$38,000
Cost per unit ($38,000 ÷ 40,000)	$ 0.95

Because Dept. A is presently operating at 80% of its total capacity, the company can save $2,000 ($40,000 purchased cost – $38,000 cost to make), or $0.05 per part ($1.00 – $0.95), by making the 40,000 parts rather than buying them. If the 80% capacity level in Dept. A is a short-run condition, this factor must be considered before the final decision is made. The estimated savings may not be realized if the excess capacity of the department will soon be required for the company's regularly manufactured products.

DISTRIBUTION COSTS

LEARNING OBJECTIVE 7
Identify the appropriate techniques to analyze and control the distribution costs incurred in selling and delivering products.

Cost accounting is frequently thought of as a method of accounting only for the costs of manufacturing. However, "cost" as a general term covers more than merely manufacturing costs; it should include all of the costs of doing business. In other words, efficient control of all costs should cover both the production costs and the distribution costs. **Distribution costs** include the costs incurred to sell and deliver the product.

In recent years, state and federal laws prohibiting discriminatory sale prices and increasing competition have forced accountants to devote more time to the study of distribution costs. An attempt is being made to determine, by means of close and careful analysis, the answers to a variety of questions:

1. How much of the selling and administrative expense is allocable to each type of product sold?
2. How much of the selling and administrative expense is allocable to each particular sales office?
3. How much of the selling and administrative expense is allocable to each salesperson?
4. How much of the selling and administrative expense is allocable to each order sold?

To illustrate some of the difficulties encountered, assume that a company that sells bakery products also operates a fleet of delivery trucks to distribute the finished items. Each driver is a salesperson; therefore, each truck is a combination sales and delivery truck. At each stop, the driver takes an order from the store manager for bread, cakes, cookies, and other bakery products carried on the truck and then stocks the shelves. In one store, fifteen minutes may be spent selling four dozen loaves of bread, two dozen breakfast rolls, and a dozen boxes of doughnuts. In another store, the salesperson may need forty-five minutes to sell only a dozen loaves of bread.

Suppose that the daily costs of the operation are $50 for the salesperson-driver's salary, $30 for truck depreciation, $15 for gasoline and oil, and $5 for miscellaneous operating expenses. How much of the total truck expense is chargeable to each sale? Should it be allocated on the basis of the number of sales made? Should it be allocated on the basis of the time spent at each stop by the driver? What is the cost of selling a loaf of bread, a dozen doughnuts, or a package of breakfast rolls?

These questions are not academic, and businesses devote a considerable amount of time attempting to arrive at meaningful answers to such questions. The following example will show the usefulness of distribution cost studies.

Assume that a company is making three products, A, B, and C. The manufacturing cost per unit follows:

$$
\begin{array}{ll}
A & \$10 \\
B & 15 \\
C & 5
\end{array}
$$

During one month, 1,000 units of each product are sold at $15, $18, and $6 each, respectively. The gross margin for the month would be $9,000 ($39,000 – $30,000). If the selling and administrative expense for the month is $4,000, the net income for the month would be $5,000, a result that management would probably regard as satisfactory.

Now assume that an activity-based costing study indicates that the distribution cost per product is as follows:

Expense	A	B	C	Total
Selling expenses:				
Salaries	$ 300	$200	$ 300	$ 800
Commissions			500	500
Advertising	600	200	200	1,000
Telephone and telegraph	40		60	100
Sales manager's salary	133	133	134	400
Miscellaneous selling expense	127	17	56	200
Total selling expense	$1,200	$550	$1,250	$3,000
Administrative expense	300	350	350	1,000
Total	$1,500	$900	$1,600	$4,000
Number of units	÷1,000	÷1,000	÷1,000	
Cost per unit	$1.50	$0.90	$1.60	

To arrive at these figures, the company must identify the most appropriate cost driver for each expense and allocate these expenses to the products. For example, sales salaries might be allocated to the products on the basis of time reports showing the amount of time devoted to selling each product. Advertising might be allocated on the basis of the number of square inches of advertising space purchased for each product. The sales manager's salary might be allocated evenly among the products. Miscellaneous selling expense might be allocated on the basis of the number of orders received for each product or the value of each product sold.

Using the preceding cost and sales data, it becomes apparent that a profit is actually being made only on Products A and B. Product C is being sold at a loss. The following table, based on the sales for the month, shows the extent of the gain and loss:

Product	Cost to Make	Cost to Sell	Total Cost	Selling Price	Profit (Loss)
A	$10,000	$1,500	$11,500	$15,000	$3,500
B	15,000	900	15,900	18,000	2,100
C	5,000	1,600	6,600	6,000	(600)
Total	$30,000	$4,000	$34,000	$39,000	$5,000

As a result of the analysis of distribution costs, management determines that the company might make more money by selling less. If the sale of Product C were discontinued, it appears that the overall company profit would be greater by the amount of the loss being sustained on C. However, if a more intensive study were undertaken, it may show that Products A and B could not sustain their profit margins if the inescapable costs charged to Product C, such as the sales manager's salary, had to be charged to A and B. Also, the intangible benefits derived from continuing to carry Product C must be considered. Frequently, the intangible factors play a major role in determining whether one action or another is more justified. The overall effect on the company usually determines such decisions.

The following Real-World Example describes how the use of activity-based costing concepts can help managers determine which of their distribution channels is the most profitable.

You should now be able to work the following: Questions 4-16; Exercises 10-7 to 10-15; and Problems 10-2 to 10-10.

DISTRIBUTION CHANNEL PROFITABILITY

Distribution costs are a fact of life for almost every manufacturer, distributor, and supplier. As major retailers, wholesalers, distributors, and manufacturers reconfigure their supply chains, all participants in the supply chain need to understand the revenue and cost trade-offs associated with the various channels through which they deliver products and services. . . . The sections below describe how two companies facing different competitive issues could use the [activity-based costing] approach to develop their strategic responses.

A specialty chemical manufacturer supplied products to a broad range of customers in the food, consumer products, and manufacturing industries. The products were made primarily in-house. . . . Customers could opt for several delivery and pricing options including customer pick-up, bulk delivery, or less-than-truckload (LTL) delivery.

It recently had become known that a new competitor was planning to enter a key segment of the company's market. The vice president of sales & marketing . . . believed that the targeting segment provided a significant portion of the division's profit although the financial report indicated that it was not very profitable due to above average discounts. The head of sales and marketing decided to sponsor a study to understand the "true" profitability of the various delivery options and customer groups. . . .

The study team uncovered several significant findings:

- The large customers did provide a disproportionate percentage of the division's profits, despite their much lower gross margin, due primarily to less customer service, lower bad credit expenses, and reduced handling charges on large orders.
- Cost differentials within the large customer grouping depended on the use of the product. Customers in the food industry consumed more technical marketing, demanded more research support, and required a finer-grade product, which slowed process run rates.
- The "true" cost difference among the different delivery options was surprising. . . . The study revealed that the customer pick-up option after adjustment for freight charges actually cost less than the other delivery options due to much lower damage claim losses and reduced freight scheduling costs.
- The gross sales generated by small customers did not cover even the cost of selling and servicing these accounts. . . . Smaller customers often relied on the company's assistance. . . .
- While [several of the large-volume outsourced products] appeared profitable, the study indicated they were unprofitable once the inbound logistics cost and purchasing cost were taken into account.

. . . The head of sales & marketing worked with the vice president of operations, R&D, and finance to develop the following set of responses:

1. Technical resources were shifted away from smaller customers and assigned to work exclusively on the large consumer product and manufacturing accounts. The sales force then attempted to discover customer problems that could be solved by making these valuable resources available to the customers. . . .
2. The customer pick-up delivery price was lowered to attract more volume through this channel. This move was intended to attract the largest-volume users of the product—consumer product and manufacturing. . . .
3. The company began to look actively for other suppliers for the products they outsourced so as to improve the profitability of this operation. . . .

Kenneth H. Manning, "Distribution Channel Profitability," *Management Accounting,* January 1995, pp. 44–48.

KEY TERMS

Absorption costing, p. 398
Break-even analysis, p. 407
Break-even point, p. 407
Common cost, p. 404
Contribution margin, p. 400
Contribution margin ratio, p. 412
Cost-volume-profit (CVP) analysis, p. 407
Differential cost analysis, p. 414
Direct costing, p. 398
Direct (traceable) cost, p. 404
Distribution costs, p. 416
Full costing, p. 398

Gross margin, p. 400
Gross profit, p. 400
Indirect (nontraceable) cost, p. 404
Marginal income ratio, p. 412
Margin of safety, p. 412
Margin of safety ratio, p. 412
Period cost, p. 398
Product cost, p. 398
Segment, p. 404
Segment margin, p. 404
Variable costing, p. 398

SELF-STUDY PROBLEM

BREAK-EVEN POINT; ABSORPTION AND DIRECT COSTING

RIVER PRODUCTS COMPANY

River Products Company has a maximum productive capacity of 100,000 units per year. Normal capacity is 90,000 units per year. Standard variable manufacturing costs are $20 per unit. Fixed factory overhead is $450,000 per year. Variable selling expense is $10 per unit and fixed selling expense is $300,000 per year. The unit sales price is $50.

The operating results for the year are as follows: sales, 80,000 units; production, 85,000 units; and beginning inventory, 5,000 units. All variances are written off as additions to (or deductions from) the standard cost of sales.

Required:
1. What is the break-point expressed in dollar sales?
2. How many units must be sold to earn a net income of $50,000 per year?
3. Prepare a formal income statement for the year under the following:
   a. Absorption costing. (Hint: Don't forget to compute the volume variance.)
   b. Direct costing.

SOLUTION TO SELF-STUDY PROBLEM

1. To compute the break-even point in sales dollars, you must first identify the total fixed costs, the variable cost per unit, and the selling price per unit and put them into the following formula:

$$\text{Break-even sales volume} = \frac{\text{Fixed costs}}{1 - (\text{Variable costs} \div \text{Sales})}$$

$$= \frac{\$450,000 + \$300,000}{1 - [(\$20 + \$10) \div \$50]}$$

$$= \frac{\$750,000}{1 - .60}$$

$$= \frac{\$750,000}{.40}$$

$$= \$1,875,000$$

2. To solve for the target volume in units, you must first identify the total fixed costs, the desired net income, the unit sales price, and the unit variable cost and put them into the following formula:

$$\text{Target volume in units} = \frac{\text{Fixed costs} + \text{Net income}}{\text{Unit sales price} - \text{Unit variable cost}}$$

$$= \frac{\$750,000 + \$50,000}{\$50 - \$30}$$

$$= \underline{40,000} \text{ units}$$

3a. Before preparing an income statement under absorption costing, you must:
(1) Compute the standard production cost per unit:

$$\text{Standard production cost per unit} = \text{Variable cost} + \text{Fixed cost}$$

$$= \$20 + \frac{\$450,000}{90,000 \text{ units}^*}$$

$$= \$25$$

*Note that the fixed overhead per unit is based on normal capacity.

(2) Compute the ending inventory:

Beginning inventory	5,000
Add production	85,000
Inventory available for sale	90,000
Less sales	80,000
Ending inventory	10,000

(3) Determine the unfavorable volume variance:

Normal capacity	90,000
Actual production	85,000
Volume variance in units	5,000
Fixed overhead per unit	× $5
Unfavorable volume variance	$25,000

River Products Company
Absorption Costing Income Statement
For the Year Ended December 31, 20—

Sales (80,000 × $50)			$4,000,000
Less cost of goods sold:			
Beginning inventory (5,000 × $25)	$ 125,000		
Cost of goods manufactured (85,000 × $25) . .	2,125,000		
Goods available for sale	$2,250,000		
Ending inventory (10,000 × $25)	250,000		
Cost of goods sold at standard	$2,000,000		
Add unfavorable volume variance	25,000		
Cost of goods sold			2,025,000
Gross margin			$1,975,000
Selling expenses:			
Variable (80,000 × $10)	$800,000		
Fixed	300,000	$1,100,000	
Net income			$ 875,000

3b. Before preparing an income statement under direct costing, you must:
  (1) Realize that the variable production cost per unit is only $20.
  (2) Use the contribution margin format for your income statement, where
       Sales – Variable costs = Contribution margin
                    Contribution margin – Fixed costs = Net income

River Products Company
Direct Costing Income Statement
For the Year Ended December 31, 20—

Sales		$4,000,000
Variable costs:		
Beginning inventory (5,000 × $20)	$ 100,000	
Cost of goods manufactured (85,000 × $20)	1,700,000	
Goods available for sale	$1,800,000	
Ending inventory (10,000 × $20)	200,000	
Variable cost of goods sold	$1,600,000	
Variable selling expense	800,000	
Total variable expenses		2,400,000
Contribution margin		$1,600,000
Fixed costs:		
Fixed factory overhead	$450,000	
Fixed selling expense	300,000	750,000
Net income		$ 850,000

(Note: Problem 10-6 is similar to this problem.)

QUESTIONS

1. What is the difference between absorption costing and direct costing?

2. What effect will applying direct costing have on the income statement and the balance sheet?

3. What are the advantages and disadvantages of using direct costing?

4. Why are there objections to using absorption costing when segment reports of profitability are being prepared?

5. What are common costs?

6. How is a contribution margin determined and why is it important to management?

7. What are considered direct costs in segment analysis?

8. What is cost-volume-profit analysis?

9. What is the break-even point?

10. What steps are required in constructing a break-even chart?

11. What is the difference between the contribution margin ratio and the margin of safety ratio?

12. What is differential cost analysis?

13. What is the importance of make-or-buy studies for a company?

14. What are distribution costs?

15. What is the purpose of the analysis of distribution costs?

16. In cost analysis, what governs which costs are to be included in the study?

EXERCISES

E10-1
Computing unit cost
and cost of
inventory—direct and
absorption costing
Objective 1

Piersall Products Company uses a process cost system and applies actual factory overhead to work in process at the end of the month. The following data came from the records for the month of March:

Direct materials	$200,000
Direct labor	$100,000
Variable factory overhead	$ 80,000
Fixed factory overhead	$ 60,000
Selling and administrative expenses	$ 40,000
Units produced	25,000
Units sold	15,000
Selling price per unit	$ 25

There were no beginning inventories and no work in process at the end of the month.

From the information presented, compute the following:

1. Unit cost of production under absorption costing and direct costing
2. Cost of the ending inventory under absorption costing and direct costing

E10-2
Comparative income
statements—direct
and absorption
costing
Objective 1

Using the information presented in E10-1, prepare comparative income statements for March (a) under absorption costing and (b) under direct costing.

E10-3
Using direct costing
and absorption
costing
Objective 1

The chief executive officer of Cleaver Corporation attended a conference in which one of the sessions was devoted to direct costing. The CEO was impressed by the presentation and has asked that the following data of Cleaver Corporation be used to prepare comparative statements using direct costing and the company's absorption costing. The data follow:

Direct materials	$ 90,000
Direct labor	120,000
Variable factory overhead	60,000
Fixed factory overhead	150,000
Fixed marketing and administrative expense	180,000

The factory produced 75,000 units during the period and 60,000 units were sold for $600,000.

1. Prepare an income statement using direct costing.
2. Prepare an income statement using absorption costing.

E10-4
Using direct and
absorption costing
Objective 1

The following production data came from the records of Hoops Company for the year ended December 31, 20—:

Materials	$480,000
Labor	260,000
Variable factory overhead	44,000
Fixed factory overhead	36,800

During the year, 40,000 units were manufactured but only 35,000 units were sold.

Determine the effect on inventory valuation by computing the following:

1. Total inventoriable costs and the cost of the 35,000 units sold and of the 5,000 units in the ending inventory, using direct costing
2. Total inventoriable costs and the cost of the 35,000 units sold and of the 5,000 units in the ending inventory, using absorption costing

E10-5
Determining income by absorption costing
Objective 1

A company had income of $50,000, using direct costing for a given period. Beginning and ending inventories for the period were 18,000 units and 13,000 units, respectively. If the fixed overhead application rate was $2 per unit, what was the net income, using absorption costing?

E10-6
Adjusting direct cost income to absorption net income
Objective 1

The fixed overhead budgeted for Hamlet Company at an expected capacity of 500,000 units is $2,500,000. Direct costing is used internally and the net income is adjusted to an absorption costing net income at year-end. Data collected over the last three years show the following:

	First Year	Second Year	Third Year
Units produced	502,000	498,000	495,000
Units sold	496,000	503,000	495,000
Net income—(direct cost)	$500,000	$521,000	$497,000

Determine the adjustment each year to convert the direct costing income to an absorption costing net income. Compute the absorption costing net income for each year.

E10-7
Segment reporting by division
Objective 3

Fraternity Company has two divisions, Alpha and Beta. For the month ended March 31, Alpha had sales and variable costs of $500,000 and $225,000, respectively, and Beta had sales and variable costs of $800,000 and $475,000, respectively. Alpha had direct fixed production and administrative expenses of $40,000 and $25,000, respectively, and Beta had direct fixed production and administrative expenses of $60,000 and $35,000, respectively. Fixed costs that were common to both divisions and couldn't be allocated to the divisions in any meaningful way were selling, $33,000, and administration, $27,000.

Prepare a segmented income statement by division for the month of March.

E10-8
Computing break-even
Objective 4

Standard Company has a sales price per unit for its only product at $13. The variable cost per unit is $5. In year 20A, the company sold 80,000 units, which was 5,000 units above the break-even point.

Compute the following:

1. Total fixed expenses (Hint: First compute the contribution margin per unit.)
2. Total variable expense at the break-even volume

E10-9
**Computing break-
even plus net income**
Objective 4

Avalon Company sells its only product for $50 per unit. Fixed costs total $600,000 per year. Variable expenses are $1,120,000 when 40,000 units are sold.

How many units must be sold to make a net income of $40,000?

E10-10
**Using break-even
analysis**
Objective 4

A new product is expected to have sales of $100,000, variable costs of 60% of sales, and fixed costs of $20,000.

1. Using graph paper, construct a break-even chart and label the sales line, total cost line, fixed cost line, break-even point, and net income and net loss areas.
2. From the chart, identify the break-even point and the amount of income or loss if sales are $100,000.

E10-11
Using CVP analysis
Objectives 4, 5

A company has sales of $1,000,000, variable costs of $400,000, and fixed costs of $300,000. Compute the following:

1. Contribution margin ratio
2. Break-even sales volume
3. Margin of safety ratio
4. Net income as a percentage of sales

E10-12
**Using break-even
analysis**
Objectives 4, 6

A company has prepared the following statistics regarding its production and sales at different capacity levels.

Capacity level	60%	80%	100%
Units	60,000	80,000	100,000
Sales	$240,000	$320,000	$400,000
Total costs:			
Variable	$120,000	$160,000	$200,000
Fixed	150,000	150,000	150,000
Total costs	$270,000	$310,000	$350,000
Net profit (loss)	$ (30,000)	$ 10,000	$ 50,000

1. At what point is break-even reached in sales dollars? In units?
2. If the company is operating at 60% capacity, should it accept an offer from a customer to buy 10,000 units at $3 per unit?

E10-13
**Using differential cost
analysis—special
customer order**
Objective 6

Joyce-Ann Company manufactures basketballs. The company's forecasted income statement for the year, before any special orders, follows:

	Amount	Per Unit
Sales	$8,000,000	$10.00
Manufacturing cost of goods sold	6,400,000	8.00
Gross profit	$1,600,000	$ 2.00
Selling expenses	600,000	.75
Operating income	$1,000,000	$ 1.25

Fixed costs included in the forecasted income statement are $4,000,000 in manufacturing cost of goods sold and $400,000 in selling expenses.

A new client placed a special order with Joyce-Ann, offering to buy 100,000 basketballs for $5.00 each. The company will incur no additional selling expenses if it accepts the special order. Assuming that Joyce-Ann has sufficient capacity to manufacture 100,000 more basketballs, by what amount would operating income be increased or decreased as a result of accepting the special order? (Hint: First compute the variable cost per unit relevant to this decision.)

E10-14
Deciding to make or buy
Objective 6

JR Company needs 20,000 units of a certain part to use in its production cycle. The following information is available:

Cost to JR to make the part:

Direct materials	$ 4
Direct labor	16
Variable factory overhead	12
Fixed factory overhead applied	6
Total	$38
Cost to buy the part from Coldwater Company	$36

If JR buys the part from Coldwater instead of making it, JR could not use the released facilities in another manufacturing activity. Seventy percent of the fixed factory overhead applied will continue regardless of what decision JR makes.

1. In deciding whether to make or buy the part, what are the total relevant costs per unit to make the part?
2. What decision should JR make?

E10-15
Using comparative net income analysis
Objectives 3, 7

Hook Manufacturing Company wishes to determine the profitability of its products and asks the cost accountant to make a comparative analysis of sales, cost of sales, and distribution costs of each product for the year. The accountant gathers the following information, which will be useful in preparing the analysis:

	Product X	Product Y	Product Z
Number of units sold	30,000	20,000	20,000
Number of orders received	5,000	2,500	1,000
Selling price per unit	$50	$75	$100
Cost per unit	$30	$50	$ 75

Advertising expenses total $600,000 for the year, an equal amount being expended to advertise each product. The sales representative's commission is based on the selling price of each unit and is 8% for Product X, 12% for Product Y, and 16% for Product Z. The sales manager's salary of $75,000 per year is allocated evenly to each product. Other miscellaneous selling and administrative expenses are estimated to be $15 per order received.

Prepare an analysis for Hook Manufacturing Company that will show in comparative form the net income derived from the sale of each product for the year.

PROBLEMS

P10-1
Absorption and direct costing income statements
Objective 1

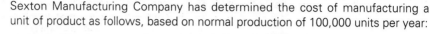

Sexton Manufacturing Company has determined the cost of manufacturing a unit of product as follows, based on normal production of 100,000 units per year:

Direct materials	$ 5
Direct labor	4
Variable factory overhead	3
Fixed factory overhead	3
	$15

Operating statistics for the months of March and April include the following:

	March	April
Units produced	12,000	6,000
Units sold	6,000	10,000
Selling and administrative expenses (all fixed)	$12,000	$12,000

The selling price is $18 per unit. There were no inventories on March 1, and there is no work in process on April 30.

Required:

Prepare comparative income statements for each month under each of the following:

1. Absorption costing (Include under- or overapplied fixed overhead)
2. Direct costing

P10-2
Segmented income statement
Objective 3

Greek Manufacturing Company manufactures two products, Alpha and Beta, which are sold in two territories designated by the company as East Territory and West Territory. The income statement prepared for the company shows the product-line segments.

Greek Manufacturing Company
Income Statement

	Total	Alpha		Beta	
Sales	$1,000,000	$600,000	100%	$400,000	100%
Less variable expenses	600,000	420,000	70	180,000	45
Contribution margin	$ 400,000	$180,000	30%	$220,000	55%
Less direct fixed costs	200,000	50,000		150,000	
Segment margin	$ 200,000	$130,000		$ 70,000	
Less common fixed costs	120,000				
Net income	$ 80,000				

The territorial product sales are as follows:

	East	West
Alpha	$400,000	$200,000
Beta	200,000	200,000
Total	$600,000	$400,000

The direct expenses of Alpha ($50,000) and Beta ($150,000) are not identifiable with either of the two territories. The common fixed costs are partially identifiable with East Territory, West Territory, and the general administration as follows:

East Territory	$ 54,000
West Territory	36,000
General administration	30,000
Total common fixed costs	$120,000

Required:

1. Prepare a segmented income statement by territories. The direct fixed costs of the product lines should be treated as common fixed costs on the segmented statement being prepared.
2. What is the significance of this analysis?

P10-3
Segment Reporting
Objective 3

Tic-Tac Manufacturing Company has two product lines. The income statement for the year ended December 31 shows the following:

Tic-Tac Manufacturing Company
Product Line and Company Income Statement
For the Year Ended December 31, 20—

	Cris	Cross	Total
Sales	$40,000	$60,000	$100,000
Less variable expenses	16,000	24,000	40,000
Contribution margin	$24,000	$36,000	$ 60,000
Less direct fixed expenses	16,000	14,000	30,000
Product margin	$ 8,000	$22,000	$ 30,000
Less common fixed expenses			12,000
Net income			$ 18,000

The products, Cris and Cross, are sold in two territories, North and South, as follows:

	East	West
Cris sales	$24,000	$16,000
Cross sales	18,000	42,000
Total sales	$42,000	$58,000

The common fixed expenses are traceable to each territory as follows:

North fixed expenses	$ 4,000
South fixed expenses	6,000
Home office administrative fixed expenses	2,000
Total common fixed expenses	$12,000

The direct expenses of Cris, $16,000, and of Cross, $14,000, are not identifiable with either of the two territories.

Required:

1. Prepare income statements segmented by territory for the year that includes a column for the entire company.
2. Why are direct expenses of one type of segment report not direct expenses of another type of segment report?

P10-4
Segment Reporting
Objective 3

West-Southern Publishing Company prepares income statements segmented by divisions, but the chief operating officer is not certain about how the company is actually performing. Financial data for the year follow:

	Segments		
	Textbook Division	Professional Division	Total Company
Sales	$360,000	$820,000	$1,180,000
Less variable expenses:			
Manufacturing	$ 64,000	$410,000	$ 474,000
Selling and administrative	8,000	41,000	49,000
Total	$ 72,000	$451,000	$ 523,000
Contribution margin	$288,000	$369,000	$ 657,000
Less direct fixed expenses	30,000	440,000	470,000
Net income	$258,000	$ (71,000)	$ 187,000

The Professional Division appears to be floundering and the CEO believes a closer look should be taken concerning its operating effectiveness. Additional data regarding this division follow:

	Accounting	Executive	Management
Sales	$280,000	$280,000	$260,000
Variable manufacturing expenses as a percentage of sales	60%	40%	50%
Other variable expenses as a percentage of sales	5%	5%	5%
Direct fixed expenses	$100,000	$150,000	$100,000

The Professional Division's accounting books are sold to auditors and controllers.

The current data on these two markets follow:

	Sales Market	
	Auditors	Controllers
Sales	$60,000	$220,000
Variable manufacturing expenses as a percentage of sales	60%	60%
Other variable expenses as a percentage of sales	16%	2%
Direct fixed expenses	$30,000	$ 50,000

Required:

1. Prepare an income statement segmented by products of the Professional Division, including a column for the division as a whole. (Hint: To obtain the common fixed expenses, start with the total direct expenses in the Professional Division.)
2. Prepare an income statement segmented by markets of the accounting books of the Professional Division.
3. Evaluate the accounting books of the Professional Division. Should all books be kept or should some books be discontinued?

P10-5
Break-even analysis
Objectives 1, 4

The production of a new product required Melissa Manufacturing Company to lease additional plant facilities. Based on studies, the following data have been made available:

Estimated annual sales—24,000 units

Estimated costs:	Amount	Per Unit
Materials	$ 96,000	$4.00
Direct labor	14,400	.60
Factory overhead	24,000	1.00
Administrative expense	28,800	1.20
Total	$163,200	$6.80

Selling expenses are expected to be 20% of sales and net income is to amount to $1.20 per unit.

Required:

1. Calculate the selling price per unit. (Hint: Let "X" equal the selling price and express selling expense as a percent of "X".)
2. Prepare an absorption costing income statement for the year.
3. Calculate the break-even point expressed in dollars and in units, assuming that administrative expense and factory overhead are all fixed but other costs are fully variable.

P10-6
Break-even point: absorption and direct cost analysis. Similar to self-study problem.
Objectives 1, 4

Jombo Company has a maximum productive capacity of 210,000 units per year. Normal capacity is 180,000 units per year. Standard variable manufacturing costs are $10 per unit. Fixed factory overhead is $360,000 per year. Variable selling expense is $5 per unit and fixed selling expense is $252,000 per year. The unit sales price is $20.

The operating results for the year are as follows: sales, 150,000 units; production, 160,000 units; beginning inventory, 10,000 units. All variances are written off as additions to (or deductions from) the standard cost of sales.

Required:

1. What is the break-even point expressed in dollar sales?
2. How many units must be sold to earn a net income of $100,000 per year?
3. Prepare a formal income statement for the year under the following:
    a. Absorption costing (Hint: Don't forget to compute the volume variance.)
    b. Direct costing

P10-7
Contribution margin and break-even analysis
Objective 4

Palmer, Inc. produces and sells a product with a price of $100 per unit. The following cost data have been prepared for its estimated upper and lower limits of activity:

	Lower Limit	Upper Limit
Production (units)	4,000	6,000
Production costs:		
Direct materials	$ 60,000	$ 90,000
Direct labor	80,000	120,000
Overhead:		
Indirect materials	25,000	37,500
Indirect labor	40,000	50,000
Depreciation	20,000	20,000
Selling and administrative expenses:		
Sales salaries	50,000	65,000
Office salaries	30,000	30,000
Advertising	45,000	45,000
Other	15,000	20,000
Total	$365,000	$477,500

Required:

1. Classify each cost element as either variable, fixed, or semivariable. (Hint: Recall that variable expenses must go up in direct proportion to changes in the volume of activity.)
2. Calculate the break-even point in units and dollars. (Hint: First use the high-low method illustrated in Chapter 4 to separate costs into their fixed and variable components.)
3. Prepare a break-even chart.
4. Prepare a contribution income statement, similar in format to the statement appearing at the top of page 411, assuming sales of 5,000 units.
5. Recompute the break-even point in units, assuming that variable costs increase by 20% and fixed costs are reduced by $50,000.

P10-8
Calculating break-even point, contribution margin ratio, and margin of safety ratio
Objectives 4, 5

Evita Company is considering building a manufacturing plant in Mexico. Predicting sales of 100,000 units, Evita estimates the following expenses:

	Total Annual Expenses	Percent of Total Annual Expenses That Are Fixed
Materials	$19,000	10%
Labor	26,000	20%
Overhead	40,000	40%
Marketing and administration	14,000	60%
	$99,000	

A Mexican firm that specializes in marketing will be engaged to sell the manufactured product and will receive a commission of 10% of the sales price. None of the U.S. home office expense will be allocated to the Mexican facility.

Required:

1. If the unit sales price is $2, how many units must be sold to break even? (Hint: First compute the variable cost per unit.)
2. Calculate the margin of safety ratio.
3. Calculate the contribution margin ratio.

P10-9
Make or buy
Objective 6

Bugs-Off Corporation produces and sells a line of insect repellants that are sold usually in the summer months. Recently, the chief operating officer has become interested in possibly manufacturing a repellant that can prevent a person from being attacked if sprayed by a "pepper" repellant. The appeal of this product is that it would have year-around sales and would help stabilize the income of the company.

The product, however, must be sold in a specially designed spray can that will be safe from being discharged accidently. The product will be sold in cartons that hold 24 cans of the repellant. The sales price will be $96 per carton. The plant is now operating at only 65% of its total capacity, so no additional fixed costs will be incurred. However, a $100,000 fixed overhead charge will be allocated to the new product from the company's present total of fixed costs.

Using the current estimates for 100,000 cartons of "Pepper" as a standard volume, the following costs were developed for each carton, including the cost of the can:

Direct materials	$12
Direct labor	6
Overhead (includes allocated fixed charge)	4
Total cost per carton	$22

Bugs-Off Corporation has requested a bid from a manufacturer of speciality dispensers for a purchase price of an empty can that could be used for the new product. The speciality company offered a price of $4 for a carton of cans. If the proposal is accepted, Bugs-Off estimates that direct labor and variable overhead costs would be reduced by 10% and direct materials would be reduced by 20%.

Required:

1. Should the Bugs-Off Corporation make or buy the special cans? (Hint: First compute the costs that could be saved by buying the cans.)
2. What would be the maximum purchase price acceptable to Bugs-Off Corporation for the cans?

P10-10
Differential cost analysis
Objective 6

Clear Company manufactures household products such as windows, light fixtures, ladders, and work tables. During the year it produced 10,000 Model 10X windows but only sold 5,000 units at $40 each. The remaining units cannot be sold through normal channels. Cost for inventory purposes on December 31 included the following data on the unsold units:

Materials	$10.00
Labor	5.00
Variable overhead	3.00
Fixed overhead	2.00
Total cost per window	$20.00

Clear can sell the 5,000 windows at a liquidation price of $10.00 per window, but it will incur a packaging and shipping charge of $6.00 per window.

Required:

1. Identify the relevant costs and revenues for the liquidation sale alternative. Is Clear better off accepting the liquidation price rather than doing nothing?
2. Assume that the Model 10X can be reprocessed to another size window, Model 20X, which will require the same amount of labor and overhead as was required to initially produce, but sells for only $25. Determine the most profitable course of action—liquidate or reprocess?

GLOSSARY

A

Absorption costing. A method of accounting for manufacturing costs that charges both fixed and variable costs to the product; also referred to as the "full cost" method.

Accounting information system. A set of procedures designed to provide the financial information needed within a business organization.

Activity-based costing (ABC). A method of applying overhead to products that considers non-volume-related activities that create overhead costs as well as volume-related activities.

Adjusted sales value. A basis for allocating joint costs which takes into consideration the cost of processing after split-off.

Algebraic distribution method. A method for allocating service department costs to production departments using algebraic techniques. While this method may provide the most accurate distribution of costs, it is more complicated than the other methods and the results obtained may not justify the additional effort involved.

Applied Factory Overhead. The account credited when applying estimated overhead to production; the debit is to Work in Process. Use of a separate "applied" account avoids confusion with actual overhead costs charged to Factory Overhead, the control account in the general ledger.

Attainable standard. A performance criterion that recognizes inefficiencies that are likely to result from such factors as lost time, spoilage, or waste.

Average cost method. A commonly used procedure for assigning costs to the ending inventories under a process cost accounting system. Under this method, ending inventories are valued using an average unit cost, computed as follows: (cost of beginning work in process + current period production costs) divided by the total equivalent production for the period.

B

Backflush costing. The name for the accounting system used with JIT manufacturing. Costs are not "flushed out" of the accounting system until goods are completed and sold.

Bar codes. These are symbols that can be processed electronically to identify numbers, letters, or special characters.

Billing rates. The hourly rates that a firm charges its clients for the various categories of professional labor worked on the job.

Bonus pay. An amount paid to employees in addition to regular earnings for outstanding performance, as a result of higher-than-usual company profits, or for a variety of other reasons.

Break-even analysis. An analytical technique based on the determination of a break-even point expressed in terms of sales revenue or sales volume.

Break-even point. The point at which sales revenue adequately covers all costs to manufacture and sell the product but no profit is earned.

Budget. Management's operating plan expressed in quantitative terms, such as units of production and related costs.

Budget for manufacturing costs. Budget of the costs of materials, labor, and factory overhead for each month (or shorter period) of the coming year.

Budget for receivables. Shows when cash can be expected from the turnover of inventory and receivables.

Budget variance (two-variance method). The difference between budgeted factory overhead at the capacity attained and the actual factory overhead incurred.

Budgeted income statement. A summary of anticipated revenues and expenses for the coming year based on budgets for sales, manufacturing costs, and nonmanufacturing expenses (selling, administrative, and other).

Budgets for administrative, selling, and other expenses. Individual budgets showing anticipated expenses for administrative, selling, and other nonmanufacturing activities; prepared after the level of activity for sales and production have been determined.

By-products. Secondary products with relatively little value that are obtained in the process of manufacturing the primary product.

C

Capacity variance. It reflects an under- or overabsorption of fixed costs by measuring the difference between actual hours worked, multiplied by the standard rate, and the budget allowance based on actual hours worked.

Capital expenditures budget. A plan for the timing of acquisitions of buildings, equipment, and other operating assets during the year.

Carrying costs. The costs incurred as a result of maintaining (carrying) inventories. These costs generally include: materials storage and handling costs; interest, insurance, and taxes; losses from theft, deterioration, or obsolescence; and record keeping and supplies.

Cash budget. Budget showing the anticipated flow of cash and the timing of receipts and disbursements based on projected sales, manufacturing costs, and other expenses.

Clock card. A preprinted card used to record the total amount of time spent in the factory by an employee.

Common cost. The term used in segment analysis to describe a cost that cannot be traced to, or specifically identified with, a particular business segment.

Contribution margin. The difference between sales revenue and variable costs.

Contribution margin ratio. The relationship of contribution margin to sales.

Contributory plans. Pension plans that require a partial contribution from the employees.

Control. The process of monitoring the company's operations and determining whether the objectives identified in the planning process are being accomplished.

Controllable variance. The amount by which the actual factory overhead costs differ from the standard overhead costs for the attained level of production.

Conversion cost. The combined cost of direct labor and factory overhead, which is necessary to convert the direct materials into finished goods.

Cost accounting. The branch of accounting that focuses on providing the detailed cost data that management needs in controlling current operations and planning for the future.

Cost accounting system. A set of methods and procedures used by a manufacturing organization to accumulate detailed cost data relating to the manufacturing process.

Cost and production report. A summary of cost and production data for a particular cost center.

Cost behavior. The determination of whether costs are fixed or variable.

Cost/benefit decision. A decision as to whether the benefit received from pursuing a certain course of action exceeds the costs of that action.

Cost center. A unit of activity, such as a department, to which costs may be practically and equitably assigned.

Cost driver. The basis used to allocate each of the activities in activity-based costing such as number of setups and number of design changes.

Cost of production summary. A report that summarizes production costs for a period for each department and provides the information necessary for inventory valuation.

Cost performance report. It compares the budgeted costs for a job with its actual costs and indicates the variance for each line item.

Cost-volume-profit analysis. An analytical technique that uses the degrees of cost variability for measuring the effect of changes in volume on resulting profits.

D

Debit-credit memorandum. A document used to notify the vendor that materials received do not correspond with materials ordered.

Defective units. Units of product with imperfections that are considered correctable because the market value of the corrected unit will be greater than the total cost incurred for the unit.

Department-type analysis sheet. One form of factory overhead analysis sheet; a separate analysis sheet is maintained for each department, with individual amount columns for each type of overhead expense.

Differential cost analysis. A study that highlights the significant cost data of alternatives.

Differential costs. The costs that are highlighted from a series of alternative solutions that compare different sets of relevant cost data.

Direct charge. A charge that can be exactly measured and charged to a specific department.

Direct (traceable) cost. The term used in segment analysis to describe a cost that can be traced to a specific business segment.

Direct costing. A method of accounting for manufacturing costs that charges the product with only the costs that vary directly with volume: direct materials, direct labor, and variable factory overhead. This method is also referred to as "variable costing."

Direct distribution method. A method for allocating service department costs to production departments. No attempt is made to determine the extent to which service departments provide services to each other; instead, all service department costs are distributed directly to the production departments.

Direct labor. The cost of labor for employees who work directly on the product being manufactured.

Direct labor cost method. A method of applying factory overhead to production based on the amount of direct labor cost incurred for a job or process.

Direct labor hour method. A method of applying factory overhead to production based on the number of direct labor hours worked on a job or process.

Direct materials. Materials which become part of the product being manufactured and which can be readily identified with a certain product.

Distribution costs. Costs incurred to sell and deliver a product.

E

Economic order quantity. The optimal (most economical) quantity of materials that should be ordered at one time; represents the order size which minimizes total order and carrying costs.

Efficiency variance. The difference between overhead applied (standard hours at the standard rate) and the actual hours worked multiplied by the standard rate; indicates the effect on fixed and variable overhead costs when actual hours worked are more or less than standard hours allowed for the production volume.

Employee earnings record. A form prepared for each employee showing the employee's earnings each pay period and cumulative earnings for each quarter and for the year.

Equivalent production. The number of units that could have been completed during a period using the total production costs for the period.

Expense-type analysis sheet. One form of factory overhead analysis sheet; a separate analysis sheet is used for each type of overhead expense with individual amount columns for each department.

F

Factory ledger. A separate ledger containing all the accounts relating to manufacturing, including the inventory accounts; it is maintained at the factory and tied to the general ledger through a special account.

Factory overhead. All costs related to the manufacturing of a product except direct materials and direct labor; these costs include indirect materials, indirect labor, and other manufacturing expenses such as depreciation, supplies, utilities, maintenance, insurance, and taxes.

Factory overhead analysis sheets. A subsidiary record of factory overhead expenses; replaces a subsidiary factory overhead ledger. Analysis sheets are commonly used by larger enterprises with several departments and many different types of overhead expenses.

Factory overhead ledger. A subsidiary ledger containing the individual factory overhead accounts; the total of the individual account balances in the subsidiary ledger should equal the balance in the control account, Factory Overhead, in the general ledger.

Favorable variance. The difference between actual and standard costs when actual costs are less than standard costs.

Federal Insurance Contributions Act (FICA). Federal legislation requiring both employers and employees to pay social security taxes on wages and salaries.

Federal Unemployment Tax Act (FUTA). Federal legislation requiring employers to pay an established rate of tax on wages and salaries to provide for compensation to employees if they are laid off from their regular employment.

Financial accounting. The branch of accounting that focuses on the gathering of information to be used in the preparation of external financial statements; i.e., balance sheet, income statement, and statement of cash flows.

Finished goods. The inventory account that represents the total cost incurred in manufacturing goods that are complete but still on hand at the end of the accounting period.

First-in, first-out (FIFO). An inventory costing method based on the assumption that materials issued are taken from the oldest materials in stock. Thus, materials issued are costed at the earliest prices paid for materials in stock and ending inventories are costed at the most recent purchase prices.

Fixed costs. Manufacturing costs that remain constant when production levels increase or decrease; examples include straight-line depreciation, periodic rent payments, insurance, and salaries paid to production executives.

Flexible budget. A budget that shows expected costs at different production levels.

Flow of costs. The order in which materials are actually issued for use in the factory.

Flow of materials. The order in which unit costs are assigned to materials issued.

Forecast of sales. A budget of projected sales expressed in both units and dollars; serves as a basis for preparation of all other budgets.

For-profit service businesses. These are businesses that sell services rather than products, such as airlines and accountants.

Four-variance method. The analysis of fixed and variable factory overhead costs based on the computation of a spending variance and an efficiency variance for variable costs and a budget variance and a volume variance for fixed costs.

Full cost method. See Absorption costing.

G

Gainsharing plan. A type of group bonus plan in which the efforts of a work group determine the level of incentive compensation, if any, for the group.

General factory overhead expenses. Overhead expenses that cannot be identified with a specific department and must be charged to departments by a process of allocation.

Gross margin. The difference between sales revenue and cost of goods sold; also referred to as "gross profit."

Gross profit. See Gross margin.

Gross profit percentage (or mark-on percentage). A percentage of manufacturing cost per unit; the percentage is applied to manufacturing cost to determine the gross profit which, in turn, is added to manufacturing cost to determine selling price.

H

High-low method. A method used to isolate the fixed and variable elements of a semivariable cost; involves comparison of a high volume and its related cost with a low volume and its related cost to determine the variable amount per unit and the fixed element.

Holiday pay. An amount paid to employees for designated holidays on which the employee is not required to work.

Hourly rate plan. A wage plan under which an employee is paid an established rate per hour for each hour worked.

I

Ideal standard. A performance criterion that reflects maximum efficiency, with no allowance for lost time, waste, or spoilage.

Incentive wage plan. A wage plan modified to increase worker productivity by paying a bonus rate per hour when an employee meets or exceeds established production quotas.

Indirect (nontraceable) cost. See Common cost.

Indirect labor. The wages and salaries of employees who are required for the manufacturing process but who do not work directly on the units being produced; examples include department heads, inspectors, materials handlers, and maintenance personnel.

Indirect materials. Materials and supplies necessary for the manufacturing process that cannot be readily identified with any particular product manufactured or whose relative cost is too insignificant to measure.

Individual production report. A daily report prepared for each employee when labor costs are calculated on a piece-rate basis. The report shows the employee's work assignment and the number of units completed.

Inventory report. A form prepared when making a physical count of inventory on hand and used to reconcile differences between recorded inventory and the inventory quantities determined by physical count.

J

Job cost ledger. A subsidiary ledger that consists of the individual job cost sheet.

Job cost sheet. A form used to accumulate costs applicable to each job under a job-order cost accounting system.

Job-order cost system. A method or system of cost accounting that is appropriate for manufacturing operations that produce custom-made or special-order goods. Manufacturing costs are accumulated separately for each job and recorded on a job cost sheet.

Joint costs. The costs of materials, labor, and overhead incurred during the production of joint products.

Joint products. Two or more products that are obtained from the same manufacturing process and are the primary objectives of the process.

Just-in-time inventory system. A system that significantly reduces inventory carrying costs by requiring that raw materials be delivered by suppliers to the factory at the exact time that they are needed for production.

L

Labor cost standard. A predetermined estimate of the direct labor cost required for a unit of product based on estimates of the labor hours required to produce a unit of product and the cost of labor per unit.

Labor cost summary. A form showing the allocation of total payroll to Work in Process and Factory Overhead.

Labor efficiency (usage) variance. The difference between the actual number of direct labor hours worked and the standard hours for the actual level of production at the standard price.

Labor rate (price) variance. The difference between the average hourly direct labor rate actually paid and the standard hourly rate, multiplied by the number of hours worked.

Last-in, first-out (LIFO). An inventory costing method based on the assumption that materials issued are the most recently purchased materials. Thus, materials issued are costed at the most recent purchase prices and ending inventories are costed at the prices paid for the earliest purchases.

Lead time. The estimated time interval between the placement of an order and the receipt of materials.

Liabilities budget. Shows how the cash position will be affected by payment of liabilities.

M

Machine hour method. A method of applying factory overhead to production based on the number of machine hours used for a job or process.

Make-up guarantee. An amount paid to employees under a modified wage plan when established production quotas are not met during a work period. The make-up guarantee is charged to the factory overhead account.

Management by exception. As relates to variance analysis, it is the practice of examining significant unfavorable or favorable differences from standard.

Manufacturers. They convert raw materials into finished goods by using labor, technology, and facilities.

Manufacturing (or production) costs. All costs incurred in the manufacturing process; the costs are classified into three basic elements: direct materials, direct labor, and factory overhead.

Manufacturing process. The activities involved in converting raw materials into finished goods through the application of labor and incurrence of various factory expenses.

Margin of safety. The amount that sales can decrease before the company will suffer a loss.

Margin of safety ratio. A relationship computed by dividing the difference between the total sales and the break-even point sales by total sales.

Marginal income ratio. See Contribution margin ratio.

Mark-on percentage. A percentage of the manufacturing cost per unit.

Materials. The inventory account that represents the cost of all materials purchased and on hand to be used in the manufacturing process, including raw materials, prefabricated parts, and supplies.

Materials control. Procedures incorporated in the system of internal control that are designed to physically protect or safeguard materials (physical control) and to maintain the proper balance of materials on hand (control of the investment in materials).

Materials cost standard. A predetermined estimate of the cost of the direct materials required for a unit of product.

Materials ledger. See Stores ledger.

Materials price variance. The difference between the actual unit cost of direct materials and the standard unit cost, multiplied by the actual quantity of materials used.

Materials quantity (usage) variance. The difference between the actual quantity of direct materials used and the standard quantity for the actual level of production at standard price.

Materials (or stores) requisition. A form, prepared by authorized factory personnel and usually approved by the production department supervisor, to request materials from the storeroom; represents authorization for the storeroom keeper to issue materials for use in production.

Merchandisers. Wholesalers or retailers who purchase finished goods for resale.

Mixed costs. See Semifixed and Semivariable costs.

Modified wage plan. A wage plan that combines certain features of the hourly rate and piece-rate plans.

Moving average. An inventory costing method based on the assumption that materials issued at any time are withdrawn from a mixed group of like materials, and no attempt is made to identify materials as being from the earliest or most recent purchases. Under this method, an average unit price is computed each time a new lot of materials is received, and the new unit price is used to cost all issues of materials until another lot is received and a new unit price is computed.

N

Non-contributory plans. Pension plans that are completely funded by the employer.

Nonvalue-added activities. Operations that include costs but do not add value to the product, such as moving, storing, and inspecting.

Normal capacity. The level of production that will meet the normal requirements of ordinary sales demand over a period of time; frequently used for budget development because it represents a logical balance between maximum capacity and the capacity demanded by actual sales volume.

Normal losses. Units lost due to the nature of the manufacturing process. Such losses are unavoidable and represent a necessary cost of producing goods.

Not-for-profit service agencies. These include charities, governmental units, and some health care facilities that provide services at little or no cost to the user.

O

Observation method. A technique used to classify a semivariable cost as either fixed or variable; involves examination and analysis of past relationships between the expense and production volume. Based on the observed pattern of cost behavior, a decision is made to classify the expense as either a fixed or variable cost, depending on which it more closely resembles.

Optical scanners. Devices that read bar-coded materials, such as employee identification badges.

Order costs. The costs incurred as a result of ordering materials; includes salaries and wages of employees involved in purchasing, receiving, and inspecting materials; communications costs such as telephone, postage, and forms; and record-keeping costs.

Order point. The point at which an item of inventory should be ordered; occurs when a predetermined minimum level of inventory on hand is reached. Determining an order point requires consideration of usage, lead time, and safety stock.

Outliers. Nonrepresentative data points that may be wrongly selected when using the high-low method.

Overapplied (or overabsorbed) factory overhead. The amount by which applied factory overhead exceeds actual factory overhead expenses incurred; represented by a remaining credit balance in Factory Overhead.

Overtime pay. The amount earned by employees at the regular hourly rate for hours worked in excess of the regularly scheduled time.

Overtime premium. An additional pay rate added to the employee's regular rate for hours worked in excess of the regularly scheduled time.

P

Payroll department. The department responsible for maintaining payroll records and determining each employee's gross and net earnings.

Payroll record. A form prepared each pay period showing the earnings of each employee for the period.

Payroll taxes. Taxes imposed on employers, including social security tax and federal and state unemployment taxes.

Peanut-butter costing. The practice of assigning costs evenly to jobs via an overhead rate when, in fact, different jobs consume resources in different proportions.

Pension costs. The costs incurred by an employer to provide retirement benefits to employees.

Performance report. A periodic summary of cost and production data that are controllable by the manager of a particular cost center.

Period costs. All costs that are not assigned to the product, but are recognized as expense and charged against revenue in the period incurred.

Periodic inventory system. A method of accounting for inventory that requires estimating inventory during the year for interim statements and shutting down operations to count all inventory items at the end of the year.

Perpetual inventory system. A method of accounting for inventory which provides a continuous record of purchases, issues, and balances of all goods in stock.

Piece-rate plan. A wage plan under which an employee is paid a specified rate for each unit or "piece" completed.

Planning. The process of establishing objectives or goals for the organization and determining the means by which the objectives will be attained.

Practical capacity. The level of production that provides complete utilization of all facilities and personnel, but allows for some idle capacity due to operating interruptions such as machinery breakdowns, idle time, and other inefficiencies.

Predetermined factory overhead rate. A percentage or amount determined by dividing budgeted factory overhead cost by budgeted production; budgeted production may be expressed in terms of machine hours, direct labor hours, direct labor cost, or units. The predetermined rate is an estimate used in applying factory overhead to production.

Price. In the context of variance analysis, refers to the cost of materials or the hourly wage rate for direct labor.

Prime cost. The combined costs of direct materials and direct labor incurred in manufacturing a product.

Process cost system. A method or system of cost accounting that is appropriate for manufacturing operations that produce continuous output of homogeneous products. Manufacturing costs are accumulated separately for each department and are recorded on a cost of production report.

Process costing. The act of assigning costs to a unit of activity within the factory.

Product costs. Costs that are included as part of inventory costs and expensed when goods are sold.

Production department. A department in which actual manufacturing operations are performed, and the units being produced are physically changed.

Production department supervisor. The employee who is responsible for supervising the operational functions of a production department.

Production report. A report, used in a process cost accounting system and prepared by the department head, showing: beginning units in process; number of units completed during the period; ending units in process and their estimated stage of completion.

Production work teams. A recent concept where output is dependent upon contributions made by all members of the work crew.

Professional labor budget. A budget for which the budgeted hours required for each client service area are multiplied by the budgeted rate for each category to obtain the total wages expense for each category of professional labor.

Purchase order. A form, prepared by the purchasing agent and addressed to the chosen vendor, that describes the materials ordered, credit terms and prices, and the date and method of delivery; represents the vendor's authorization to ship goods.

Purchase price variance. The difference between the actual cost of materials and the standard cost.

Purchase requisition. A form, usually prepared by the storeroom keeper or employee with similar responsibility, that is used to notify the purchasing agent that additional materials are needed; represents the agent's authority to purchase materials.

Purchasing agent. The employee who is responsible for purchasing the materials needed for production. An individual in any organization who is responsible for the purchasing function.

R

Receiving clerk. The employee who is responsible for supervising incoming shipments of materials and making sure that all incoming materials are checked as to quantity and quality.

Receiving report. A form prepared by the receiving clerk for each incoming shipment of materials. The clerk identifies the materials, determines the quantity received, and records this information on the receiving report as well as the name of the shipper, date of receipt, and the number of the purchase order identifying the shipment.

Relative sales value. A basis for allocating joint costs proportionally based on the respective selling prices of the separate products.

Responsibility accounting. The assignment of accountability for costs or production results to those individuals who have the authority to influence costs or production.

Retailers. A type of merchandiser who sells products or services to individuals for consumption.

Return shipping order. A form prepared by the purchasing agent when goods are to be returned to the vendor.

Returned materials report. A form prepared to accompany materials being returned to the storeroom that had been previously requisitioned but were not used in production.

S

Safety stock. The estimated minimum level of inventory needed to protect against stockouts.

Scattergraph method. A method that estimates a straight line along which the semivariable costs will fall by drawing the line by visual inspection through the data points plotted on the graph.

Schedule of fixed costs. A listing of fixed overhead costs, such as depreciation, insurance, and property taxes; provides the source from which fixed costs can be allocated to the various departments. Since fixed costs are assumed not to vary in amount from month to month, a schedule can be prepared in advance for several periods; at the end of a period, a journal entry can be prepared to record total fixed costs from the information provided in the schedule.

Scrap materials. By-products that are generated in the manufacturing process; usually, such materials have some value and their costs and revenues are accounted for separately.

Segment. A division, a product line, a sales territory, or other organizational unit that can be separately identified for reporting purposes and profitability analysis.

Segment margin. The term used in segment analysis for the excess of segment revenue over direct costs assigned to the segment; common costs are excluded in computing segment margin.

Semifixed costs. Costs that tend to remain the same in dollar amount over a certain range of activity but increase when production exceeds certain limits.

Semivariable costs. Manufacturing costs that are somewhat responsive to changes in production, but do not change proportionally with increases or decreases in volume; examples include indirect materials, indirect labor, repairs and maintenance, and power.

Sequential distribution method. A method for allocating service department costs to production departments, recognizing the interrelationship of the service departments. Costs are first allocated, sequentially, to other service departments and then to production departments. The sequence may begin by distributing the costs of the service department that renders the greatest amount of service to all other service departments. Alternatively, the costs of the service department with the largest total overhead can be distributed first.

Service department. A department within the factory that does not work directly on the product but provides needed services to other departments; examples include a department that generates power for the factory; a maintenance department that maintains and repairs buildings and equipment; and a cost accounting department that maintains factory accounting records.

Shift premium. An additional rate of pay added to an employee's regular rate as compensation for working an evening or night shift.

Spending variance. See Budget variance. The difference between the actual factory overhead for variable costs and the actual hours multiplied by the standard variable rate.

Split-off point. The point where joint products become separately identifiable; may occur during, or at the end of, the manufacturing process.

Spoiled units. Units of product with imperfections that cannot be economically corrected; they are sold as items of inferior quality or "seconds."

Stage of completion. The fraction or percentage of materials, labor, and overhead costs of a completed unit that have been applied during the period to goods that have not been completed.

Standard. A norm or criterion against which performance can be measured.

Standard cost accounting. See Standard cost accounting system.

Standard cost accounting system. A method of accounting for manufacturing costs that can be used in conjunction with either a job order system or process cost system. Standard costing makes it possible to determine what a product should have cost as well as what the product actually cost.

Standard costs. The costs that would be incurred under efficient operating conditions and are forecast before the manufacturing process begins. The predetermined standard costs are compared with actual manufacturing costs incurred and used by management as a basis for evaluating operating efficiency and taking corrective action when necessary.

Standard production. The volume on which the initial calculation of standard costs is based.

Standard unit cost for factory overhead. The result of estimating factory overhead cost at the standard, or normal, level of production, considering historical data and future changes and trends.

Static budget. A budget that is prepared for only one level of activity.

Step costs. See Semifixed costs.

Step-down method. See Sequential distribution method.

Step variable cost. A type of semivariable cost that remains constant in total over a range of production and then abruptly changes.

Stockout. Running out of an item of inventory; may occur due to inaccurate estimates of usage or lead time or other unforeseen events, such as the receipt of damaged or inferior materials from a supplier.

Storeroom keeper. The employee who is responsible for the storing and maintaining of materials inventories.

Stores (or materials) ledger. A subsidiary ledger supporting the Materials control account in the general ledger. The individual accounts in the stores ledger are used to record receipts and issues of materials and show the quantity and cost of materials on hand.

Stores requisition. See Materials requisition.

Summary of factory overhead. A schedule of all factory overhead expenses incurred during a period; prepared from the factory overhead analysis sheets, the schedule shows each item of overhead expense by department and in total.

Summary of materials issued and returned. A form used to record all issuances of materials to the factory, returns of materials previously requisitioned, and returns of materials to the vendors (sellers). The summary, when completed at the end of a period, provides the information needed to record the cost of materials for the period.

T

Theoretical capacity. The maximum number of units that can be produced with the completely efficient use of all available facilities and personnel.

Three-variance method. The analysis of factory overhead costs based on the computation of efficiency, capacity, and budget (spending) variances.

Throughput time. The time that it takes a unit to make it through the production process.

Time ticket. A document used to record the time spent by an employee on specific assignments. The time ticket is the basis for allocating the cost of factory labor to jobs or departments.

Timekeeping department. The department responsible for determining the number of hours for which employees should be paid and the type of work performed by employees.

Transferred-in costs. The portion of a department's total costs that were incurred by and transferred from a prior production department.

Two-variance method. The analysis of factory overhead costs based on the computation of the volume variance and the budget variance.

U

Under- and Overapplied Factory Overhead. An account used to accumulate differences from period to period between actual and applied factory overhead. At the end of the year, the balance in this account may be closed to Cost of Goods Sold (if the amount is relatively small) or allocated on a pro rata basis to Work in Process, Finished Goods, and Cost of Goods Sold (if the amount is material).

Underapplied (or underabsorbed) factory overhead. The amount by which actual factory overhead exceeds applied factory overhead; represented by a remaining debit balance in Factory Overhead.

Unfavorable variance. The difference between actual and standard costs when actual costs exceed standard costs.

Unit cost. The cost of manufacturing one unit of product.

Units from the prior department. Units that are completed units as to the transferor department and raw materials as to the transferee department.

Usage. The quantity of materials used or the number of direct labor hours worked.

V

Vacation pay. An amount paid to employees during their vacation periods as part of the employees' compensation for services to the employer.

Variable costing. See Direct costing.

Variable costs. Manufacturing costs which vary in proportion to changes in production volume; includes direct labor, direct materials, and some types of factory overhead.

Variance. The difference, during an accounting period, between the actual and standard or budgeted costs of materials, labor, and overhead.

Velocity. The speed with which units are produced in a manufacturing system. It is the inverse of the throughput time.

Vendor's invoice. A form, usually received from the vendor before goods are delivered, confirming a purchase of materials and representing a "bill" for the ordered goods. The purchasing agent should compare the invoice with the related purchase order to verify the description of materials, price, terms of payment, method of shipment, and delivery date.

Volume variance. The difference between budgeted fixed overhead and the fixed overhead applied to work in process; the result of operating at a level of production different from the standard, or normal, level.

W

Waste materials. See Scrap materials.

Wholesalers. A type of merchandiser who purchases goods from manufacturers and sells to retailers.

Work in process. The inventory account that includes all the manufacturing costs incurred to date for goods that are in various stages of production but are not yet completed.

Work shift. A regularly scheduled work period for a designated number of hours.

INDEX